# BREAKING RULES

THE SOCIAL AND SITUATIONAL DYNAMICS OF
YOUNG PEOPLE'S URBAN CRIME

# CLARENDON STUDIES IN CRIMINOLOGY

Published under the auspices of the Institute of Criminology, University of Cambridge; the Mannheim Centre, London School of Economics; and the Centre for Criminological Research, University of Oxford.

**GENERAL EDITOR: LUCIA ZEDNER**
(*University of Oxford*)

**EDITORS: MANUEL EISNER, ALISON LIEBLING, AND PER-OLOF WIKSTRÖM**
(*University of Cambridge*)

**ROBERT REINER, JILL PEAY, AND TIM NEWBURN**
(*London School of Economics*)

**IAN LOADER AND JULIAN ROBERTS**
(*University of Oxford*)

RECENT TITLES IN THIS SERIES:

# Breaking Rules

The Social and Situational Dynamics of
Young People's Urban Crime

*by*

**PER-OLOF H. WIKSTRÖM**
**DIETRICH OBERWITTLER**
**KYLE TREIBER**
**BETH HARDIE**

OXFORD
UNIVERSITY PRESS

# OXFORD

UNIVERSITY PRESS

Great Clarendon Street, Oxford, OX2 6DP,
United Kingdom

Oxford University Press is a department of the University of Oxford.
It furthers the University's objective of excellence in research, scholarship,
and education by publishing worldwide. Oxford is a registered trade mark of
Oxford University Press in the UK and in certain other countries

First Edition published in 2012
First published in paperback 2013

Impression: 1

British Library Cataloguing in Publication Data

Data available

Library of Congress Cataloging in Publication Data
Library of Congress Control Number: 2012934414

ISBN 978-0-19-959284-5
ISBN 978-0-19-968709-1 (pbk.)

Printed in Great Britain by
CPI Group (UK) Ltd.' Croydon, CR0 4YY

# Preface

'The aim of science is to find *satisfactory explanations* of whatever strikes us as being in need of explanation' (Popper 1985: 132, original emphasis). In this book, we aim to contribute to the explanation of acts of crime by advancing the understanding of the social and situational dynamics of crime.

People are different, but so are the environments in which they live and take part. There is little doubt that the social environment plays an important role in how we act: it shapes and forms personal characteristics and experiences that influence how we react (propensity) and it provides circumstances to which we react (exposure). However, our understanding of the role of the social environment in crime causation is still rudimentary and leaves much unexplored. A particular aim of this research is to employ new theory developed to capture the person–environment interaction in crime causation, and advance more adequate methods for studying it.

This book is the first major presentation of key findings from the ESRC-financed Peterborough Adolescent and Young Adult Development Study (PADS+). The study follows a cohort of approximately 700 young people randomly selected from the UK city of Peterborough, focusing on the role of the interplay between their personal characteristics and experiences, and the features of the environments in which they live and take part, in their crime involvement. The study is guided by the recently developed Situational Action Theory (SAT), an action theory specifically created to account for the person–environment interaction in the explanation of moral action such as crime (see, eg, Wikström 2006, 2010a, 2010b, 2011a).

In this book we will concentrate on the role of the *social environment* and its interaction with personal factors in the explanation of young people's involvement in *acts of crime* during the early to mid-adolescent period (ages 13–17). A second book will focus on the role of the social environment in young people's development and change, dealing with questions such as how young people acquire different crime propensities, and how environmental factors (exposure) shape and form the extent and nature of their crime involvement and its changes.

The present research aim is to expand beyond conventional neighbourhood and place-based approaches in the empirical study of environmental effects on crime by utilizing new methodologies (and new combinations of methodologies) that capture (1) young people's exposure to different kinds of environments (their activity fields), and (2) the crime propensity–criminogenic exposure interaction in crime causation (the analysis of crime occurrences by kinds of people in kinds of settings).

We hope that the theory (SAT), the new methodologies, and the substantive findings presented in this book will help stimulate new integrated ways of thinking about crime and its causes and new avenues for integrated research and thinking about crime-prevention policies.

Per-Olof H. Wikström
University of Cambridge
3 September 2011

# Foreword

*Clarendon Studies in Criminology* aims to provide a forum for outstanding empirical and theoretical work in all aspects of criminology and criminal justice, broadly understood. The Editors welcome submissions from established scholars, as well as excellent PhD work. The *Series* was inaugurated in 1994, with Roger Hood at its first General Editor, following discussions between Oxford University Press and three criminology centres. It is edited under the auspices of these three criminological centres: the Cambridge Institute of Criminology, the Mannheim Centre for Criminology at the London School of Economics, and the Centre for Criminology at the University of Oxford. Each supplies members of the Editorial Board and, in turn, the Series Editor.

*Breaking Rules: The Social and Situational Dynamics of Young People's Urban Crime* is a major contribution to criminology. Per-Olof Wikström, Dietrich Oberwittler, Kyle Treiber and Beth Hardie have set themselves the task of remedying what they see as the fragmented and poorly integrated state of theorizing about the causes of crime. In so doing, they advance criminological knowledge in two related ways. First, the book presents a full and systematic statement of 'situational action theory', a theory of why individuals break moral rules that Wikström has developed in several important papers over recent years. The theory aims to integrate individual and environmental perspectives on crime causation by proposing that acts of crime (which are defined as moral rules stated in law) are the result of a perception-choice process guided by the interaction between a person's propensity to commit crime and their exposure to criminogenic settings. Secondly, the book offers a first major presentation of key findings from the Peterborough Adolescent and Young Adult Development Study (PADS+) - an ongoing longitudinal study of a cohort of 700 young people in Peterborough which combines interviews with young people and parents, analysis of official data, time-space diaries and a community survey. The result is a rich, detailed dissection of the distribution and causes of youth offending in Peterborough, and a major empirical demonstration of the explanatory power of situational action theory.

Theoretical and empirical studies of the causes of crime have in recent years been relatively under-represented in the *Clarendon Studies in Criminology*. The Editors are pleased to be able to go some way to making good this imbalance and welcome this important addition to the *Series*.

Ian Loader
University of Oxford
March 2012

# Acknowledgements

The Peterborough Adolescent and Young Adult Development Study (PADS+) is financed by the *UK Economic and Social Research Council* (ESRC). Some additional funding (for the 2005 Peterborough Community Survey) has also been provided by the Youth Justice Board for England and Wales and Peterborough City Council.

PADS+ has benefited from the time and efforts of a large number of people who have assisted in numerous tasks, such as extracting official data, facilitating the arrangement of interviews, and generally supporting the process of setting up and carrying out the research. We would like to express our sincere thanks to the following schools, colleges, and other local organizations for their kind assistance:

**Schools and colleges:**
Arthur Mellows Village College
Bretton Woods School (now closed)
Bushfield Community College
Deacon's School (now closed)
Hereward School (now closed)
Jack Hunt School
John Mansfield School (now closed)
Ken Stimpson Community School
Marshfields School
New College Stamford
Orton Longueville School
Peterborough College of Adult Education
Peterborough High School
Peterborough Regional College
St John Fisher RC School
Stanground College
The King's School
The Voyager School
Thomas Deacon Academy
Walton School (now closed)

**Peterborough City Council** (including the following departments):
Office of the Chief Executive
Children's Services
Economic and Community Regeneration (no longer exists)
Electoral Services
GIS Support Services
Youth Offending Service (particularly Mark Garratt and Adrian Alban)

**Cambridgeshire Constabulary** (including the following departments):
Management of Police Information
Northern Division Intelligence Unit (particularly Gillian Atherton)
Police National Computer Bureau (particularly Shirley Barnes, Gill Hughes, and Andy Plumb)

**Others:**
Cambridge Youth Offending Service
Huntingdonshire District Council
Peterborough Central Library

To ensure the highest possible data quality, PADS+ has employed only its own specially trained and qualified research staff for data collection (all of whom hold a degree in a social or behavioural science). It is no small task to keep track of and motivate more than 700 young people to take part in a longitudinal study. The fact that the study has a retention rate of 97 per cent over the first six waves of annual data collection (one wave of parent interviews, and five subsequent waves of young people's interviews) is by all standards an outstanding achievement, and can be attributed mostly to the dedication and professionalism of the PADS+ research staff. We would like to thank all those who have contributed to the study over the years. Below are listed all PADS+ researchers/research assistants who contributed significantly to the initial parent interviews (indicated by 'P') and/or the first five waves of young people's interviews (indicated by the number of the wave/s they took part in):

David Butterworth      (P)
Charlotte Read          (P)
Alpa Parmar             (P)
Nicola Every            (P,1)
Lindsay Whetter         (P,1,2)

| | |
|---|---|
| Helen McKinnon | (1,2,3) |
| Aase Villadsen | (1,2,3,4) |
| Kyle Treiber | (1,2,3,4) |
| Louise Neil | (2,3) |
| Beth Hardie | (3,4,5) |
| Andrea Egerton | (4) |
| Caroline Moul | (4,5) |
| Seran Davies | (5) |
| Harsha Patel | (5) |
| Neema Trivedi | (5) |

The current team of research assistants (Jenni Barton-Crosby, Lauren Bates, Beverley Garrigan, Harriet Ludford, and Loveday Newman) have helped in the compilation of some official statistics for this book.

Beth Hardie was responsible for managing the Peterborough Community Survey (PCS) in 2005.

Professor Jost Reinecke (University of Bielefeld) has kindly given us some valuable expert advice on aspects of the structural equation modelling applied in this book. Associate Professor Vania Ceccato (Royal Institute of Technology, Stockholm), as a part of the initial research team, helped lay the groundwork for the geospatial methodologies we use. In the set-up phase of PADS+, Professor Magda Stouthamer-Loeber (University of Pittsburgh) and the team of the Pittsburgh Youth Study kindly shared with us their experiences of how to ensure high quality data collection in longitudinal research.

Former Chief Superintendent David Harvey and former Head of the Peterborough Youth Offending Service Bob Footer played an invaluable role in providing practical support facilitating our research. We would also like to thank Professor John Spencer (University of Cambridge) for providing legal advice, for example in matters concerning consent and disclosure.

Finally, we would like to express our gratitude to all the young people of Peterborough who have made this study possible by volunteering information about themselves and their lives repeatedly over the years. Without their contribution this study would not have been possible. Similarly, we would like to thank all the respondents of the Peterborough Community Survey who volunteered information about themselves and their neighbourhoods.

## Advance Praise for Breaking Rules

*Breaking Rules* is among the most significant works in criminology in decades. It sets the standard for sophisticated and innovative measurement, for careful and well-executed research design, and for clarity and precision of presentation. It both presents and explicates an innovative theory of crime, one that is broad in scope and appropriately ambitious. The data and their analyses are of vital importance to cumulative knowledge in criminology. With this book, Situational Action Theory takes its place as among the most important perspectives in modern criminology and the study provides data of unprecedented scope and quality. *Breaking Rules* represents the best tradition of the science of criminology and as such it commands the attention of the field.

Professor Michael R. Gottfredson
University of California

*Breaking Rules* is a truly impressive book that combines all of the features of first-rate scholarship in the social sciences. The theorizing, in the form of Situational Action Theory (SAT), is creative. The methodological procedures are carefully crafted and skillfully executed to serve the theoretical objectives of the research. Moreover, the extensive and rich analyses of the data from the Peterborough Adolescent and Young Adult Development Study (PADS+) yield compelling insights about who commits crimes, when, where, and—most importantly—why.

Professor Steven F. Messner
University at Albany

Criminology has produced a staggering amount of data and findings. Correlates of crime are everywhere but theoretical interpretation of their meaning is fraught with disagreement. Wikström and colleagues cut through the fog with a compelling new theory and multi-faceted longitudinal study of adolescents that lays bare the fundamental importance of situational dynamics and their interaction with both person-level characteristics and the larger social environment of the city. The theoretical emphasis on situation and individual action in context is original and the empirical analysis is carefully constructed to assess major hypotheses. *Breaking Rules* is a breakthrough that deserves a wide readership.

Professor Robert J. Sampson
Harvard University

# Table of Contents

# List of figures

# List of tables

# PART 1

# Analysing Crime as Situational Action: Theory, Methods, Key Constructs, and Basic Findings

**Chapter 1** introduces *Situational Action Theory* (SAT), the theory guiding the research presented in this book; its background, key concepts, and propositions; and its application to the study of urban crime. **Chapter 2** describes the design, methodologies, and data of the *Peterborough Adolescent and Young Adult Development Study* (PADS+), the study upon which the research findings presented in this book are based. **Chapter 3** introduces and discusses the measurement of the key constructs of the study—crime, crime propensity, and criminogenic exposure—and presents some basic findings regarding the distribution of crime, crime propensity, and criminogenic exposure, and their relationships, in the study population.

# 1

# Situational Action Theory

Criminology is a fragmented discipline and its key theoretical and empirical insights are poorly integrated. There is not even clear agreement about what its theories aim to explain, ie what crime is. This state of affairs hampers the development of a sound understanding of crime and its causes and hinders advancement of effective crime prevention strategies and policies. *Situational Action Theory* (SAT) was developed to overcome key shortcomings identified in prominent criminological theories (briefly detailed in sections 1.1 and 1.2 below). SAT builds upon and aims to integrate, within an adequate action theory framework, main insights from criminological theory and research as well as theory and research from relevant social and behavioural sciences more generally (see, eg, Wikström 2006, 2010a, 2010b, 2011a). In this book SAT serves as the analytical framework for our research into the social and situational dynamics of young people's urban crime.

## 1.1 Criminology: A fragmented and poorly integrated discipline

A key problem with criminological theorizing and research is that it is fragmented. One need only consult any criminological textbook (or take part in any major criminological conference) to be convinced of the discipline's theoretical fragmentation.

While a good deal is known about the correlates of delinquency and crime, there is surprisingly little agreement about the causes.

(Farrington 1988: 75)

The study of deviance and crime has traditionally been characterized by a multitude of seemingly unrelated and competitive theories.

(Liska et al. 1989: 1)

No simple theory in the crime/deviance area… has proven to be more than minimally satisfactory in overall explanatory ability, in applicability to a wide range of deviance, or in empirical support for its tenets. All are plausible, yet they fail as general theories.

(Tittle 1995: 1)

...criminology risks being a field of study in which many ideas are developed and all are chosen—in which all theories have equal claim to legitimacy and in which only the most highly specialized scholars can separate the theoretical wheat from the chaff.

(Cullen et al. 2008: 2)

The problem of fragmentation and poor integration is also well reflected when it comes to empirical research.

...there is no shortage of factors that are significantly correlated with offending and antisocial behavior; indeed, literally thousands of variables differentiate significantly between official offenders and nonoffenders or correlate significantly with self-reported offending.

(Farrington 1992: 256)

...when factors become too numerous... we are in the hopeless position of arguing that everything matters.

(Matza 1964: 23–24)

...a major problem with the risk factor prevention paradigm is to determine which risk factors are causes and which are merely markers or correlated with causes.

(Farrington 2000: 7)

A discipline that is fragmented, theoretically and empirically, is of little help to politicians, policy makers, and practitioners who want to base their policies and interventions on the best available scientific knowledge about crime causation.

For decades, theoretical fragmentation in criminology has contributed to generally ineffective, fragmented and shortsighted public policies. Without a holistic understanding of the causes of crime, policy makers will continue to shift the focus of control efforts back and forth from individual-level to macro-level causes as the political pendulum swings from right to left. This erratic approach feeds the desperate belief that the problem of crime is intractable.

(Vila 1994: 314)

It is clear that to get out of the current stalemate of disparate theory and research and develop as a discipline, criminology needs to integrate key theoretical insights and relevant empirical findings within a framework that can more effectively focus research and policy on the role of causally relevant factors and processes and their interactions in crime causation.

One of the key divides in existing criminological theorizing and research is between person-oriented and environment-oriented approaches. There is a lack of advanced theorizing that attempts to analytically integrate key insights from these two explanatory approaches. The role of the social environment, and particularly *how* it interacts with personal characteristics and experiences in crime causation, is surprisingly poorly developed and under-researched.

...more is to be gained by linking those traditions than by their continued separate development and testing.

(Reiss 1986: 29)

Existing research tells us more about the development of criminal potential than about how that potential becomes the actuality of offending in any given situation.

(Farrington 2002: 690)

Many contemporary efforts that purport to pursue the goal of theoretical integration might better be described as attempts at prediction. Variables from two or more theories are included in the same prediction equation, but there is little concern with relating the concepts to one another.

(Messner et al. 1989: 18)

Criminology lacks an accepted and general theoretical structure for guiding integrative inquiry into the causes of crime.

(Wikström and Sampson 2006: 1)

Person-oriented and environment-oriented approaches are potentially helpful for identifying important explanatory factors but, taken separately, do not provide fully developed explanations of crime *as an action*. Rather, person-oriented approaches mostly aim to explain the emergence of personal differences affecting people's tendency to commit acts of crime (their crime propensity), while environment-oriented approaches generally aim to explain place (and time) differences in the occurrence of acts of crime (or crime rates) as an outcome of criminogenic features of the environment. Typically, neither explains the actual *causal process* that directly links a person (crime propensity) and a setting (criminogenic exposure) to an act of crime. To do so requires the integration of causally relevant personal and environmental factors and analysis of their interaction within the context of an adequate action theory. However, developed action theory is a rarity in criminological theories.

If criminological theories refer at all to theories of action they mostly make general references to the importance of choice without giving any more developed account of its role within the theory, typically alluding to self-interest, pleasures and pain, costs and benefits and similar grounds for action.

(Wikström 2006: 70)

Even theories that explicitly deal with the person–environment interaction as a rule lack a developed account of how (through what process) personal and environmental factors interact in causing acts of crime. This problem is clearly illustrated by two of the currently most influential criminological theories: Gottfredson and Hirschi's (1990) general theory of crime (or, as it is often referred to, self-control theory) and Cohen and Felson's (1979) routine activity theory.

Both theories suggest that crime occurs because of the intersection of people (in Gottfredson and Hirschi's case, those with low self-control; in Cohen and Felson's case, motivated offenders) and opportunities to offend (in Gottfredson and Hirschi's case, opportunities to achieve quick, easy rewards with minimal effort through force or fraud; in Cohen and Felson's case, opportunities to interact with a suitable target in the absence of a capable guardian). However, although both theories recognize the role of personal and environmental factors, they largely focus on the role of one, essentially disregarding (or only paying lip-service to) the other, and, crucially, do not specify in any detail the process by which the two interact in producing acts of crime (see, for example, Clarke and Felson 1993: 1–4; Gottfredson and Hirschi 2003).

There is clearly a strong case for integrating key insights from person-oriented and environment-oriented approaches and, arguably, this is best achieved by means of an adequate action theory that can account for *how* (through what process) the interplay between person (propensity) and environment (exposure) affects actions (eg acts of crime), and thereby help identify which are the causally relevant personal and environmental factors among all the hundreds of empirically demonstrated crime correlates (for a recent overview of crime correlates, see Ellis et al. 2009).

## 1.2 Key common shortcomings in criminological theory

To advance criminological theory there are (at least) four main tasks that need to be addressed to create a comprehensive and integrated explanation of the causes of crime (Wikström 2010a):

(1) to define what crime is (what it is the theory aims to explain);
(2) to specify what it is that moves people to engage in acts of crime (to present an adequate action theory);
(3) to specify which (and how) personal and environmental factors interact in moving people to engage in acts of crime (to properly integrate key insights from personal and environmental explanatory approaches);
(4) to specify the role of broader social conditions (macro factors) and individual development (life histories) in crime causation (to analyse their influence not as causes but as causes of the causes).

Criminological theories are not always clear about what they aim to explain and, crucially, the definition of *crime* is rarely (though it should be) the starting point for the development of their explanations (but cf. Gottfredson and Hirschi 1990[1]). Without a clear definition of crime (what it is one aims to explain) it is difficult to develop an unambiguous theory of *crime causation*. A theory has to be a theory about *something*, causes have to cause *something*, and an explanation has to explain *something* (Wikström 2010a). Depending on how crime is defined (what it is a theory of crime aims to explain) relevant causes and explanations will vary.

There is a lack of a generally accepted definition of crime within the discipline of criminology. The concept of crime is differently defined in different theories (and sometimes not at all or only vaguely) and observers have questioned whether different theories of crime causation really aim to explain the same thing (eg Akers 1989: 25). Without a clear common definition of what criminological theory should explain it is difficult to analytically compare and empirically test which proposed theory is the best (most true)

---

[1] However, the starting point for Gottfredson and Hirschi's theory (their definition of crime) is problematic. They define crime as 'acts of force and fraud undertaken in the pursuit of self-interest' (Gottfredson and Hirschi 1990: 15). One major problem is their definition includes an element of explanation: 'in the pursuit of self-interest' (see further Wikström and Treiber 2007).

explanation of crime (because it is unclear if they aim to explain the same thing).

Some scholars have questioned whether it is possible to develop a general theory of crime. Wilson and Herrnstein (1985: 21) argue 'that it is difficult to provide a true and interesting explanation for actions that differ so much in their legal and subjective meaning'. This objection is correct if one focuses on explaining the many different kinds of *acts* that constitute crime (eg shoplifting, rape, drunken driving, insider trading, plane hijacking); but if one focuses on explaining the *rule-breaking* (which is common to all crimes) this objection becomes less of a problem. A general theory of why people act in compliance with or breach rules of conduct is certainly possible.

People are the source of their actions and to explain their acts of crime we need an adequate *action theory* that explains what moves people to comply with or breach rules of conduct. Criminology lacks a generally accepted action theory; in fact, most criminological theories lack any developed theory of action.[2] Typically, criminological theory (and research) lists factors supposed to influence people's crime involvement without specifying in much detail *how* (the process by which) these factors affect the occurrence of acts of crime. Many criminological theories appear to be theories about the causes of crime propensity (theories about the causes of *one* factor affecting people's acts of crime) rather than theories explaining crime events.

To explain acts of crime we need to understand the process (mechanism) that produces acts of rule-breaking. An *action theory* is a theory that details the process (the mechanism) that produces action. Correctly specifying the process that moves people to act in one way or another (eg to follow or breach rules of conduct) is crucial to identifying which of all the many crime correlates are causally relevant for the outcome and which are only *markers* (factors merely correlated with causally relevant factors) or *symptoms* (factors merely associated with the outcome). According to SAT, this process

---

[2] Some prominent criminological theorists have alluded that their theories are compatible with some variant of rational choice theory (eg, Felson 1986; Hirschi 1986). However, they do not develop the potential for integration in any detail. Applications of [rational] choice theory can typically be found in particular research areas, such as deterrence (eg, Nagin and Pogarsky 2003) and situational crime prevention (eg, Clarke 1980). See McCarthy (2002) more generally on the use (and lack of use) of [rational] choice theory within criminology.

is one of *perception of action alternatives and choice* (Wikström 2006). Only those factors that influence the perception–choice process that moves people to act are causally relevant in the explanation of action. Consequently, *only* those factors that directly (or indirectly, as causes of the causes) influence the perception–choice process that moves people to follow or breach rules of conduct (stated in law) are causally relevant in the explanation of acts of crime (see further Wikström 2011a).

Criminological theories (and research) tend to analyse the causes of crime as if the influence of personal and environmental factors on acts of crime were independent. This is a mistake. There can be no proper explanation of action (eg acts of crime) without considering the person–environment *interaction*. Environments do not act. People act, but, importantly, they do not act in a social vacuum. People act in response to settings (the parts of the environment that they directly experience). There are no personal or environmental factors that are sufficient to cause action on their own; they only become activated as part of the person–environment interaction. The explanation of the causes of acts of crime requires an understanding of how (through what processes) the *situational dynamics* (person–setting interactions) influence people to follow or breach rules of conduct. The crucial question is what personal and environmental factors are causally relevant, that is what personal and environmental factors interact to influence the perception–choice process by which people are moved to follow or breach rules of conduct.

In the analysis of crime causation it is important to distinguish between the causes and the 'causes of the causes' of acts of crime. Criminological theories (and research) are not always fully clear about this central analytical distinction. Analysis of the *causes of the causes* of acts of crime primarily concerns the explanation of why people come to have different crime propensities, why environments (places) come to vary in their criminogeneity, and why different kinds of people (according to their crime propensity) come to be exposed to different kinds of settings (environments) with particular criminogenic features.

Person–setting interactions take place in, and are dependent on, the wider social context. To explain the *social dynamics* of crime requires an understanding of how (through what processes) systemic factors (such as residential and activity differentiation) influence the occurrence of particular (and the frequency of particular) person–setting interactions in which people develop (their crime propensities) and act (commit acts of crime). In other words, the analysis of the social dynamics (as a study of the causes of the causes) helps explain *why* certain kinds of people are exposed to certain kinds of settings (in which they develop and act), while the analysis of the situational dynamics (as a study of the causes) helps to explain *why* certain person–setting combinations are likely to make people (follow or) breach particular rules of conduct.

To understand why and how particular kinds of interactions emerge at particular times and places we need an ecological approach. We need to understand how processes of *social selection* (and their interplay with self selection) introduce kinds of people to kinds of settings (and how these kinds of settings emerge). This, in turn, will help explain spatial and temporal patterns and concentrations of acts of crime.

All in all, developing an adequate theory of crime causation requires the realization that

(1) crimes are actions—specifically, actions that breach rules of conduct—and should, therefore, be explained as such;

(2) people are the source of their actions; therefore, to explain their actions, we need an adequate action theory that explains what moves people to act in compliance with or breach rules of conduct;

(3) people's actions are an outcome of a perception–choice process initiated and guided by the person–environment interaction (where this interaction is the input to the perception–choice process); therefore, we require a situational action theory to understand the situational dynamics of crime;

(4) people's interactions occur in a wider social context; therefore, we need an ecological perspective to grasp the social dynamics of crime. Understanding the role of this wider social context helps explain why certain kinds of environments (settings in which people develop and act) emerge and, crucially, why certain kinds of people are exposed to certain kinds of settings (what interactions take place).

A proper study of crime causation thus calls for an *ecological action approach* that takes into account actors, action contexts, and their interaction, and how that interaction is dependent on the wider social context. Moreover, there is a need to take more seriously issues of human agency and causation (Wikström 2011a). SAT aims to provide such a framework.

## 1.3  Situational Action Theory: Basic constructs and propositions

According to SAT, people are essentially rule-guided creatures (Wikström 2010a). People express their desires (and needs) and their commitments, and respond to frictions, within the context of rule-guided choice. To explain human action (such as acts of crime) we therefore need to understand how the process of rule-guidance influences what action alternatives people perceive and what choices they make in relation to the motivations (temptations and provocations) they experience.

### 1.3.1  Outline of the basic situational model

SAT proposes that acts of crime (C) are ultimately an outcome of a perception–choice process ($\rightarrow$) that is initiated and guided by the interaction (x) between a person's crime propensity (P) and criminogenic exposure (E):

$$P \, x \, E \rightarrow C$$

*Acts of crime* are defined as acts that break moral rules of conduct stated in law. The *perception–choice process* is a process of perceiving action alternatives and making choices in relation to a motivation (a temptation or provocation). This process can be either predominantly automated (expressing a habit) or reasoned (making a judgement) depending on the familiarity of the circumstances and the congruence of the rule-guidance in the setting in which the person takes part. What action alternatives people perceive (eg if they see an act of crime as an action alternative) and, on that basis, what choices they make (eg if they choose an act of crime) in relation to particular motivations, depends on the *interaction* between their crime propensity and the criminogenic features of the settings to which they are exposed.

SAT maintains that a person's *crime propensity* depends on the extent to which his or her relevant morality (moral rules and their attached moral emotions) and ability to exercise self-control encourage breaching moral rules of conduct (stated in law); and that a setting's criminogenic features depend on the extent to which that setting's (perceived) moral norms and their enforcement (or lack of enforcement) encourage the breach of moral rules (stated in law). A person's *criminogenic exposure* is the extent to which he or she takes part in settings with criminogenic features. Crime propensity and criminogenic exposure are the key direct causally relevant factors in the explanation of a person's acts of crime. The factors that influence (1) the development of a person's crime propensity, (2) the emergence of criminogenic settings (environments), and (3) people's exposure to criminogenic settings are analysed in SAT as *the causes of the causes*. Below we develop these arguments in more detail.

### 1.3.2  Explaining crime as moral action

SAT maintains that acts of crime are best explained as moral actions, that is actions guided by moral rules. A *moral rule* is a rule of conduct that states what is the right or wrong thing to do (or not to do) in a particular circumstance. The *law* is a set of moral rules of conduct. Acts of *crime* are acts that breach moral rules of conduct stated in law. This is what all crimes, in all places, at all times, have in common. To explain acts of crime we thus need to explain *why* people comply with or breach rules of conduct (stated in law). That is what a theory of crime causation should explain.

A theory of crime causation is a special case of a general theory of moral action. Explaining acts of crime is not different from explaining why people breach moral rules more generally. The explanatory process is the same. The only difference between an act of crime and another breach of a rule of conduct is that the former is *stated in law*. If we can explain why people comply with or breach rules of conduct in general we can also explain why people comply with or breach moral rules stated in law. As Ehrlich ([1936] 2008: 39) points out, 'the legal norm... is merely one of the rules of conduct, of the same nature as all other rules of conduct'. In this context it is important to stress that SAT does not require the existence of the law, only the existence of moral rules. While, in principle, it is possible to abolish the law (and, hence, there would be no breaches of moral rules *stated in law*), it is not conceivable that moral rules can be abolished (because people are essentially rule-guided creatures; see further Wikström 2010a).

The explanation of crime as moral action has the great advantage of being *applicable to all kinds of crime*, from shoplifting to major company fraud, from bar fights to mass shootings, from civil disobedience to roadside bombings, to mention just a few examples. The key explanatory *factors* and causal *processes* involved are the same; it is only the input to the process, its *content* (the applicable moral rules), that may vary depending on what kind of moral action we want to explain (Wikström 2010a). For example, the perception–choice process that makes a person lie to a friend, shoplift or blow up an airplane is the same (he or she has to see the action as an alternative and then chose to carry it out) but the relevant moral rules that guide the process may be very different.

One great advantage of explaining crime as moral action is that it *avoids the problem that some actions are defined as crimes at some times, or in some places, but not at other times, or in other places*, because what is explained is why a person performs an action that breaches a rule of conduct (eg drives at 100 mph on a road with a 70 mph speed limit), not why he or she performs the particular action in itself (drives at 100 mph). Thus, for example, the issue of why homosexual acts may be criminalized in some jurisdictions but not in others, or the fact that they have previously been criminalized in a jurisdiction but no longer are, does not present any problems for the theory. SAT does not aim to explain why particular rules of conduct exist (eg why cannabis smoking is illegal) but why people follow or breach particular rules of conduct (eg why people smoke cannabis when it is illegal). To explain why certain actions are considered acts of crime is an important criminological topic, but not one it is necessary to address when the aim is to explain why people comply with or breach rules of conduct stated in law.

Explaining crimes as moral action does not (necessarily) involve any judgement about whether or not existing moral rules (including laws) are good (virtuous) or bad (reprehensible). SAT does not entail a '*moralistic' approach* to the study of crime. The theory does not address the issue of *what is* right (good) or wrong (bad) to do (or not to do), but focuses on *how* moral rules (rules about what it is right and wrong to do or not to do) guide human action. The basic argument is that people's actions (such as acts of crime) are best explained as moral actions, actions guided by moral rules (whatever the rules and their origins).

However, this does not imply any position of *moral relativism* (that all moral rules are equally likely to occur and endure). There are most likely important grounds for why some particular kinds of moral rules emerge, for example relating to *human nature* and the problem of creating *social order*. There is probably no coincidence that most societies (of some complexity) regulate, for example, ownership, sexual behaviour, and the use of violence (albeit the nature of these regulations may vary over time and between juris-dictions).

Morality is not only a question about what rules of conduct a person holds, but also about how much he or she *cares* about adher-ing to specific moral rules. It is reasonable to expect a correspon-dence between a person's *moral values* (what actions he or she regards as good or bad) and his or her *moral rules* (what actions he or she considers right or wrong to do). People who agree with a rule of conduct generally consider it a good thing to comply with the rule and a bad thing not to. However, the degree to which a person finds particular actions good (virtuous) or bad (reprehensible) may vary. He or she is likely to care more about some rules of conduct than others. For example, a person may consider it wrong both to run a red light and to break into another person's house, but he or she may consider running a red light less reprehensible. People also vary in how important they consider adhering to a particular moral rule. For example, some people may find it unthinkable to snitch on a friend, while others may not find it that big a deal (even if, in prin-ciple, they consider it wrong to do so).

The strength of a person's particular moral rules may be seen as reflected in the *moral emotions* he or she attaches to breaching a particular moral rule. People vary in how much *shame* (feeling bad in front of others) and *guilt* (feeling bad in front of oneself) they feel for having conducted (or, in the case of guilt, even having merely thought of conducting) a particular kind of action. In the analysis of people's morality, SAT uses the concept of moral rules (indicat-ing what a person perceives as right and wrong to do) and moral emotions (indicating the strength of particular moral rules) to capture a person's morality.

### 1.3.3  Elements of the situational model: Person, setting, situation, and action

People act, they act within settings, and the interaction of people and settings creates situations, to which their actions are a (deliber-ate or habitual) response. The key elements of the situational model of SAT are thus (1) a person, (2) the setting, (3) the situation, and (4) an action. A *person* is defined as a body with a biological and psychological makeup, experiences, and agency (powers to make things happen intentionally). The environment is all that lies

outside the person. A *setting* is defined as the part of the environment (the configuration of objects, persons, and events) that, at any
given moment in time, is accessible to a person through his or her
senses (including any media present). A *situation* is defined as the
perception of action alternatives and process of choice, which
emerges from the person–setting interaction. *Action* is defined as a
bodily movement or a sequence of bodily movements, under the
person's guidance (eg speaking, hitting, pinching, running, or laugh-
ing). Reflexes are not counted as actions. The situation lies at the
core of SAT's explanation of moral action (including acts of crime),
not the person or the environment (setting), but the perception–
choice process that arises from their interaction. That is why the
theory has been labelled *Situational Action Theory*.

SAT fully recognizes the important fact that people are different
(have different propensities), and that environments (places) are
different (provide different kinds of exposure) but, crucially, argues
that particular combinations of kinds of people and kinds of settings
will tend to create particular kinds of situations (perception–choice
processes) that, in turn, will tend to encourage particular kinds
of action (for example particular kinds of acts of crime). A key argument of SAT is that any explanation that focuses on (or ignores)
either personal or environmental factors will fall short as an explanation of acts of crime.

## 1.3.4 Crime propensity and criminogenic exposure

SAT proposes that people vary in their propensity to engage in acts
of crime (and particular acts of crime) as a consequence of their
morality and ability to exercise self-control. *Crime propensity* is
the tendency to see and, if so, to choose acts of crime (a particular
act of crime) as a viable action alternative in response to a motivation (temptation or provocation). People who easily see acts of
crime as action alternatives they readily choose to carry out may
be regarded as crime prone, while those who rarely or never see acts
of crime as action alternatives may be regarded as crime averse.
This general reasoning may be applied to specific types of crime,
in which case we can talk about a *crime-specific propensity* (eg a
propensity to shoplift to get desired goods or a propensity to use
violence to forward political ends).

According to SAT, a person's crime propensity fundamentally
depends on his or her *morality* (his or her moral rules and their

attached moral emotions). People vary in how important it is for them to abide by the rules of law (and rules of conduct more generally). However, they also, crucially, vary in their *action-relevant moral rules* (the specific moral rules of relevance to breaking particular kinds of rules of conduct, such as the use of violence, and the specific circumstances in which such use may be seen as a morally justifiable action alternative), and the strength of these moral rules (as indicated by the shame and guilt attached to violating the rule). The likelihood that a person will perceive a particular crime as an action alternative in response to a motivator depends on his or her action relevant moral rules and their strength.

While people's morality is the basic personal factor of relevance for their crime propensity, their *ability to exercise self-control* is also of importance in cases in which they are externally encouraged to break a moral rule they themselves hold (this point will be further elaborated in section 1.3.7). A person's ability to exercise self-control depends on his or her executive capabilities (see further Wikström and Treiber 2007), but is also influenced by momentary personal factors such as alcohol and drug intoxication or high levels of stress or emotion. All in all, a person's crime propensity may be seen as the outcome of the interaction between his or her morality and ability to exercise self-control.

However, propensity is not action. Even those with the highest crime propensity spend very little of their time awake engaging in acts of crime (see Wikström and Butterworth 2006: 212–13; Wikström et al. 2010: 80). For crime propensity to be triggered into action it has to interact with action-relevant features of a setting. Settings present different *moral contexts*, that is different *moral norms* and *levels of enforcement* (through formal and informal monitoring and intervention and their associated potential consequences), which means they differ in the extent to which they encourage or discourage breaches of rules of conduct (stated in law) in relation to the opportunities they provide and the level of friction they create. The moral norms of a setting will vary in the degree to which they correspond with the rules of conduct stated in law (for example the moral norms of some settings may encourage cannabis smoking even when doing so is illegal). Settings that tend to encourage acts of crime (or particular acts of crime) may be regarded as *criminogenic settings*. Just as we can speak about people's crime-specific propensities we can also speak about settings' *crime-specific criminogenic features*.

The influence of a setting's moral context on action is always a question of its *perceived* moral context. Although it is reasonable generally to assume a rather close correspondence between the actual and perceived moral norms of a setting and their enforcement, people may misinterpret which moral norms apply to a setting, and the efficacy of their enforcement, particularly if they operate in new and unfamiliar settings. Some settings may also be more diffuse (or conflicting) than others in terms of the available cues regarding which moral norms apply and the level to which they are enforced. All in all, a person's *criminogenic exposure* may be seen as his or her encounters with settings in which the (perceived) moral norms and their (perceived) levels of enforcement (or lack of enforcement) encourage breaches of rules of conduct (stated in law) in response to particular opportunities or frictions.

### 1.3.5 The perception–choice process

SAT proposes that human actions, such as acts of crime, are an outcome of a perception–choice process initiated and guided by the *causal interaction* of (crime) propensity and (criminogenic) exposure (see Figure 1.1). The factors that influence a person's perception of action alternatives and process of choice (ie his or her propensity and exposure) are the factors that are causally relevant for his or her actions. A *causally relevant factor* in the explanation of action is a factor that when manipulated will change the relevant input into the perception–choice process and, hence, influence a person's (automated or deliberate) choice of action. The perception–choice process may be regarded as a two-stage process in which the perception of action alternative sets the boundaries for the choice process by providing the alternatives among which a person makes a choice.

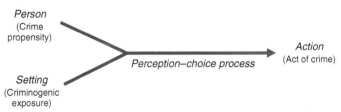

**Figure 1.1 The causes of the perception–choice process in crime causation**

*Perception* (ie the information we get from our senses) is what links a person to his or her environment (on perception generally, see Maund 2003). Perception is selective (filtered) and depends not only on the features of the setting in which a person takes part, but also on his or her relevant previous experiences and personal characteristics (such as preferences). People in the same setting differ in what they attend to and how they process and evaluate this information. In the explanation of action, an important aspect of perception is the perception of action alternatives that emerge as an outcome of the person–environment interaction. People vary significantly in what kind of action alternatives they perceive in response to a particular motivator in a particular setting, and, crucially, whether such action alternatives include acts that break rules of conduct, such as an act of crime (see further Wikström 2006). Understanding *why* people vary in the action alternatives they perceive in a particular setting is central to the explanation of why they follow or break rules of conduct.

People make choices among the action alternatives they perceive. A *choice* is the formation of an intention to act in a particular way (eg forming an intention to take a CD from a shop without paying). Intention and action are not the same because even if a person has formed an intention to act in a particular way the action may (particularly in prolonged action sequences) be interrupted or prevented before it is carried out, eg a security guard may suddenly turn up, or the person may detect a CCTV camera he or she had not previously noticed, making him or her change his or her mind about carrying out the theft. Moreover, actions may succeed or fail, and they may have intended and unintended consequences (see Wikström 2006).

Most action theories tend to focus on factors that influence people's *choice* between action alternatives (eg why they chose an act of crime to satisfy a particular desire, instead of a legal action), while paying little or no attention to why people differ in what *action alternatives* they perceive in the first place (eg why some people see an act of crime as an action alternative to satisfy a particular desire while others do not). SAT insists that the perception of action alternatives is of more fundamental importance to people's actions than the process of choice between perceived action alternatives. It is *only* when people perceive an act of crime as an action alternative that the process of choice becomes relevant for the explanation of whether or not they commit an act of crime.

This is a crucial insight because the main reason why most people, most of the time, do not engage in most acts of crime is that they generally *do not perceive* crime as an action alternative. For example, most people who walk by an unsupervised and unlocked car with the keys in the ignition do not see this as an opportunity to steal the car. Thus the main reason why most people abide by the law most of the time is not that they regularly *choose not to* commit an act of crime because, for example, they fear the consequences. Rather, they just do not perceive crime as an action alternative. However, this does not imply that the process of choice is unimportant in the explanation of crime. On the contrary, when people do see crime as an action alternative the process of choice is crucial to the outcome (ie whether or not an act of crime will result).

### 1.3.6 Rational deliberation and habit

If people do not see an act of crime as an alternative for acting upon a motivation there will be no act of crime. On the other hand, if they do see an act of crime as an action alternative the outcome may, or may not, be an act of crime depending on the process of choice. SAT proposes that there are basically two kinds of processes of choice; habitual or rational deliberate processes (Treiber 2011; Wikström 2006).[3] In the first case (habit), the actor perceives only *one* causally effective action alternative (the act of crime) and automatically forms an intention to carry out that action. To see only one causally effective alternative means the person makes no active consideration of any other action alternative (although he or she is likely to be loosely aware, in the back of his or her mind, that there are other possibilities). In the second case (rational deliberation), the actor sees *several* potent action alternatives, including at least one that involves an act of crime, and whether or not he or she will form an intention to engage in an act of crime depends on the outcome of his or her deliberation (see Figure 1.2). Let us briefly develop these arguments.

People are not merely puppets at the sole mercy of psychological and social forces. It is therefore essential to aim to model how (the process by which) social and psychological forces impact people's actions. However, the role of human agency is poorly treated in

---

[3] There is plenty of evidence for the existence of a dual process of human reasoning of this kind (see, eg, Evans and Frankish 2009).

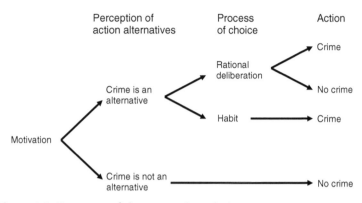

**Figure 1.2  Key steps of the perception–choice process**

criminological theory and research, if at all. That people are moved to action by making a choice implies that they have *agency*, that is the (context–dependent) power to make things happen intentionally. SAT recognizes that human action exhibits elements of free will and predictability and incorporates voluntaristic and deterministic processes into its explanation of acts of crime.

People express agency through habit or rational deliberation. Depending on the circumstances, their actions are thus more or less strongly determined. When people act out of *habit* they essentially react (in a stimulus-response fashion) to environmental cues (they only perceive one causally effective action alternative). They 'allow' the setting to determine their actions by triggering associative mechanisms developed through repeated previous exposure to similar circumstances. When people *deliberate* they actively weigh pros and cons of different alternatives for action (the process of deliberation may at its most elaborate even involve discussing the problem with, and taking advice from, other people).

When people deliberate they may be thought of as exercising '*free will*', meaning there is no predetermined alternative for action they automatically apply; instead they actively choose among perceived action alternatives. However, this does not mean that people choose without constraint when deliberating because, crucially, the choice among alternatives (to act upon a motivation) is a choice among the alternatives they perceive (and people vary in what alternatives they perceive in relation to a particular motivation in a particular setting). In other words, *they exercise 'free will' within the constraint of perceived action alternatives*. When people act based on deliberation they are likely to be aware of why they act as they do (although they may not be fully aware of why they perceive the particular action alternatives amongst which they choose). When people act habitually, they do not exercise 'free will' since no active choice among action alternatives is involved in the action process (see further Wikström 2006). Moreover, when people act out of habit they may be unaware of why they act as they do (although they may be able post factum to 'rationalize', more or less correctly, why they acted as they did).

SAT accepts that rationality (at times) plays a role in guiding human action. According to SAT, when (and only when) people deliberate they aim to act *rationally*. To act rationally means to choose the action alternative that is 'the best means of satisfying the agent's desires [*or commitments, or responding to a provocation*], given his beliefs about the available options and their consequences' (Elster 2007: 193, text in italics and brackets added by the authors).[4] Rational choice theories, thus, specify 'that in acting rationally, an actor is engaging in some kind of optimization' (Coleman and Fararo 1992: xi). Rationality does *not* (necessarily) assume that people (always) act out of *self-interest*.[5] As Elster (2007: 193) comments, 'the confusion of rationality and egoism is a crude error, although one that is facilitated by the practise of some rational-choice theorists'. When people act out of habit, rationality does not come into play because there is no weighing of pros and cons among several action alternatives (to choose *the best* alternative requires that a genuine choice among alternatives is made). Habitual action may even be *irrational*, that is people may act in ways they would not consider in their best interest had they deliberated.

Habitual action is oriented towards the *past* as it involves drawing upon previous experiences to guide current actions, while rational deliberate action is oriented towards the *future* as it involves trying to assess the best potential outcome of different perceived action alternatives. When people operate in *familiar* circumstances with *congruent* rule-guidance the perception–choice process tends to be habitual (they tend to see only one causally effective action alternative).

---

[4] It is difficult to imagine it would be otherwise *when people deliberate*, ie, that people's choices would be random or they would *aim* not to choose the best alternative (as they see it).

[5] Or, for that matter, that a choice of action is (always) guided by the aim to acquire pleasure and/or avoid pain.

In other words, people tend to do what they normally do in such circumstances without giving it much thought. When people act in *unfamiliar* circumstances, and/or they experience *conflicting* rule-guidance, the perception–choice process tends to be rational deliberate (that is, people aim to choose the best among several perceived action alternatives). The level of deliberation preceding a (rational) choice may vary dramatically depending on the importance and circumstances of the choice. Only rarely will such deliberation involve a full-blown process of rational choice that 'requires that benefits and costs of all courses of action be specified, then postulating that the actor takes the "optimal" action, the action that maximizes the differences between benefits and costs' (Coleman and Fararo 1992: xi). Although most actions are likely to be predominantly habitual or deliberate in nature, many actions, particularly in prolonged action sequences, may include elements of both habit and rational deliberation (eg people may drift back and forth between habitual and deliberate action guidance).

The extent to which acts of crime (and particular types of acts of crime) are an outcome of habit or rational deliberation is largely unknown (ie not researched), although there are good reasons to believe that many acts of crimes are expressions of habit rather than the result of rational deliberation, as are human actions in general (see, eg, Forgas and Laham 2005; Wood and Quinn 2005). A major reason for persistent offending, for example, may be that people have developed habits that encourage the breaking of particular rules of conduct (stated in law) in particular circumstances:

> The notion of habitual choice may in fact be particularly relevant to the explanation of chronic offending, as habituation suggests stability in the interactions between individuals and the settings they encounter, leading to enduring patterns of behavior, which could arguably include persistent offending.
>
> (Wikström and Treiber 2009b: 411)

### 1.3.7 Situational factors: Motivation, the moral filter, and controls

The key *situational factors* influencing the perception–choice process in the situational model of SAT are (1) motivation, (2) the moral filter, and (3) controls (Wikström 2010a). Their roles in the process of action are briefly described in Table 1.1.

**Table 1.1 Key situational factors in the perception–choice process**

1. **Motivation** initiates action processes
2. The **moral filter** provides *action alternatives* (in response to a particular motivation)
3. **Controls** influence the *process of choice* when there is conflicting rule-guidance (regarding perceived action alternatives)

Motivation

*Motivation* is defined as goal-directed attention. Motivation is a necessary but not sufficient factor in the explanation of why people break particular rules of conduct. To act people must first be motivated to do so, yet there are no particular motivations that always make people break a particular rule of conduct. For example, people may kill others for greed or revenge, or they may shoplift for excitement or to get money to buy drugs. If certain mobile telephones become popular (many people prefer them) that may explain why many such telephones are stolen, but not why some people who prefer them choose to steal them while others do not.

Motivation is a situational concept; it is an outcome of the person–environment interaction (on motivation and action generally, see Heckhausen and Heckhausen 2008). The two main kinds of relevant motivators, according to SAT (Wikström 2006, 2010a), are

(1) *temptations*, which are either
   (a) the outcome of the interaction between a person's desires (wants, needs) and opportunities to satisfy a desire (want, need), or
   (b) the outcome of the interaction between a person's commitments and opportunities to fulfil a commitment;
(2) *provocations*, which occur when a friction (an unwanted external interference) makes a person annoyed or angry with its perceived source (the extent to which depends on his or her sensitivity to particular unwanted interferences).

Motivators may include negative or positive *emotions*; temptations will often be associated with positive emotions (eg excitement), while provocations will usually be associated with negative emotions (eg anger). Motivators vary in strength. A strong motivator is one that has strong (positive or negative) emotions attached to it.

It is a mistake to assert, as general strain theory seems to (eg Agnew 2006: 2), that acts of crime only emerge from negative emotions, caused by strains and stressors (see Wikström 2010a). It is not difficult to think of examples of acts of crime linked to positive emotions such as excitement and fun (a point well made, for example, by Katz 1988).

### The moral filter

What action alternatives a person perceives in response to a particular motivator (temptation or provocation) depends on the interaction between a person's relevant moral rules (and their associated moral emotions) and the (perceived) relevant moral norms (and their enforcement) of the setting in which he or she takes part. The personal moral rules and the moral norms of a setting that are relevant in the explanation of acts of *crime* (particular acts of crime) are those that are *law relevant* (ie that concern actions that adhere to or break rules of conduct stated in law). Whether or not personal moral rules or the moral norms of the setting are the most potent influence may vary by circumstance, but there is always a minimal influence from both. People care more about certain moral rules (feel more shame and guilt if violating them), and certain moral norms are more salient (more relevant, commonly shared, and effectively upheld and enforced) in some settings than in others.

A person's moral engagement with the moral context of a particular setting creates a *moral filter*, defined as the moral rule-induced selective perception of action alternatives, circumscribing what actions are perceived as appropriate in response to a particular motivator (Figure 1.3). The moral filter is applied to motivation either habitually (through the exercise of a moral habit) or as part of rational deliberation (providing action alternatives for a moral judgement). Whether the moral filter is applied automatically or deliberately depends on, as previously discussed, whether the actor operates in familiar circumstances with congruent rule-guidance, in new or unfamiliar circumstances, and/or in circumstances where the rule-guidance is unclear or conflicting.

The moral filter may encourage or discourage breaking a moral rule (such as a law). If a person's moral rules and the moral norms of the setting encourage adhering to a particular rule of conduct when acting upon a motivation, it is unlikely the person will see breaking that rule of conduct as an alternative. On the other hand, if a person's moral rules and the moral norms of the setting encourage

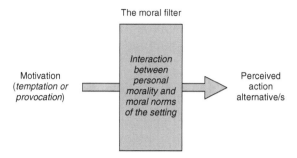

**Figure 1.3  The role of the moral filter**

breaking a particular rule of conduct when acting upon a motivation, it is likely the person will perceive breaking that rule of conduct as an alternative. Thus, if there is a correspondence between a person's moral rules and the (perceived) moral norms of a setting, the action alternatives a person perceives are likely to be in accordance with those rules. This is what is referred to as SAT's *principle of moral correspondence*. However, a person's moral rules do not always correspond with the moral norms of a setting, in which case controls becomes important for what actions may follow upon a particular motivation.

## Controls

SAT proposes that controls *only* come into play in the explanation of acts of crime when people (1) deliberate and (2) there is conflicting rule-guidance between personal moral rules and the moral norms of the settings regarding whether or not to engage in an act of crime. When people (as a result of the application of the moral filter) do not see an act of crime as an action alternative, or they see only one causally effective alternative, which is an act of crime (and therefore act out of habit), controls are irrelevant. Controls 'oppose something in support of something else' (Mele 2001: 121) and thus (in the explanation of crime) require a circumstance in which a person deliberates over action alternatives that include an act of crime. Again, if an act of crime is not perceived as an action alternative, or an act of crime is committed out of habit, no control is involved. This is referred to in SAT as *the principle of the conditional relevance of controls* (Wikström 2010a).

Control is conceptualized in SAT as the process by which a person manages conflicting rule-guidance in his or her choice of action in relation to a particular motivation. What controls thus aim to control is the adherence to moral rules when a person deliberates about alternatives for acting upon a motivation (Wikström 2010a). Controls may be internal in origin (through the process of self-control) or external in origin (through the process of deterrence). *Self-control* is defined as an (inner-to-outer) process by which a person succeeds in adhering to a personal moral rule when it conflicts with the moral norms of the setting (a typical example would be withstanding peer pressure to smoke cannabis when doing so conflicts with one's own rules of conduct). *Deterrence* is defined as an (outer-to-inner) process by which the (perceived) enforcement of a setting's moral norms (by creating concern or fear of consequences) succeeds in making a person adhere to the moral norms of the setting even though they conflict with his or her personal moral rules (a typical example would be a person who finds shoplifting morally unproblematic and considers doing so but, because of environmental cues that make him or her consider the risk and consequences of getting caught, refrains).

The principles of moral correspondence and the conditional role of controls are illustrated as four ideal cases in Figure 1.4. Box 1 represents a particular moral rule of conduct (eg a law that prohibits smoking cannabis). Box 2 represents the person's moral rules relevant to that particular moral rule (eg personal moral rules relevant to whether it is right or wrong to smoke cannabis) and Box 3 represents the moral norms of the setting applicable to that particular moral rule (eg the moral norms that encourage or discourage smoking cannabis). The signs indicate whether or not there is correspondence (+) or conflict (–) in moral rule-guidance. As shown in Figure 1.4, a person's *ability to exercise self-control* only comes into play when the moral norms of the setting encourage him or her to break a rule of conduct but his or her personal moral rules discourage doing so in response to a motivation (example 3), while the *efficacy of deterrence* only comes into play when a person's moral rules encourage rule-breaking but the moral norms of the setting discourage doing so (example 4). In examples 1 and 2, controls are not relevant because there is a moral correspondence between the person's moral rules and the moral norms of the setting that either discourages (example 1) or encourages (example 2) breaking a particular rule of conduct.

Control theories in criminology tend to conflate moral rules and controls in the explanation of acts of crime (see Wikström 2010a).

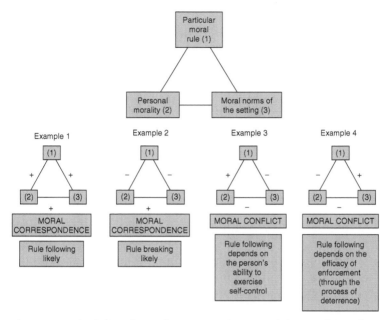

**Figure 1.4  Principles of moral correspondence and the conditional relevance of controls**

SAT maintains the importance of distinguishing the two analytically, as they play different roles in crime causation. Moral rules influence the perception of action alternatives, while controls (may) play a role in the process of choice. Moreover, some control theories tend to focus on control as a personal characteristic (eg self-control as a trait) and generally ignore its situational nature (see Wikström and Treiber 2007).

SAT stresses the importance of distinguishing analytically between:

(1) controls as (situational) processes of self-control and deterrence in the management of conflicting rule-guidance;
(2) people's ability to exercise self-control and the capacity of settings to create effective deterrence (Wikström 2010a).

People vary in their ability to exercise self-control and settings vary in their capacity to create effective deterrence. A person's ability to exercise self-control depends on his or her executive functions (general cognitive abilities) but also on temporary personal factors like intoxication or extreme stress or emotions (see Wikström and Treiber 2007). A setting's capacity to create effective deterrence (ie concern or fear of consequences) depends on the level of enforcement of relevant moral norms (ie the effectiveness of monitoring and intervention and the likelihood and severity of sanctions).

### 1.3.8  Summing up the key constructs of the situational model, their relationships and roles in the action process

The key constructs of the situational model of SAT (and their relationships) are summarized in Table 1.2. The second column specifies the key personal characteristics (the factors causally relevant to a person's particular crime propensity), and the third the key setting features (the factors causally relevant to a setting's particular criminogeneity). People vary in their desires, commitments, and sensitivities (to particular frictions) as well as their morality (moral rules and their attached moral emotions) and ability to exercise self-control. Settings vary in the opportunities they provide and the frictions they create as well as in the moral norms and levels of enforcement that apply to particular opportunities and frictions. The first column specifies the situational factors that emerge out of the interaction between the relevant personal characteristics and setting features (eg the moral filter is an outcome of the interaction between personal morality and [perceived] moral norms of the setting). Finally, the

**Table 1.2  Key constructs of the situational model and their relationships**

| Situation | = | Person | x | Setting | Affects |
|---|---|---|---|---|---|
| Motivator: | | | | | |
| 1. Temptation | | a. Desires (needs)<br>b. Commitments | | Opportunity<br>Opportunity | Goal-directed attention |
| 2. Provocation | | Sensitivity | | Friction | |
| Moral filter | | Morality | | Moral norms | Perception of action alternatives |
| Control | | Ability to exercise self-control | | Capacity to enforce moral norms | Process of choice |
| | | Propensity | x | Exposure | = | Action |

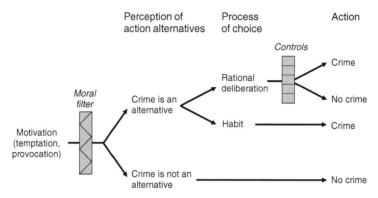

**Figure 1.5  The role of the moral filter and controls in the action process**

Source: Wikström, P-O H. (2011a), 'Does everything matter? Addressing the problem of causation and explanation in the study of crime'. In J. M. McGloin, C. J. Sullivan, and L. W. Kennedy (eds), *When crime appears: The role of emergence* (London: Routledge).

fourth column specifies what aspect of the action process is affected by particular situational factors (eg the moral filter affects the perception of action alternatives). The role of the moral filter and controls in the action process is illustrated in Figure 1.5.

## 1.4  Situational Action Theory: The causes of the causes

SAT proposes that the *situation* is the appropriate level to analyse and explain acts of crime because the causes of acts of crime are situational (ie acts of crime are an outcome of a perception–choice process initiated and guided by the interaction of crime propensity and criminogenic exposure in relation to a particular motivation). However, this does not render the role of *social systemic* factors and processes, and factors and processes in a person's *life history*, unimportant in the explanation of crime. SAT insists though that these factors should be analysed as *causes of the causes* rather than causes of acts of crime, and that to effectively analyse the causes of the causes we first need to know what the causes are (for more on the problem of causation and explanation in the study of crime, see Wikström 2011a). The argument is simple: if we do not understand the causes it is difficult (if not impossible) to understand the causes of the causes. The processes through which the causes and the causes of the causes are linked in the explanation of crime, according to SAT, is summarized in the following points, and illustrated in Figure 1.6.

(1) Crime is ultimately an outcome of a perception–choice process.
(2) This perception–choice process is initiated and guided by relevant aspects of the person–environment interaction.
(3) Processes of social and self selection place kinds of people in kinds of settings (creating particular kinds of interactions).
(4) What kinds of people and what kinds of environments (settings) are present in a jurisdiction is the result of historical processes of personal and social emergence.

The focus of this chapter so far has been the causal factors (propensity and exposure) that initiate and guide the causal (perception–choice) process that moves people to engage in acts of crime. The remainder of the chapter will focus on the problem of identifying and understanding the causes of the causes and, particularly, how this can be applied to a study of crime in the urban environment. The main argument advanced is that the problem of the causes of the causes (of action) is best analysed in terms of processes of (social and personal) *emergence*, and processes of (social and self) *selection*.

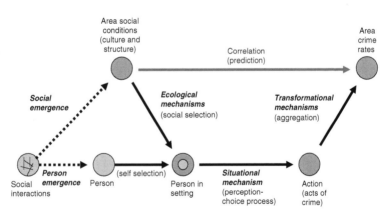

**Figure 1.6  Key causal mechanisms in the study of crime causation, as suggested by SAT**

**Source:** Wikström, P-O H. (2011a), 'Does everything matter? Addressing the problem of causation and explanation in the study of crime'. In J. M. McGloin, C. J. Sullivan, and L. W. Kennedy (eds), *When crime appears: The role of emergence* (London: Routledge).

### 1.4.1 Social and personal emergence

The concept of *emergence* essentially refers to how something becomes as it is (on the topic of emergence generally, see Bunge 2003; Kaidesoja 2009; Sawyer 2005), for example, how a person acquires a particular crime propensity against the backdrop of his or her psychosocial development, or how an environment (setting) acquires a particular criminogeneity against the backdrop of socio-ecological factors. It refers to the occurrence of higher-order qualities that are not reducible to the lower-order processes that constitute the entity in question. However, even if these higher-order qualities are not reducible to lower-order processes, they may be explained by such processes. As Bunge (2003: 21) maintains, 'it is a mistake to define an emergent property as a feature of a whole that cannot be explained in terms of the properties of its parts'. In fact, 'some of the most interesting and toughest problems, in any science, are to discover mechanisms of emergence and submergence' (ibid.: 22).[6]

Cultural and structural characteristics of an area (eg a nation or a city), such as general and localized systems of formal and informal rules of conduct (including their application and enforcement), and patterns of social and spatial differentiation of kinds of people and kinds of activities, may be regarded as emergent properties of historical processes of social interactions, while people's characteristics (such as their propensities) may be regarded as emergent properties of (life) historical processes of personal social interactions in social context (with a biological foundation).

*Personal emergence* is a 'kinds of people' question, and a natural criminological focus is how people acquire different crime propensities. SAT proposes, as previously discussed, that people's morality and ability to exercise self-control are the key relevant personal aspects affecting their crime propensity and, therefore, the *processes* by which people acquire their morality and ability to exercise self-control are of prime criminological interest (see eg Wikström 2005). These include:

(1) moral education (how people come to acquire particular moral rules and related moral emotions through processes of

---

[6] The concept of submergence refers to how something loses its emergent properties (eg, how a crime prone person becomes crime averse, or how a criminogenic environment loses its criminogeneity).

instruction, trial and error, sanctions, and observations of reactions to and sanctioning of others' actions); and

(2) cognitive skills development (how people come to acquire particular cognitive skills, for example, through processes of cognitive nurturing and training) relevant to their ability to exercise self-control.

Central to the analysis of the processes of social interaction that influence criminologically relevant aspects of moral education and cognitive skills development are the role of key social institutions (as prime agents of socialization and nurturing), such as the family and school, but also peer networks (see Wikström and Sampson 2003: 131–5). The impact of these institutions is likely to vary depending on the stage of a person's biological maturation and social and cognitive development. The concept of 'time windows' is useful in this context, as stated by Bloom (1964: vii): 'variations in the environment have the greatest quantitative effect on a characteristic at its most rapid period of change and least effect on the characteristic during the least rapid period of change'.

One can, of course, go even further back in the causal chain and (as an analysis of the 'causes of the causes of the causes') examine the dependence of the nature and efficacy of criminologically relevant aspects of socialization and nurturing provided by the family, school, and peer networks on the broader social institutions of politics, religion, and economics in which they are embedded (see Messner 2012). Arguably, such knowledge would rely largely on insights from non-criminological research. In this book we do not aim to investigate the problem of how people acquire differential crime propensities but take the fact that people have different crime propensities as a starting point for our analysis of environmental influences on people's acts of crime.

*Social emergence* is a 'kinds of settings' question, and a natural criminological focus is how environments (in a particular jurisdiction) become different in features relevant to their criminogeneity. SAT proposes, as previously discussed, that an environment's (setting's) criminogenic features depend on the extent to which its moral norms and their enforcement encourage breaking rules of conduct (stated in law) in relation to the opportunities it provides and the frictions it generates. Of prime criminological interest, therefore, are the *processes* by which environments (settings) come to have (1) particular moral norms and (2) specific levels of moral norm enforcement (through monitoring and intervention),[7] in relation to (3) the particular opportunities and frictions they present.

The theory and research tradition within criminology that most clearly focuses on exploring and explaining the social emergence of moral contexts of settings conducive to acts of crime (and, in the longer term, the development of people's crime propensity) is the social disorganisation tradition. Originating from the classic Chicago School (eg Park et al. [1925] 1967), and its study of crime and other social problems in the urban area (eg Shaw and McKay [1942] 1969), this tradition has evolved over many years into its present form (eg Bursik 1988; Kornhauser 1978; Sampson 2006a).

The social disorganization tradition's primary focus is on how processes of urban residential segregation (mainly on economic grounds[8]) create neighbourhood differentiation in terms of population disadvantage, heterogeneity, and turnover, and, in turn, consequences for the efficiency of local social institutions (eg families and schools) and the strength of residents' social cohesion (social and moral integration). These latter factors are seen to impact the efficacy of neighbourhood collective socialization of children and young people, and the efficacy of momentary informal social control (monitoring and interventions) regulating residents' and visitors' behaviour (see, eg, Kornhauser 1978: 70–82). In this book we make no attempt to analyse and study the emergence of residential segregation (and its dependency on the wider political and economic context) but focus on how the resulting residential differentiation and its key social consequences help create spatial differences in the occurrence of criminogenic settings (eg areas with poor collective efficacy).

A basic idea of the social disorganization perspective is that differences between social environments (eg neighbourhoods, communities) in the rate of resident offenders (particularly young

---

[7] Note that moral norms of a setting can either encourage or discourage breaking rules of conduct (stated in law) and, hence, that effective enforcement of moral norms, depending on whether or not the moral norms support law-abiding action, can either encourage or discourage acts of crime. Lack of effective enforcement of moral norms is only criminogenic when the moral norms support law abidance.

[8] But more recently the impact of urban planning and local housing markets and policies (eg, the provision and location of social housing) have also been stressed as important influences on the pattern of residential social differentiation (see, eg, Baldwin and Bottoms 1976; Sampson 1990; Wikström 1991).

offenders) and the rate of crime events can be explained 'in terms of variations in the abilities of local communities to regulate and control the behavior of their residents' and visitors (Bursik and Grasmick 1993). More specifically, the theory asserts that socially disorganized environments do not have the capacity to regulate and control behaviour effectively. Kornhauser (1978: 63) defined social disorganization as a lack of 'a structure through which common values can be realised and common problems solved' (where law abidance may be regarded as a typical common value and people committing acts of crime as a chief example of a common problem).

Sampson and colleagues have further developed the modern social disorganization perspective by suggesting the concept of *collective efficacy*[9] (eg Sampson et al. 1997; Sampson et al. 1999; Sampson 2006b) to describe residents' willingness to intervene for the common good (ie their potential to exercise informal social control if needed) as the result of shared expectations and mutual trust in the community. A key argument is that residents are less likely to enforce rules of conduct in neighbourhoods with poor collective efficacy, that is 'in a neighborhood context where the rules are unclear and people mistrust or fear each other' (Sampson 2011: 232). The concept of collective efficacy thus subsumes the concepts of social cohesion (a community's ability to generate moral and social integration among its residents; Sampson 1993) and informal social control (monitoring and intervention). The structural sources of collective efficacy are largely seen to be the same as those discussed by Shaw and McKay ([1942] 1969) and Kornhauser (1978) as the structural sources of social disorganization (ie population disadvantage, heterogeneity, and turnover), although Sampson (1987, 1993) has highlighted the importance of family disruption (ie single parent households) as an additional important structural factor.

While the social disorganization tradition (in which we include collective efficacy theory) has contributed substantially to our understanding of the role of the social environment in crime causation, it has some general limitations as a theory of crime causation.

---

[9] It has (to our knowledge) never been made fully clear how the concepts of social disorganization and collective efficacy relate to each other, although the latter (collective efficacy) is clearly more focused on the local processes influencing whether or not people abide by rules of conduct, while the former (social disorganization) is more clearly focused on the structural conditions of importance for the emergence of these processes.

According to SAT, it is analytically important to clearly differentiate between the environment's long-term (cumulative) effect, as a *context of development*, on the formation and shape of people's crime propensities (eg through moral education), and its short-term (momentary) effect, as a *context of action*, on people's perceptions and choices relevant to their engagement in acts of crime (eg through the enforcement of law-relevant moral rules). However, social disorganization/collective efficacy theory does not always effectively differentiate between these two key analytical problems in its theorizing (but cf. Wikström and Sampson 2003). In this book, we focus on urban environments (urban settings) as *contexts of action* (and leave the problem of analysing their role as contexts of development, relevant to the development of people's crime propensities, to be addressed in future publications).

Social disorganization/collective efficacy theory does not explain why *acts* of crime occur. The influence of neighbourhood structural characteristics and social processes on crime are mainly analysed at the area level (explaining area *rates* of acts of crime) and therefore do not tell us that much about how (through what processes) structural characteristics are linked to individual acts of crime. Wikström and Sampson (2003: 127) suggest 'what has been missing is a concept that directly links the community context to individual development and actions... behavior-setting is a concept that may provide such a linkage'.[10]

SAT stresses the importance of understanding the role of the person–environment interaction in crime causation. Traditionally, the social disorganization perspective tends to ignore the role of *individual differences*, that is, the differential effect of particular kinds of environments on particular kinds of people's actions (although more recently the importance of this aspect has been increasingly emphasized by some scholars working in the social disorganization tradition; see, for example, Harding et al. 2011). Moreover, and crucially, social disorganization theory does not provide any situational model that explains *how* the *interaction* between people and environments moves people to engage in acts of crime. Interestingly, Kornhauser concludes her seminal

---

[10] To avoid confusion with Barker's (1968) concept of *behaviour setting* (which has a somewhat different meaning), SAT refers to *settings* (rather than behaviour settings). However, it should be acknowledged that SAT's concept of setting is partly inspired by Barker's concept of behaviour setting.

assessment of social disorganization (and cultural deviance) theory by arguing for the need 'to search for the root causes of delinquency in social structure and situation' (1978: 253). However, the role of the emergence of situations conducive to acts of crime, and its dependency on social structure, has not figured much in subsequent work in this tradition, although it is a challenge that is taken up by SAT.

The concept of *neighbourhood*, the key analytic unit of social disorganization theory, is rarely well defined. Originally, neighbourhoods were seen as 'natural areas' emerging as a result of the process of residential segregation (Park [1925] 1967; Zorbaugh 1961). Bursik and Grasmick (1993: 6) characterize a neighbourhood as 'a small area embedded within a larger area in which people inhabit dwellings' where 'there is a collective life that emerges from the social networks that have arisen among the residents and the sets of institutional arrangements that overlap these networks' and 'some tradition of identity and continuity over time'. Sampson (2011: 228) defines a neighbourhood as 'a variably interacting population of people and institutions in a common place', and goes on to say that he thus chooses to 'define neighborhoods geographically and leave the nature and extent of social relations problematic' (ibid.: 229). The problem of the unit of analysis when studying the impact of environments on individual action will be further discussed in section 3.3.1 (see also section 2.8.2).

Social disorganization/collective efficacy theory tends to primarily focus on residents' characteristics and relationships (eg cohesion), when explaining the influence of neighbourhood social features on rates of crimes (and residents' crime propensity). However, the moral norms of an area (setting) and their enforcement depend not only on residents' characteristics and relationships, but also on those of visitors to the area, as well as the kinds of activities that take place in the area, and the circumstances under which people take part in those activities. The social cohesion amongst people present in an area, and the nature of an area's social life, may vary substantially depending on its particular combination of residents, visitors, and activities, which has implications for the homogeneity of its (law-relevant) rules of conduct and their level of enforcement (or lack of enforcement). Compare, for example, the social life of a purely residential area with that of the city centre with a large transient non-residential population. Taking into account the role of activities (and area visitors) also puts emphasis on the short-term *temporal* dimension of settings' moral contexts; eg the moral context of a specific area may be conducive to rule-breaking at particular times of the day but not at others as the kinds of people present and kinds of activities taking place may vary.

While social disorganization/collective efficacy theory helps us understand why some environments are more criminogenic than others (in particular, as it relates to residents' varying capacity to uphold law-relevant moral norms), it does not particularly help us to understand the processes by which people (and different kinds of people) become exposed to criminogenic environments within a jurisdiction (other than as a function of their home location). Arguably, acts of crime are an outcome of the person–environment interaction and, therefore, considering only the criminogenic features of environments tells only part of the story. People are differently influenced by criminogenic features of settings depending on their crime propensity. This is a problem that is helpfully addressed as a problem of selection.

### 1.4.2 Social and self selection

Selection is a 'kinds of people in kinds of settings' question. The concept of *selection* relates to the ecological processes responsible for introducing particular kinds of people to particular kinds of settings (and thus creating the situations to which people respond through their actions). Particular patterns of selection are an outcome of the interaction of processes of social selection and self selection.

*Social selection* refers to the social forces (dependent on systems of formal and informal rules and differential distribution of personal and institutional resources in a particular jurisdiction) that enable (encourage or compel) or restrict (discourage or bar) particular kinds of people from taking part in particular kinds of time and place-based activities. *Self selection* refers to the preference-based choices people make to attend particular time and place-based activities within the constraints of the forces of social selection (eg people do not always have the resources, or are allowed, to take part in some activities they prefer). What particular preferences people have developed may be seen as an outcome of their life history experiences. The extent to which particular preferences can be materialized depends on the person's context specific agency.[11] Depending on the circumstances, social or self selection can be more influential in explaining why a particular person takes part in a particular setting.

Selection is often discussed as a potential problem of bias in statistical analysis of environmental effects on people's actions. The main idea seems to be that because people select environments it is not the effect of the environment (kinds of environments) that is of importance for their actions but the fact that they (kinds of people) have self selected to be in the particular environment. A not uncommon idea seems to be that the same personal characteristics (eg poor ability to exercise self-control) that lead people to self select into certain environments also explain why they get into trouble in those environments.

Within the framework of SAT, selection is not treated as a (potential) bias but as an important explanatory factor (ie as a key cause of the causes, explaining why particular kinds of people are exposed to particular kinds of settings). SAT maintains that it is a mistake to confuse the processes by which people come to take part in particular settings (selection processes) with the effects of these settings (environmental effects) on their actions (and development) (Wikström 2006: 88; see also Sampson 2011: 244).

The criminological approach most relevant to the problem of (social) selection is *routine activity theory* (RAT), which emerged as a key theoretical approach in the late 1970s (eg Cohen and Felson 1979). Routine activities refer to generalized patterns of social activities in a society (ie spatial and temporal patterns in family, work, and leisure activities). RAT is based on two key ideas: (1) that the structure of routine activities in a society influences what kinds of situations (person–environment interactions) emerge; and (2) that people commit acts of crime in response to situational conditions (opportunities).

---

[11] People start life with little agency but generally significantly develop (albeit at different rates) their capacity to make things happen intentionally throughout childhood and adolescence. People who have acquired strong human capital (eg, skills), financial capital (eg, money), and social capital (eg, resourceful networks) generally have a greater potential to (and greater *belief* that they can) self select the activities (in places) they prefer. However, a person's agency may vary significantly between his or her different life domains (eg, family, work, and leisure) and between particular settings within those domains.

The situational model of RAT defines what constitutes an *opportunity*, that is the convergence of a motivated offender and a suitable target in the absence of a capable guardian (Cohen and Felson 1979; Felson and Cohen 1980). It is, in principle, an interactional model that by its logic requires all three elements to be present simultaneously for a crime to occur. A 'capable guardian' is a person (perceived to be) willing and capable to intervene to stop acts of crime, in other words a person (perceived to be) ready and able to exercise (formal or informal) social control. What constitutes a 'suitable target' is never made fully clear other than that 'target suitability is likely to reflect such things as value (ie the material or symbolic desirability of a personal or property target for offenders), physical visibility, access, and the inertia of a target against illegal treatment by offenders (including the weight, size, and attached or locked features of property inhibiting its illegal removal and the physical capacity of personal victims to resist attackers with or without weapons)' (Cohen and Felson 1979: 591).

A major shortcoming of RAT is that the theory does not specify how (through what causal process) the people–environment convergence brings about an act of crime. If this question is touched upon at all, proponents of RAT generally seem to allude to some version of rational choice theory (eg Felson and Cohen 1980). This argument is not well developed and RAT and rational choice theory have (to our knowledge) never been properly integrated (see Clarke and Felson 1993: 1–14).

Another major limitation of RAT is the poor treatment of the role of individual differences in the interaction process, something that is perhaps understandable against the background of the following claim by Clarke and Felson (1993: 2): 'the routine activity approach offered a thought experiment: to see how far one could go in explaining crime trends without ever discussing any of the various theories about criminal motivation'. However, the concept of motivated offenders seems to acknowledge that people differ in their propensity to engage in acts of crime (see Felson 2002), although some scholars who work in this tradition seem to take the rather extreme position that all people are motivated offenders, that is that acts of crime are solely a function of momentary influences on action by environmental conditions with no input of (differential) individual propensity (Wilcox et al. 2003).

Closely related to routine activity theory is Brantingham and Brantingham's (1993) *crime pattern theory*, a theory that more

specifically focuses on the prediction of spatial and temporal variation in crime events. The theory's basic assumption (similar to
RAT's situational model) is that 'crime is an event that occurs when
an individual with some criminal readiness level encounters a
suitable target in a situation sufficient to activate the readiness
potential (ibid.: 266).

The concept of readiness seems to conflate the concepts of motivation (as a situational concept) and propensity (as a more stable
individual characteristic); 'readiness to commit a crime is not a
constant: it varies from person to person; and it varies for each
individual person across time and space as the backcloth varies'
(ibid.: 266). The fact that readiness 'varies from person to person'
indicates an assumption of (at least) somewhat stable individual
propensity differences, while the fact that readiness is also seen to
vary over time and space for a specific person indicates an assumption of situationally induced motivation. SAT emphasizes the analytic importance of clearly distinguishing between the concepts of
propensity and motivation in the explanation of crime.

A key contribution of crime pattern theory is the idea that it is
possible to predict crime occurrences from people's (offenders')
activity space. 'Crime is not randomly distributed in time and space.
It is clustered, but the shape of the clustering is greatly influenced by
where people live within a city, how and why they travel or move
about a city, and how networks of people who know each other
spend their time' (P. J. Brantingham and Brantingham 2008: 91). SAT
agrees with the explanatory importance of people's activity space,
but prefers the concept of activity field. The concept of activity field
incorporates that of activity space but also takes into account the
circumstances in which people are exposed to particular environments. Environmental influences on people's crime are not primarily
a question of where people spend time and when, but, crucially,
a question of the features of the settings (environments) in which
people take part, and the circumstances under which they do so.

While crime pattern theory shares many key important insights
with routine activity theory it also shares some of the same basic
explanatory problems facing routine activity theory. Just like RAT,
it does not specify in any detail the causal process by which the
convergence of people and environments moves people to action
(other than alluding to rational choice theory). It is more a theory
about why crime events occur at particular places and times than
about why and how the convergence of particular kinds of people

with particular kinds of environments causes acts of crime. Nor does it specify in any depth the role of individual differences in the person–environment interaction (other than acknowledging that people have a different 'readiness' to engage in acts of crime).

## 1.5 Explaining urban crime patterns

SAT aims to incorporate and develop key insights from routine activity/crime pattern theory and social disorganization/collective efficacy theory within an emergence–selection framework. These theories make seminal contributions to our understanding of crime causation, but mainly as theories of the causes of the causes of crime; they help us understand the *social mechanisms* that explain how criminogenic settings emerge and how people are introduced to criminogenic settings. However, as already discussed, neither says much about the *situational mechanisms* that move people to engage in acts of crime, or the role of individual differences in that process. SAT aims to overcome these problems by integrating the role of social mechanisms (processes of emergence and selection) and situational mechanisms (perception–choice processes) in its comprehensive explanation of urban crime (and crime more generally) and its causes. The fundamentals of SAT's explanation of urban crime are outlined below.

Historic processes of social emergence (for example as a result of political and economic processes affecting social group efficacy in the competition over desirable space and city planning) help explain why a city has a particular urban structure (a particular pattern of residential and activity differentiation creating a particular mosaic of social environments). Historical processes of personal emergence (developmental processes in local social contexts), and processes of selective in- and out-migration, help to explain an urban area's population's mix of personal characteristics and experiences. Historical processes of social and personal emergence are not unrelated since changes in the social environment mean changes in the social contexts that may be relevant to what experiences people have and what characteristics they develop (eg different generations growing up in the same city, or even in the same neighbourhood, may have very different social experiences). Contemporaneous processes of social and self selection help explain why certain kinds of people are introduced at a certain rate to certain kinds of settings (Figure 1.6).

People are crime prone depending on the extent to which their morality and ability to exercise self-control encourages breaking rules of conduct stated in law. Settings are criminogenic depending on the extent to which their moral norms and their levels of enforcement (or lack of enforcement) encourage breaking rules of conduct stated in law. Acts of crime tend to occur when crime prone people are introduced to criminogenic settings in which they experience temptations or provocations.

Processes of social and personal emergence that affect the occurrence of criminogenic settings (the occurrence of settings with moral norms and levels of enforcement/lack of enforcement encouraging crime) and people's crime propensities (moral education and cognitive nurturing encouraging crime), and processes of social and self selection (expressed in people's activity fields) that influence the convergence of crime prone people and criminogenic settings, are all factors of importance for the explanation of the rate of crime in a city and its variation across different areas.

Concentrations of crime events in time and space ('hot spots') in an urban area are essentially consequences of concentrations in time and space of interactions between crime prone people and criminogenic settings (against the backdrop of a set of particular temptations and provocations of relevance for what kinds of crimes may occur at a particular location), creating the situations to which crime prone people may (habitually or after deliberation) respond with acts that break the rules of conduct stated in law.

Changes in the level of crime in a particular urban area (or in certain parts of an urban area) are seen to be a result of (1) changes in the prevalence of crime prone people among its population (and its visitors), or (2) changes in the extent of its criminogenic settings, or (3) changes in the nature of the selection processes that affect the rate by which crime prone people are exposed to its criminogenic settings. Such changes are an outcome of changes in processes of social emergence (as they affect the prevalence of criminogenic settings), or changes in processes of personal emergence (as they affect the prevalence of crime prone people), or changes in contemporaneous processes of social and self selection (as they affect the frequency of interactions between crime prone people and criminogenic settings) which, in turn, may be related to political and economic changes in the larger society in which the urban area is embedded and on which it depends.

In this book we will not deal with the role of historical processes of social and personal emergence in crime causation, but rather focus on how processes of social and self selection (as manifested in people's activity fields) can explain the spatial and temporal distribution of young people's crime in urban areas. In a nutshell, SAT proposes that contemporaneous urban crime patterns can be explained by the fact that the social dynamics created by the differentiated urban environment, and related processes of social and self selection, help create varying intersections of kinds of people in kinds of settings in different parts of the city, at different times of the day, creating different situational dynamics (perception–choice processes), some of which are more likely to result in acts of crime (or particular kinds of acts of crime), thus explaining concentrations of crime (and particular kinds of crime) in time and space.

**2**

# The Peterborough Adolescent and Young Adult Development Study

The *Peterborough Adolescent and Young Adult Development Study* (PADS+) is an investigation into the social lives and crime of 700 young people in the UK city of Peterborough. Its overall aim is to advance knowledge about the role of the social environment and its interaction with personal characteristics and experiences in crime causation.

One of the biggest shortcomings of criminological research to date is a lack of adequate research into how the *interplay* between people's crime propensity and criminogenic exposure affects their crime involvement and criminal careers. As Sampson (1997: 32) points out, 'few studies have successfully demonstrated a unified approach to the individual and community level dimensions of crime', while Brooks-Gunn et al. (1993: 354) note that 'the bulk of developmental research has focused on the most proximal environments, specifically the family and peer group... and has largely ignored neighbourhood contexts'.

PADS+ was specifically set up to help overcome these kinds of problems by introducing a research design and new methodologies that enable the exploration of people's exposure to social environments and its interaction with their personal characteristics and experiences in predicting their crime involvement. In this chapter we outline and discuss the design of, methodologies used, and data collected for, PADS+. In the next chapter (chapter 3) we introduce and discuss in some detail the key constructs (and their measures) used for the analyses presented in this book.

## 2.1 The research design

### 2.1.1 Why Peterborough?

... a great city tends to spread out and lay bare to the public view in a massive manner all the human characters and traits which are ordinarily obscured and suppressed in smaller communities... It is this fact, perhaps, more than any other, which justifies the view that would make of the city a laboratory or clinic in which human nature and social processes may be conveniently and profitably studied.

(Park [1925] 1967: 45–6)

To study young people's social lives means looking beyond their homes and neighbourhoods to capture everywhere they spend their time. To do so comprehensively requires a self-contained study area in which they can act out all major aspects of their lives. A city is just such an environment. An urban area, such as a city, is a habitat that provides all the amenities necessary for physical and social life. Studying social lives in cities is important not only because cities provide the right kind of self-contained environment, but also because most people live in urban areas, even though such areas cover a small proportion of the land mass. For example, in 2001, 80.4 per cent of people in England lived in urban settlements (Countryside Agency et al. 2004), yet urban areas covered only 8.9 per cent of the UK land mass (Pointer 2005).

Peterborough is a modestly sized city (containing, according to the 2001 census, about 156,000 inhabitants) situated in an area of sparsely populated fenland and relatively isolated from other urban centres. This increases the likelihood that its residents will spend the majority of their time within its boundaries. In support of this contention, our analyses (using a space–time budget; see section 2.5) show that the young people in the PADS+ sample spent 93 per cent of their time awake within the study area during the study period.

To study the differential effects of environments on young people's lives requires a certain degree of variation in physical and social characteristics (see G. J. Duncan and Raudenbush 1999). This calls for a study area large enough to encompass an adequate range of environments. For its size, Peterborough presents a considerable diversity of social environments. It is constructed around a number of townships, such that its urban area is spread out across the cityscape, forming unique social communities and environments. It is designed to separate industrial, commercial, and residential areas, which further differentiates its physical and social geography. It also includes environments at both ends of the social spectrum; for example, it contains some of the most affluent as well as some of the most disadvantaged residential areas in the country (see sections 4.1, 4.2, and 4.3 for a more in-depth description of Peterborough's social, physical, and historic landscape).

An additional consideration in the selection of a study area was its proximity to the research headquarters in Cambridge. For practical reasons the study area needed to be within commuting distance for researchers. A number of nearby urban areas were considered, including Luton and Colchester. Peterborough was selected because it met the criteria of being a self-contained but socially diverse city and, crucially, because following the *Peterborough Youth Study* (see Wikström and Butterworth 2006), which served as a pilot for PADS+, a number of useful contacts had been forged with local agencies, including the police, the local council, and local schools, which proved influential in the implementation of the study.

### 2.1.2  Why adolescence?

Adolescent development cannot be understood apart from the context in which young people grow up... In order to understand how adolescents develop in contemporary society, [we] need first to understand the world in which adolescents live and how that world affects their behaviour and social relationships.

(Steinberg 2011: xv)

This book deals with the relationship between social life and crime in adolescence. Across the lifespan people pass through several development phases, including childhood, adolescence, and young adulthood. In studying the relationships between social environments and crime events, adolescence proves particularly informative, as it is the time period during which young people increasingly, but differentially, spend time outside the typically more structured environments of their childhood.

During adolescence, young people expand their activity fields, coming into contact with a wider range of social contexts (see, for example, Osgood et al. 2005: 55–7). During childhood their activities are concentrated around the home and school but as they gain mobility and personal freedom they begin to move further afield, exerting greater agency in their selection of social environments, and greater autonomy in interacting with them. At the same time, their peers play an increasingly important role in how they spend their time. They also reach physical maturity, fully realizing important cognitive capacities linked to personal control and social behaviour, the groundwork for which is laid during childhood.

Adolescence is also a key developmental phase for crime involvement. Studies from Europe and North America (eg Farrington and

Wikstrom 1994; Laub and Sampson 2003: 86; Le Blanc and Fréchette 1989: 61–3; McVie 2005; Piquero et al. 2007: 48; Tracy et al. 1990: 216; Wikström 1990) consistently show a sharp rise in crime involvement during the early to mid teen years with a peak in offending prevalence between ages 14 and 17. Studies which use self-report data tend to show a peak on the earlier end of this spectrum,[1] while those which use official data tend to show a peak at the latter end[2] (potentially an artefact of how official data is recorded; see, for example, Le Blanc and Fréchette 1989: 63). Data on the age crime curve (based on police recorded prevalence) for England and Wales in 2006 (the mid-point of PADS+ Phase 1 data collection) is shown in Figure 2.1; here 16-year-olds have the highest prevalence rate.[3]

[1] For example, Le Blanc and Fréchette (1989: 62) found that self-reported crime involvement in the Montreal Two-Sample Longitudinal Study peaked at age 15. Hales et al. (2009: 1) reported a peak in self-reported offending between ages 14 and 16 across all years of the Home Office Crime and Justice Survey; McVie (2005: 8), for the Edinburgh Study of Youth Transitions and Crime (ESYTC), found a self-reported peak in crime at age 14; and Flood-Page et al. (2000: vi) reported a self-reported peak at age 14 for boys and girls (once fraud and workplace theft were excluded) in the Home Office Youth Lifestyles Survey.

[2] Tracey, Wolfgang, and Figlio (1990: 213) recorded a peak prevalence in official police contacts at age 16 in two birth cohorts (1945 and 1958), as did Le Blanc and Fréchette (1989: 62) for judicial data in their Montreal Study, and Laub and Sampson (2003: 86) for recorded offences using the Gluecks' *Unravelling Juvenile Delinquency* data. Piquero, Farrington, and Blumstein (2007: 48) found a peak in convictions just a year later, at age 17, in the Cambridge Study in Delinquent Development (CSDD), while Wikström (1990: 68) reported a peak in crimes known to the police at age 19 in Stockholm, but noted 'the figure for the age of 17 is close to it, with a dip at age 18, so the peak age in offenders might be said to be at ages 17–19 years.'

[3] Within the study period (2004–08), the time between the offence and completion of the criminal case was between 80 and 100 days on average, with the majority of cases being completed in fewer than 70 days (or approximately two and a half months; see Ministry of Justice 2010). For persistent young offenders, these averages were even lower (between 50 and 75 days in Cambridgeshire) following a pledge by the fledgling Labour government in 1997 to reduce the time from arrest to sentence for persistent young offenders, which since 2005 had been applied to all Criminal Justice System areas (see Ministry of Justice 2008). While Crown Court cases take significantly longer to complete (around 200 days on average, or around six and a half months) this still means the lag between offenders' age at the time of their offence and their age at the time of their conviction is minimal and unlikely to significantly affect conclusions about the age of the criminal population.

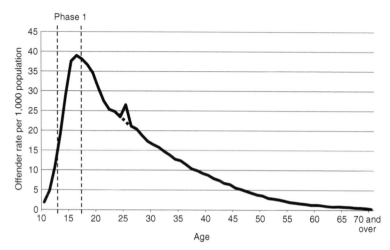

**Figure 2.1 Prevalence of people found guilty or cautioned for indictable offences in England and Wales in 2006 by age at conviction[a,b]**

[a] Criminal Justice System Statistics, Justice Statistics Analytical Services, Ministry of Justice. Rates are calculated using mid-year population estimates for 2006 (see chapter 2, footnote 6).

[b] Missing age and date of birth data are automatically defaulted to age 25 (personal correspondence). The dotted line suggests the likely actual trend.

Figure 2.1 also shows that the prevalence of younger people found guilty or cautioned for offences is very high in comparison to older people. This is a well-replicated and stable finding (eg Bottoms et al. 2004; Piquero et al. 2007). In England and Wales in 2006, 3.8 per cent of 15-year-olds were cautioned or found guilty of offences compared to 1.6 per cent of 30-year-olds, 0.6 per cent of 45-year-olds and just 0.1 per cent of 60-year-olds.[4] In 2007, the rate of offences among 17-year-olds in England and Wales was six times that of the entire population (6,433 versus 1,082 offences per 100,000). Young people are therefore responsible for a large proportion of crime. Annually in England and Wales, at least one-fifth of crimes where an offender is cautioned or convicted are committed by offenders aged between 10 and 17 (Budd et al. 2005). Young people are also over-represented in arrest data. Of the 1,429,800 arrests in England and Wales in 2005–06, 39 per cent were of

---

[4] Source: Justice Statistics Analytical Services, Ministry of Justice.

10–20-year-olds,[5] although this age group only made up 16 per cent of the population aged over 10.[6] This age distribution is very stable across years and at a local level.

Self-report studies also show an even stronger skew; Budd et al. (2005), for example, found that even though 10- to 17-year-olds comprised only 14 per cent of the sample (aged 10 to 65), they were responsible for 35 per cent of all self-reported incidents. This even higher concentration of self-reported crime amongst young people indicates that youth crime is perhaps particularly absent from official crime statistics. Of the 30 per cent of 10- to 17-year-olds who admitted a recent offence in the Home Office 2006 Offending, Crime and Justice survey, only 5 per cent had been arrested (Roe and Ash 2008). More than half of crimes in 2007–08 in England and Wales were not brought to police attention, and this is particularly the case for less serious crime, such as vandalism and assault without injury (Jansson et al. 2008). These kinds of crimes are particularly prevalent among young people, including those in the PADS+ sample (see section 3.1.1).

### 2.1.3 Exploring the person–environment interaction

Guided by the key propositions of Situational Action Theory (SAT) (see chapter 1), PADS+ is specifically designed to advance knowledge about:

(1) the role of the interaction between people's crime propensity and exposure to criminogenic settings in crime causation;
(2) the factors (causes of the causes) that influence the emergence of people's different crime propensities and varying criminogenic exposure, and the factors that affect their patterns of convergence in time and space;
(3) the role of changes in crime propensity and criminogenic exposure for people's crime involvement and criminal careers, and the factors that influence such changes.

In this book we will focus on exploring (1) the role of the interaction between crime propensity and criminogenic exposure in crime causation, (2) the personal characteristics and experiences that

---

[5] Home Office.
[6] Office for National Statistics mid-year population estimates 2006 <www.statistics.gov.uk/statbase/product.asp?vlnk=15106>.

affect young people's differential exposure to criminogenic settings, and (3) aspects of the urban milieu that influence the (spatio-temporal) patterns of convergence of crime prone young people and criminogenic settings. A subsequent book will investigate the factors that influence the emergence of young people's different crime propensities, the role of changes in young people's crime propensity and criminogenic exposure for their crime involvement and criminal careers, and the factors that influence such changes.

To study the interaction between kinds of people and kinds of settings in crime causation requires, in addition to data on participants' crime involvement, relevant data on their personal characteristics and experiences; small area social environments (resembling settings) in the study area; and, crucially, people's exposure to different kinds of settings in the study area. Collecting these three distinct kinds of data was the main challenge faced in designing PADS+, and selecting, or developing, appropriate methodologies, as no previous study has ever done so.[7] An overview of the research design and key methodologies is shown in Figure 2.2.

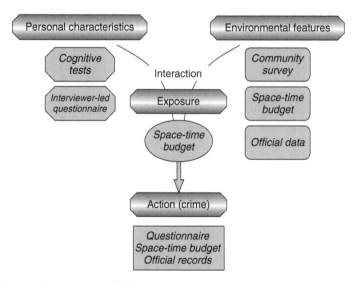

**Figure 2.2  Overview of the PADS+ research design and key methodologies**

---

[7] The Peterborough Youth Study (Wikström and Butterworth 2006) piloted the space–time budget technique but did not combine it with a small area community survey.

Data on young people's *personal characteristics and experiences*, for example, their morality and ability to exercise self-control, was collected through annual[8] interviewer-led questionnaires (section 2.4.1) and one-to-one cognitive measures (section 2.4.2), as part of the main cohort study (with some data collected from initial parents' interviews—see section 2.3—including some retrospective data on participants' childhoods).

Data on *small area environments* (approximating settings) in Peterborough, such as their levels of collective efficacy, was collected through a special community postal survey carried out in the middle of the study period (2005) across a large sample of Peterborough residents aged 18 and older (see section 2.8). A random sample was taken for each output area[9] in Peterborough (and some nearby villages) to ensure that data points covered all settings in the study area. Additional data on these output areas were collected from the census and other official sources, including data on land use and residents' demographic characteristics. In addition to the data on more 'stable' characteristics of these output areas, data on the particular *circumstances* in which young people encountered them (eg with whom, doing what) was collected through a space–time budget (see section 2.5).

Space–time budgets were not only utilized to collect information about the circumstances in which young people took part in settings but, crucially, young people's *exposure* to different kinds of settings (their activity fields). Space–time budgets were completed annually through one-to-one interviews and covered a four-day period, measuring participants' activities and their circumstances hour by hour by geographic location (output area). Matching space–time budget and community survey data at the output area level enabled the construction of measures of criminogenic exposure such as time spent unsupervised with peers (data from space–time budgets) in an area with poor collective efficacy (data from the community survey).

Data on crime involvement was collected through the interviewer-led questionnaires (self-reported annual offending; see section 2.4.1), space–time budgets (self-reported crimes during the four days studied for each year; see section 2.5.1), and official criminal justice records (see section 2.6). Space–time budget crime data

---

[8] During Phase 2 data collection was biennial (see Figure 2.4).
[9] Output areas are a geographic unit defined in section 2.8.2.

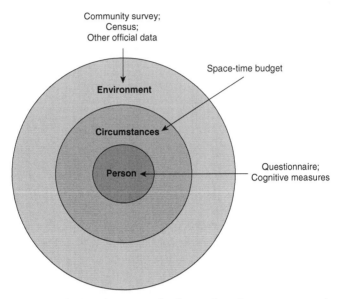

**Figure 2.3  Exploring the person in the setting: Data sources and methodologies**

made it possible directly to link, in time and space, acts of crime to specific features of settings (for example, being unsupervised with peers), and consequently also made it possible, for the first time ever (as far as we are aware), to study directly the convergence in time and space of people's crime propensity, criminogenic exposure, and acts of crime (some preliminary findings have been published in Wikström et al. 2010).

PADS+ is not only focused on exploring the direct causes of acts of crime but also the factors (causes of the causes) that may affect the development of a person's crime propensity (such as aspects of his or her family and school experiences) and his or her exposure to criminogenic settings (such as levels of parental monitoring), and the factors that may affect these factors (eg the factors that affect parental monitoring levels—the causes of the causes of the causes, so to speak). Many of the measures included in PADS+ target potential causes of the causes. The following sections describe in more detail each data source and methodology. We pay particular attention to the description of the space–time budget (section 2.5) and small area community survey (section 2.8), as these are not standard methodologies used in the study of crime.

## 2.2 The cohort study

PADS+ is an (ESRC-financed) longitudinal study that has followed a random sample of 716 young people (who were living in Peterborough in 2002) since 2003, through adolescence, and now into young adulthood. Interview data from the young people, which includes data from the interviewer-led questionnaire, cognitive measures, and the space–time budget, was collected annually between 2004 and 2008 and again in 2010 (with the next wave scheduled for 2012; see section 2.4 and Figure 2.4). This followed an initial wave of data collection from participants' parents in 2003, which collected in-depth data about participants' families' social situations at the time of their enrolment in the study, and retrospective information on their childhood experiences and critical life events via a structured interview (see section 2.3). Data from the first five young people's waves (2004–08) and the parents' wave (2003) comprise Phase 1 (adolescence) and characterize the young people and their social lives from ages 13 to 17. This book will deal only with Phase 1 data.

### 2.2.1 The sample and response rates

PADS+ utilized a random sample to capture the general spectrum of personal and social circumstances, as its aim is to study the relationship between young people's varying social lives and their differential crime involvement. The study sought to sample from the entire cohort of young people living in Peterborough (postcodes PE1 to PE7) poised to enter school year 7 in 2002 (who would have been turning 12 around the time of the parents' interview in 2003[10]). By combining data from the local education authority with information provided from independent schools[11] and Peterborough's Youth

[10] The age of the cohort is based on the school year, rather than the calendar year (young people in the sample turned 12 before the beginning of the 2003–04 school year, 13 before the 2004–05 school year, etc.). This means that many participants had already had their birthdays when they were interviewed in the first term of the calendar year, ie they were, on average, 13 when interviewed in 2003, 14 in 2004, etc. Their self-reported crime, on the other hand, referred to the previous calendar year, during which, on average, they were approximately one year younger (12 in 2003, the time period for which they reported crime in 2004, etc.). Hence, when we refer to the study period, we refer to ages 13–17, while our crime data refers to ages 12–16. See section 3.1.6 for further discussion of this difference.

[11] Although independent schools are sometimes reluctant to take part in longitudinal research, all such schools in Peterborough agreed to take part, including those for young people with special educational needs.

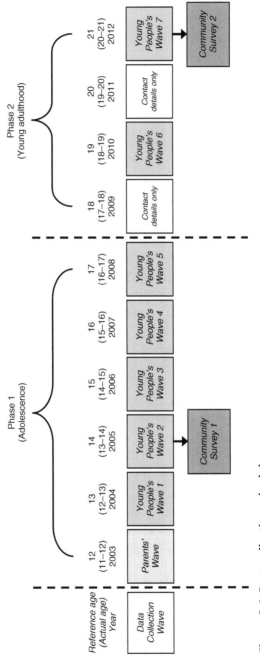

**Figure 2.4  Data collection schedule**

Offending Service on young people in alternative education or out-side education,[12] 2,349 young people were identified. It is impor-tant to combine such data sources as samples taken only from state schools may be biased towards the middle of the spectrum, while young people at both ends (eg the very affluent who opt for public education, or those with behavioural difficulties who are excluded from or leave education early), who may be of particular interest to this kind of research, may be overlooked.[13]

Of these 2,349 young people, 72 lived outside the specified post-code areas, four were unable to participate due to severe disabili-ties, and three lived on travellers' sites and were deemed unlikely to remain in Peterborough for the duration of the study. This left 2,270 young people from which to draw the study sample. The study aimed to achieve a sample of approximately 750 young people (about one-third of the cohort) in order to ensure adequate statistical power.

The parents' interviews were piloted with 25 randomly selected guardians, in order to trial the interview format, questions, and timing. For the main sample 1,000 of the 2,270 young people were then randomly selected. Young people from nine of the pilot families were selected in this 1,000; those from the remaining 16 families were then added. However, by the time they were con-tacted, 25 of the resulting 1,016 had moved out of the designated study area, leaving 991 families eligible for inclusion in the parents' data wave in 2003.

Written active consent was sought from the parents or guardians of all 991 young people for their children to take part (and to collect data from their children's school records[14]). Although active consent is more difficult to obtain than passive consent (by which participants are automatically included in the sample unless they opt out) it is regarded as more ethical. To encourage participation, families were sent an introductory letter from the Director for Education and Children at the Peterborough City Council, follow-up

---

[12] Sources were asked to update their data before sampling took place.

[13] However, the vast majority of young people in the United Kingdom attend state schools.

[14] Throughout Phase 1, PADS+ collected data on the participants' SAT (Standard Attainment Test) and GCSE (General Certificate of Secondary Education) exam performances and any other qualifications gained (such as vocational or founda-tion level courses) from the participants, their schools, and the local education authority (LEA).

letters, and contacted by telephone and home visits where necessary. Parents were paid £20 for taking part in the interview and a considerable effort was made to accommodate them in regards to interview time and location. Communications were also undertaken in Urdu, Gujerati, and Hindi where relevant/requested, to accommodate Peterborough's relatively sizeable Asian community.

In the end, 716 families agreed to participate (see Table 2.2). This represents 72.3 per cent of the eligible sample and 31.5 per cent of the total cohort, satisfying the study's goals to interview approximately one-third of the young people in this age group in Peterborough and achieve a sample with adequate statistical power. Young people whose parents did not take part in the parents' wave (2003) were not included in the study, as parent interview data was critical for establishing their social circumstances at the start of the study, as well as providing key retrospective information about their circumstances and experiences since birth.

### 2.2.2  Key characteristics of the sample and the question of selection bias

The sample distribution across key socio-demographic dimensions is shown in Table 2.1. From this table we can draw two important conclusions. First, the sample demonstrates substantial variation across all the factors shown, satisfying the aim to study people from a wide range of social backgrounds. Second, and crucially, once this data is compared with official data, we see that the sample, as far as we can assess, is generally socio-demographically representative of the population from which it is drawn, and therefore appears largely socially unbiased by non-response.

The distributions shown in Table 2.1 generally correspond with those of the equivalent population as measured by the 2001 census.[15] The sample was almost evenly split by gender, as was the case in the general population (in 2001, 49.8 per cent of the 12-year-olds in Peterborough were female). The sample was also ethnically representative of Peterborough, which had a slightly higher representation of young ethnic minorities than the national average,

---

[15] Note that these comparisons are not always drawn across identical categories, but are as close an approximation as we could construct, and that census data was collected in 2001, while the parents' data was collected in 2003; it is possible that some changes in distribution may have occurred in the intervening years.

**Table 2.1 Key socio-demographic characteristics of the sample at age 12[a]**

| Characteristics | Number | Per cent |
|---|---|---|
| **Sex** | | |
| Male | 357 | 49.9 |
| Female | 359 | 50.1 |
| **Family ethnicity** | | |
| White | 594 | 83.0 |
| Asian | 73 | 10.2 |
| Black | 6 | 0.8 |
| Mixed | 43 | 6.0 |
| **Family structure** | | |
| Two biological parents | 436 | 60.9 |
| Two parents (including step parent/s) | 111 | 15.5 |
| Single parent | 156 | 21.8 |
| Adopted/foster care/institution | 13 | 1.8 |
| **Family occupational social class[b]** | | |
| Lower working | 157 | 22.0 |
| Working | 276 | 38.7 |
| Lower middle | 241 | 33.8 |
| Upper middle/upper | 40 | 5.6 |
| **Highest educational level of either parent** | | |
| Not completed compulsory school | 100 | 14.0 |
| Completed compulsory school | 286 | 39.9 |
| Completed A-levels | 205 | 28.6 |
| University degree | 125 | 17.5 |
| **Household income** | | |
| 0–5,000 | 20 | 2.8 |
| 5,001–10,000 | 84 | 11.7 |
| 10,001–15,000 | 95 | 13.3 |
| 15,001–20,000 | 81 | 11.3 |
| 20,001–25,000 | 79 | 11.0 |
| 25,001–30,000 | 82 | 11.5 |

*(continued)*

**Table 2.1** *(Continued)*

| Characteristics | Number | Per cent |
| --- | --- | --- |
| **Household income** | | |
| 30,001–35,000 | 54 | 7.6 |
| 35,001–40,000 | 53 | 7.4 |
| 40,001–45,000 | 41 | 5.7 |
| 45,001–50,000 | 40 | 5.6 |
| 50,001–55,000 | 17 | 2.4 |
| 55,001–60,000 | 17 | 2.4 |
| 60,001–65,000 | 13 | 1.8 |
| 65,001–70,000 | 11 | 1.5 |
| 70,000 + | 28 | 3.9 |
| **Household tenure** | | |
| Owner | 496 | 69.3 |
| Renting from a private landlord | 53 | 7.4 |
| Renting from the council/a social authority | 165 | 23.0 |
| Other | 2 | 0.3 |

[a] Data taken from the parents' interviews (2003).
[b] Lower working class = unskilled workers; working class = skilled workers and lower ranking white collar employees; lower middle class = officials and small scale entrepreneurs; upper and upper middle class = large-scale entrepreneurs, high-ranking officials, and high-ranking white collar employees (adapted from Janson 1980a).

with a particularly large Asian population (Head 2004); 10 per cent of our participants' families and 10 per cent of all Peterborough households with dependent children were Asian. Single parent families made up 22 per cent of the sample, compared to 25 per cent of Peterborough households with dependent children. Of the 628 mothers who took part in the parents' interviews, 19 per cent reported not completing compulsory education, which is comparable to the 22 per cent of Peterborough females in an equivalent age group (25–54). The distribution of household incomes for the sample (in 2003) is consistent with the mean income of £25,100 reported for the Peterborough Unitary Authority (in 2002) (CACI 2002). Finally, 23 per cent of the families in the sample rented from the council or a social authority, a very similar proportion to that of Peterborough families with dependent children (24 per cent).

Taken together, these findings indicate no strong selectivity due to non-response in the PADS+ sample; hence it appears that the families that declined to participate did not substantially bias the study sample's social composition.

## 2.2.3 Attrition and retention rates

Attrition is always a concern for longitudinal research (Goldstein 2009). Previous research has shown that in criminological studies crime rates and patterns of relationships between predictors and outcomes may be affected by the loss of uncooperative, reluctant, or elusive participants (Burton et al. 2006; Thornberry et al. 1993). Two key ways to maintain participation are (1) tracking participants (maintaining contact with them over the study duration), and (2) motivating them to continue taking part (Farrington et al. 1990; Stouthamer-Loeber and van Kammen 1995).

To ensure contact with participants was not lost between data waves, their contact details were updated at every interview, making use of their most regular forms of communication, such as mobile phones, emails, and social networking websites, as well as their home addresses and phone numbers. Details were also taken about where participants expected to be living over the following year, as well as information about several alternative contacts, such as friends and relatives, and participants' written permission to ask those contacts for their details. Peterborough schools could be incredibly helpful when young people went 'off the radar', so an effort was made to stay in contact with schools and particularly school staff who were familiar with the study, such as those who helped organize school interviews. When all else failed, visits were undertaken to participants' last-known addresses.

The primary incentive for young people to take part was a payment of £10 for their participation in each of Waves 1 to 4, increased to £20 in Wave 5.[16] Most interviews took place at school, and most young people appeared unconcerned about missing their regular classes for the 1.5-hour interview; for those young people who were not in school, interviews were arranged, as much as possible, at a convenient time and place. An increasing number of young people left school in each wave, particularly in Wave 5 when they

---

[16] By Wave 5 participants had reached a stage in life when £10 might not be as attractive an economic incentive, as many had left school and held jobs.

were old enough to end their compulsory education. These young people were more mobile and more difficult to maintain contact with, which is why slightly more young people were uncontactable in Wave 5 (see Table 2.2).

For young people who were particularly difficult to track and motivate, tracking methods were tailored on a case-by-case basis. The importance of the study and their continued involvement was emphasized and, if necessary, they were recontacted later in the wave (see Burton et al. 2006 on refusal conversion; Farrington et al. 1990 on situationally influenced refusals).

These strategies were clearly successful, as only 23 (3.2 per cent) of the original 716 participants were not taking part five years later at the end of Phase 1 (see Table 2.2). Of those who left the study, their reasons for attrition were as follows: 10 refused to take part, 11 were uncontactable, one was deemed unable to take part due

**Table 2.2  Phase 1 response and retention rates (and reasons for attrition)**

| PADS+ Wave | Year | Young person's age | N | Non-response/attrition | | | Response/ retention rate |
|---|---|---|---|---|---|---|---|
| | | | | Refused[b] | Uncontactable | Other | |
| Parents' | 2003 | 12 | 716 | 223 | 52 | 0 | 72.3% |
| 1 | 2004 | 13 | 710 | 4 | 1 | 1 | 99.2% |
| 2 | 2005 | 14 | 707 | 2 | 1 | 0 | 98.7% |
| 3 | 2006 | 15 | 703 | 1 | 3 | 0 | 98.2% |
| 4 | 2007 | 16 | 703[a] | 1 | 0 | 1 | 98.3%[b] |
| 5 | 2008 | 17 | 693[a] | 3 | 8 | 0 | 96.9%[b] |

[a] Young people were regained in these waves who had not taken part in the previous wave (two were regained in 2007, and one in 2008). This means a total of 26 participants did not take part in all five waves (in addition, seven of the young people lost in 2008 were regained in 2010). For regained participants, retrospective crime data was also collected for the wave that they had missed and included in Phase 1 (except for those who were regained in 2010, when the data collection was biennial).

[b] The young person who died between Waves 3 and 4 is excluded from the sample, so the eligible sample decreases to 715 from Wave 4 onwards for the calculation of these retention rates.

to severe disabilities, and one young person sadly died between Waves 3 and 4.[17] This attrition was not apparently biased by gender or ethnicity: 13 were male and 10 female; 21 described themselves as white British and two described themselves as Asian. The study's extremely high retention rate of 97 per cent over five waves ensures minimal risk for the introduction of selectivity into the sample due to attrition, rendering analysis of the attrition for selection bias largely irrelevant.

## 2.3 Parents' interviews

The parents' interviews comprised the first wave of data collection and had two main aims: (1) to collect data on the young people's social circumstances at age 12, the beginning of the study; and (2) to collect retrospective information on the young people up to age 12. This provided a baseline for pre-existing differences.

The parents' interviews were administered one-to-one with the young person's primary guardian. To maximize consistency, participants' mothers were encouraged to complete the interview. Research suggests that mothers typically possess more accurate and detailed knowledge about their children (for example, their daily lives, activities, peers, etc.) than fathers or other guardians (see, for example, Crouter et al. 1999; Updegraff et al. 2001; Waizenhofer et al. 2004). Although interviewing both parents (or guardians, where applicable) would have been ideal, the additional knowledge gained was unlikely to outweigh the added time and expense. In cases where the mother was not the primary caregiver or unable to complete the interview (12 per cent), the father (10 per cent) or another guardian (for example, a grandparent or step parent; 2 per cent) was interviewed instead.

During the interview, parents were asked about themselves, their family, their neighbourhood, and their children. For each question, they were shown a card with a list of possible responses and their answers were recorded directly into fieldwork computers. Parents' interviews were typically conducted in the parent's home. This allowed interviewers to observe some key features of the neighbourhood and household environments, which were documented in internal and external assessments after the interview.

[17] This person is excluded from the eligible sample used for retention rate calculations from Wave 4 onward; see Table 2.2.

When necessary, parents' interviews were conducted in different languages, including Urdu, Gujerati, and Hindi.

## 2.3.1 Key constructs

The parents' interviews collected data on their children's current social circumstances and important developmental events and influences (Table 2.3). This included data on important dimensions of family resources, about which we might expect at least some young people would lack accurate knowledge, such as their parents' education and occupations and their household income. Subsequent family changes (for example, parental separation) were recorded and updated through the young people's interviews.

## 2.4  Young people's interviews

At the centre of PADS+ research are the annual[18] young people's interviews. Each interview lasted approximately 1.5 hours and was generally conducted in two 45-minute blocks. During one 45-minute block, participants completed the interviewer-led young people's questionnaire; during the other, they completed the space–time budget and cognitive tests. While the latter must be completed one-to-one with a researcher, the interviewer-led questionnaire could be administered simultaneously to several participants. The maximum questionnaire group size was set at four. Four participants completed the one-to-one interview while four filled out the questionnaire; these groups then swapped activities for the second half of the interview. This allowed five researchers to complete up to eight interviews in a 1.5-hour block. This method was particularly conducive to interviews conducted in schools, where there were many participants in attendance. It was later adapted for use in public locations, such as the city library, for participants who could not attend school interviews. Of course, when necessary, the entire interview was completed with a single researcher at the young person's convenience.

## 2.4.1 Interviewer-led questionnaires

The PADS+ interviewer-led questionnaire methodology was developed to take advantage of the respective strengths of (and minimize

---

[18] Biennial since Phase 2 (2009).

**Table 2.3  Key constructs from the parents' interview**

| Domain | Construct |
| --- | --- |
| Neighbourhood | Area of residence (output area) |
| | Type of tenure |
| | Informal social control |
| | Social cohesion |
| | Intergenerational closure |
| | Youth disorder |
| Childhood events | Young person's birth complications |
| | Young person's critical life events |
| | Young person's childhood behaviour problems |
| | Young person's accidents and injuries |
| Family | Family structure |
| | Parent's educational attainment |
| | Parent's occupational social class |
| | Household income |
| | Parent's employment status |
| | Family ethnicity |
| | Parent's religion |
| | Family social capital |
| | Family cohesion |
| | Family bonds |
| | Nurturing of the young person |
| | Affection for the young person |
| | Aspirations for the young person |
| | Parental monitoring of the young person |
| | Discipline of the young person |
| School | Young person's school bonds |
| | Young person's truancy |
| Peers | Parent's approval of young person's friends |
| | Young person's peers' crime involvement |
| Personal | Parent's moral rules |
| | Parent's self-control |
| | Parent's shame |

the weaknesses of) pen-and-paper questionnaires and one-to-one interviews as data collection methods. Questionnaires, for example, are cost-effective and provide respondents with a greater sense of anonymity, while the interactive nature of interviews enables the researcher to provide instructions and answer questions when clarification is needed.

Young people's questionnaires were administered by one researcher to small groups of up to four young people. The groups were situated so that the young people could not see each others' answers but could be supervised by one researcher. The questionnaire was divided into short, topical sections and participants completed one at a time, waiting at the end of each section until everyone in the group was finished. At the beginning of each section the researcher provided a brief introduction including instructions about how to complete the section and clear definitions for key constructs (such as family or neighbourhood). This was to ensure the young people understood what they needed to do and, as much as possible, what the questions were asking. Participants were also encouraged to seek clarification if they were unsure about anything in the questionnaire, and the researcher was on hand to answer. The researcher then concluded each section by having the young people check they had not missed any questions. Although the interviewer-led questionnaire method is more intensive than more traditional pen-and-paper surveys where respondents fill in their answers on their own, it kept potential problems with internal non-response, reliability, and consistency in participants' answers to a minimum (see Table 2.8).

### Key constructs from the interviewer-led young people's questionnaire

The interviewer-led questionnaire collected a broad range of data on the young people's current circumstances and experiences including a number of scales measuring key personal characteristics, such as those relating to morality and self-control (Table 2.4). The questionnaire also collected the bulk of the study's self-reported data on crime and drug use. This included prevalence, frequency, age of onset, as well as some information on the circumstances of offending.

### 2.4.2 Cognitive measures

Cognitive measures are an established method for gauging various cognitive abilities. In PADS+, measures tapped into *executive capabilities* (see Wikström and Treiber 2007), higher order cognitive processes involved in information processing and decision making relevant to action (Damasio 1994; Fuster 1997; Goldberg 2001; Ishikawa and Raine 2003; Morgan and Lilienfeld 2000; Nigg and Huang-Pollock 2003; Stuss and Levine 2002). In Waves 1, 3, and 5 several tests were administered relevant for deliberation, tapping into information maintenance and processing abilities; in Waves 2 and 4 tests targeted more emotional capabilities, tapping into intuitive learning capacities (Table 2.5). These exercises were selected and adapted to be age appropriate and were administered in the

**Table 2.4  Key constructs from the young people's questionnaire**

| Domain | Construct[a] |
|---|---|
| Neighbourhood | Area of residence (output area)<br>Informal social control<br>Social cohesion<br>Intergenerational closure |
| Family | Bonds<br>Cohesion (Waves 4–5)<br>Informal social control (Wave 4–5)<br>Running away<br>Monitoring<br>Discipline |
| School | Bonds<br>Cohesion (Waves 4–5)<br>Informal social control (Waves 4–5)<br>Truancy<br>Bullying (Waves 2–4) |
| Work | Bonds (Wave 5)<br>Truancy (Wave 5)<br>Bullying (Wave 5) |
| Peers | Peer crime involvement<br>Out-of-school activities<br>Intimate relationships (Wave 4–5)<br>Intimate relationship violence (Wave 4–5) |
| Personal | Morality 1 (wrongfulness of specific actions)<br>Morality 2 (principles)<br>Ability to exercise self-control<br>Shame (Waves 2–5)<br>Guilt (Waves 2–5)<br>Deterrence perceptions: Risk of getting caught (Waves 2–5)<br>Deterrence perceptions: Consequences (Waves 2–5)<br>Temptation (Waves 3–5)<br>Contact with professionals/authorities (Waves 3–5)<br>Religion (Wave 5) |
| Decision making | Theft scenario (Waves 1–3)<br>Violence scenario (Waves 1–3) |

(continued)

**Table 2.4** *(Continued)*

| Domain | Construct |
|---|---|
| Crime | Theft from a person<br>Shoplifting<br>Vandalism<br>Arson<br>Robbery<br>Assault<br>Residential burglary<br>Non-residential burglary<br>Theft of or from a car (Wave 1)<br>Theft of a car (Waves 2–5)<br>Theft from a car (Waves 2–5)<br>Carrying a weapon (Waves 2–5)<br>Carrying a weapon at school (Waves 2–5) |
| Substance use | Alcohol<br>Tobacco<br>Inhalants<br>Cannabis<br>Amphetamines<br>Ecstasy<br>Heroin<br>Cocaine<br>Crack<br>LSD |

[a] Asked in all waves unless indicated.

**Table 2.5  Cognitive measures used in PADS+**

| Measure | Construct |
|---|---|
| Count span | Working memory capacity (Waves 1, 3, 5)<br>(see Daneman and Carpenter 1980) |
| Dual task processing | Working memory processing efficiency (Waves 1, 3)<br>(see Baddeley et al. 1991) |
| Iowa Gambling Task (IGT) | Somatic markers (Waves 2, 4)<br>(see Bechara et al. 1994; Bechara et al. 2000a;<br>Bechara et al. 2000b) |
| Trail Marking Task A, B | Cognitive flexibility (Wave 5)<br>(see Army Individual Test Battery 1944) |

one-to-one block of the interview, so that one researcher could instruct each participant on how to complete the exercise, monitor participants' progress, and answer any questions. The cognitive tests selected are well-known and have been tested on various populations, including adolescents.

## 2.5  Space–time budget

The space–time budget is the most innovative methodology used in PADS+, and one of the most important research tools utilized in this book (together with the small area community survey; see section 2.8), therefore we provide a more detailed introduction. The fundamental purpose of the space–time budget in PADS+ was to measure (by geographical location and time) participants' exposure to different settings by measuring (1) which settings they take part in, and (2) the circumstances under which they encounter those settings, from which we can analyse (3) their activity fields—the constellation of settings to which they are exposed during a specific time period, including how much time they spend in each of those settings.

Other methods used in criminology for measuring exposure are arguably not as specific in measuring the time young people spend in particular settings (for example, surveys that ask 'how often' a person spends time in a setting, such as the city centre, eg 'once or twice a week'), nor as specific in measuring characteristics of the settings to which they are exposed (ie do not specify in detail who they are with and what they are doing). The reliability of such survey measures of activity compares poorly with other more specific measures of time use (Niemi 1993; J. P. Robinson 1985; J. P. Robinson and Bostrom 1994). As far as we are aware, space–time budgets were first used in criminological research in the Peterborough Youth Study, which served as a pilot for PADS+ (see Wikström and Butterworth 2006), although space–time budgets have since been replicated by the Study of Peers, Activities and Neighbourhoods (SPAN), conducted in the city of The Hague, in the Netherlands (see, eg, Wikström et al. 2012).

A space–time budget can collect detailed time-specific, spatially-located data, for example, on who is present in a setting, what activities are taking place in that setting, and what kind of place the setting represents. This data can then be geographically matched to community survey and official data, providing further detail on the environment in which the setting is embedded (see further section 2.8).

Adequately measuring exposure to different settings is of key importance for studying the impact of the wider social environment on young people's behaviour. Data from PADS+ shows that young people spent more than half their time awake outside their home output areas,[19] and 90 per cent of their crimes occurred during this 50 per cent of their time. Thus, while the home environment is obviously a key location in young people's lives and activity fields, data on environments beyond their homes and neighbourhoods, and the time they spend (and what they do) in those environments, is crucial in the explanation of their crime involvement.

Another advantage of space–time budgets is they can be used to directly relate instances of behaviour to the environments in which they take place (J. Anderson 1971: 360). Moreover, 'to be really useful, activity analyses should be linked to other types of analysis... and this demands careful integration of diary and questionnaire design' (J. Anderson 1971: 357). Using personal data from the questionnaire and cognitive measures described above, we can analyse features of the *intersections* between young people with particular personal characteristics and settings with particular environmental characteristics to analyse which kinds of young people commit acts of crime in which kinds of settings (as we do in chapter 7).

Space–time budgets originated from time budgets. 'A time-budget is a systematic record of a person's use of time over a given period' (J. Anderson 1971: 353; see also Szalai 1966b: 3). Time budgets date back to the 1920s, when they were used to compare temporal aspects of work and leisure across different social classes (for discussion see J. Anderson 1971; Andorka 1987; Juster and Stafford 1991; Szalai 1966b). Major time-use surveys began in the 1960s with Szalai's multinational comparative time budget research project (see Szalai 1966a; Szalai 1966b, 1972) and developed into major ongoing surveys such as the Multinational Time Use Study,[20] the American Time Use Survey,[21] and the Panel Study of Income Dynamics Child Development Supplement.[22] These kinds of surveys have a number

---

[19] See section 2.8.2 on this geographic unit.
[20] MTUS (Fisher et al. 2010); see also <www.timeuse.org>.
[21] ATUS (Phipps and Vernon 2009); see also <www.bls.gov/tus>.
[22] PSID CDS (Stafford 2009); see also <http://psidonline.isr.umich.edu/Studies.aspx>.

of applications as they measure comparative aspects of human activity, particularly social behaviour, and the lifestyles of different social groups (Andorka 1987; Belli et al. 2009; Harms and Gershuny 2009; Juster and Stafford 1985, 1991; Pentland et al. 1999). Following an analysis of the validity and reliability of diaries and other time-use measures, Robinson (1985: 60) concluded that 'the burden of evidence clearly points to the strong likelihood that time diaries are the only viable method of obtaining valid and reliable data on activities' (for discussion of the superiority of the time budget method, see also Belli et al. 2009; Juster 1985; Juster and Stafford 1991; Marini and Shelton 1993; Mulligan et al. 2005; Phipps and Vernon 2009; J. P. Robinson 1985; Stafford 2009).

'As a logical extension of [the time budget], a space–time budget includes the spatial coordinates of activity locations' (J. Anderson 1971: 353). However, despite their applicability to a number of disciplines, space–time budgets[23] are time consuming to implement, therefore economically onerous and, as a consequence, rarely used in any discipline (J. Anderson 1971; Goodchild and Janelle 1984; Pearce 1988).

They have proved most useful for tourism,[24] urban planning,[25] and transportation[26] research, typically using larger spatial units and recording less detail about the circumstances of activity than the PADS+ space–time budget, and only being used to measure certain aspects of people's movement and activity patterns. In contrast, PADS+ and its pilot (Wikström and Butterworth 2006), and only a handful of studies from other disciplines (eg Dijst 1999; Hanson and Hanson 1980; Schönfelder and Axhausen 2003), have collected empirical data which can be used to test theories of human activity and movement (such as that of Hägerstrand 1970). Further, the PADS+ space–time budget goes beyond measuring movement patterns to also measure features of the settings in which people spend time—what we refer to as a person's *activity field*—the constellation of settings, and their characteristics, which a person encounters during a particular period of time. Activity fields differ from *activity* or *action spaces*—comprehensive, two-dimensional

---

[23] Including methodologies such as travel and trip diaries.

[24] eg Dietvorst 1994; Fennell 1996; Thornton et al. 1997.

[25] eg J. Anderson 1971; Janelle et al. 1988; Mey and Heide 1997; Tomlinson et al. 1973.

[26] eg Forer and Kivell 1981; M. Fox 1995; Hanson and Hanson 1980; Schönfelder and Axhausen 2003.

spatial units representing a person's movements over a particular period of time (see P. L. Brantingham and Brantingham 1981; Dijst 1999; Golledge and Stimson 1997; Schönfelder and Axhausen 2003)—in that activity fields focus on the environmental characteristics a person encounters (rather than the geographical aspects of a person's movement in space). By analysing activity fields, we can identify differences in how people spend their time, ie their exposure to different kinds of settings (configurations of particular environments and circumstances). This means that within criminology, studies such as PADS+ are uniquely capable of providing true tests of spatial theories of crime (such as 'pattern theory'; see P. L. Brantingham and Brantingham 1993).

### 2.5.1 The PADS+ space–time budget

PADS+ space–time budget data was collected on an hourly basis covering four days during the previous week. Data was taken every hour for a continuous period of 24 hours on each day. This continuous measurement is essential when measuring people's general activity patterns and exposure to particular settings over time.[27] The Peterborough Youth Study collected data on an hourly basis covering seven days, with the aim of capturing the natural weekly rhythm of young people's activities, but their experiences suggested that four days were sufficient to capture young people's general activity patterns and personal variation (Wikström and Butterworth 2006: 207-37). Findings from other studies support this decision. For example, the American Time Use Survey (ATUS) found that activities between Monday and Thursday are essentially identical (Stewart 2006: 55–6; see also Stinson 2000: 999–1001).

In PADS+, data was collected about the Friday and Saturday before the interview and the two other most recent weekdays (see Table 2.6) to cover key times for structured and unstructured activities. The two most recent weekdays were chosen to minimize difficulties in participants' recall. Friday daytime resembles most other weekdays; however, Friday and Saturday evenings differ considerably from other weeknights and are a particularly interesting

---

[27] As opposed to studies with different research aims that allow researchers to collect data only for random or specified points during a period of time, such as the beeper or experience sampling method (see Larson and Verma 1999).

**Table 2.6 Days covered by the space–time budget interview**

| Day of the interview | Days covered by the interview | | | |
|---|---|---|---|---|
| Monday | Saturday | Friday | Thursday | Wednesday |
| Tuesday | Monday | Saturday | Friday | Thursday |
| Wednesday | Tuesday | Monday | Saturday | Friday |
| Thursday | Wednesday | Tuesday | Saturday | Friday |
| Friday | Thursday | Wednesday | Saturday | Friday |
| Saturday | Friday | Thursday | Wednesday | Saturday |

time during which to study young people's less structured activities (particularly, leisure activities). Sunday was not chosen as a weekend day as activities on Sunday are constrained by the upcoming school/work week, such that Sunday evenings to some degree reflect a school/work night.

This method proportionately over-represents activities on Fridays and Saturdays. Thus to draw any conclusions on a weekly or yearly basis, the data must be weighted appropriately. However, for most analyses in this book we are interested in comparative counts of hours, which do not require weighting as all young people provide data on a comparable period of time.

The accuracy of participant recall is an important consideration in a detailed diary like the space–time budget. Limiting the interview to four days, rather than seven, reduced demands on participants' memory, and consequently may have increased the reliability of the data. A shorter interview is also less likely to lose participants' interest, which can potentially damage response rates. Previous research has shown a link between response rates and a higher burden of longer interviews (see, for example, J. Anderson 1971: 357; Gershuny et al. 1986: 20; Harms and Gershuny 2009: 8). Ultimately, it appears that the additional data gathered in a longer interview does not outweigh the additional time and participant effort required. Even a four-day space–time budget interview can take up to 45 minutes.

Four days amounts to 96 hours of data per participant per year, and up to 20 days of data for those who took part in all five Phase 1 waves (480 hours). In total, 3,491 space–time budget interviews were conducted during Phase 1 (335,136 hours). Space–time budget data was still collected for participants who moved outside the study area,[28] and for time spent outside the study area, simply without the spatial element (data relevant to the setting and circumstances was still collected). However, for the analyses presented in this book, many of which involve the environmental context and therefore regularly make use of the spatial element of the space–time budget data, a small number of interviews (accounting for 1.6 per cent of the total hours) with 32 participants were excluded because they were living so far away (including in other countries) that they spent *no time at all* in the study area (further description excludes these interviews). This left a total of 329,952 hours (of which 205,885 hours were spent awake).

Although the study area was designed to include most areas where the sample spent time, some young people, who attended school and spent time in the study area, lived in rural areas and villages not included in the study area. This makes it all the more remarkable that the participants spent 93 per cent (190,972 hours) of their time awake within the study area, and that almost half of those hours spent outside the study area were attributable to 65 young people who lived outside the study area during the study period.[29] Participants actually living within the study area spent 96 per cent of their time awake within the study area. This suggests that the study area is a natural area that contains the vast majority of places local young people visit or spend time in during their daily lives. This also means that there were few hours we cannot link geographically to external environmental data.

The problem of seasonal variation in activity patterns (eg summer holidays compared to school terms) was avoided by completing the

[28] In Waves 1–3, some time budget interviews (excluding the spatial element) were not conducted with the small number of young people who had moved so far from Peterborough that they spent no time in the study area, but in Waves 4 and 5, time budget data was collected from this small but growing number of participants. Combined with the general attrition from the study (Table 2.2), time budget or space–time budget data was taken every year from 675 (94.4 per cent of) participants, and space–time budget data was taken every year from 657 (91.9 per cent of) participants. All 693 participants taking part in Wave 5 completed time budget or space–time budget interviews (480 hours per participant).

[29] At the start of the study, 39 individuals lived outside the study area but, as required by the sampling criteria, attended school there. In later waves, more individuals moved into rural areas and other villages not included in the study area (Wave 1, 2 and 3 = 40, Wave 4 = 69, Wave 5 = 79). Therefore, 214 interviews were conducted over five waves with 65 different participants who lived outside, but near, the study area.

majority of interviews in the first quarter of each year. Every effort was also made to interview young people following a 'normal' school/work week, which was defined as a week in which no more than one of the interview days was spent on holiday, ill at home, in hospital, or under other extenuating circumstances (such as an intensive Youth Offending Team intervention that limited the young person's movement). Of the Phase 1 interviews 95 per cent were completed for such 'normal' weeks.

For each hour of each day of the interview, data was collected on the young person's geographic *location* (coded at the output area level so that it could be matched with data from the Peterborough Community Survey and the census; see section 2.8.2); the *functional place* (eg home, school, workplace, skate park, shopping centre); *who the young person was with* (eg peers, parents, other adults, siblings); and the young person's *main activity* (eg talking face-to-face, revising, sleeping, watching television) (see Figure 2.5). A categorical coding system was developed with hundreds of codes to represent functional places, people, and activities (as detailed in appendix A2 on space–time budget coding). One of the major advantages of this system is its capacity to create 'complex constructions' (see Stafford 2009: 23) which combine categories, such as certain activities with certain people in certain places. This *combination* of codes is central to the space–time budget methodology, and the amount of detail it is able quantitatively to represent. For example, in isolation, the very common activity 'socializing face to face' is not particularly informative, as it could refer to chatting with parents at home on a Saturday morning, or drinking with friends in a park in an area with poor collective efficacy on a Friday night. It is only by combining all data components, such as functional place, people present, activity, and time, that the detailed circumstances of settings become clear and we can define and select particular kinds of circumstances for analysis (as we do in chapter 6).

The size of the time unit used for temporal (and temporal–spatial) analysis should be determined by the type of research. An hour was chosen as the unit of time for PADS+. Hours are a standard unit that is easily quantified and interpreted, allowing simple calculation of measures of exposure to particular settings. Although some space and/or time budget research (eg Schönfelder and Axhausen 2003) also divides its data into equal time segments for ease of activity space analysis, some studies measure the beginning and end time, and therefore exact duration, of each activity (I. G. Cullen and

| | | | | | | | Extra Incidents | | | | | | | | | | |
|---|---|---|---|---|---|---|---|---|---|---|---|---|---|---|---|---|---|
| **Monday** | | | | | | | Alcohol / Drugs | | | Victimisation | | | Offending | | | Weapons | |
| | | | | | | | No ○ | | | No ○ | | | No ○ | | | No ○ | |
| | | | | | | | Yes ○ | | | Yes ○ | | | Yes ○ | | | Yes ○ | |
| | | | | | Truancy | Truancy | Incident | | | Incident | | | Incident | | | Incident | |
| Hour | Geocode | Place | Activity | Who | School | Work | 1 | 2 | 3 | 1 | 2 | 3 | 1 | 2 | 3 | 1 | 2 | 3 |
| 6 | | | | | | | | | | | | | | | | | | |
| 7 | | | | | | | | | | | | | | | | | | |
| 8 | | | | | | | | | | | | | | | | | | |
| 9 | | | | | | | | | | | | | | | | | | |
| 10 | | | | | | | | | | | | | | | | | | |
| 11 | | | | | | | | | | | | | | | | | | |
| 12 | | | | | | | | | | | | | | | | | | |
| 13 | | | | | | | | | | | | | | | | | | |
| 14 | | | | | | | | | | | | | | | | | | |
| 15 | | | | | | | | | | | | | | | | | | |
| 16 | | | | | | | | | | | | | | | | | | |
| 17 | | | | | | | | | | | | | | | | | | |
| 18 | | | | | | | | | | | | | | | | | | |
| 19 | | | | | | | | | | | | | | | | | | |
| 20 | | | | | | | | | | | | | | | | | | |
| 21 | | | | | | | | | | | | | | | | | | |
| 22 | | | | | | | | | | | | | | | | | | |
| 23 | | | | | | | | | | | | | | | | | | |
| 0 | | | | | | | | | | | | | | | | | | |
| 1 | | | | | | | | | | | | | | | | | | |
| 2 | | | | | | | | | | | | | | | | | | |
| 3 | | | | | | | | | | | | | | | | | | |
| 4 | | | | | | | | | | | | | | | | | | |
| 5 | | | | | | | | | | | | | | | | | | |

**Figure 2.5  PADS+ space–time budget data entry form (sample day)**

Godson 1975; Phipps and Vernon 2009; Stafford 2009). For PADS+, however, there was less interest in the exact timing of activities, as the aim was rather to represent important changes in the circumstances, such as who was present and where the activity was taking place. An hour is specific enough to capture the diversity of places and activities in which young people spend their time, while maintaining the focus on where they spend *most* of their time and their *main* activities. Using a smaller unit would tend to collect a lot of irrelevant data (for example time spent making cups of tea) and would extend the interview significantly, potentially impacting participation (see Harms and Gershuny 2009: 8). It would also tax participants' recall, potentially reducing reliability. Hours are salient reference points in the day, which makes it easier for young people to remember what happened in each. Some precision is, however, lost in using hours as a unit of time; activities that take less than the majority of an hour, or secondary activities (eg listening to music while doing homework) may be underrepresented (J. P. Robinson 1985). This is true of many activities of particular interest to PADS+, such as acts of crime, which rarely take up an entire hour, or drug and alcohol use, which may be secondary activities. However, this problem was avoided by separately collecting specific data about crime events and other incidents of particular interest.

For each day covered in the interview, participants were asked whether or not they had taken any drugs or drunk any alcohol; whether or not they had experienced altercations, such as witnessing a fight or being involved in an argument; whether or not they had been the victim of any crime; whether or not they had themselves committed any acts of crime; and whether or not they carried a weapon (see appendix on space–time budget coding, section A2.4). These events were coded by the hour in which the event occurred (see Figure 2.5) and specific details were recorded, such as what kinds of drugs, alcohol, or weapons were used, who was involved in fights or arguments, what property the offender vandalized or stole, etc.[30] This information could then be linked to details about the setting recorded in the space–time budget, features of the geographical area provided by the small area community survey (PCS), and census and land use data (see section 2.10), as well as data on personal characteristics and experiences from the young people's questionnaire and cognitive measures. All together, this provided a considerable amount of detail about the intersections between young people with particular personal characteristics and settings with particular environmental characteristics.

---

[30] The space–time budget data entry form (see Figure 2.5) allows for the recording of up to three incidents of each type during the hour, for example the consumption of beer, spirits, and cannabis. In the extremely unusual event that more than three incidents of any type occurred in one hour, additional codes allow for incidents to be grouped, for example the consumption of a combination of different types of alcohol, cannabis, and ecstasy.

## 2.5.2 One-to-one interview

Although much space and time budget research is done using self-completion diaries, the one-to-one interview method has many advantages for the kind of research conducted in PADS+ (Loosveldt 2008; Phipps and Vernon 2009). Researchers could consistently and accurately record recollections at the correct level of detail, aid participants' recall, and maintain overall control over the interview (for example, researchers were able to manage distractions and threats to confidentiality, and engage the respondent to ensure careful and honest responses).

Researchers employed a natural method whereby participants were guided to describe the chronology of events, and then coded these events as they were described. Research into the time budget methodology (Belli et al. 2009; Juster 1985; Niemi 1993; Stafford 2009) suggests this is a preferable method of eliciting information from participants compared to, for example, methods that focus on particular activities in turn (eg 'how long did you spend watching television that day'). It reduces processing biases that arise when using methodologies that require participants, for example, to add up the number of hours spent in an activity or make judgements about time, as well as problems related to social desirability (which may avoid, for example, underreporting activities that may be seen as less socially acceptable).

This method also avoids certain problems inherent in self-completion diaries. Arguably, young people cannot be expected to self-complete a space–time budget using the same multitude of codes accurately, consistently, or reliably, especially when it comes to identifying their geographic location, a critical element for the purposes of PADS+.[31] Studies that utilize self-completion diaries are less able to ensure that the diary and instructions are interpreted the same way by all participants (Niemi 1993), is completed by the intended participant, and includes the correct amount of detail

---

[31] Geospatial technology, such as GPS tracking and radio telemetry, not commonly available when PADS+ was designed, can also be used to record participants' geographical locations. However, while such technology may collect very specific space and time data, it cannot collect information on activities or settings. It is also difficult to be certain participants have actually carried the devices as required. As a consequence, an interview may still be necessary. This plus the added cost of equipping young people with expensive technology makes this method currently impractical.

(see also Loosveldt 2008). In a one-to-one interview, a researcher can ask for clarification or further detail, and potentially reduce participants' reticence or confabulation.

Perhaps more significantly, the one-to-one format allowed researchers to help participants recall their activities and locations.[32] For example, a researcher could lead participants backwards or forwards through a day or a week to help them if they were struggling to remember some movements and activities. Researchers could also support participants' recall based on their activities during other days in the interview or by making reference to memorable external events, such as much discussed sports fixtures or unusual weather, and request further details about circumstances to ensure they were accurately coded. Researchers could also make conversational data checks, such as retrospective verification of inconsistent aspects of the chronology provided (for discussion of similar recall techniques, see also Phipps and Vernon 2009). Interviewers reported that generally young people were good at recalling their activities and movements.

To assist researchers in geocoding each hour each young person spent to the appropriate output area, a number of tools were developed for use in the field. Details on key locations such as home and school were prepared prior to the interview and then checked with participants. Detailed, alphabetized lists of streets located in a single output area were compiled, as well as categorized listings of specific places, particularly those relevant to young people, such as schools, parks, sports venues, shops, pubs, and landmark public buildings. When a street ran through several output areas or an appropriate landmark was not available, researchers used maps and street atlases of Peterborough to help participants find where they were. These locations could then be referred to maps of Peterborough wards which were subdivided into output areas to identify the correct output area for that hour. On the few occasions where it was impossible to determine an exact location in the field, researchers took additional notes on landmarks and addresses

---

[32] Although methods that record activities in real time, such as diaries that are carried around and completed throughout the day, may reduce recall issues (J. P. Robinson 1985), they are plagued by problems caused by both lack of compliance, which reduces their effectiveness (Phipps and Vernon 2009; Stone and Broderick 2009), and participants' heightened awareness that activities are being recorded, which may impact on data quality.

which could be further researched back in the office. As a last resort (for example, when a young person knew the general area but not their exact location), more general codes were utilized to provide as much detail as possible (such as the ward or village). However, these general codes were rarely used, as even in the most difficult cases an iterative process usually led to at least the identification of an output area that, if not containing the exact location, was very near. Generally, participants, especially as they matured, were knowledgeable about the city and able to provide helpful information about local sites and activities with which researchers were not familiar.

Because of the demands of the one-to-one space–time budget interview, researchers were carefully selected and trained in-house (see further section 2.7.1 and Lessler et al. 2008). Most took part in several waves, such that the 3,491 space–time budget interviews conducted during Phase 1 were carried out by only 10 different researchers, which no doubt had an impact on the reliability and consistency of the space–time budget data.

## 2.6  Criminal justice records data

In addition to self-reported crime data collected through questionnaires and space–time budgets, data was also collected on police-recorded crimes and criminal justice interventions. Written consent was acquired from all participants who took part in Wave 5 (2008, when all participants were over 16) to access their criminal justice data.[33] Total crime and incident data was also collected for the entire study area, including all crime data for young people. Criminal justice data was taken from several sources, including the Youth Offending Service, the Police National Computer, and Cambridgeshire Constabulary (Table 2.7).[34]

Peterborough Youth Offending Service gave full access to participants' records on their Youth Offending Information

---

[33] All 693 participants in Wave 5 consented to allow PADS+ to access criminal justice data about them. For the remaining 23 participants who had left the study before this point, except for one individual who gave consent but did not take part in Wave 5, we have not collected any criminal justice data.

[34] Table 2.7 shows criminal justice data collected to date (spring 2011). However, we plan to collect additional kinds of criminal justice data, such as antisocial behaviour orders.

**Table 2.7  Details of criminal justice data collected for Phase 1**

| Source | Information about | Data covers |
|---|---|---|
| Youth Offending Service | Participants | Offence details<br>Disposals<br>Intervention records<br>Case diaries<br>Court reports<br>Police interviews<br>ASSET assessments[a] |
| Police National Computer | Participants | Offences<br>Disposals |
| Peterborough Police | Participants | Offence/incident details<br>(incl. if suspect or offender)<br>Victimization details<br>Offence witnessed details<br>Custody record |
| | Crime | Offence details |
| | Young people's crime[b] | Offence details[c]<br>Offender(s) details[c] |
| | Non-crime incidents[d] | Incident details[c] |

[a] Structured assessment tools used by Youth Offending Teams in England and Wales.
[b] Offenders aged 10–21
[c] Data only available since April 2004 (see text).
[d] Includes calls for service from the public regarding non-crime incidents, and also non-crime incidents discovered by the police. This data is used for only a few analyses in this book (eg noisy neighbours: see Figure 2.8).

System (YOIS), which is a case-management system that records detailed qualitative and quantitative information regarding offences, interventions, assessments, disposals, and contacts with a caseworker, police or court, for all young offenders in Peterborough. Cambridgeshire Constabulary provided details and comprehensive contextual information from their Crime File system about incidents and offences in Peterborough where a participant was the offender, victim, witness, suspect, or otherwise involved.

Although data collected locally from Cambridgeshire Constabulary and the Peterborough Youth Offending Service contained considerable contextual detail, information about offences that occurred outside Peterborough and by young people who had moved to other parts of the country were not included. For data at the national level,[35] we accessed the Police National Computer (PNC[36]). The comprehensiveness of PNC data for police-recorded crime makes it the most appropriate source for the crime analyses in this book. The PNC database was searched using the dates of birth, names, and any aliases of the 694 consenting participants. Offence type and disposal information was collected for 74 participants who had been convicted by a court or given a final warning or reprimand by the police[37] for PNC recordable offences (up to June 2009).[38]

In addition to data on police-recorded crimes by PADS+ participants, data on police-recorded crime in Peterborough, including crime by all known young offenders, was also collected. Cambridgeshire Constabulary recorded 132,087 crimes occurring in Northern Division (Peterborough and the surrounding area) between January 2003 and the end of 2007. Access to this crime

[35] Offences committed outside the United Kingdom are not usually recorded on the PNC. This is highly unlikely to lead to any underestimation of participants' offending, except for those young people who moved out of the country during the study period ($N$ = 5). However, these young people's police recorded and self-reported levels of crime involvement are consistent with the rest of the sample; hence their data has not been excluded.

[36] The PNC is a national information system maintained and delivered by the National Policing Improvement Agency (NPIA: <www.npia.police.uk/en/10508. htm>), which contains data on people, vehicles, crimes, and stolen property. It is accessible electronically to the police and other criminal justice agencies.

[37] For the most part during the study period, cautions were not given to offenders under 18, so only convictions, final warnings, and police reprimands were recorded for PADS+ participants. Police reprimands (also known as juvenile cautions) are a formal verbal warning for young people (under 18) who admit they are guilty of a minor first offence. Final warnings are like reprimands but the young person is also assessed to determine the causes of his or her offending behaviour and a short programme of activities is identified to address these causes. Information about the final warning programme is not held on the PNC, but is recorded by the YOS.

[38] Recordable offences are those deemed disclosable (for example, in criminal records bureau checks). Non-recordable offences were therefore not disclosed to PADS+ from the PNC, and are not analysed in this book, but may appear in the Cambridgeshire Constabulary Crime File data. Examples of non-recordable offences include those for which a 'ticket' was given (eg a penalty notice for disorder or a fixed penalty notice). These fines are given to those over the age of 16 for a range of offences (eg speeding, driving without insurance, shoplifting, public order offences), most often to juveniles or for a first-time offence that would receive a fine in court. A small number of non-recordable offences are disclosable if they coincide with other, recordable, offences and are dealt with using the same disposal.

data,[39] including offender details for crimes by known offenders aged 10–21, was requested and kindly granted. A small number (3.6 per cent) of crimes were immediately excluded because they occurred in the rural areas and villages near the city that are within Northern Division but not included in the study area. Some other more minor amendments were also made to the data,[40] with the advice and support of analysts at the Cambridgeshire Constabulary Northern Division Intelligence Unit.

An important feature of these data for our analyses is their spatial location. There were exceptionally few crimes (0.4 per cent[41]) for which spatial coordinates were missing. These crimes were excluded (many of which occurred in rural locations outside the study area). There was also little evidence for false crime concentrations or systematic bias in the assignment of coordinates. According to the force protocol it is not acceptable for officers to apply generic coordinates to crimes where an exact location cannot be determined. In these cases, officers are instructed to use address or location points of the nearest place, which in most cases is within a very short distance. Detailed assessment of the crime patterns shows no crime concentrations at key landmarks that might be used as 'dumping grounds' for crimes with difficult to code locations.[42]

---

[39] Access was not requested for data on fraud and forgery, which excluded around 7,800 crimes.

[40] A small number of crimes (2.1 per cent) were excluded as they were considered duplicates for our purposes (eg the recovery location of a stolen car). Some crimes (0.4 per cent) were duplicated annually because they were identified as ongoing crimes (eg harassment and theft of electricity). A very small number of crimes (0.1 per cent) were excluded because they were erroneously included in the data provided by the police (eg they were reported, but did not occur, during the study period).

[41] The provision of coordinates improved over time: 0.74 per cent of coordinates were missing from the 2003–March 2004 data and just 0.20 per cent from the April 2004–07 data.

[42] We found a small concentration of crime at the main Thorpe Wood Police Station in Longthorpe, which is visible as an isolated hotspot in Figure 5.1. Looking more closely at the crimes occurring there, it is clear this had not resulted from officers applying the coordinates of the police station to crimes with unknown or problematic locations but to crimes that occurred in connection with police arrests or when the offender was in custody. Half involved criminal damage (eg of a cell or police car while in custody), 26 per cent were violent offences (eg assault of a police officer), 17 per cent were possession of cannabis, and the rest were crimes such as attempting to pervert the course of justice and intimidating a witness.

During the study period (in April 2004), Cambridgeshire Constabulary changed the system used to record crime. The recording methods and definitions remained largely the same for the purposes of PADS+ analyses, and any major differences in crime type coding between these periods was absorbed during the process of aggregation into crime category groups.[43] However, the way the data was held and presented by the two systems varied, which led to some data extraction inconsistencies that did affect the data relating to young offenders, which unfortunately meant it was too problematic to use the pre-April 2004 young people's crime and offender data. Therefore, we excluded data from 2003 and January to March 2004. However, a comparison of the annual stability of this data suggests the omission of data from the three months in 2004 is not a problem for our analyses.

For the analyses presented in this book, crime types that matched as closely as possible the self-report data collected from the participants were selected. These are violent crimes such as robbery and assault, crimes equivalent to vandalism such as criminal damage and arson, residential and non-residential burglary, theft of and from a car, and shoplifting. The resultant police-recorded crime data covers the period from January 2003 to December 2007 (93,666 crimes). The young people's crime data (2,555 crimes by offenders aged 13–17) and young offender data (1,162 offenders aged 13–17), as presented in chapter 5, covers the period from April 2004 to December 2007.

## 2.7  Data quality

The quality of the data can be seen as the keystone of a project's success, and perfection should be the standard to strive for on all levels of the operation.

(Stouthamer-Loeber and van Kammen 1995: 114)

To draw robust conclusions in any piece of research requires high quality data; consequently, data quality has remained a top

---

[43] Differences between the two time periods were analysed and we were satisfied that no bias existed. For example, scatterplots of output area level frequencies of crimes (by crime type) before and after April 2004 showed a high level of stability in their spatial distribution (beyond the effect of random variation due to the small absolute numbers of crimes). These results satisfied us that changes in the recording system did not introduce a (spatial) bias into the police data.

priority throughout PADS+. We are firm believers in the 'garbage in, garbage out' mantra. Data quality cannot be discerned in the presentation of most findings (regardless of the sophistication of the statistical analyses employed), which may, if data quality is low, be misleading.

A number of strategies were employed to help improve PADS+ data quality. One was to develop new or improve existing methodologies, like the interviewer-led questionnaire and one-to-one space–time budgets. A second was to use only our own specially trained researchers for the data collection. A third was to take issues of trust and confidentiality very seriously to make participants as comfortable as possible and willing to provide accurate information even on sensitive topics. Finally, a considerable effort was made to monitor and clean the collected data to ensure it was accurately recorded.

### 2.7.1 Researcher training and selection

The intensity of an ongoing longitudinal study like PADS+ places demands not only on participants, but also researchers (see also Lessler et al. 2008). As well as carrying out the data collection, PADS+ research staff had to communicate regularly with participants and their families, as well as local schools and other agencies like the Youth Offending Service and the Cambridgeshire Constabulary, often regarding sensitive material, and do so in a friendly, professional, patient, and flexible manner. A multitude of office-based skills were also required, such as being able to develop and adhere to protocols, handle and manipulate large datasets, and exhaust all avenues when tracking participants. Consequently, researchers were sought who would engage with the research and have an invested interest (see also Lessler et al. 2008); temporary staff (eg those paid by completed interview) or, as commonly used, a private survey company, were, therefore, not considered, in favour of full-time staff who worked directly for the study.

Researchers were selected who had a strong university educational background in a social or behavioural science and experience working with young people, conducting interviews, and handling sensitive and confidential material. Researchers were trained in-house by senior researchers and members of the research team with prior fieldwork experience. Training in the space–time budget interview was particularly important, due to the complexity of this methodology.

## 2.7.2  Participant trust and confidentiality

PADS+ participants were asked to report personal and often sensitive information truthfully to research staff (such as acts of crime). An effort was therefore made to ensure they felt secure in the confidentiality of their information and the impartiality of the research team.

Instilling confidence and gaining participants' trust began in the parents' wave, when contact was first made with the young people and their families. Parents were first approached under the auspices not only of the University of Cambridge, a well-known and respected centre for research, but also with a letter of support from the Director for Education and Children at the Peterborough City Council, in order to demonstrate the legitimacy of this research.

Because it is necessary to maintain personal details in order to track participants and link their data year to year, protocols were established to protect confidentiality. Random identifiers were used on all data and data collection material; these could only be linked to participants via a single file kept securely in the Cambridge office. Participants were also assured that none of the personal information they provided would be shared with people outside the research team, such as family members or authorities, and all researchers signed confidentiality agreements. A good indication of participant trust is the fact that *none* of the young people, when asked at Wave 5 (ages 16 or 17) to provide written consent for the PADS+ researchers to access their criminal justice records, refused such consent. The study's high retention rate is another good indicator of participant trust (Table 2.2).

Honesty is always a concern in self-report studies, especially those that tackle sensitive material. However, the validity and reliability of self-report measures of young people's crime are fairly well established for certain robust methodologies, such as the instruments and collection strategies employed by PADS+ (for a review see Hindelang et al. 1981; Huizinga and Elliott 1986; Junger-Tas and Marshall 1999; Thornberry and Krohn 2000). Analyses of patterns of responses in PADS+ data across waves and with data on police-recorded crimes supports the contention that participants did not simply fabricate their information. Participants with an official record, on average, self-reported significantly more crime than those who did not have an official record (see section 3.1.2 for further detail). The distribution of crimes reported in the space–time budget was also consistent in space (Figure 7.1) and time (see Figure 7.2) with police-recorded data on youth crime in Peterborough (see section 7.2).

### 2.7.3 Data checks: Missing values and consistency

The complexity of the data collected by PADS+ means that much can be done during and after fieldwork to improve its quality. One potential threat to data quality is internal non-response, which is rarely discussed, although it has the same detrimental effect on data quality as attrition.

Several steps were taken to reduce internal non-response during data collection. For the interviewer-led questionnaire, researchers were clear and consistent in their instructions to young people, and informed by experiences from the Peterborough Youth Study and earlier waves. For example, participants were clearly instructed to write a specific number when asked how many times they had done something, rather than generalities such as 'a lot' or 'loads'; they were given advice on how to quantify their activities by their frequency (eg weekly, monthly, etc.). They were also asked to check they had answered all questions at the end of each section. The internal non-response across all methodologies, as illustrated in Table 2.8, is generally very low for the data from the parents' and young people's questionnaires. Because the space–time budget was completed through a one-to-one interview, researchers coded the data as precisely as possible, and there is virtually no missing data.

Back in the office, protocols were developed for inputting paper-and-pen data, such as that from the questionnaire, to improve consistency, and subsequently to check input data for errors and inconsistencies. Similar procedures were also established for the space–time budget and imparted to researchers during training to increase consistency of encoding in the field. Many elements of the space–time budget data could also be checked after its collection. For example, the geocodes used for the participants' schools and homes were specifically checked. These are key locations in which young people spend a considerable percentage of their time, and using the correct geocode was particularly critical for linking space–time budget data with other environmental data.

The array of codes for each hour was also checked to ensure they made sense; for example, the spatial location of a young person

**Table 2.8  Internal non-response on parents' and young people's questionnaires**

| Questionnaire | Year | N questions | Internal non-response[a] | | | |
|---|---|---|---|---|---|---|
| | | | Mean % | Median % | Minimum % | Maximum % |
| Parents' | 2003 | 209 | 0.2 | 0.0 | 0.0 | 5.6 |
| 1 | 2004 | 163 | 0.7 | 0.6 | 0.0 | 3.5 |
| 2 | 2005 | 159 | 0.0 | 0.0 | 0.0 | 0.6 |
| 3 | 2006 | 181 | 0.1 | 0.0 | 0.0 | 1.8 |
| 4 | 2007 | 234 | 0.0 | 0.0 | 0.0 | 0.6 |
| 5 | 2008 | 228 | 0.0 | 0.0 | 0.0 | 0.9 |
| Total | Phase 1 | 1,174 | 0.2 | 0.0 | 0.0 | 5.6 |

[a] Percentage of missing answers on specific questions.

watching a film at the cinema should correspond to a cinema location.[44] By checking for congruence it was possible to correct minor mistakes that would reduce data quality. This latter kind of cleaning was undertaken shortly after the interview when researchers could best recall the interview and verify any necessary changes.

Some simple tests of the accuracy of certain aspects of the space–time budget geocoding were also run. One such test involved checking that the spatial location (output area) assigned by researchers to hours spent on school premises contained, as is to be expected, a school or some kind of education establishment. Analysis showed that over the entire study period, 56,289 space–time budget recorded hours[45] occurred on school premises,

---

[44] Due to the complex nature of the space–time budget, these checks are not always straightforward. For example, 94.4 per cent of 411 hours spent in the study area watching films at the cinema were coded at an output area containing a cinema. The remaining 5.6 per cent may represent errors in geocoding; however, these hours were spread across four output areas that all contain venues that may occasionally be used to show films (eg theatres), so the geocoding may, in fact, be correct.

[45] Spent awake and within the study area.

and that 99.4 per cent of these hours were recorded as occurring in 26 (5 per cent of) output areas that contain known education establishments.[46] The distribution of these hours across these output areas varied, depending on the size and type of the establishment, and whether the school was open for the whole of the study period, which further confirms the accuracy of the space–time budget.

For larger scales created from a battery of items in the questionnaire it was possible to *impute missing items* using a regression method. This was only undertaken on scales with more than eight items and only if the answers to no more than two of those items were missing. However, the need for and number of imputations made was generally very low; for example, for the personal morality scale and the ability to exercise self-control scale used in this book (see sections 3.2.1 and 3.2.2) the number of imputations made by wave varied between zero and seven cases (morality) and zero and five cases (self-control), with one notable exception, the self-control scale for Wave 1 for which imputations were made in 32 cases.[47]

## 2.8  Small area community survey (PCS)

Space–time budgets (see section 2.5) allow us to analyse where young people are (at what geographical locations), and under what circumstances (eg doing what with whom). However, they do not provide data about the social and built environment in which young people encounter particular circumstances (Figure 2.3). Space–time budget data therefore needed to be complemented with relevant environmental data with which it can be geographically matched. Such data were collected from official records (eg census and land use data) and by means of a special community survey

---

[46] Though some of the remaining 0.6 per cent of hours on school premises may represent coding error, some may also have occurred at very small independent education establishments unknown to researchers at the time of analysis.

[47] After Wave 1 the items for this scale were placed in a table with shading in alternating rows so that participants were less likely to miss items. Additional reminders for participants to check their answers were also introduced at key points during the questionnaire (such as this scale), which possibly influenced the reduction in internal non-response after this wave (Table 2.8).

(the Peterborough Community Survey) conducted in 2005. The main focus of the community survey was to gather small area data not regularly included in official statistics (such as area levels of informal social control) by using residents as observers of selected social conditions in the environment immediately surrounding their home.

Using an independent sample to report on the social environments of Peterborough avoided the potential for same-source bias (see G. J. Duncan and Raudenbush 1999). Using area residents meant we could tap into knowledge acquired over time (in most cases, over many years) which may provide a more representative characterization of the environment across different times of the day, weeks, and years. Other methods, such as systematic social observation (see, eg, Reiss 1971; Sampson and Raudenbush 1999) may only provide a more (time and resource) limited snapshot (problems which are particularly exaggerated in recent efforts to utilize technology like Google Earth[48]).

In this section we present the key constructs, design, and sampling of the 2005 *Peterborough Community Survey* (PCS).

### 2.8.1 Key constructs

Two kinds of data were collected by the community survey (see Table 2.9): data on small area social conditions (eg social cohesion and informal social control); and data on respondents themselves, which could be used in ecometric analyses to test the reliability of the environmental measures (see section 3.3.2).

### 2.8.2 Units of analysis: Output areas

The common unit of analysis used in this study for environmental variables is the output area (OA). Output areas are small enough geographical units to serve as proxies for settings. They form the base unit of output for the UK census, making them the smallest unit available for national statistics. Output areas are created using combinations of postcode polygons, which are designed to minimize between-output area variation in size, geographical area, and

---

[48] As presented in the sessions on '*Bringing innovative geographical data on neighbourhood quality into longitudinal studies of crime development*' at the Stockholm Criminology Symposium 2011.

**Table 2.9 Key constructs from the Peterborough Community Survey**

| Domain | Construct |
|---|---|
| Home setting (output area) | Area of residence (output area) |
| | Informal social control |
| | Formal social control |
| | Social cohesion |
| | Intergenerational closure |
| | Youth problems |
| | Youth presence |
| | General disorder |
| | Problem neighbours |
| | Local services |
| Respondents | Sex |
| | Age |
| | Ethnicity |
| | Employment |
| | Education level |
| | Social capital |
| | Morality |
| | Self-control |
| | Household tenure |
| | Household characteristics |
| | Free time spent in area |
| | Time lived in area |
| | Local friends |
| | Victimization |
| | Offending |
| | Fear of crime |

population density, and within-area variation in key social statistics (Martin 1998, 2000), although they are fundamentally geographical units, and are not intended to represent neighbourhoods or communities, which may have different boundaries. Typically, they cover around 6.8 hectares (0.068 km$^2$) and contain about 300 residents (220 adults) living in 125 households (see Table 2.10).

Output areas are a much smaller area unit than is typically used in community surveys in criminological studies. For example, in its community survey, the Edinburgh Study of Youth Transitions in Crime (ESYTC) used 'neighbourhoods' as the unit of analysis, with each neighbourhood encompassing approximately 45 OAs and an average population of around 5,000 (more than 16 times the average population of an output area) (A. M. Brown 2004; D. J. Smith et al. 2001; D. J. Smith and McVie 2003). Longitudinal research on

**Table 2.10  Area and population statistics for OAs in the study area**

|  | Minimum | Maximum | Mean | SD | Skewness (SE) | Median |
|---|---|---|---|---|---|---|
| Area (hectares) | 2.4 | 430.5 | 12.3[a] | 24.4 | 11.2 (.10) | 6.8 |
| Total population | 106 | 560 | 296 | 60.9 | .32 (.11) | 293.5 |
| Population 18+ | 89 | 429 | 221 | 37.3 | .44 (.11) | 219 |
| Households | 48 | 234 | 124 | 15.1 | .61 (.11) | 124 |

[a] A few large rural output areas dramatically skew the mean (75 per cent of OAs cover less than the mean area).

youth crime in the US typically uses comparably large units. For example, the Pittsburgh Youth Study (PYS) analysed key aspects of community social characteristics in 90 'neighbourhood units' (created by aggregating US census tracts) with an average population of 4,000 (more than 13 times the average population of an output area) (Loeber and Wikström 1993; Wikström and Loeber 2000); while the Project on Human Development in Chicago Neighbourhoods (PHDCN) combined 865 US census tracts into 343 'neighbourhood clusters' with an average population of 8,000 (more than 26 times that of an output area) (Morenoff et al. 2001; Sampson et al. 1997).

In addition, one of the most prominent longitudinal studies in the United Kingdom, the Cambridge Study in Delinquent Development (CSDD; see, for example, Piquero et al. 2007), does not include a community survey and refers to only one working class London neighbourhood. Similarly, the Environmental Risk Longitudinal Twin Study (see, for example, Odgers et al. 2009) is not linked to a particular study area but draws its sample from across England and Wales, surveying on average three other residents in each participant's postcode.

The main reason the PCS aimed for much smaller areas was to obtain (on theoretical grounds) units resembling settings as much as possible (see section 1.3.3). Arguably, large area units cannot adequately represent settings, and therefore the environmental features that directly influence action. Consequently, PADS+ focused on the smallest units available that can still be linked to official data and used in the space–time budget—*output areas*.[49]

---

[49]   For more on the argument that 'small is better', see Oberwittler and Wikström (2009).

## 2.8.3 Observational space

the density of information per unit area for a given household tends to exhibit distance-decay properties with the household's location as the centre of the density surface.

(L. A. Brown and Moore 1970: 8)

Community survey data was collected at the address level but aggregated to the output area level in order to be matched with official and space–time budget data. However, community survey respondents were not asked to report on the features of their output area (few are likely to be familiar with the concept of output areas and have any knowledge of their home output area's geographical boundaries). Instead, they were asked to report on an easily defined and explicit area, ie

the area within a short walking distance (say a couple of minutes) from your home. That is the street you live in and the streets, houses, shops, parks and other areas close to your home.

This area is referred to as their home area *observational space*, which should amount to an area approximately 200 metres in diameter. Such a small area is likely to be homogenous in its social environmental character, and it is reasonable to assume that residents can make accurate and detailed observations on this scale (eg L. A. Brown and Moore 1970). The overlap between (hypothetical) observational spaces and the boundaries for the output area is not perfect (see Figure 2.6). However, despite this slight imperfection, it is reasonable to assume that residents' average responses provide a good measure of the social conditions in their output area.

## 2.8.4 Sampling strategy

The community survey study area was defined as the area from which the PADS+ participants were randomly selected (see section 4.1, Figure 4.1, for the geographical boundaries of the study area). The space–time budget was designed to measure in which settings (in which output areas) in the study area PADS+ participants spent time; community survey data was therefore required for each of these settings (and each output area). The sampling strategy was designed to procure a sufficient number of responses from the 518 output areas in this study area.

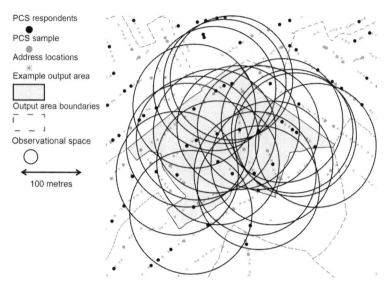

PCS respondents

PCS sample

Address locations

Example output area

Output area boundaries

Observational space

100 metres

**Figure 2.6 Illustration of the sampling and observational spaces for residents in an output area**

The initial sampling frame consequently needed to be drawn from a comprehensive list of people living in the study area and their home addresses, so they could be linked to their prospective output areas. The most complete and accurate list of names and addresses available for research purposes in the United Kingdom in 2005 was the electoral register (ER), a list of the names and addresses of all UK residents eligible and registered to vote. However, it presented a few limitations.

Some people living in the United Kingdom are not eligible to register to vote; this includes young people under the age of 18, prisoners,[50] homeless people with no 'declaration of local connection', and people who do not have British, Republic of Ireland, European Union, or Commonwealth citizenship (regardless of their residential status or nationality).

Some eligible people do not register to vote. Research into UK voter registration shows a gradual increase over several decades to

---

[50] Prisoners serving a sentence are ineligible, while remand prisoners can join the register.

a stable rate of around 90–93 per cent[51] (see, for example, Electoral Commission 2005, 2009). This is comparable to voter registration rates found in other countries with similar registration systems, although registration rates in the United States are only around 65 per cent. Registration rates vary between different groups (such as those on low incomes, from black and ethnic minority groups, and mobile young people living in rented accommodation[52]) and areas (such as those characterized by social disadvantage, over-crowding, or a high proportion of multi-occupant housing, students, members of the armed forces, homeless people, and travellers) (Electoral Commission 2005; Rallings et al. 2000). Although these discrepancies cause selection in the sample, the strategy to sample a minimum number for each output area (see further below) means that while groups that are underrepresented on the electoral register may be under sampled, *areas* in which fewer people register will not be.

Perhaps the most significant shortcoming of the electoral register is that some people who are registered 'opt out' of appearing on the available register. The opt-out system was introduced in 2002 and since then the full electoral register has only been available for the purposes of voting administration, prevention and detection of crime by police and law enforcement agencies, and credit assessment, leaving only the edited electoral register (EER), available for public use. In 2004, the national opt-out rate stood at 26 per cent; however, this varied substantially across different councils, largely due to varying methods and levels of publicity for the opt-out system (Equifax 2006). At the time, Peterborough had an opt-out rate of 30 per cent, slightly higher than the national average, which may be explained by the City Council's policy to automatically opt out voters who had opted out previously. Analysing opt-out rates for the 19 electoral wards in the study area,[53] we found they ranged from 20.9 per cent to 35.3 per cent, and were very strongly negatively correlated with deprivation scores from the 2000 Index of

---

[51] In the United Kingdom, the incentive to register is increased by the inclusion of the electoral register in credit reference checks.

[52] The Electoral Commission (2005) reports that 81 per cent of black and ethnic minority respondents claimed to have registered, compared to 94 per cent of those from other ethnic groups, while 83 per cent of 18–34-year-olds claimed to have registered, compared to 98 per cent of those over the age of 55.

[53] Data on any lower level of aggregation was not available.

Deprivation[54] ($r = -.73$. $p = .000$),[55] meaning the opt-out rate tended to be highest among those who live in advantaged areas. As with voter non-registration, higher opt out among certain social groups may cause them to be under-sampled; however, *areas* where these people are concentrated will not be, due to the strategy to sample a minimum number from each output area (see further below).

Using address information from the EER, residents could be located in their home output areas.[56] A sufficient number of residents needed to be sampled from each output area. Community surveys like the PCS have to strike a balance between sampling many areas or many respondents within each area in order to maximize statistical power within financial resource limitations. Two main strategies are possible: sampling fewer, larger areas, but more respondents within each; or sampling more, smaller areas, but fewer respondents within each. A number of studies have shown that more statistical power is gained by opting for more areas with fewer respondents (Murray et al. 2004; Snijders and Bosker 1999). Snijders and Bosker (1999) suggest that for some hypotheses, just 8–15 respondents per area are sufficient for adequate statistical power in multilevel models including area level effects.[57] Against this background, and the fact that the study area encompasses a large number of areas (518), a minimum of 10 respondents were aimed for per output area.

### 2.8.5 Methodology: The postal survey

A postal survey was utilized because they are able to reach a large number of people at a minimal cost, are accessible to most adults

---

[54] The Index of Deprivation (ID 2000) is an earlier version of the Index of Multiple Deprivation 2004 described in chapter 2, footnote 58 and Noble et al. (2004).

[55] Very little independent research has been conducted on electoral register opt out. However, according to Direct Marketing Association findings and personal correspondence with the Director of External Affairs at consumer credit reporting agency Equifax and the government Electoral Commission, more affluent people are most likely to opt out, as are younger people.

[56] Just 1.6 per cent of addresses failed to geocode. This process was completed using the Royal Mail Postcode Address File (PAF®, registered trademark of Royal Mail) and Ordnance Survey Addresspoint (by permission of Ordinance Survey on behalf of HMSO. © Crown copyright and database right 2005. All rights reserved).

[57] For more on statistical power analysis in complex survey designs, such as multilevel sampling, see Murray et al. (2004) and Raudenbush (1999).

(unlike internet or telephone surveys), can be completed at respondents' convenience (increasing the likelihood they will be completed) and if conducted effectively can achieve good response rates (de Leeuw and Hox 2008; Dillman 1978, 1998). Nonetheless, response rates have traditionally posed a challenge for UK postal surveys (see, for discussion, Moser and Kalton 1971). Response rates between 30 and 40 per cent are not uncommon (Punch 2003), and a response rate of 50 per cent may be considered very good for a UK self-administered postal survey (Stoop 2005). In Peterborough, previous postal surveys report response rates lower than 5 per cent (the Peterborough Crime and Disorder Survey 2004, which was sent to every household via the council magazine; see Clements et al. 2006) to a mediocre 33 per cent (the City Council's Rural Crime and Disorder Survey 2003).

To trial the community survey and measure the expected response rate, a small pilot was performed. Forty questionnaires were mailed to three different output areas in the city characterized by low, medium, and high deprivation, as research shows a positive correlation between area deprivation and non-response (Goyder 1987; Goyder et al. 1992; Goyder et al. 2002; Groves and Couper 1998). Output area deprivation was determined using Office of the Deputy Prime Minister (ODPM) Indices of Multiple Deprivation (IMD) 2004.[58] The outcome supported the expectation that more deprived areas would have lower response rates: response rates were 41 per cent for the area with high deprivation, 60 per cent for the area with medium deprivation, 62 per cent for the area with low deprivation, and 55 per cent overall. It was therefore decided to generally sample 22 people per output area and to oversample by 50 per cent in deprived areas (ie to sample 33 people) to reach the goal of a minimum of 10 respondents in all output areas.

### 2.8.6 Motivating people to take part

A considerable body of literature was drawn upon to design strategies for increasing participation in the community survey,

[58] Devised by the Social Disadvantage Research Centre (SDRC) at the University of Oxford, the IMD 2004 is a weighted and aggregated index created using seven diverse deprivation domains that can be measured distinctly: income, employment, health deprivation and disability, education skills and training, barriers to housing and services, crime, and the living environment (see Noble et al. 2004). The higher the score, and the lower the rank, the more deprived the area.

improving data quality, and reducing non-response (for discussion and reviews of empirical findings, see, for example, de Leeuw and Hox 2008; Dillman 1978, 1998, 2000; Dillman et al. 2008; Edwards et al. 2002; Groves et al. 1992; Groves et al. 2002; Groves et al. 2004; Porter 2004; Stoop 2005). Some of the methods utilized included:

(1) The questionnaire was designed to be as accessible as possible to facilitate participation and reduce item non-response (see Dillman 1998; Dillman et al. 2002; Groves et al. 2002; Jenkins and Dillman 1997; Redline and Dillman 2002; Redline et al. 2005). The initial mailing included a clear personalized cover letter stating the survey's aim to know about the social conditions of their neighbourhoods and the potential benefits this knowledge could provide to the local community.[59]

(2) Findings suggest that responses are normally higher on surveys linked to government agencies or academic institutions, namely due to greater trust in their legitimacy and accountability (Edwards et al. 2002; Moser and Kalton 1971). Special permission was obtained to use the Peterborough City Council and University of Cambridge logos on the cover letter, which was signed by a number of sponsors from the local government, local agencies, and the police constabulary.[60] Questionnaires were also sent to respondents in University of Cambridge envelopes.[61]

(3) Awareness of the survey was raised through a series of media releases, including an article in the Peterborough City Council Newsletter (delivered to every household in the unitary authority), an interview feature on the BBC Radio Cambridgeshire Breakfast Show, and articles in a number of local papers.

---

[59] Personalizing questionnaires and letters has been shown to increase response rates on postal surveys (see Edwards et al. 2002), while drawing attention to respondents' civic duty and personal interests has been found to increase their willingness to take part (see, for example, Dillman 1978; 2000: 14-21; Goyder 1987; Groves et al. 1992: 484).

[60] Sponsorship by those known to and respected by the target population has been shown to increase participation (Dillman et al. 2002; Groves et al. 1992; Moser and Kalton 1971).

[61] Research has shown that postal questionnaires sent from universities typically achieve (31 per cent) higher response rates than those sent from other sources (Edwards et al. 2002).

(4) Ethnic minorities are often a problematic group in survey research (Goyder 1987; Groves and Couper 1998; Stoop 2005: 64). Efforts were made to counteract a number of potential causes of poor response rates from minority groups (see Johnson et al. 2002; Stoop 2005). For example, to accommodate the language difficulties of the largest minority population in Peterborough copies of the cover letter were sent in English and Urdu to residents in areas characterized by a high concentration of Pakistani residents, offers were made to send the Urdu version to residents in other parts of the city, and the opportunity was provided for respondents to complete the survey in Urdu over the phone.[62]

(5) Reminder letters can improve response rates (de Leeuw and Hox 1988; Dillman 1991) and were sent to non-respondents in output areas from which the minimum 10 desired responses were not yet obtained, changing the nature of appeals in successive letters (Dillman 2000). Initially, reminder letters emphasized how many local residents had already returned the survey;[63] later letters highlighted the fact that few residents in their small area had returned surveys.[64] Additional copies of the survey were sent if area response rates remained low.

Overall, the sampling and non-response reduction strategies appear comparatively successful, as reflected by the reasonable size and distribution of the final sample. Table 2.11 shows the breakdown of the sampling procedure from selection of the sampling frame to the final response rate.

### 2.8.7 The final sample

The EER compiled in the autumn of 2004 was used for the sampling frame. This provided 75,041 names and addresses in the study area. One adult per household was then randomly sampled to maximize the distribution of respondents across each output area. To reduce any negative effects on PADS+ retention rates, 384 adults were removed who were living at the addresses of PADS+ participants.

---

[62] The entire survey was not translated as the majority of respondents could be expected to have some level of English, as the sample was taken from the electoral register and therefore could not include newly arrived immigrants or refugees.

[63] This drew upon the 'social validation heuristic' (see Groves et al. 1992).

[64] This played upon the 'scarcity principle' (see Groves et al. 1992).

**Table 2.11 Breakdown of the sampling frame and sample**

|  | Study area (518 OAs) |
| --- | --- |
| Total population (2001 census) | 152,205 |
| Total population over the age of 18 (2001 census) | 114,423 |
| Population of the EER | 75,041 (66% of total 18+) |
| Sampling frame (one person per household) | 35,853 (31% of total 18+) |
| Random sample | 12,681 (11% of total 18+) |
| Ineligible | 231 (2% of sample) |
| Response rate (for eligible random sample) | 6,615 (53% of sample) |

In addition, 1,626 young people who were registered but did not turn 18 until 2005 were also removed. This derived an initial sampling frame of 35,853 (see Table 2.11).

Matching each address with its output area, a random sample of 22 residents was selected from each output area, except the most deprived, from which a random sample of 33 residents[65] was selected (for a geographical illustration of the relationship between addresses, addresses sampled, and those included in the final sample, see Figure 2.6). The rationale for the larger samples from the disadvantaged areas was based on the findings from the pilot showing a lower response rate in disadvantaged areas. IMD scores used to determine deprivation were only available at the time of the sampling at the super output area level, so the output areas were stratified by disadvantage based on super output area scores. Super output areas (SOAs), an official census output unit, are aggregates of OAs (five on average). Any OA in the 25 most deprived SOAs was designated as deprived, which amounted to 125 OAs.

This sampling strategy left a random sample of 12,681 (see Table 2.11). However, 231 sampled residents were ineligible[66] to

---

[65] Additional adjustments to the sample including oversampling in output areas with abnormally large populations caused by recent residential development, undersampling when there were not enough cases in the sampling frame to fulfil the sample quota, and undersampling in rural areas (18 rather than 22 residents) which are generally more affluent and had a higher response rate (59 per cent).

[66] Some studies confuse ineligible and non-contactable respondents, which may lead to inflated response rates (see Stouthamer-Loeber and van Kammen 1995). For the PCS sample, eligibility was always assumed in cases where there was no response of any kind and ineligibility could not be determined.

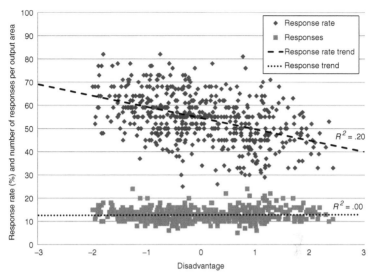

**Figure 2.7  Number and percent of community survey respondents per output area by disadvantage[a]**

[a] Disadvantage here is measured at the output area level using a measure, created from 2001 census data, which became available after the sample was stratified by deprivation using data at the super output area level.

participate because they had either moved[67] or died since the compilation of the EER. This meant the final sample included 12,450 eligible residents (see Table 2.11), of which 6,615 returned responses, amounting to a valid response rate of 53 per cent for the whole study area.

On average, 13 responses were received per output area and more than 10 responses from 94.2 per cent of output areas. Only five OAs (1 per cent) received fewer than eight responses (the lowest being five). This meant that PCS responses were well spread across the city and adequately represented all OAs. The fact that the strategy to oversample in deprived areas worked well is illustrated in Figure 2.8, showing that while the response rate declined by area disadvantage, the actual number of respondents included in the study did not (ie was fairly even across levels of disadvantage).

[67] For example, to a new home, abroad with the army, into a nursing home, or into hospital (permanently or for an extended period).

Although there were relatively few respondents per output area, because of the small population of output areas and the number sampled, the sample represents a much larger proportion of the population than most comparable community surveys. More than 4 per cent of the total population, and nearly 6 per cent of the adult population, of the study area took part in the PCS, compared to 0.4 per cent of the population of the study area of the ESYTC Community Survey (see A. M. Brown 2004; McVie and Norris 2006; D. J. Smith et al. 2001; D. J. Smith and McVie 2003), and 0.3 per cent of the population of the study area (343 neighbourhood clusters) surveyed in the PHDCN (see Morenoff et al. 2001: 526–7). The population was well represented across all output areas, with a mean rate of 6.0 per cent of the adult population per output area taking part (representing, on average, every tenth household (10.4 per cent) in the output area).

### 2.8.8  Residents as social observers: Issues of validity and reliability

The goal of the small area community survey was to acquire a sample of capable social observers who could provide valid and reliable information about selected social conditions of their home area observational space. It is therefore crucial that variation in respondents' social observations was due primarily to variation in their environments, and not them as people.

To test whether or not respondents reliably reported on the specified observational space surrounding their home, they were asked about the presence of key structures such as schools and police and fire stations within their observational space. The findings support the assertion that respondents generally referred only to the very small area around their home, ie only reported the presence of a school, police station, or fire station if it was located close to home (see Oberwittler and Wikström 2009: 46).

The fact that some people do not register to vote, that some groups are excluded from the electoral register (eg those who are not eligible to vote, with no home address, or in prison), that some people opt out of appearing on the available register, and that, albeit being a good result for a UK postal survey, just over half of the resulting sample took part in the survey, leaves room for potential problems with selection bias. Analysis of the key demographics of the sample (Table 2.12) demonstrated reasonable variation,

**Table 2.12  Key demographics of PCS respondents**

| Construct | N | Percentage of sample |
|---|---|---|
| **Sex** | | |
| Male | 2,884 | 43.6 |
| Female | 3,685 | 55.7 |
| Missing | 46 | 0.7 |
| **Household composition** | | |
| No children in household | 4,239 | 64.1 |
| Children living in household (w/cohabiting adults) | 1,792 | 27.1 |
| Children living in household (lone adult) | 501 | 7.6 |
| Missing | 83 | 1.3 |
| **Ethnicity** | | |
| White | 5,993 | 90.6 |
| Asian | 377 | 5.7 |
| Black | 99 | 1.5 |
| Mixed | 48 | 0.7 |
| Chinese/other | 44 | 0.8 |
| Missing | 54 | 0.8 |
| **Highest education level (or equivalent)** | | |
| University degree | 747 | 11.3 |
| A levels | 1,185 | 17.9 |
| GCSEs | 2,587 | 39.1 |
| No/lower qualifications | 1,525 | 23.1 |
| Missing/unknown | 571 | 8.6 |
| **Employment** | | |
| Full-time employed | 2,926 | 44.2 |
| Part-time employed | 844 | 12.8 |
| Full-time education | 115 | 1.7 |
| Housewife/husband | 403 | 6.1 |
| Retired | 1,806 | 27.3 |
| Unable (medical) | 327 | 4.9 |
| Unemployed | 135 | 2.0 |
| Missing | 59 | 0.9 |

*(continued)*

**Table 2.12** *(Continued)*

| Construct | N | Percentage of sample |
|---|---|---|
| **Caught or arrested?** | | |
| No | 5,966 | 90.2 |
| Yes, once or twice | 510 | 7.7 |
| Yes, many times (3+) | 59 | 0.9 |
| Missing | 80 | 1.2 |
| **Tenancy** | | |
| Own | 4,854 | 73.4 |
| Private rent | 416 | 6.3 |
| Rent from council/association | 1,190 | 18.0 |
| Family/friends | 54 | 0.8 |
| Sheltered/social housing | 15 | 0.2 |
| Equity share/part own | 11 | 0.2 |
| Other | 29 | 0.4 |
| Missing | 46 | 0.7 |

although a comparison of the sample characteristics with those of the general population of the study area (according to the 2001 census) showed there was some social selectivity in the sample.[68] The crucial question then is whether the noted selectivity significantly affected the validity of the measures of small area social conditions.

The comparison between the sample and the population statistics showed that, where selection did arise, it generally favoured respondents who were likely to have more free time. For example, while only approximately 12.3 per cent of the population of the study area according to the 2001 census was retired, 27.3 per cent of the PCS respondents were retired. As this suggests, the PCS sample had a higher proportion of older people than the population of the study area: 50.4 per cent of the sample were aged 50+, compared to 40.2 per cent of the population; and 32.4 per cent were aged 60+, compared to 24.6 per cent of the population. However, the sample

---

[68] Note that the intervening time between the 2001 census and the 2005 community survey may account for some differences in these distributions.

was well distributed across the adult age bracket, with a mean age of 50.7 years and a standard deviation of 17.9, suggesting that the majority of the sample was between 30 and 70 years old, an age group one would expect to have little foreseeable difficulty effectively observing the area around their residence.

The PCS sample was slightly less likely to be 'economically active' (employed either full or part-time) than the general population (57.0 per cent versus 69.3 per cent), mainly because of the overrepresentation of retirees (other categories, such as full-time students, housewives/husbands, unemployed, and unable to work were comparable). The sample was also slightly better educated than the general population, with 68.3 per cent holding qualifications, compared to only 50.3 per cent of the population.

On other fronts the sample was very similar to the general population, such as in household composition (61.4 per cent of the PCS sample did not have children living in the household, versus 67.0 per cent of the population; and 7.6 per cent of the PCS sample were lone parents, versus 8.5 per cent of the general population), household tenure, and ethnicity (5.7 per cent, 1.5 per cent and 90.6 per cent of the PCS sample were Asian, black, or white, respectively, compared to 7.1 per cent, 1.3 per cent and 89.5 per cent of the general population). The latter in particular suggests the participant recruitment techniques were effective, as the underrepresentation of minority groups is frequently cited as a problem in survey research (Goyder 1987; Groves and Couper 1998; Johnson et al. 2002; Stoop 2005: 64).

The fact that the sample somewhat overrepresented people who were retired and better educated (and excluded those under 18, who were not eligible to vote, had no home address, or were in prison) may not necessarily be of any great concern. There is, to our knowledge, no strong reason to believe that economically active and less well-educated people would be better social observers than people who are retired and better educated, as well as there is no reason to believe that the groups excluded from the register would be better social observers than those included. In this context it is crucial to bear in mind that selection is only a problem for the study in so far as it leads to bias in the measures of home area environments.

However, there are good reasons to believe that people living in the same environment may differ somewhat in their ability to assess its social conditions. People may vary in their knowledge of the area, for example, as a consequence of how much time they spend at home and how long they have lived in the area. The fact that most respondents (91.4 per cent) had lived at their current address for more than a year, and many for much longer (mean = 15.7 years, standard deviation = 12.5 years) minimizes this risk. People may also vary in how much time they spend in the immediate area outside their home (at different times of the day) and how much contact they have with their neighbours. For example, those with children may have more contact with neighbours and more knowledge about what goes on in their immediate surroundings. Finally, there may be differences between people in their ability to accurately assess social conditions like social cohesion and informal social control. For these reasons there is a risk that some selection bias may be introduced. To test this we carried out ecometric analyses (see section 3.3.2). Our findings support the contention that residents' perceptions of the social features of their neighbourhoods were largely independent of their socio-demographic characteristics.

We were also able, in some instances, to check the accuracy of respondents' observations of local social conditions using independent external data, and generally observed agreement between the two. For example, there was a strong correspondence between the distributions of PCS respondents' reports of problematic neighbours and police incident data concerning nuisance neighbours[69] (Figure 2.8; for details on how maps in this book are created see technical appendix, section A1.2).

Taken all together, we are confident that our measures of selected social conditions of settings (output areas), such as their levels of social cohesion, informal social control, and disorder, adequately represent area variation in those conditions.

## 2.9  Summary and conclusion

In this chapter we have introduced and presented in some detail the data and methodologies of the Peterborough Adolescent and Young Adult Development Study (PADS+). The most innovative aspect of PADS+ is the use of a space–time budget methodology in

---

[69] One output area in the Hampton area proved to be a major outlier (by more than nine standard deviations). This is likely to be a result of large-scale housing development in the area after 2005, leading to a mismatch between PCS data (measured in 2005) and police incident data (covering the period from April 2004 to December 2007).

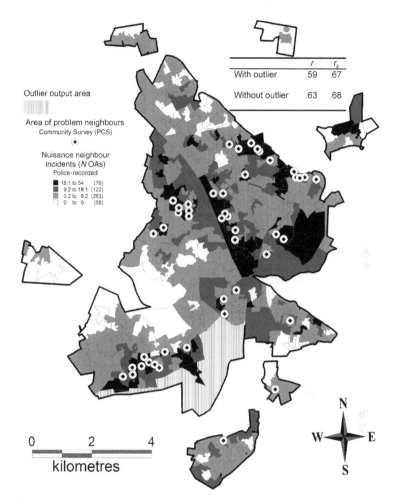

| | $r$ | $r_s$ |
|---|---|---|
| With outlier | .59 | .67 |
| Without outlier | .63 | .68 |

Outlier output area

Area of problem neighbours
Community Survey (PCS)

Nuisance neighbour
incidents (*N* OAs)
Police-recorded

| | | |
|---|---|---|
| ■ | 18.1 to 54 | (76) |
| ■ | 9.2 to 18.1 | (122) |
| ■ | 0.2 to 9.2 | (263) |
| □ | 0 to 0 | (56) |

0    2    4
kilometres

N
W    E
S

**Figure 2.8   Spatial distribution of police recorded incidents concerning nuisance neighbours[a] compared to PCS reports of problem neighbours,[b] with zero-order and rank correlations[c,d]**

[a] Total number of police recorded incidents of nuisance neighbours per output area from April 2004 to December 2007 (thematic mapping boundaries determined by standard deviations).
[b] Areas are defined as having problem neighbours if the average response for an OA to the following question was two or more: *Would you say that in your neighbourhood (the area within a short walking distance from your house) there is a problem with people who cause problems for or disturb their neighbours (for example, neighbours who are noisy or aggressive)?* 1 = 'No, no problem at all'; 2 = 'Yes, somewhat of a problem'; 3 = 'Yes, a big problem'.
[c] Correlations use the average PCS response score per output area regarding problem neighbours and the nuisance neighbour incident count.
[d] On choloropleth maps see technical appendix, section A1.2.1.

combination with a small area community survey, which enables the measurement of settings (ie the features of and circumstances in which people take part in small area environments) and people's exposure to settings (their activity fields—the configuration of settings, or particular kinds of settings, they take part in during a specific time period). Combined with more traditional data on people's personal characteristics (and their social situation), space–time budget and small area community survey data makes it possible to explore the role of the interaction between personal characteristics (crime propensities) and environmental features (criminogenic exposure) in crime causation in a way that has not been possible in previous research. In the next chapter we introduce the key measures of crime propensity, criminogenic exposure, and crime involvement used in this study and present an initial test of the basic propositions of SAT regarding the importance of the interaction between crime propensity and criminogenic exposure for people's crime involvement.

# 3

# Young People's Crime, Crime Propensity, and Criminogenic Exposure: Key Constructs and Basic Findings

The basic proposition of Situational Action Theory (SAT) is that acts of crime are an outcome of the interaction between people's crime propensity and criminogenic exposure. To test key propositions of SAT we therefore need to have adequate measures of participants' crime involvement, crime propensity, and criminogenic exposure. The main aims of this chapter are to:

(1) introduce and discuss the methods used in PADS+ to measure crime, crime propensity, and criminogenic exposure;
(2) present basic findings about, and the relationship between, young people's crime involvement, crime propensity, and criminogenic exposure and, thereby, conduct an initial test of some key propositions of SAT.

As the main focus of this book is to analyse the role of criminogenic exposure (and its interaction with crime propensity) in the prediction of crime events, this particular topic will be developed (spatially, temporally, and situationally) in greater depth in subsequent chapters.

## 3.1 Crime

Crimes are acts that break rules of conduct stated in law. In PADS+ three key measures were used to study participants' crime involvement: (1) annual self-reported incidences of crime from the (annual) small group questionnaire (see section 2.4.1), subsequently referred to as *self-reported crime*; (2) self-reported incidences of crime over the four days covered each year by the annual space–time budget (see section 2.5.1), subsequently referred to as *space–time budget crimes*; and (3) data about convictions, warnings, and reprimands recorded by the police on the Police National Computer (PNC) (see section 2.6), subsequently referred to as *police-recorded crimes*. In other chapters data is also used from other official sources, measuring total counts of crime in Peterborough during the study period, as well as crimes committed by known young offenders of a similar age to PADS+ participants (see sections 2.6 and 5.1 for details).

Different sources of crime data present different problems as measures of people's actual crime involvement (for general discussion, see, eg, Hindelang et al. 1981; Hood and Sparks 1970: 11–79). A main concern for police-recorded data is the problem of the *dark figure*—not all crimes committed are recorded by the police. In addition, only a small proportion of police-recorded crimes have a known and recorded offender (the problem of low *clearance*[1]). Moreover, the dark figure and clearance rates vary between crime types and the circumstances under which particular crimes take place (depending on factors such as the crime's seriousness and third party visibility, and, in crimes against a person, the relationship between victim and offender). Violent crimes are a good example of acts for which the dark figure and clearance rate will vary according to the circumstances (see Wikström 1985: 36–55). Violent crimes between people who know each other are less likely to be reported to the police (and therefore have a higher dark figure); however, if they are reported, the offender can (with the main exception of homicide[2]) almost always be identified by the victim (therefore they have a higher clearance rate). On the other hand, violent crimes between strangers are more likely to be reported to the police (and therefore have a lower dark figure), but in many cases the offender cannot be identified (therefore they have a lower clearance rate).

---

[1]  We use the concept of clearance here to refer to cases in which a reported crime is cleared by the identification of the offender/s (clearance by arrest). Clearance is sometimes used in a more general sense; for example clearance rates sometimes include cases in which an act reported as a crime is later found not to be a crime in the legal sense, and is therefore cleared from the books.

[2]  Other examples include cases in which the victim is unconscious or under the influence of alcohol or drugs and cannot remember what happened.

Police data may also reflect different stages of the criminal justice process (from crime reporting to formal sanction) and it is, therefore, necessary to consider to what stage police-recorded data refers. The police-recorded data for PADS+ participants reflects the final stage, covering crimes for which an offender has been formally sanctioned, that is warned, reprimanded, or convicted.[3] Participants who have been formally sanctioned, as well as others who have not, may have had other contact with the police, eg they may have been questioned or arrested without having been formally warned, reprimanded, or convicted for the crime in question. It is a reasonable assumption, and one borne out by our data (see section 3.1.2), that more frequent and serious offenders are more likely to be police recorded than less frequent and serious offenders (although many offences by frequent offenders may not be officially recorded).

It is clear that if we want a reasonably accurate estimate of a population of young people's crime involvement, data on police-recorded crime are not an ideal source; these data will significantly underestimate the prevalence and, particularly, the magnitude of young people's crime involvement.[4] Arguably, the best source of adequate data about a population's crime involvement (ie prevalence and frequency of crime) is a well-executed self-report study, simply because an offender is the best source of information about his or her own crimes. The main concerns with self-report data are participants' *accuracy of recall* and *honesty* in reporting their crime involvement. The extent to which participants are honest and can accurately recall their crimes is the extent to which self-report data provides a representative picture of their crime involvement.

The PADS+ field research team made a concerted effort to create trust and ensure anonymity to promote honesty in response and took measures to facilitate accurate recall as much as possible[5] (as described in section 2.7.2). We generally report the exact figures of participants' self-reported crimes, although we are, of course, well

[3] There are other sanctions that are not included in PNC data; see section 2.6.

[4] Although data on police-recorded crimes may in many cases give an adequate representation of the *variation*, for example, between people, places, and times in relative (but not absolute) levels of crime.

[5] Precise recall may, for example, be particularly difficult for very frequent offenders in the case of longer recall periods such as the annual period used in the questionnaire. For example, it may be difficult for participants accurately to recall whether crimes they committed at the early part of the recall period fell within or before this period (especially if they committed many acts of crime).

aware, as the reader should be, that they are likely to have some imprecision. What is important for our analyses is not that the figures are exact but that they are in the right order of magnitude (eg that an offender who self-reports 112 crimes has actually committed about 112 crimes). The patterns apparent in the self-report data, and their relationship to offenders' police-recorded crimes do not give any cause for particular concern regarding the general reliability of our self-report data (see section 3.1.2). The findings appear reasonable and consistent, and (when comparable[6]) in line with what is already known about young people's crime involvement (eg Farrington et al. 2006; Le Blanc and Fréchette 1989; Loeber and Farrington 1998), further supporting the supposition that self-report data (collected using rigorous and well-executed methods) provides the best and closest approximation of young people's real levels of crime involvement.

The (annual) self-report data was restricted to certain selected crime categories (Table 3.1), and excludes, for example, fraud, sex, and traffic crimes. Data was also collected about young people's illegal drug use as well as their alcohol consumption and smoking (which generally constitute law-breaking across most of the ages included in this study under most circumstances). However, for various reasons we have decided not to analyse these kinds of rule-breaking in this book. The key assumption we make is that the overall prevalence and frequency of the included crime types accurately represent the overall *variation* among young people in their breaches of rules of conduct stated in law.[7]

Self-report questions about crime involvement refer to 10 different types of crime: shoplifting, theft from a person, residential burglary, non-residential burglary, theft from a car, theft of a car, vandalism, arson/fire-setting, assault, and robbery from a person (see Table 3.1). Participants were asked whether they had committed the crime in question during the last year and, if so, how many times they had done so. These questions were introduced by a field

---

[6] Although there are many cross-sectional studies of young people's self-reported crime there are rather few longitudinal studies of self-reported offending (see, eg, Farrington 2001; McVie 2005). Most research on age-related patterns in offending is based on crime data recorded by criminal justice agencies such as the police or courts (eg Farrington and Wikström 1994; Piquero et al. 2007; Wikström 1990).

[7] Analysis of young people's police data generally supports this assertion. The most common crime types that are not covered by the questionnaire are public disorder, harassment, affray, and breaches of punishment (ie previous sanctions).

**Table 3.1  Definitions of self-reported crime types and corresponding crime categories recorded by the PNC during the study period**

| Crime | Self-reported (PADS+ questionnaire) | Police-recorded (PNC data[a]) |
|---|---|---|
| Shoplifting | *Have you, during the year (200X), stolen anything from a shop (for example, a CD, clothes, cosmetics or any other things)?* | Theft (shoplifting) |
| Theft from a person | *Not counting events in which you broke into a car, house or non-residential building or shop-lifted, have you during the year (200X) stolen anything from another person (for example, money, a mobile telephone, a bicycle, a wallet or a purse, a hand-bag, jewellery, a watch)?* | Theft from a person |
| Theft from a car[b] | *Have you, during the year (200X) broken into a car to steal something?* | Theft from a motor vehicle Attempted theft from a motor vehicle |
| Theft of a car[b] | *Have you, during the year (200X) stolen a car?* | Taking a motor vehicle without consent Aggravated vehicle taking, causing damage to property other than a vehicle, under £5,000 Being carried in a motor vehicle taken without consent |
| Residential burglary | *Have you, during the year (200X) broken into someone's house or flat to steal something?* | Burglary and theft (dwelling) |
| Non-residential burglary | *Have you, during the year (200X) broken into a non-residential building to steal something (for example, broken into a shop, school, warehouse, office)?* | Burglary with intent to steal (non-dwelling) Burglary and theft (non-dwelling) |
| Robbery | *Have you during the year (200X) used a weapon, hit or threatened to hurt someone, to take money or other things from them?* | Robbery |

*(continued)*

**Table 3.1  Definitions of self-reported crime types and corresponding crime categories recorded by the PNC during the study period** (*continued*)

| Crime | Self-reported (PADS+ questionnaire) | Police-recorded (PNC data[a]) |
|---|---|---|
| Assault | *Not counting events when you took money or other things from someone, have you during the year (200X)* <u>*beaten up or hit someone*</u> *(for example, punched, stabbed, kicked or head-butted someone)? (Do not count fights with your brothers or sisters).* | Battery Assault occasioning actual bodily harm Common assault Assault on a constable |
| Vandalism | *Have you, during the year (200X)* <u>*damaged or destroyed things not belonging to you*</u> *for fun or because you were bored or angry (for example, smashed windows or street lights, scratched the paint off cars, sprayed graffiti on a wall, damaged a bicycle)?* | Destruction of or damage to property (£5,000 or less, or unknown value) |
| Arson/ fire- setting | *Have you in the last year (200X)* <u>*set fire to something you were not supposed to set fire to*</u> *(for example, started a fire in a school/college/ university, started a fire in an empty building, set fire to a house, started a fire in a playground, started a fire in a wood)?* | |

[a] Listed are only those categories of crime actually committed by a participant between ages 12 and 16.
[b] Theft of and from a car are combined in the analyses presented in this book.

researcher supervising the questionnaire using the following instructions (the example text is from the 2006 interviewer-led small group questionnaire):

Now I would like you to answer some questions about things you may or may not have done. The questions will ask about things that happened in 2005, that is, in the second and third term of year 9, the summer break and the first term of year 10.

When you answer these questions do not include anything that happened after New Year's Eve. [Here the supervisor stopped and asked the subjects if this was all clear and if they had any questions. When he or she was convinced that they all understood the time frame he or she would continue the introduction.] The questions follow the same format. First they ask you to answer yes or no whether you have done something. If you answer yes, you need to say how many times you did it in 2005. If you answer no, you need to go on to the next question. Please remember that nobody, not your family, not your teachers, not the police nor anybody else will be told what you have told us. You can be sure that what you tell us will remain secret.

Although data was collected for all of the participants' police-recorded crimes (ie all their convictions, warnings, and reprimands), in this chapter we only present findings about crimes comparable to the self-reported crime types. Table 3.1 compares self-reported and police-recorded crime categories. Unless otherwise stated, data on police-recorded crimes used in this chapter refers only to these crime types.

### 3.1.1 The extent of crime involvement

Most young people (70.4 per cent) self-reported at least one crime between the ages of 12 and 16. However, few reported a high frequency of offending and a large group (29.6 per cent) reported no crimes at all. Altogether, those who self-reported at least one crime were responsible for 15,970 crimes committed between ages 12 and 16 (Table 3.2). Given that the sample represents about one-third of the full age cohort in Peterborough, we would expect the entire age group (of about 2,100 young people) to report about 48,000 crimes between the ages of 12 and 16, an average of 26 crimes per day. As is to be expected, the amount of police-recorded crime by the sample was much lower. Only 7.8 per cent of the sample had been warned, reprimanded, or convicted for one of the studied crime types during the same time period (and only 8.9 per cent for any crime type).

The most common types of self-reported crimes were (in rank order) assault, shoplifting, and vandalism; together these represented 71 per cent of all included crimes reported by young people between ages 12 and 16. The picture is largely the same for police-recorded crimes; the most common types (in rank order) were also assault, vandalism, and shoplifting, which together accounted for 80 per cent of all (comparable) police-recorded crimes.

A major difference between self-reported and police-recorded crimes concerned arson/fire-setting. PADS+ participants self-reported 1,737 such acts but had no police-recorded cases. It is

**Table 3.2  Basic descriptors for self-reported (*N* = 693) and police-recorded (*N* = 694)[a] crimes during Phase 1**

| Crime type | Prevalence (per cent of offenders) | Mean frequency (crimes per offender) | Rate[b] (per 1,000 young people) | Number of crimes | Percent of all crimes | Maximum |
|---|---|---|---|---|---|---|
| **Self-reported crimes** | | | | | | |
| Shoplifting | 34.3 | 15.4 | 5,300 | 3,673 | 23.0 | 400 |
| Theft from person | 25.1 | 5.7 | 1,400 | 992 | 6.2 | 79 |
| Theft of or from car | 8.2 | 18.1 | 1,500 | 1,030 | 6.4 | 311 |
| Residential burglary | 5.1 | 3.7 | 200 | 128 | 0.8 | 21 |
| Non-residential burglary | 6.8 | 5.0 | 300 | 235 | 1.5 | 30 |
| Robbery | 13.0 | 5.0 | 600 | 450 | 2.8 | 65 |
| Assault | 56.4 | 11.1 | 6,300 | 4,341 | 27.2 | 215 |
| Vandalism | 37.8 | 12.9 | 4,900 | 3,384 | 21.2 | 356 |
| Arson/ fire-setting | 36.1 | 6.9 | 2,500 | 1,737 | 10.9 | 75 |
| *All crimes* | *70.4* | *32.7* | *23,000* | *15,970* | *100.0* | *913* |
| **Police-recorded crimes[c]** | | | | | | |
| Shoplifting | 2.7 | 1.2 | 33 | 23 | 20.0 | 3 |
| Theft from person | 0.4 | 1.3 | 6 | 4 | 3.5 | 2 |
| Theft of or from car | 1.3 | 1.2 | 16 | 11 | 9.6 | 2 |
| Residential burglary | 0.3 | 2.0 | 6 | 4 | 3.5 | 3 |
| Non-residential burglary | 0.4 | 1.0 | 4 | 3 | 2.6 | 1 |
| Robbery | 0.1 | 1.0 | 1 | 1 | 0.9 | 1 |
| Assault | 3.3 | 1.8 | 60 | 42 | 36.5 | 5 |
| Vandalism | 2.4 | 1.7 | 39 | 27 | 23.4 | 3 |
| Arson/ fire-setting | 0.0 | 0.0 | 0 | 0 | 0.0 | 0 |
| *All crimes* | *7.8* | *2.1* | *166* | *115* | *100.0* | *8* |

[a] One young person has police-recorded but not self-reported data for Phase 1 because he or she dropped out of the study but gave us permission to check his or her criminal justice records.
[b] Self-reported crime rates are rounded to the nearest 100.
[c] Crimes for which the young person was convicted, warned, or reprimanded (of the studied crime types).

possible that many self-reported cases refer to minor events of fire-setting, which are unlikely to catch police attention. The lack of police-recorded arson is consistent with the fact that few young people self-reported having been caught or arrested by the police for arson/fire-setting compared to other crime types (Table 3.6).

A majority of the young people self-reported acts of assault (56.4 per cent). Bearing in mind the age of the sample, it is likely that most cases of assault involved violence towards or fights with other young people (many in the school context). This is supported by data about victims of assault collected via the questionnaire,[8] which shows that the majority of victims were known to the offender, and a high proportion were pupils at the offender's school, especially during early adolescence (Table 3.3). The changing circumstances of young people's assault over the study period are indicated by the fact that the proportion of victims who were strangers increased with the offender's age, while the proportion of victims who were pupils at the offender's school sharply decreased.

Although a large majority of young people self-reported acts of crime during the study period, the distribution of crime is highly skewed (Figure 3.1); while most offenders reported very few crimes, a small group were responsible for a large proportion. For example, the 5.5 per cent of the offenders self-reporting 100 or more crimes over the five years were responsible for 47 per cent of all crimes in that same period. These 27 young people (3.8 per cent of the entire sample) self-reported a total of 7,523 crimes between the ages of

**Table 3.3 Victim–offender relationships for self-reported assaults[a] by age**

| Age (year) | Victim known | | Victim unknown | Total |
|---|---|---|---|---|
| | Known to the offender | *Pupil at the offender's school* | Stranger | |
| 13 (2004) | 89.5 | *56.6* | 10.5 | 100.0 |
| 14 (2005) | 85.2 | *52.9* | 14.8 | 100.0 |
| 15 (2006) | 76.4 | *39.5* | 23.6 | 100.0 |
| 16 (2007) | 71.5 | *28.5* | 28.5 | 100.0 |

[a] Data on victims was collected for the most recent act of violence.

[8] In Waves 2–5.

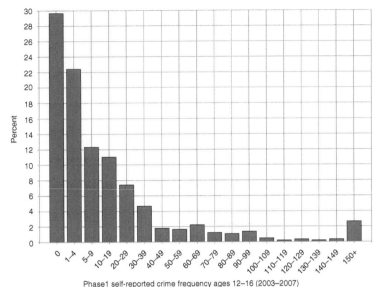

Phase1 self-reported crime frequency ages 12–16 (2003–2007)

**Figure 3.1 Distribution of young people's Phase 1 self-reported crime frequency (*N* = 693)**

12 and 16, about one crime per week, on average, over the five years (not an unreasonable figure for the most frequent offenders in a cohort). The most frequent offender self-reported 913 crimes during Phase 1, about three crimes, on average, per week.

Young people's self-reported crime involvement in any given year consistently correlated with their self-reported crime involvement in any other year during Phase 1 (Table 3.4). These correlations were strong between proximate years, but declined somewhat with increasing age difference, indicating that some individual change in crime involvement took place. These correlations between crime frequencies in proximate years also grew stronger as the young people aged, as self-reported crime became more concentrated in a smaller group of persistent offenders.

The nature of young people's crime involvement varied with their crime frequency. Infrequent offenders (the 49 per cent of offenders who self-reported fewer than 10 crimes over the five years) were rarely involved in acts of serious theft (defined as theft of and from cars, and burglaries). In fact, they were responsible for only 1 per cent of all serious thefts, meaning the remaining 51 per cent of offenders who reported 10 or more crimes were responsible for 99 per cent of all serious thefts.

**Table 3.4 Zero-order correlations[a] for self-reported crime frequency by age[b]**

| Age[c] | 12(13) | 13(14) | 14(15) | 15(16) | 16(17) |
|--------|--------|--------|--------|--------|--------|
| 12(13) | 1.0 | | | | |
| 13(14) | .55 | 1.0 | | | |
| 14(15) | .47 | .60 | 1.0 | | |
| 15(16) | .35 | .50 | .66 | 1.0 | |
| 16(17) | .31 | .45 | .56 | .67 | 1.0 |

[a] All correlations significant at the .000 level or better.
[b] N varies between 693 and 707 depending on age combinations.
[c] Age at crime involvement (age when reporting crime involvement).

Although most young people reported at least occasional offences during Phase 1, it is worthwhile to highlight again the substantial minority (29.6 per cent) of the sample who self-reported no crimes between ages 12 and 16, showing that it is not a necessary condition of adolescence to be involved in crime.

### 3.1.2 Comparing police-recorded and self-reported offenders

Participants' police-recorded crimes refer to acts for which they received a formal conviction, warning, or reprimand, as recorded on the Police National Computer (PNC; see section 2.6).[9] Almost all young people (52 out of 54, or 96.3 per cent) who had a police record also self-reported acts of crime (Table 3.5). The two young people

[9] Other forms of contact that young people may have had with the police as a result of offending, but which are not recorded or disclosable by the PNC, include the Guardian Awareness Programme (for young people under 16) and penalty notices for disorder or fixed penalty notices for 16- and 17-year-olds. Both typically result when young people are caught by the police for minor, 'one-off' offences (eg traffic violations, public order offences, and shoplifting). In the Guardian Awareness Programme, parents or guardians are informed of their child's misconduct through formal letters from the police, while penalty notices for disorder or fixed penalty notices typically incur a fine. These outcomes are often determined on a case-by-case basis and have been put into place to deflect young people away from the criminal justice system and to make better use of police resources. Because these kinds of sanctions are not disclosed with PNC data, our measure of police-recorded crime may slightly underestimate the rate of minor offences, and the prevalence of minor or one-time police-recorded offenders.

who had a police record but no self-reported crimes, therefore, seem to have underreported their crimes in the questionnaire,[10] unless they were actually innocent of their police-recorded crimes.

**Table 3.5  Phase 1 self-reported and police-recorded crime prevalence**

|  |  | Police-recorded offender *(%)* | | Total |
| --- | --- | --- | --- | --- |
|  |  | No | Yes |  |
| Self-reported offender *(%)* | No | 203 *(29.3)* | 2 *(0.3)* | 205 *(29.6)* |
|  | Yes | 436 *(62.9)* | 52 *(7.5)* | 488 *(70.4)* |
| Total |  | 639 *(92.2)* | 54 *(7.8)* | 693 *(100.0)* |

Assuming that the self-reported crimes give a roughly accurate estimate of the number of offenders in the sample and their rates of offending, it is possible to provide a rough estimate of the proportion of offenders caught by the police, and the proportion of their crimes that lead to a formal sanction. About one in nine (10.7 per cent) of those self-reporting a crime (between ages 12 and 16) also received police sanctions (between ages 12 and 16), but for fewer than 1 per cent of their total crimes (0.7 per cent). This means, on average, young people received police sanctions for one crime in every 140 crimes they self-reported (see Table 3.6). However, many of their other crimes are likely to have come to the attention of the police, although they were either not identified as the offender or sanctioned (in most cases probably because they were not identified).

Interestingly, the proportion of offenders with a police record (10.7 per cent) is very similar to the proportion of offenders (10.9 per cent) who reported being caught or arrested by the police for their last self-reported crime (at ages 15 and 16; Table 3.6). It should be noted in this context that most police records referred to acts committed when offenders were at the older end of the studied ages (Table 3.10).

The question of what differentiates self-reported offenders with and without a police record is interesting both from a methodological and substantive point of view. A comparison between self-reported

---

[10]  One offender was convicted for an act of vandalism in 2006 (age 15) and one was warned/reprimanded for an act of non-residential burglary in 2007 (age 16).

**Table 3.6 Percentage of participants who reported being caught or arrested by the police the last time they committed a particular type of crime[a]**

| Crime type | Percentage caught or arrested | Number of offenders |
|---|---|---|
| Shoplifting | 15.2 | 184 |
| Theft from a person | 6.8 | 88 |
| Theft of or from a car | 26.9 | 52 |
| Residential burglary | 15.8 | 19 |
| Non-residential burglary | 9.1 | 22 |
| Robbery | 14.0 | 50 |
| Assault | 11.4 | 297 |
| Vandalism | 10.1 | 197 |
| Arson/fire-setting | 1.8 | 162 |
| All crimes | 10.9 | 1071 |

[a] Data combines reports at age 16 and 17 (2007 and 2008) referring to crimes committed at ages 15 and 16.

offenders recorded by the police and those not recorded clearly shows that those with a police record tended to be much more criminally active (Table 3.7): their average crime frequency was about five times higher; they had, on average, been involved in crime during one more year between the ages of 12 and 16; and they were much more versatile in their crime involvement (they had, on average, committed acts covering five different crime types of the nine key crime categories, compared to a mean of three for self-reported offenders without a police record) (Table 3.7). These findings are further supported by the fact that there were strong correlations between offenders' crime frequency, duration, and versatility; very frequent offenders not only demonstrated a longer duration of crime involvement (as may be expected), but they also tended to be much more versatile in their offending (Table 3.8).

Extending the comparison to specific categories of crime shows that for virtually all types of crime, self-reported offenders who had a police record had a higher crime prevalence and frequency than those who did not (Table 3.9). The most notable exception was assault, where the difference in prevalence (but not frequency) between police-recorded and other self-reported offenders was

**Table 3.7 Phase 1 crime frequency, mean duration,[a] and versatility[b] of police-recorded (N = 52) and other self-reported offenders (N = 436)**

|  | Police-recorded offender | | Eta | Prob. |
|---|---|---|---|---|
|  | No | Yes |  |  |
| Crime frequency | 22.3 | 124.0 | .39 | .000 |
| Crime duration | 2.8 | 3.8 | .22 | .000 |
| Crime versatility | 2.9 | 5.2 | .34 | .000 |

[a] Duration = number of years self-reporting crime (maximum = five).
[b] Versatility = number of different crime categories committed (maximum = nine).

**Table 3.8 Zero-order correlations[a] between self-reported offenders' (N = 488) Phase 1 crime frequency, duration,[b] and versatility[c]**

|  | Frequency | Duration | Versatility |
|---|---|---|---|
| Crime frequency | 1.0 |  |  |
| Crime duration | .43 | 1.0 |  |
| Crime versatility | .58 | .69 | 1.0 |

[a] All correlations significant at the .000 level or better.
[b] Duration = number of years with at least one crime (maximum = five).
[c] Versatility = number of different crime categories committed (maximum = nine).

non-significant. The difference in prevalence and frequency was particularly strong for more serious property crimes of theft of and from cars and residential and non-residential burglary (with the exception of frequency for the latter). A logistic regression analysis (not shown), predicting whether or not offenders had a police record based on their frequency of the nine studied crime types, showed that two crime categories significantly predicted a police record: theft of and from a car (odds ratio = 1.20) and residential burglary (odds ratio = 1.62), the overall explained variance (Nagelkerke's $r^2$) being .27. In other words, offenders involved in serious theft were more likely to be police recorded.

About half (52 per cent) of police records for PADS+ participants refer to convictions, and the other half (48 per cent) to warnings and reprimands (Table 3.10). The likelihood of having a police record increased with age over the study period, and convictions were much more common at the older end of the studied ages

**Table 3.9 Self-reported crime prevalence and frequency[a] between police-recorded (*N* = 52) and other offenders (*N* = 436) during Phase 1**

| Crime type | | Police-recorded offender | | | |
| --- | --- | --- | --- | --- | --- |
| | | No | Yes | Phi (*Eta*)[b] | Prob. |
| Shoplifting | Prevalence | 45.2 | 80.0 | .21 | .000 |
| | *Frequency* | *10.8* | *38.5* | *(.27)* | *.000* |
| Theft from a person | Prevalence | 33.3 | 56.0 | .14 | .002 |
| | *Frequency* | *5.0* | *9.4* | *(.17)* | *.024* |
| Theft of and from a car | Prevalence | 8.2 | 42.0 | .32 | .000 |
| | *Frequency* | *3.0* | *43.9* | *(.37)* | *.005* |
| Residential burglary | Prevalence | 4.6 | 30.0 | .30 | .000 |
| | *Frequency* | *1.6* | *6.3* | *(.47)* | *.004* |
| Non-residential burglary | Prevalence | 6.2 | 40.0 | .35 | .000 |
| | *Frequency* | *4.4* | *5.8* | *(n.s.)* | *n.s.* |
| Robbery | Prevalence | 15.5 | 44.0 | .22 | .000 |
| | *Frequency* | *4.0* | *8.2* | *(.21)* | *.043* |
| Assault | Prevalence | 79.2 | 88.0 | n.s. | n.s. |
| | *Frequency* | *9.2* | *25.8* | *(.24)* | *.000* |
| Vandalism | Prevalence | 51.6 | 72.0 | .12 | .006 |
| | *Frequency* | *7.8* | *44.9* | *(.36)* | *.000* |
| Arson/fire-setting | Prevalence | 49.1 | 70.0 | .13 | .005 |
| | *Frequency* | *6.5* | *9.5* | *(n.s.)* | *n.s.* |

[a] Crimes per offender having committed the crime in question.
[b] Prevalence (Phi), frequency (Eta).

(police records being dated to the offence, and not the sanction[11]). This may reflect factors such as a reduction in leniency as offenders get older, and/or the increasing severity of their crimes (but changes in police practices over the study period may also be relevant). One implication is that police-recorded data mainly refers to acts of crime in later adolescence (few young people had received a police

[11] Although, as described in chapter 2, footnote 3, the time between offence and sanction was rarely more than a few months.

**Table 3.10  Self-reported and police-recorded crimes by age and formal sanction**

| Age (year) | Self-reported | Police-recorded | | |
|---|---|---|---|---|
| | | Total | Convictions | Reprimands and warnings |
| 12 (2003) | 1,964 | 1 | 0 | 1 |
| 13 (2004) | 3,413 | 7 | 0 | 7 |
| 14 (2005) | 3,248 | 21 | 11 | 10 |
| 15 (2006) | 3,733 | 38 | 15 | 23 |
| 16 (2007) | 3,612 | 48 | 34 | 14 |
| Total | 15,970 | 115 | 60 | 55 |

record at age 12 or 13, and none received convictions). This should be borne in mind when we present findings about police-recorded crime by young people across Peterborough (not only those included in the PADS+ sample) in subsequent chapters.

Most young people self-reported a substantial degree of crime involvement before they acquired their first (PNC) police record (Table 3.11). The great majority (91 per cent) of those with a PNC record had self-reported crimes in previous years—45 on average (not including self-reported crimes in the year in which they acquired their first police record). This finding is at odds with the idea that young people's persistent crime involvement is mainly initiated by their being officially labelled as a 'criminal' (ie recorded by the police). Bear in mind there are also a significant number of young people who self-reported many offences during Phase 1 but had not yet acquired a police record.

### 3.1.3 Versatility

We have already observed that very frequent offenders also tend to be more versatile. An oblique factor analysis[12] of the nine studied crime types confirms the lack of any strong specialization among all young offenders (Table 3.12). Two highly correlated factors were extracted, together explaining 51 per cent of the variance. The first may be interpreted as an acquisitive crime factor with the highest loadings on shoplifting and residential burglary, while the

---

[12] A factor analysis allowing the factors to be correlated.

**Table 3.11 Descriptives for young people's self-reported crime prior to the year they acquired their first police record**

|  | Year of first police-recorded crime[a] | | | | Total |
|---|---|---|---|---|---|
|  | 2004 | 2005 | 2006 | 2007 |  |
| N participants who acquired a police record for the first time | 5 | 13 | 23 | 12 | 53 |
| N participants who acquired a police record for the first time but self-reported no crimes in previous years | 0 | 1[b] | 4[c] | 0 | 5 |
| *(Percentage of participants who acquired a police record for the first time who self-reported crimes in previous years)* | *(100.0)* | *(92.3)* | *(82.6)* | *(100.0)* | *(91.0)* |
| Mean self-reported crimes in previous years by participants who acquired a police record for the first time | 7 | 48 | 33 | 94 | 45 |
| Standard deviation | 9.5 | 72.5 | 38.0 | 104.3 | 69.7 |

[a] Self-reported crimes were first reported in 2003 so the first year we can assess self-reported crime frequency prior to the acquisition of a police record is 2004. One young person did acquire a police record for the first time in 2003, and in 2003 he or she self-reported 20 acts of crime.
[b] This young person self-reported eight crimes in 2005 when he or she received a police record.
[c] Two of these young people self-reported crimes in 2006, and two were the young people who did not self-report crimes in any year.

second factor may be interpreted as an aggressive crime factor with the highest loadings on personal robbery and assault. However, as already mentioned, the two factors are highly correlated, so overall the result can be interpreted as showing that young (frequent) offenders mostly tended to be 'jacks of all trade' when it came to traditional crimes of the types included in this study, albeit with some slight individual variation as to whether or not aggressive crimes tended to play a recurrent role in their crime involvement.

### 3.1.4 Age of onset and crime involvement

Analysing offenders' age of onset of crime involvement and its relationship to their patterns of crime involvement during adolescence (ages 12 to 16) shows that the emergence of new offenders decreased sharply with age, and that those who experienced an early onset

**Table 3.12 Factor analysis (oblique rotation; promax) of self-reported crime frequencies by crime type (N = 693)[a]**

| Crime | Factor I (Acquisitive crimes) | Factor II (Aggressive crimes) | h² |
|---|---|---|---|
| Shoplifting | **.79** | .35 | .63 |
| Theft from a person | **.65** | **.55** | .50 |
| Theft of or from a car | **.68** | .33 | .47 |
| Residential burglary | **.79** | .19 | .67 |
| Non-residential burglary | **.53** | **.51** | .37 |
| Robbery | .18 | **.73** | .64 |
| Assault | **.55** | **.79** | .63 |
| Vandalism | **.59** | **.51** | .42 |
| Arson/fire-setting | .23 | **.51** | .26 |
| Explained variance | 39.0 | 11.8 | |
| Interfactor correlation = .48 | | | |

[a] Loadings .50 and higher in bold.

(before the age of 12) were responsible for the bulk of crimes reported by the sample between the ages of 12 and 16.

In the first wave of data collection participants were asked not only whether or not they had committed particular crimes during the previous year but also how old they were the first time they ever committed a particular crime. Based on these data an age of onset variable was created identifying those who reported a crime at any age before the age of 12, then, for each subsequent year, new first-time offenders at each age.

The majority (56 per cent) of self-reported offenders reported acts of crime before the age of 12 (41 per cent of the entire sample; see Table 3.13). Of those with an early onset, 4.5 per cent (3.1 per cent of all young people) only self-reported a crime before the age of 12 but no crime for the subsequent studied ages. The age of onset data clearly revealed the strong decline with age of the emergence of new offenders (Table 3.13).[13] The prevalence of self-reported crimes

---

[13] One complication here is that the data on age of onset before age 12 refers to the subject's age, while the age of onset data for ages 12 to 16 refers to the calendar year in which the subject reached the particular age (so, for example, when we talk about age 12 the subject would have been 11 for parts of the year). This means, since all

**Table 3.13  Self-reported age of onset for all participants (N = 693) and offenders only (N = 511)**

| Age of onset | Percentage | | Percentage (offenders only) | |
|---|---|---|---|---|
| No crimes | 26.3 | | – | |
| Before 12 (before 2003) | 41.4 | *(35.2)*[a] | 56.2 | *(47.8)*[a] |
| 12 (2003) | 12.5 | *(18.7)*[a] | 17.0 | *(25.4)*[a] |
| 13 (2004) | 9.7 | | 13.1 | |
| 14 (2005) | 4.8 | | 6.5 | |
| 15 (2006) | 3.7 | | 5.1 | |
| 16 (2007) | 1.6 | | 2.1 | |
| Total | 100.0 | | 100.0 | |

[a] Value if participants reporting their first crime at age 11 committed that crime in the year they turned 12 (2003) (see chapter 3, footnote 13).

by crime type for crimes committed before the age of 12 is presented in Table 3.14.

The earlier a participant's onset the more likely he or she also reported an act of crime in subsequent years (see Table 3.15). The fact that the emergence of new offenders decreased by age (Table 3.13), and that those with an early onset were more likely than those with a later onset to report acts of crime in subsequent years, meant that those with an early onset (before age 12) tended to be the most prevalent offenders at all ages throughout adolescence (ages 12 to 16) (Table 3.15). Even at age 16, offenders with an age of onset before the age of 12 constituted a majority (61.9 per cent) of all offenders.

Table 3.15 shows that with increasing age the proportion of new offenders declined. For example, only 5 per cent of offenders at age 16 emerged for the first time at that age. Moreover, Table 3.15 also shows that as their age of onset increased fewer offenders went on to offend in subsequent years. For example, while 77.7 per cent of

offenders reporting an age of onset at 11 have been classified as having an age of onset before age 12, there is some underestimation of those with an age of onset at 12 (the year in which they became 12) when comparing with the other ages of onset (ie 13 to 16) based on calendar year. The figures in brackets and italics in Table 3.13 show the alternative percentage if all those with a reported age of onset at 11 are classified as having an onset as 12 instead of before age 12. The main relevance is that if one is *only* comparing the age of onset groups based on the calendar year, the true figure for those with an age of onset at 12 is somewhere between the two figures shown.

**Table 3.14  Crime prevalence, total and by crime type, before the age of 12 ($N$ = 693)**

| Crime | Percentage |
|---|---|
| Shoplifting | 11.4 |
| Theft from a person | 13.4 |
| Theft of or from a car | 1.0 |
| Residential burglary | 0.4 |
| Non-residential burglary | 1.3 |
| Robbery | 2.6 |
| Assault | 25.0 |
| Vandalism | 22.7 |
| Arson/fire-setting | 10.5 |
| All crimes | 41.4 |

**Table 3.15  Crime prevalence in subsequent years (and percentage of offenders at each age) by age of onset**

| Age of onset[a] | Crime prevalence (percentage of all offenders) | | | | | |
|---|---|---|---|---|---|---|
| | Before 12 | 12 | 13 | 14 | 15 | 16 |
| Before 12 | 100.0 | 77.7 | 75.4 | 67.8 | 61.4 | 51.1 |
| (before 2003) | *100.0* | *70.2* | *62.6* | *59.9* | *58.5* | *61.9* |
| 12 (2003) | | 100.0 | 59.8 | 58.6 | 48.3 | 36.8 |
| | | *29.8* | *16.4* | *17.1* | *15.1* | *14.7* |
| 13 (2004) | | | 100.0 | 53.7 | 50.7 | 35.8 |
| | | | *21.1* | *12.0* | *12.3* | *11.0* |
| 14 (2005) | | | | 100.0 | 39.4 | 30.3 |
| | | | | *11.0* | *4.7* | *4.6* |
| 15 (2006) | | | | | 100.0 | 23.1 |
| | | | | | *9.4* | *2.8* |
| 16 (2007) | | | | | | 100.0 |
| | | | | | | *5.0* |

[a] Refers to the year in which participants turned the stated age.

those with an age of onset before age 12 went on to offend at age 12, only 23.1 per cent of those with an age of onset at 15 went on to offend at age 16.

The impact of those with an early onset on the sample's crime during adolescence (ages 12 to 16) is even more striking if one considers the number of crimes reported at each age (see Table 3.16). Those with an age of onset before 12 were responsible for 82.7 per cent of all self-reported crime between ages 12 and 16. This was not purely a consequence of their having more criminally active years (if all age of onset groups were equally active each year of crime activity the crimes by the early age of onset group over the five years would have been 3,992 crimes rather than the 13,212 they actually reported). Rather, their high proportion of crimes between ages 12 and 16 was

Table 3.16  **Number of self-reported crimes committed at specific ages (and age-specific crime frequency of offenders) by age of onset**

| Age of onset[a] | Number of crimes (offenders' crime frequency) | | | | | | Total | % |
|---|---|---|---|---|---|---|---|---|
| | Before 12 | 12 | 13 | 14 | 15 | 16 | | |
| Before 12 (before 2003) | N/A[b] | 1,709 | 2,870 | 2,584 | 2,864 | 3,185 | 13,212 | 82.7 |
| | | 5.9 | 10.0 | 8.9 | 10.0 | 11.1 | | |
| 12 | | | 255 | 221 | 349 | 282 | 180 | 1,287 | 8.1 |
| | | | 2.9 | 2.5 | 4.0 | 3.2 | 2.1 | | |
| 13 | | | | 322 | 221 | 266 | 132 | 941 | 5.9 |
| | | | | 4.7 | 3.5 | 4.0 | 2.0 | | |
| 14 | | | | | 94 | 247 | 80 | 421 | 2.6 |
| | | | | | 2.8 | 7.5 | 2.4 | | |
| 15 | | | | | | 74 | 11 | 85 | 0.5 |
| | | | | | | 2.8 | 0.4 | | |
| 16 | | | | | | | 24 | 24 | 0.1 |
| | | | | | | | 2.2 | | |
| Total | N/A[b] | 1,964 | 3,413 | 3,248 | 3,733 | 3,612 | 15,970 | 100.0 |

[a] Refers to the year in which participants turned the stated age.
[b] Only prevalence data is available before age 12.

predominantly due to their having a higher prevalence (Table 3.15) and a much higher crime frequency (Table 3.16).

### 3.1.5 Crime trends ages 12 to 16

The sample's overall self-reported crime increased significantly between the ages of 12 and 13 and only marginally between ages 13 and 16 (Figure 3.2). However, this overall trend obscures the fact that there were different trends in offender prevalence and frequency. While both offender prevalence and frequency increased between ages 12 and 13, after that offender *prevalence* declined while offender *frequency* still increased, meaning that the percentage of participants who offended (after age 13) fell with age, but those who were offending tended to become much more active with age.

Recall that, as previously shown, the emergence of new offenders declined with age (Table 3.13) and those with an early age of onset tended to have a longer duration (ie more crime-active years; Table 3.15) and a higher frequency of crime involvement than those with a later onset (Table 3.16). Also recall that very frequent offenders tended to be more versatile than other offenders (Table 3.8). The overall picture is, thus, one of a gradual increase by age across adolescence in the concentration of the sample's crime involvement within a small group of very frequent, persistent, and versatile offenders with an early age of onset.

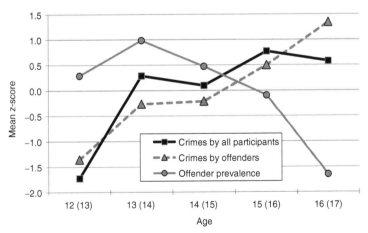

**Figure 3.2  Crimes by all participants, crimes by offenders, and offender prevalence (z-scores) by age of crime commission (and age of self-reporting)**

### 3.1.6 The problem of the comparability of the reference period for crime counts and other data

Most items on the questionnaire asked young people to answer in reference to themselves at the time the questionnaire was administered (eg about their self-control, morality, and time spent in different settings); most were administered in the first quarter of each year. Some items, however, including self-reported measures of crime involvement, referred to the previous calendar year, which is why we compared these self-reported crimes with police-recorded (PNC) crimes between ages 12 and 16. There is no consistent policy for dealing with this mismatch in longitudinal research. Many studies (eg the ESYTC) compare data collected in the same year, even if some is more retrospective than others (D. J. Smith 2004). Others (eg Loeber et al. 2008; Moffitt et al. 2001) aggregate data into 'omnibus' or 'block' variables covering a number of years. Most of our analyses in this book resemble the latter, using Phase 1 variables. However, when we analyse relationships year by year, we generally employ the former technique.

In studying the annual relationship between factors such as a person's crime propensity and exposure to criminogenic settings, which are measured at the time of the interview, and self-reported crime data,[14] which is measured for the year prior to the interview, the key question is whether the latter (eg retrospective data covering crime during 2004 reported during the first quarter of 2005) is indicative of participants' crime involvement at the time of the interview (eg the first quarter of 2005), or should be analysed in relation to data from the previous interview (so that, for example, data covering crime during 2004 collected during the first quarter of 2005 is analysed in relation to propensity and exposure data collected in the first quarter of 2004). Comparing the two approaches shows that which strategy is adopted makes little difference for the magnitude of the correlation between crime and crime propensity or criminogenic exposure (except for criminogenic exposure in 2007;[15] see Table 3.17). Generally the correlation was marginally stronger if data about propensity and exposure were correlated with crime data collected at the same point in

[14] Space–time budget self-reported crime data does not experience the same problem, as it refers to acts committed in the week just prior to the interview.

[15] When young people aged out of compulsory education and began to gain employment in significant numbers.

**Table 3.17  Zero-order correlations[a] between crime propensity and criminogenic exposure[b] with crime involvement,[c] comparing crime data for the previous or same year**

| Crime data refers to...[d] | Year of measurement | | | | | | | |
|---|---|---|---|---|---|---|---|---|
| | 2004 | | 2005 | | 2006 | | 2007 | |
| | Propensity | Exposure | Propensity | Exposure | Propensity | Exposure | Propensity | Exposure |
| Previous year (2003) | .56 | .28 | | | | | | |
| Same year (2004) | .50 | .29 | | | | | | |
| Previous year (2004) | | | .61 | .28 | | | | |
| Same year (2005) | | | .53 | .28 | | | | |
| Previous year (2005) | | | | | .57 | .35 | | |
| Same year (2006) | | | | | .50 | .30 | | |
| Previous year (2006) | | | | | | | .53 | .30 |
| Same year (2007) | | | | | | | .50 | .19 |

[a] All correlations significant at the p = .000 level.
[b] Correlations with criminogenic exposure include only participants who completed space–time budgets in all five waves.
[c] Crime variable logged.
[d] Previous year refers to crime data collected retrospectively in the same interview as propensity and exposure data; same year refers to data collected during the interview in the subsequent wave.

time (but referring to the previous year). A measure of the previous year's crime involvement taken early the following year may be indicative of current crime involvement, a contention supported by the fact that the correlation between self-reported crime on the questionnaire and the space–time budget (collected at the same time but referring, respectively, to crime the previous year and crime in the previous week) did not dramatically differ (Table 3.18).

One significant drawback of correlating crime data collected in Wave n + 1 with variables measured in Wave n is the loss of one year of comparative data, as it means there is no crime data available for comparison with data collected in the final year.

In this study we generally explore the relationships between crime involvement and personal and exposure variables at the point (year, age) when the data was collected (generally 2004–08, ages 13–17). The mismatch when using crime data from the annual questionnaire (which refers to 2003–07, ages 12–16) we do not believe has any significant impact on findings regarding the relationships between this data and other variables. Any impact on Phase 1 variables, which dominate our analyses, are even more negligible.

**Table 3.18  Zero-order correlations[a] between self-reported crime from the questionnaire[b] and space–time budget crime, comparing crime data for the previous or same year**

| Questionnaire crime data refers to...[c] | Space–time budget crimes | | | |
|---|---|---|---|---|
| | 2004 | 2005 | 2006 | 2007 |
| Previous year (2003) | .24 | | | |
| *Same year (2004)* | .22 | | | |
| Previous year (2004) | | .38 | | |
| *Same year (2005)* | | .26 | | |
| Previous year (2005) | | | .19 | |
| *Same year (2006)* | | | .23 | |
| Previous year (2006) | | | | .36 |
| *Same year (2007)* | | | | .44 |

[a] All correlations significant at the $p$ = .000 level.
[b] Questionnaire self-reported crime data logged.
[c] Previous year refers to crime data collected retrospectively in the same interview as propensity and exposure data; same year refers to data collected during the interview in the subsequent wave.

## 3.2 Crime propensity

According to SAT, one key factor in the explanation of young people's crime involvement is their crime propensity, defined as their tendency to see, and if so, to choose to break a rule of conduct (stated in law). The proposed key personal factors that influence a person's crime propensity are his or her morality and ability to exercise self-control (see sections 1.3.4, 1.3.7, and 1.3.8). This section presents the scales used in PADS+ to measure young people's generalized morality and ability to exercise self-control, and the composite measure of generalized crime propensity constructed from them. Key findings are also presented for these basic constructs: the distribution of crime propensity in the population, the changes in crime propensity by age, and the basic relationship between crime propensity and crime involvement.

The scales of personal morality and ability to exercise self-control may be regarded as *generalized* measures, since participants are asked to report on their general rather than situation-specific views on the wrongfulness of particular actions and self-control relevant reactions. The assumption is that young people's generalized responses will have some relationship to how they would generally apply their morality (exercising moral habits or making moral judgements) and their ability to employ self-control (ie to manage conflicting rule-guidance) in specific situations, and, crucially, that the particular combination of the two, as a measure of participants' generalized crime propensity, will have some relationship to their likelihood to see, and choose, crime as an action alternative when confronted with a criminogenic setting.

### 3.2.1 The generalized morality scale

Table 3.19 reports the items included in the morality scale,[16] the average 'wrongfulness' ranking among the items (higher values mean items were assessed as more wrong), and their stability or change with age. Table 3.19 also reports the scale's mean score and (Cronbach's) alpha (a measure of its internal consistency) at each age. The alphas are all highly satisfactory.

---

[16] The morality scale is a modified version of the pro-social values scale used by Rolf Loeber in the Pittsburgh Youth Study.

The morality scale included a range of items that represent various acts of rule-breaking (legal and illegal) and differ by type and level of seriousness. The findings show that there was, in fact, substantial and reasonable variation regarding how wrong young people considered different actions to be (Table 3.19). For example, at age 13 participants ranked stealing a pencil from a classmate as the least wrong act (with a mean score of 1.56—ie somewhere between 'a little wrong' and 'wrong'), while they ranked using a weapon or force to get money or things from another person as the most wrong (with a mean score of 2.91—ie 'very wrong').

The overall morality scale shows, on average, a general decrease between ages 13 to 16 followed by a stabilization in young people's judgement of the wrongfulness of the included acts (Table 3.19). Looking into the specific items that make up the morality scale, participants, on average, became more morally lenient as they grew older regarding substance use, particularly the use of alcohol but also cigarettes and cannabis. They also tended to become more lenient regarding infractions they regarded as the least wrong at age 13 (such as skipping school, skipping doing homework for school, skateboarding in a place where skateboarding is not allowed, and stealing a pencil from a classmate). However, actions (except smoking cannabis) that were ranked as the most wrong at age 13, with an average score above 2.5 (ie personal robbery, burglary, shoplifting, and vandalism), stayed the highest ranked and changed little in their score.

Grouping the items (based on participants' initial ranking at age 13) into minor moral infractions (items 1–6 and 9–10) and serious moral infractions (items 11–13 and 15–16), as well as substance use infractions (items 7–8 and 14), and analysing their age trends (Figure 3.3), clearly illustrates that substance use morality had the strongest average decline (declining at all ages);[17] followed by minor moral infractions, which, on average, declined from age 13 to 16 and then levelled out;[18] and finally more serious moral infractions, which, on average, declined slightly between ages 13 and 15, and then eventually levelled out.[19]

[17] All age differences are statistically significant (outside the 95 per cent confidence interval).
[18] All differences except those between ages 16 and 17 are statistically significant.
[19] Only the change between 13 and 14, and 14 and 16 is statistically significant.

**Table 3.19 Mean scores for the morality scale and individual items by age and change from scores at age 13**

| How wrong it is for someone your age to...[a] | Mean | | | | |
|---|---|---|---|---|---|
| | *Change from age 13* | | | | |
| | 13 | 14 | 15 | 16 | 17 |
| 1. Steal a pencil from a classmate | 1.56 | 1.33 | 1.18 | 1.12 | 1.13 |
| | | *−0.23* | *−0.38* | *−0.44* | *−0.43* |
| 2. Skip doing homework for school | 1.60 | 1.34 | 1.18 | 1.06 | 1.09 |
| | | *−0.26* | *−0.42* | *−0.54* | *−0.51* |
| 3. Ride a bike through a red light | 1.64 | 1.43 | 1.33 | 1.25 | 1.34 |
| | | *−0.21* | *−0.31* | *−0.39* | *−0.30* |
| 4. Go skateboarding in a place where skateboarding is not allowed | 1.65 | 1.48 | 1.23 | 1.15 | 1.14 |
| | | *−0.71* | *−0.42* | *−0.50* | *−0.51* |
| 5. Hit another young person who makes a rude comment | 1.95 | 1.79 | 1.65 | 1.58 | 1.67 |
| | | *−0.16* | *−0.30* | *−0.45* | *−0.28* |
| 6. Lie, disobey or talk back to teachers | 1.97 | 1.66 | 1.55 | 1.57 | 1.65 |
| | | *−0.31* | *−0.42* | *−0.40* | *−0.32* |
| 7. Get drunk with friends on a Friday evening | 2.16 | 1.73 | 1.25 | 0.91 | 0.75 |
| | | *−0.43* | *−0.91* | *−1.25* | *−1.41* |
| 8. Smoke cigarettes | 2.35 | 2.07 | 1.76 | 1.46 | 1.34 |
| | | *−0.28* | *−0.59* | *−0.89* | *−1.01* |
| 9. Skip school without an excuse | 2.35 | 2.14 | 1.99 | 1.79 | 1.67 |
| | | *−0.21* | *−0.36* | *−0.56* | *−0.68* |
| 10. Tease a classmate because of the way he or she dresses | 2.41 | 2.31 | 2.28 | 2.27 | 2.31 |
| | | *−0.10* | *−0.13* | *−0.14* | *−0.10* |
| 11. Smash a street light for fun | 2.69 | 2.59 | 2.53 | 2.47 | 2.55 |
| | | *−0.10* | *−0.16* | *−0.22* | *−0.14* |
| 12. Paint graffiti on a house wall | 2.71 | 2.58 | 2.48 | 2.45 | 2.52 |
| | | *−0.13* | *−0.23* | *−0.26* | *−0.19* |
| 13. Steal a CD from a shop | 2.72 | 2.59 | 2.53 | 2.49 | 2.57 |
| | | *−0.13* | *−0.19* | *−0.23* | *−0.15* |
| 14. Smoke cannabis | 2.78 | 2.56 | 2.37 | 2.19 | 2.11 |
| | | *−0.22* | *−0.41* | *−0.59* | *−0.67* |

*(continued)*

**Table 3.19** *(Continued)*

| How wrong it is for someone your age to...[a] | Mean | | | | |
|---|---|---|---|---|---|
| | *Change from age 13* | | | | |
| | 13 | 14 | 15 | 16 | 17 |
| 15. Break into or try to break into a building to steal something | 2.87 | 2.80 | 2.78 | 2.74 | 2.75 |
| | | *−0.07* | *−0.09* | *−0.13* | *−0.12* |
| 16. Use a weapon or force to get money or things from another young person | 2.91 | 2.90 | 2.87 | 2.85 | 2.87 |
| | | *−0.01* | *−0.04* | *−0.06* | *−0.04* |
| Morality scale | 36.3 | 33.3 | 31.0 | 29.4 | 29.5 |
| | | *−3.0* | *−5.3* | *−6.9* | *−6.8* |
| Alpha | .89 | .90 | .88 | .89 | .88 |

[a] 0 = Not wrong at all, 1 = A little wrong, 2 = Wrong, 3 = Very wrong.

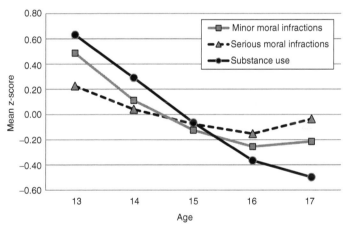

**Figure 3.3 Trends for serious, minor, and substance use morality by age (z-scores)**

### 3.2.2 *The generalized ability to exercise self-control scale*

Table 3.20 reports the items included in the (poor) ability to exercise self-control scale, participants' average 'agreement' with the items (higher values represent stronger agreement), and their stability or change by age. Table 3.20 also gives the scale's mean score and (Cronbach's) alpha for each age. The alphas are all satisfactory.

**Table 3.20 Mean scores for the (poor) ability to exercise self-control scale and individual items by age, and change from scores at age 13**

| Do you agree with the following statements about yourself?[a] | Mean | | | | |
| --- | --- | --- | --- | --- | --- |
| | *Change from age 13* | | | | |
| | 13 | 14 | 15 | 16 | 17 |
| 1. I never think about what will happen to me in the future | 0.83 | 0.70 | 0.74 | 0.64 | 0.69 |
| | | −0.13 | −0.09 | −0.19 | −0.14 |
| 2. I don't devote much thought and effort preparing for the future | 1.06 | 0.89 | 0.99 | 0.90 | 0.98 |
| | | −0.17 | −0.07 | −0.16 | −0.08 |
| 3. Sometimes I will take a risk just for the fun of it | 1.21 | 1.35 | 1.44 | 1.43 | 1.38 |
| | | 0.14 | 0.23 | 0.22 | 0.17 |
| 4. I sometimes find it exciting to do things that may be dangerous | 1.25 | 1.45 | 1.58 | 1.59 | 1.51 |
| | | 0.20 | 0.33 | 0.34 | 0.26 |
| 5. When I am really angry, other people better stay away from me | 1.43 | 1.47 | 1.47 | 1.50 | 1.42 |
| | | 0.04 | 0.04 | 0.07 | −0.01 |
| 6. I lose my temper pretty easily | 1.53 | 1.52 | 1.55 | 1.55 | 1.37 |
| | | −0.01 | 0.02 | 0.02 | −0.16 |
| 7. I often act on the spur of the moment without stopping to think | 1.64 | 1.67 | 1.72 | 1.70 | 1.69 |
| | | 0.03 | 0.08 | 0.06 | 0.05 |
| 8. I often try to avoid things that I know will be difficult | 1.42 | 1.35 | 1.33 | 1.28 | 1.27 |
| | | −0.07 | −0.02 | −0.05 | −0.01 |
| (Poor) Ability to exercise self-control scale | 10.4 | 10.4 | 10.8 | 10.6 | 10.3 |
| | | 0.0 | 0.4 | 0.2 | −0.1 |
| Alpha | .78 | .76 | .78 | .77 | .78 |

[a] 0 = Strongly disagree, 1 = Disagree, 2 = Agree, 3 = Strongly agree.

The (poor) ability to exercise self-control scale is a modified and more limited version of the self-control scale presented by Grasmick et al. (1993), including selected and some new items, intended to tap into the young person's general impulsivity (emotionality), risk-taking, and future-orientation.[20] Recall that according to SAT,

[20] No items from the physical activity, simple task, and self-centred components of Grasmick et al.'s (1993) self-control scale were included as they were regarded as theoretically less relevant to SAT.

self-control is a situational factor (see section 1.3.7); thus this scale aims to measure a person's *ability* to exercise self-control. The assumption is that a high level of impulsivity and risk-taking and a low future-orientation will affect a young person's ability to exercise self-control (ie to abide by his or her own moral rules when externally pressured to break them).

The (poor) ability to exercise self-control scale, and the mean responses to the items on the scale, showed a remarkable stability by age (Table 3.20). There was a weak tendency for older participants to be, on average, slightly more willing to take risks and engage in acts that might be dangerous, but the overall picture is one of little change. It is possible that this reflects a genetic component to this ability, and that the most important social influences on the development of this ability exert their effects before the age of 13.

### 3.2.3 The generalized crime propensity index

The generalized crime propensity index for Phase 1 (subsequently, for ease of presentation, only referred to as crime propensity) is based on the five annual measures of morality and self-control and is taken to reflect key variation among young people in their crime propensity during Phase 1 (ages 13 to 17). Crime propensity was calculated in the following manner. First, the morality variable was rescaled so high values represented weak morality (the self-control variable was already scaled so high values meant poor self-control). Second, for each sub-scale (weak morality and poor ability to exercise self-control) measurements taken in each of the five waves were merged on an add cases basis into one variable covering the whole study period (such that each person contributed five values to each variable, one from each wave, the resulting number of observations for the measure of weak morality being 3,510, and for poor ability to self-control 3,514). Third, the z-scores for these two new variables were calculated. Fourth, the z-scores of the two sub-scales of weak morality and poor self-control were added to create the composite measure for crime propensity. Fifth, to make it possible to compare age-related changes in crime propensity (as is done in Figure 3.5), the values for the composite measure of crime propensity for the whole period were split by wave (age) into five variables where each person was assigned his or her z-score (which had been calculated on the basis of the z-score distribution for all five waves) for each particular age. Sixth, the added values of these five scores constituted the participant's Phase 1 crime propensity score.

**Table 3.21 Zero-order correlations[a] for crime propensity by age[b]**

| Age | 13 | 14 | 15 | 16 | 17 |
|-----|-----|-----|-----|-----|-----|
| 13 | 1.0 | | | | |
| 14 | .69 | 1.0 | | | |
| 15 | .61 | .69 | 1.0 | | |
| 16 | .54 | .62 | .72 | 1.0 | |
| 17 | .48 | .57 | .64 | .76 | 1.0 |

[a] All correlations are significant at the .001 level or better.
[b] N varies between 686 and 702 depending on which ages are correlated.

The zero-order correlations between the crime propensity indices for each age are shown in Table 3.21. These were generally very strong but declined somewhat with the distance between ages, indicating that some individual changes over the period in relative crime propensity had taken place. Previous analyses of age-related change indicated that changes in crime propensity tended to be related to changes in crime involvement (see Reinecke and Wikström 2012; Wikström 2009).

The distribution of the crime propensity score was approximately normal, as shown in Figure 3.4. For some analyses in this

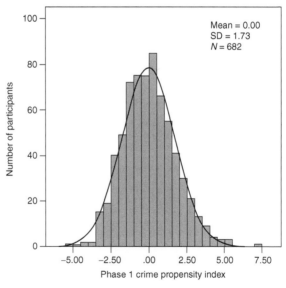

**Figure 3.4 Distribution of Phase 1 crime propensity**

**Table 3.22 Distribution of participants with high, medium, and low crime propensity**

| Propensity group | Number | Percentage |
|---|---|---|
| Low | 106 | 15.5 |
| Medium | 470 | 68.9 |
| High | 106 | 15.5 |
| Total | 682 | 99.9 |

book, findings are presented for three groups of young people: those with a high, medium, and low crime propensity, where those with a high crime propensity are defined as those whose crime propensity scores were one standard deviation or higher above the mean, and those with a low crime propensity are defined as those whose crime propensity scores were one standard deviation or lower below the mean (Table 3.22). These are, of course, somewhat arbitrary cut-off points, but these groupings heuristically help illustrate some key differences among young people according to their levels of crime propensity.

On average, young people's crime propensity generally increased between ages 13 and 15 (Figure 3.5) and then levelled out. This increase was, as previously demonstrated, mainly due to a decrease

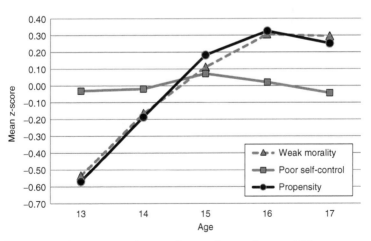

**Figure 3.5 Crime propensity, weak morality, and poor ability to exercise self-control (z-scores) by age**

in young people's morality (Table 3.19),[21] while their self-control remained rather stable over the period (Table 3.20).[22]

### 3.2.4 Crime propensity and crime involvement

Figure 3.6 shows the relationship between young people's crime propensity and their crime involvement.[23] Variation in crime propensity predicted variation in self-reported crime involvement rather well (explaining 50 per cent of the variance). Crime propensity was also very strongly correlated with duration ($r = .65$) and versatility ($r = .68$) in self-reported crime.

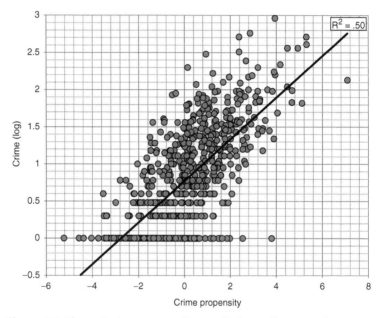

**Figure 3.6 Phase 1 crime propensity predicting self-reported crime (logged)**

---

[21] All age differences in crime propensity and weak morality were significant, with the exception of the difference between ages 16 and 17.

[22] There were no statistically significant age differences in the ability to exercise self-control.

[23] Because crime was a highly skewed variable (Figure 3.1) it is logged.

## 3.3 Criminogenic exposure

Young people vary not only in their crime propensity but also in the degree to which they are exposed to criminogenic environments. The concept of *criminogenic* refers to conditions that encourage (some) people to break rules of conduct (stated in law). According to SAT, the criminogeneity of a particular setting depends on its moral context, the (law-relevant) moral norms and the strength of their enforcement relative to the opportunities and frictions that confront people who take part in that setting (see section 1.3.4). Although the concept of a moral context (as defined in SAT) is pretty straightforward theoretically, its measurement is not.

In this section we present how criminogenic exposure has been defined and measured for this book. We will present key findings about the basic constructs: the distribution of criminogenic exposure in the population, changes in criminogenic exposure by age, and the basic relationship between criminogenic exposure and crime involvement.

### 3.3.1 Measuring criminogenic exposure

The unit of analysis is rarely a problem when we study people and their actions. A person is defined by his or her body and when we study people we study characteristics of their bodies (eg weight and height), internal to their bodies (eg personal morality and ability to exercise self-control), or their actions (eg their acts of crime). However, the unit of analysis problem becomes much more complex when we introduce the *environment* and particularly when studying environmental influences on human action such as acts of crime. There is no simple universal criterion to define the boundaries of 'the environment' (or of what it consists). In principle, a person's environment is everything external to him or herself.

Unit of analysis

SAT proposes that people (eg their development and actions) are only influenced by the part of the environment (eg people, objects, and events) that, at any given moment in time, they can access with their senses (which SAT refers to as *settings*); therefore, our environmental unit of analyses needs to, as closely as possible, approximate settings. We chose *output areas* because they are the smallest available geographical unit for which we could combine our data from different sources (ie space–time budget, community survey, and census and land use data; see further section 2.8.2). In most cases output areas are small enough in terms of land area to warrant the claim that they are reasonable proxies of settings (although there are some significant exceptions). However, people experience different degrees of exposure to particular settings; therefore, we also need to take this into consideration when assessing environmental influences on their actions.

## Exposure

People are not stationary but move around in space, encountering different kinds of settings and configurations of settings (activity fields). Even those who live at the same location may have very different activity fields and, hence, very different exposure to particular kinds of settings (a fact that is rarely taken into account in studies of environmental influences on people's crime involvement; see Wikström et al. 2010).

To measure young people's *exposure* to particular kinds of settings we use data from the space–time budget (see section 2.5.1). These data specify the amount of time, counted in hours, the young people spent in particular settings (in output areas under particular circumstances) over four days (see Table 2.6 in section 2.5.1) in each year of data collection, totalling 20 days across the 13 to 17 age period.[24] We assume time usage during these 20 days will largely reflect individual differences in general activity patterns and exposure to particular settings, such as criminogenic settings, over the study period (ages 13 to 17). Our basic unit of analysis of exposure to particular environments is thus *hours spent in particular settings (eg output areas with particular characteristics under particular circumstances).*

## Criminogenic exposure: The moral context

Although we present data about young people's general exposure to a variety of settings in subsequent chapters (see section 6.2), our core focus remains on young people's exposure to *criminogenic settings*; therefore, we needed to create a measure of such settings. According to SAT, the moral context is key to a setting's criminogeneity because it influences people's responses to the opportunities

[24] See technical appendix, section A1.4, for ways in which we quantify participants' time use.

available and the frictions they encounter in that setting. To measure the moral contexts of settings in which the young people took part, we use data from an independent community sample[25] of adults living in the study area (the Peterborough Community Survey; see further section 2.8) who acted as social observers of relevant small area conditions (ie output areas), such as social cohesion and informal social control. The community survey was conducted in the middle of the study period (2005); we assume the small area conditions at that point in time largely reflect those for the entire study period (although we are aware that a few areas have undergone significant changes; see section 4.3.2).

### 3.3.2 Collective efficacy as a measure of the moral context

We selected *collective efficacy* as our prime measure of the moral context of a setting because it is an established and tested measure (eg Duncan et al. 2003; Friedrichs and Oberwittler 2007; Sampson et al. 1997; Sampson and Wikström 2008), which combines residents' reports of social cohesion and levels of informal social control in an effort to measure their willingness to intervene in cases of crime and disorder. Collective efficacy can therefore be seen as tapping into a key aspect of the moral context—the level of enforcement of key common rules of conduct relevant to young people.

Our collective efficacy measure (as developed by Sampson and colleagues; see Sampson et al. 1997) combined information from two scales measuring small area informal social control and social cohesion (see Table 3.23). The Cronbach's alpha of the combined scales is a highly satisfactory .87. The measure was scaled so that high values meant *poor collective efficacy* (ie low social cohesion and weak informal social control). The scale is an empirical Bayes estimate adjusted for individual level socio-demographic composition as recommended by Sampson et al. (1997).

As with any social science measurement, respondents' answers regarding output area social cohesion and informal social control may not represent a 'true' picture of their area but may be biased and affected by measurement error to some extent. For example, a respondent who spends little time in his or her immediate neighbourhood and does not care about his or her neighbours will

---

[25] A random sample was taken for each of the 518 output areas of the study area (see section 2.8.7).

**Table 3.23 Items in the social cohesion and informal social control scales used to create the (poor) collective efficacy measure for output areas**

Social cohesion questions
(response categories: strongly agree, agree, disagree, strongly disagree)

1. People around here are willing to help their neighbours

2. This is a close-knit neighbourhood

3. People in this neighbourhood can be trusted

4. People in this neighbourhood generally get along with each other

5. People in this neighbourhood share the same values

Informal social control questions[a]
(response categories: very likely, likely, unlikely, very unlikely)

1. If a group of neighbourhood children were skipping school and hanging out on a street corner, how likely is it that your neighbours would do something about it?

2. If some children were spray-painting on a local building, how likely is it that your neighbours would do something about it?

3. If there was a fight in front of your house and someone was being beaten or threatened, how likely is it that your neighbours would break it up?

4. If a child was showing disrespect to an adult, how likely is it that people in your neighbourhood would tell off or scold that child?

[a] An initial analysis revealed that the inclusion of one of the original informal social control questions used by Sampson et al. (1997) significantly reduced the scale's internal consistency (Cronbach's alpha) and was therefore not included. This item asked 'Suppose that because of budget cuts the fire station closest to your home was going to be closed down by the local authority. How likely is it that neighbourhood residents would organise to try to do something to keep the fire station open?'

probably know less about community life than respondents who spend more time in their immediate neighbourhood and have more contacts with their neighbours. We therefore evaluated the setting level reliability of collective efficacy using multilevel modelling.

The first step within multilevel modelling is to compute the intraclass correlation coefficient (ICC) in a so-called 'unconditional' or 'empty model' without any individual level predictors, comparable to variance decomposition in a conventional analysis of variance. As reported in Table 3.24, 18.4 per cent of the variance of collective efficacy at the output area level was due to differences between areas. Weighted by the number of respondents, this ICC translates to a lamda ($\lambda$; ecological reliability) of .74.

Table 3.24 Intraclass correlation coefficients (ICC) and ecological reliabilities (λ) of scales measuring neighbourhood social conditions (*N* = 6,615 respondents in *N* = 518 output areas)

| Scale | Empty model | | Conditional model[a] | | | |
|---|---|---|---|---|---|---|
| | ICC | λ | ICC | λ | L1 $R^2$ | L2 $R^2$ |
| Collective efficacy | 18.4 | .74 | 17.7 | .72 | 0.8 | 5.3 |
| Social cohesion | 19.4 | .75 | 18.0 | .72 | 1.0 | 9.8 |
| Informal social control | 11.3 | .61 | 11.0 | .60 | 0.5 | 3.7 |

[a] Controlling for individual-level socio-demographic composition (age, sex, length of residence, children, ethnicity, tenancy, employment status, education status)

In a second step, individual-level variables were introduced to the multilevel model to control for output area socio-demographic composition. If differences in measurement between output areas were mainly due to socio-demographic variables, for example the fact that older respondents answered survey questions differently than younger respondents, or poorly educated respondents answered differently than highly educated respondents, this would be reflected in the so-called conditional model. The effects of individual differences in perceptions due to socio-demographic factors were entered into the multilevel model on level 1 (L1; individual respondents). The same variables may also be used as aggregated output area level variables (level 2; L2) characterizing the structural makeup of output areas (eg area social disadvantage) and may then show a distinct 'contextual' effect (see below). It is important that respondent level predictor variables are entered uncentred or grand-mean centred into the conditional model in order to be able to estimate the influence these variables have on the output area level variance (Enders and Tofighi 2007; Raudenbush and Bryk 2002: 134–49).

The stronger the effect of individual-level variables, the more the ICC would be reduced in the conditional model compared to the empty model. The conditional model in Table 3.24 reveals that socio-demographic variables had only a very small effect on output area level measurements, reducing the ICC of collective efficacy by 0.7 per cent, and ecological reliability (λ) by just .02. In terms of the share of variance that is explained in the conditional model on both levels, Table 3.24 shows that around 5 per cent of the output area level variance is explained by variation in the socio-demographic composition of output areas, and just 0.8 per cent of the variance between individual respondents is explained by socio-demographic variables. This result underlines the fact that perceptions of area social organization are largely independent of individual socio-demographic factors, and thus area differences are hardly attenuated if controlling for respondents' socio-demographic composition. What really drives area differences in these dimensions of collective efficacy, then, is the effect of the *collective* makeup of areas, such as the concentration of social disadvantage (see further section 4.3.5).

### Defining area poor collective efficacy

The 25 per cent of output areas with the highest poor collective efficacy scores were designated as having poor collective efficacy; hence, exposure to settings with poor collective efficacy refers to *time spent (hours) in the 25 per cent of output areas with the highest scores for poor collective efficacy*. Arguably, this 25 per cent cut-off is somewhat arbitrary; although it captures output areas with the highest levels of poor collective efficacy, it should be borne in mind that areas with scores just above the cut-off point will not differ dramatically from those just below the cut-off point.

### The city and local centres as weak moral contexts

One drawback of the measure of collective efficacy is the fact it is only based on residents' social observations of residents' willingness to intervene, and ignores the role of visitors to the area. This may be a particularly relevant concern for measures of collective efficacy in the city and local centres—ie areas with larger shopping complexes and entertainment venues—as well as areas dominated by offices and industry. We, therefore, decided to also use *the city and local centre environments* (settings) as an additional indicator of a weaker (law-relevant) moral context, mainly because these are areas with large non-residential populations less likely to be socially cohesive and trusting (as they generally have no investment in the area[26] and are likely to be strangers to most fellow visitors

---

[26] With the main exception of those who work in the area.

and therefore lack any strong bonds to them) and, therefore, (presumably) less inclined to exercise informal social control. The fact that high levels of crime tend to be found in such areas (see Figure 5.1) is consistent with the assumption that these public settings may have a weak (law-relevant) moral context, as well as findings from ethnographic studies of the so-called 'night-time economy' in city centres (eg Hobbs et al. 2005).

### Circumstances

Spending time in a city or local centre (eg shopping with one's parents) or in an area with poor collective efficacy (eg attending football practice) may not necessarily be very criminogenic. The relevance of a setting's moral context for a young person's crime involvement is likely to depend on the circumstances in which he or she takes part in that setting. We, therefore, also considered the *circumstances* in which young people take part in certain settings, arguing that unstructured peer-oriented activities (ie activities with peers outside of work and school that are unsupervised by adults) generally have a stronger criminogenic potential than other activities (eg structured and supervised activities), particularly if they take place in settings with weak (law-relevant) moral contexts. This measure of circumstances is constructed from space–time budget data bringing together details such as what young people are doing, who they are with, and where they are (see further sections 6.1 and 6.2 for more detailed definitions of unstructured and peer-oriented activities).

### 3.3.3 The index of criminogenic exposure

In summation, our two basic measures of *exposure to criminogenic settings* are:

(1) time spent in unstructured peer-oriented activities in areas with poor collective efficacy (number of hours over 20 days);
(2) time spent in unstructured peer-oriented activities in the city or local centres (number of hours over 20 days).

We combined these two measures to create an overall measure of criminogenic exposure by adding them together and correcting for some (geographical) overlap (eg some city and local centre output areas also had poor collective efficacy[27]). The overall criminogenic exposure measure was:

> Time spent in unstructured peer-oriented activities in the city or local centres or in an area with poor collective efficacy (number of hours over 20 days).[28]

It is important to point out that we do not expect all young people's crime to take place in these settings (clearly, other environmental conditions may be criminogenic). Our only assumption is that these are key examples of the *most* criminogenic kind of environments in which young people spend their time and, therefore, we expect them to generally have the highest rates of crime (particularly at times of the week and day during which they also present high levels of crime-relevant opportunities and frictions).

The overall distribution of criminogenic exposure among young people was highly skewed (Figure 3.7).[29] More than half (52.8 per cent) of participants spent two hours or less in criminogenic settings during the 20 studied days (and 37.1 per cent spent no time at all awake in criminogenic settings). On the other hand, only one in 10 (10.4 per cent) spent 20 hours or more in criminogenic settings. The most time any young person spent in a criminogenic setting over the 20 days was 73 hours, that is, on average, about three and a half hours per day.

The zero-order correlations by age show that those who spent more time in criminogenic settings at one age tended to do so at all other ages (particularly at proximate ages; see Table 3.25). However, the correlations by age are not as strong as those for crime propensity (Table 3.21). Possible contributory reasons for this are:

[27] Two of the four city centre and one of the six local centre output areas had poor collective efficacy. Of the 4,469 hours the young people who completed all five waves spent in the city and local centres and in areas with poor collective efficacy, 1,525 hours were overlapping, ie spent in the city and local centres with poor collective efficacy (and hence were only included once in the combined measure).

[28] By definition, all of these hours refer to hours spent awake in these settings under these circumstances.

[29] Even though young people included in these analyses completed space–time budgets in all five years ($N = 657$), not all spent 100 per cent of their time in the study area. A small number lived and/or went to school outside the study area at some point during the study period, which means their exposure may be underestimated. However, on average, the young people who completed space–time budgets in all five years spent 92.8 per cent (SD = 13.8 per cent) of that time in the study area.

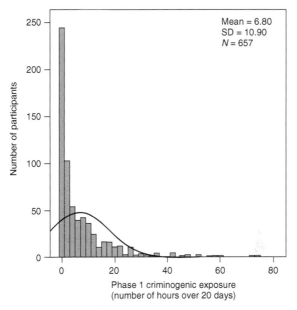

Figure 3.7 Distribution of Phase 1 criminogenic exposure

Table 3.25 Zero-order correlations[a] for criminogenic exposure by age[b] (correlations using logged variables italicized)

| Age | 13 | 14 | 15 | 16 | 17 |
|---|---|---|---|---|---|
| 13 | 1.0 | *.41* | *.35* | *.30* | *.20* |
| 14 | .33 | 1.0 | *.38* | *.32* | *.20* |
| 15 | .30 | .33 | 1.0 | *.43* | *.29* |
| 16 | .28 | .22 | .39 | 1.0 | *.29* |
| 17 | .12 | .18 | .30 | .28 | 1.0 |

[a] All correlations are significant at the .001 level or better.
[b] $N = 657$.

(1) young people's exposure is more changeable than their propensity; (2) the measure of exposure is less reliable than that of propensity, as it is based on only a four day reporting period each year (eg specific circumstances during the four-day observation period for some young people in some years may not have been representative of their normal activity patterns); and (3) the fact

that the distribution of exposure is highly skewed (in comparison to the distribution of crime propensity), which is evident as the correlations generally become stronger when the variable is logged (Table 3.25).

## Age trends in criminogenic exposure

Not only did young people's crime propensity, on average, increase from ages 13 to 17 (see Table 3.21) but so did their exposure to criminogenic settings (see Table 3.26). While the average time spent in criminogenic settings (per day) at age 13 was 9 minutes, this increased to 29 minutes at ages 16 and 17. Looking at the subscales that make up the overall criminogenic exposure measure, we find the trends are the same. The average time spent in unstructured peer oriented activities in the city and local centres increased from 2 minutes at age 13 to 17 minutes at age 17, while the average time spent in unstructured peer oriented activities in areas with poor collective efficacy increased from 8 minutes at age 13 to 25 minutes at ages 16 and 17. Most likely, this reflects general age-related changes in young people's life circumstances, including increasing mobility coupled with weakening adult supervision of their whereabouts (see chapter 6).

**Table 3.26  Average hours and minutes per day[a] spent in criminogenic settings by age (N = 657[b])**

| Age | Average time per day spent in unstructured peer-oriented activities in... | | |
|---|---|---|---|
| | City or local centres | Areas with poor collective efficacy | City or local centres or areas with poor collective efficacy[c] |
| 13 | 0:02 | 0:08 | 0:09 |
| 14 | 0:06 | 0:12 | 0:14 |
| 15 | 0:10 | 0:19 | 0:21 |
| 16 | 0:14 | 0:25 | 0:29 |
| 17 | 0:17 | 0:25 | 0:29 |

[a] Of two weekdays, one Friday, and one Saturday per year; hence activities may be overrepresented as they are more prevalent on Fridays and Saturdays.
[b] Only those who took part in all five waves of the space–time budget are included.
[c] Adjusting for overlap between the two scales.

### 3.3.4  Criminogenic exposure and crime involvement

The relationship between exposure to criminogenic settings and crime involvement (Figure 3.8) is significant (explaining 20 per cent of the variance), but not as strong as the relationship between crime propensity and crime involvement (Figure 3.6). Recall, in this context, that SAT predicts that the impact of criminogenic exposure on a person's crime involvement depends on his or her crime propensity (see section 1.3.1). Crime averse young people are not expected to be very influenced (situationally[30]) by criminogenic features of the settings in which they take part.

### 3.3.5  Peer crime involvement

In addition to our basic measures of criminogenic exposure, we can also take into account the *young people's peers' crime involvement* as an additional indicant of their exposure to criminogenic influences.

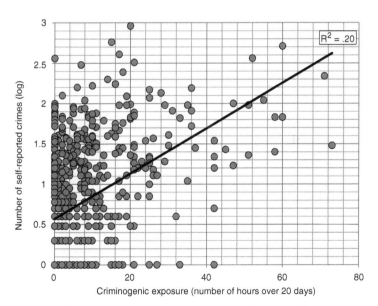

**Figure 3.8  Phase 1 criminogenic exposure predicting self-reported crimes (logged)**

---

[30] However, it is possible that long-term exposure to criminogenic environments may affect a person's crime propensity.

**Table 3.27 Percentage who were with friends the last time they committed a crime by crime type[a]**

| Crime type | Percentage committed with friends (the last time) |
|---|---|
| Shoplifting | 80.5 |
| Theft from a person | 59.6 |
| Car crime | 94.3 |
| Residential burglary | 100.0 |
| Non-residential burglary | 100.0 |
| Robbery | 74.2 |
| Assault | 72.3 |
| Vandalism | 80.2 |
| Arson/fire-setting | 95.8 |

[a] Data collected at age 16 (2007).

Young people predominantly socialize in groups and it is well known that most crimes by young people are committed in the presence of peers (eg Warr 2002). This common finding is also clearly borne out by our data, as exemplified by data collected at age 16, which captured the proportion of crime, by crime type, committed when the perpetrator was with his or her friends (Table 3.27).

Our core measures of criminogenic settings define them as settings in which a young person is engaged in unstructured *peer-oriented* activities (in the city or local centres or areas with poor collective efficacy). It is reasonable to assume that if the peers a young person socializes with tend to be crime prone, this adds to the criminogeneity of the setting.[31] The data from the space–time budget provides only limited details about the peers a young person was with (eg their gender) but no data about their personal characteristics, such as whether or not they are crime prone.

However, participants were asked in the annual questionnaire about the extent to which they knew their peers engaged in a number

[31] As we have demonstrated in Figure 3.6, there is a very strong relationship between crime propensity (morality and the ability to exercise self-control) and crime involvement. Therefore, it is reasonable to assume that peers' crime involvement is a good marker of their crime proneness, which may contribute to a moral context that may encourage rule-breaking.

of different acts of rule-breaking. These acts included skipping school or work without an excuse; getting drunk; sniffing glue, or gas, or using drugs (for example cannabis, crack or ecstasy); stealing things from shops; destroying things not belonging to them (for example smashing street lights, painting graffiti on walls, smashing windows, scratching the paint off cars); and beating up or getting into fights with others. For each item the response categories were: 'No, never', 'Yes, sometimes', 'Yes, often (every month)' and 'Yes, very often (every week)'. From the answers to these questions at each of the five waves (ages 13 to 17) an *index of peer crime involvement* for Phase 1 was created using the same method used to produce the crime propensity index (see section 3.2.3).

As might be expected, the zero-order correlation between peer crime involvement and young people's crime involvement (logged) was very strong ($r = .71, p = .000, N = 685$). In other words, young people who were frequent offenders tended to have peers who were frequently involved in crime. There was also a rather strong correlation between peer crime involvement and young people's exposure to criminogenic settings ($r = .51, p = .000, N = 652$). An interesting question is whether young people whose peers are frequently involved in crime are more affected by criminogenic exposure than those whose are not—ie whether exposure to criminogenic settings is more criminogenic for those who have 'criminogenic' peers (assuming they typically spend their unstructured peer-oriented time socializing with peers who are involved in crime).

At each level of criminogenic exposure (ie high, medium, and low), young people whose peers were frequently involved in crime self-reported more crime than others (Figure 3.9). Moreover, and crucially, the effect of criminogenic exposure tended to be much stronger for those whose peers were frequently involved in crime (ie those who were likely to take part in criminogenic settings with peers who were frequently involved in crime) as evidenced by the significant interaction effect (Table 3.28) illustrated in Figure 3.9.

Combining young people's degree of exposure to criminogenic settings and the level of their peers' crime involvement into one index (adding the two measures' z-scores) creates an index of exposure that was as strongly related to crime involvement (explaining 51 per cent of the variance) as crime propensity (Figure 3.10; and compare Figure 3.6).

**Table 3.28  Criminogenic exposure, peer crime involvement, and their interaction predicting crime involvement[a]**

|  | Beta | Prob. |
|---|---|---|
| Peer crime involvement | .43 | .000 |
| Criminogenic exposure | −.00 | n.s. |
| Interaction term | .14 | .002 |

Multiple $R^2$ x 100 = 24.9

[a] Outcome variable is not logged due to the inclusion of an interaction term.

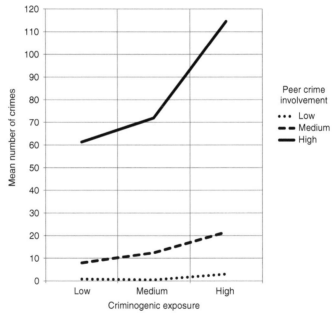

**Figure 3.9  Interaction between peer crime involvement and criminogenic exposure in predicting crime involvement[a]**

[a] Groups determined by standard deviations (high = one or more standard deviation above the mean; medium = within one standard deviation of the mean; low = one or more standard deviation below the mean).

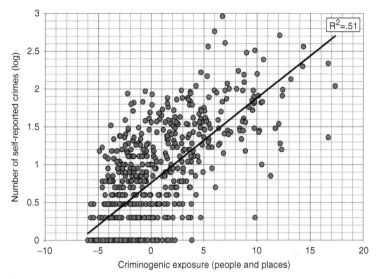

**Figure 3.10 Predicting crime involvement by an index of exposure to criminogenic people (peers who are frequently involved in crime) and places (criminogenic settings)**

## 3.4 Predicting crime involvement: The interaction between crime propensity and criminogenic exposure

A core assumption of SAT is that people's acts of crime are an outcome of the interaction between their crime propensity and criminogenic exposure. We conclude this chapter by exploring this interaction. The findings show (Table 3.29) that there was a strong interaction between crime propensity and criminogenic exposure in predicting crime involvement. The nature of the interaction is plotted in Figure 3.11. In other words, the core assumption of SAT regarding the importance of the person propensity–setting exposure interaction in crime causation was strongly supported by our data.

## 3.5 Summary and conclusion

Crime is common in adolescence but far from all young people engage in crime. In our sample, most young people reported at least one act of crime between the ages of 12 and 16, although nearly

**Table 3.29  Crime propensity, criminogenic exposure (people and places), and their interaction predicting crime involvement[a]**

|  | Beta | Prob. |
| --- | --- | --- |
| Crime propensity | .25 | .000 |
| Criminogenic exposure | .14 | .008 |
| Interaction term | .30 | .002 |

Multiple $R^2$ x 100 = 32.2

[a] Outcome variable is not logged due to the inclusion of an interaction term.

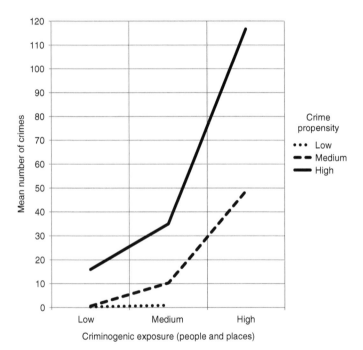

**Figure 3.11  Interaction between crime propensity and criminogenic exposure in predicting crime involvement[a]**

[a] Groups determined by standard deviations (high = one or more standard deviation above the mean; medium = within one standard deviation of the mean; low = one or more standard deviation below the mean).

one-third did not report involvement even in very minor crimes. At the same time, a very small group of young people were responsible for the majority of crimes reported in the study. This group tended to begin offending early in life (before the age of 12) and persist in their offending throughout adolescence. Very few new offenders emerged later in adolescence. Apparently, factors important for young people's persistent involvement in crime tend to exert their influence early in life. Frequent offenders tended to be 'jacks of all trades'. There was little evidence for offence specialization, although there was some variation between frequent offenders in terms of their involvement with violent crimes. Only a minority of those who self-reported offences were known to the police. Those who did have police-recorded crimes tended to be more serious offenders in terms of their self-reported frequency and versatility. Looking at age trends in offender prevalence and crimes by offenders, there was, after an initial increase in both measures between ages 12 and 13, a clear pattern of difference in development, in that from ages 13 to 16 there were fewer, albeit more active, offenders.

SAT proposes that morality and the ability to exercise self-control are the key personal factors that affect a person's crime propensity. The fact that there was a strong correlation between crime propensity (measured by an index of morality and the ability to exercise self-control) and crime involvement supports this assertion. Propensity was quite normally distributed in the PADS+ sample. As young people aged, their morality tended to decline, especially for more minor acts of rule-breaking, while their ability to exercise self-control appeared to remain stable during adolescence.

In contrast to crime propensity, criminogenic exposure was highly skewed in the PADS+ sample; few young people were frequently exposed to criminogenic settings. Exposure was measured as a combination of settings (environments) and the circumstances under which young people took part in them. The environments we propose are the most criminogenic are those with poor collective efficacy and/or those in the city and local centres (as these characteristics are assumed to indicate environments with weaker law-relevant moral contexts). The circumstances we propose are the most criminogenic are those under which young people spend time unsupervised with their peers, outside of work and school settings, in unstructured activities. There was a strong correlation between criminogenic exposure and crime involvement, which became much stronger when peer crime involvement was taken into account, to account for the fact that the presence of only crime prone peers may have significant implications for the moral context. The strong correlations between exposure and crime support the assertion that certain settings (ie those with poor collective efficacy and/or the city and local centres) under particular circumstances (ie in the presence of peers—particularly delinquent peers—during unstructured, unsupervised activities) are particularly criminogenic. Young people's exposure to criminogenic settings (ie spending time unsupervised in unstructured peer-oriented activities in the city or local centres or residential areas with poor collective efficacy) increased with age during the study period (ages 13 to 17).

A central assertion of SAT is that crime is an outcome of the interaction between crime propensity and criminogenic exposure. As predicted by SAT, our findings showed a strong interaction between crime propensity and criminogenic exposure in predicting young people's levels of crime involvement. The nature of the interaction suggests that young people with a low crime propensity are largely situationally resistant to criminogenic influences while young people with a high crime propensity are particularly situationally vulnerable.

# PART 2

# The Social Dynamics of Young People's Urban Crime

Chapter 4 introduces the city of Peterborough and its patterns of land use and residential segregation, and links these patterns to the distribution of crime and disorder at the small area level. Chapter 5 then looks in detail at the distribution of young people's crime in Peterborough, and relates this to offender home locations and features of crime and distance. Chapter 6 explores to what extent young people's different activity fields can explain their different exposure to criminogenic settings and, in turn, the distribution and concentration of young people's crime in Peterborough.

# 4

# Peterborough, Its Urban Structure, and Crime

The social milieu of an urban area, such as the city of Peterborough, is an outcome of historic processes of social emergence that create a constellation of different environments varying in their social and physical characteristics. As a result, the social conditions that people face, and therefore the content and dynamics of their social encounters, vary across an urban landscape. Social and self selective processes bring different kinds of people into contact with different environments, where they experience different opportunities and frictions in different moral contexts, with consequences for their behaviour. Hence the differential patterns of behaviour we observe across an urban landscape, such as variation in and concentrations of acts of crime, can be understood as the outcome of the particular interactions between people and settings that take place at different locations (see sections 1.4 and 1.5).

In this chapter we investigate what kinds of urban environments are the most conducive to crime, and why. It is important to bear in mind that this is only part of the story. A comprehensive explanation of why levels of crime vary between urban environments is not only a question of environments' criminogenic features, but, crucially, also a question of the extent to which, and why, people with higher crime propensities are exposed to criminogenic environments (creating the interactions that may result in acts of crime). This is a topic we will gradually introduce and explore in subsequent chapters (chapters 5 and 6). However, in this chapter the focus remains on what makes urban environments (settings) criminogenic for crime prone people.

The main aims of this chapter are to:

(1) define the study area (Peterborough) and present its key features and urban structure, patterns of land use, and residential segregation;

(2) present basic findings about the spatial variation of crime and disorder in Peterborough and its relationship to patterns of land use and residential segregation at the small area level.

A long tradition of social ecological research has highlighted the relationship between characteristics of urban environments and their levels of crime and disorder. Variations in area rates of crime and disorder are generally found to be related to patterns of *residential segregation* and *differential land use* (eg P. J. Brantingham and Brantingham 1984: 297–365; Sampson 1999: 261–3; Wikström 1998, 2007). The proposed explanations for these relationships typically focus on how particular environmental conditions (eg poor collective efficacy) promote (or fail to prevent) breaches of common rules of conduct, such as those defined in law (see sections 1.3.1 and 1.3.2).

Most previous research into the relationships between characteristics of city environments and their crime and disorder has been conducted with large area units of analysis (see sections 3.3.1 and 2.8.2), typically using only census data (although large-scale community surveys have become increasingly common). As our research is undertaken at the output area level, and combines census and community survey data, this provides a novel test of these relationships using a small unit of analysis. This is particularly important from a theoretical point of view, as, arguably, small areas (approximating settings) best reflect the social environments to which a person is exposed (settings) and that therefore directly influence his or her action (see sections 1.3.3 and 1.3.4).

Table 4.1 presents the key variables analysed in this chapter, their measurement, and their sources.

## 4.1 Peterborough: The research site

Peterborough is a cathedral city controlled by the unitary authority of Peterborough City Council within the county council area of Cambridgeshire in the Eastern region of southern England. Its contemporary urban structure represents a culmination of recent regeneration efforts and urban development building upon a long history of cultural and commercial significance. Settlements in the area date back to the Neolithic, when the area served a spiritual function (Davies et al. 2001: 6–7). Its first major industry—pottery—

**Table 4.1  Descriptions and sources for key social environmental variables**

| Variable | Description | Data source |
|---|---|---|
| **Residential segregation** | | |
| Social disadvantage | Factor score based on residents' educational qualification, social grade, employment status (employed or unemployed), and housing condition (social housing or detached) (see Table 4.2) | Census 2001[a] |
| Residential instability | Percentage of current residents who moved last year (ie all residents minus those who lived at the same address one year before) | Census 2001 |
| Asian ethnicity | Percentage of residents who are Asian or Asian-British, used as a dissimilarity measure | Census 2001 |
| Ethnic diversity index | Index of diversity, based on the four largest ethnic groups in Peterborough (white, Pakistani, Indian, black)[b] | Census 2001 |
| Family disruption | Percentage of all area households with dependent children that are lone-parent households | Census 2001 |
| Poor collective efficacy | Mean score (imputed empirical Bayes estimate) combining residents' reports of social cohesion and informal social control (see Table 3.23) | PCS 2005[c] |
| **Land use** | | |
| Non-residential land use | Percentage of residential buildings, residential gardens, and non-residential buildings that are non-residential buildings | GLUD 2005[d] |
| **Disorder and crime** | | |
| Disorder | Factor score (imputed empirical Bayes estimate) using items measuring general disorder, including disorder related to the presence of young people (see Table 4.4) | PCS 2005 |
| Drug dealing and prostitution | Factor score (imputed empirical Bayes estimate) using items measuring observed problems with, and recency of, drug taking and dealing, prostitution, and weapons carrying (see Table 4.4) | PCS 2005 |
| Police-recorded crime | Police-recorded crime count 2003–07 (selected crimes: violence, vandalism, theft of and theft from a car, residential and non-residential burglary, and shoplifting) (see section 4.2) | Cambridgeshire Constabulary |

[a] 2001 Census Standard Area Statistics (England and Wales), Office for National Statistics. Crown Copyright.
[b] Based on a technique by Gibbs and Martin (1962).
[c] Peterborough Community Survey 2005 (see section 2.8).
[d] Data on non-residential land use at the output area level provided from the Generalised Land Use Database 2005 (compiled by the Office of the Deputy Prime Minister, later the Department for Communities and Local Government) (see Department for Communities and Local Government 2007)

arose during the first century AD, when its more agricultural communities were replaced with Roman forts, which tapped into the area's rich clay deposits (ibid.: 10). The Romans were later replaced by the Anglo-Saxons and by the tenth century the Anglo-Saxon settlement of 'Burh St Peter' ('burh' meaning 'fortification'), from which Peterborough derives its name, had developed on the site of the modern-day city (ibid.: 12–13).

Parts of the city we see today were under construction by the mid twelfth century, including the cathedral square (formerly a market place) and the cathedral itself (ibid.: 14), although Peterborough would not be designated a cathedral city until 1541, under Henry VIII (ibid.: 16–17). New industries arose during the medieval period, namely weaving and woolcombing. Improvements in local roads and riverways during the Georgian period further improved commerce (ibid.: 20); Peterborough's strategic location made it accessible to northern and southern cities and during the industrial revolution it became a major railway junction between London and Birmingham, attracting a number of rail-related industries (ibid.: 23). The city again tapped into its vast local clay deposits, and became the UK's leading producer of bricks for much of the twentieth century (ibid.: 24).

These historic roots laid the foundations for the city we see today and erected many of its most memorable landmarks. However, much of its present-day social character and built environment was established much more recently, after it became a designated 'New Town' in 1968. The New Towns philosophy was born out of the success of garden cities, a movement between 1900 and 1920 to integrate the best aspects of town and country. By the 1940s, rising concerns for social welfare reform and social rebirth (embodied by the 1945 Attlee Labour administration) led to a growing consensus to halt the uncontrolled sprawl of London and other large cities. The inter-war years had made Britain a 'concrete jungle' and increasing pressure from environmental groups and the 1938 Green Belt Act set boundaries for further development. At the same time, several wartime commissions recommended the relocation of 1.5 million London residents, many of whose homes were damaged or destroyed during World War II, to 29 'New Towns' (21 in England), which would be developed in three phases between 1946 and 1970. New Towns were conceived as models for twentieth century living, 'urban utopias', which were aesthetically pleasing yet practical places to live. They would 'break down the barriers' between rich and poor by providing affordable, low-density, modern housing in self-sufficient communities replete with public green spaces and recreational facilities, separated from industrial areas, with well-planned roads and public transport networks.

In the 1950s and 1960s, the out-migration from UK urban areas was the highest in Europe, and the New Towns boomed. They were seen to embody a brighter future for war-torn Britain and many residents felt they enjoyed an improved standard of living. Although some urbanists feel the New Towns achieved their objectives (eg Hall 1981), there are growing concerns that the New Towns have outlived their original purpose and now face a host of social problems (House of Commons 2002: 7). Although the New Towns closer to London, such as Peterborough, have benefited from the strong regional economy, like most New Towns they now encompass deprived areas with high unemployment and housing needs, although this deprivation is concentrated in small areas that are interspersed with more affluent areas (House of Commons 2002: 14).

Figure 4.1 shows the main areas of the city, as well as the villages included in the study area.

One of the aims of including Peterborough in the New Towns movement was to more than double its population by the mid 1980s (House of Commons 2002). Between 1981 and 1991, Peterborough clocked an annual growth rate of 1.53 per cent, making it the third fastest[1] growing city in England (Parkinson et al. 2006).[2] During the 1990s, that growth stabilized. The 2001 census reported a city-wide population of 152,205, and a district-wide population of 156,050 (including people living in very rural areas and villages further from the city, which are not included in the PADS+ study area). Since then, the city has been growing again; mid census figures suggest a growth of 5.7 per cent across the district between 2001 and 2005, producing a 2005 district-wide population close to 165,000. This recent increase in population growth is primarily a result of extensions to existing housing developments in various parts of the city. Perhaps the most significant changes centre on development of the fourth new township, Hampton, to the south (see section 4.3.2).

---

[1] The fastest growing cities at this time were all New Towns, attesting to the success of this urban development scheme.

[2] The State of the English Cities report. Commissioned by the Office for the Deputy Prime Minister (ODPM), this is the most comprehensive study of England's cities and towns to date, covering all 56 English towns and cities with more than 125,000 inhabitants.

**Figure 4.1  Areas of Peterborough**[a]

[a] O. Refers to Orton (eg, Orton Wistow).

On the whole Peterborough is a relatively prosperous and progressive city in terms of economics and growth. Between 1995 and 2007 (prior to the recent global financial crisis) it demonstrated the highest economic growth[3] of any region in the United Kingdom except east and west inner London, and had the highest ranking for competitive industry (Oguz and Knight 2011). It forms part of the London–Stansted–Cambridge growth corridor, and has been

[3] Measured as percentage change in gross value added regional economic growth.

highlighted as one of four major growth areas across the United Kingdom for business and housing. In 2006 it was one of the leading exporters of goods outside the London area (Parkinson et al. 2006). It is the main centre of employment in Cambridgeshire, rivalled only by Cambridge as an urban centre, and traditionally boasts a high employment rate compared to other cities, both amongst its entire population and its non-white population (Parkinson et al. 2006). Historical roots in engineering and manufacturing are still evident in its modern employment structure, though due to good communication routes, cheap commercial rent, and developments in the service industry there is now no dominant employment sector in the city.

## 4.2  Land use

Land use refers to the human use of land and typically refers to the zoning of, for example, residential, commercial, industrial, and natural areas. The relationship between land use and crime and disorder has typically been studied via the environmental criminology tradition (eg P. L. Brantingham and Brantingham 1993), which focuses on routine activities (which bring certain kinds of people into certain settings) and opportunity structures (which may encourage or discourage different kinds of behaviour, including acts of crime) (see section 1.4.2). Land use affects an area's social contexts and the kinds of activities that take place in those contexts. Land use also significantly influences who takes part in which contexts by partially determining where people live, work, shop, spend their leisure time, etc., and how and when they travel (Rhind and Hudson 1980: 4).

Figure 4.2 illustrates differences in land use across the study area. Where people live is, of course, an important determinant of where they spend their time (Wikström and Sampson 2003: 130), but different kinds of environments also draw different kinds of people to them because of the resources and opportunities they provide (see P. L. Brantingham and Brantingham 1981). These environments will exhibit differences in their configuration of motivating factors (temptations, provocations) and deterrents (formal and informal social control), leading to differences in people's inclination to break rules of conduct and settings' capacities to regulate their behaviour.

Figure 4.2 shows the PADS+ study area today. The area boundaries (represented by the bold black outline) are determined by the edges of built-up areas (grey hatchmarks represent individual addresses, residential or commercial), belted in some places by

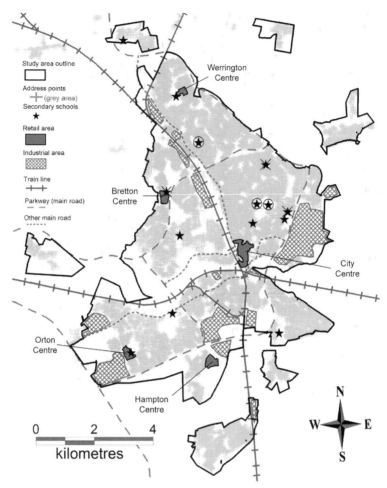

**Figure 4.2  Land use map of Peterborough**[a]

[a] Address point locations are reproduced by permission of Ordinance Survey on behalf of HMSO. © Crown copyright and database right 2005. All rights reserved. Roads, rail lines, industrial, and retail areas were defined using Land-Line, Ordinance Survey Mastermap © Crown copyright 2010.

large roadways (shown by dotted grey lines). This covers the city of Peterborough itself and six satellite villages:[4] Glinton, Newborough, Eye, Farcet, Yaxley, and Castor/Ailsworth.

[4] Most young people in the PADS+ sample lived within this study area, although sampling was based on schools and not where they lived; at the start of the study 39 (5.5 per cent) of the young people lived in rural areas not included in the study area, but all attended school in the city.

Peterborough may be seen as a multinuclear city in that it is subdivided into a number of local areas that are moderately self-sufficient (hosting local businesses, services, and schools), although the city centre remains a large draw to residents throughout the study area. To a large extent, the city is also sectorized, such that industrial, commercial, and residential areas, as well as green spaces, have been kept reasonably separate in the design of the urban space.

### 4.2.1 Residential land use

Much of the urban landscape of Peterborough is residential (grey shading in Figure 4.2 denotes the clustering of single addresses). Urban wards to the north, west and south, contain some of the oldest houses in the city, which date from the 1870s (the heydays of Peterborough's brickyards). In addition, there are a number of conservation areas and villages around Peterborough, which boast historic dwellings, although houses in the wider suburban wards mostly date from the 1960s and 1970s. Three of the self-contained New Town townships (Orton, Bretton, and Paston/Werrington—on the southwest, northwest, and north edges of the city, respectively) date from the 1970s and 1980s. The fourth township (Hampton, on reclaimed land to the south of the city) is still under construction.

### 4.2.2 Non-residential land use

The main city centre is characterized by a historic district, entertainment venues (eg pubs and nightclubs), and major shopping venues, including Queensgate Shopping Centre, a large indoor arcade. The four major townships also have their own local centres, where public amenities are concentrated, such as local businesses, services (eg healthcare centres, sports facilities), and in some cases schools (eg Werrington Centre, Orton Centre, and, prior to 2007, Bretton Centre). The shopping complex in Hampton Centre (Serpentine Green Shopping Centre) is the newest and largest, and is most like the city centre in the sense that it attracts visitors from across the whole city. Bretton Centre has also seen some recent redevelopment, while Werrington and Orton Centres are smaller and less modern. Although the latter is currently under redevelopment, during the study period (2004–08) it was particularly dilapidated. There are numerous other smaller local shopping locations throughout the city.

The city centre is the hub of entertainment in the city. Around one-third of licensed pubs and nightclubs in the study area are concentrated around the city centre. The rest are relatively evenly distributed. Other entertainment venues are dotted around the city, including one cinema complex, two bowling alleys, one ice skating rink, two outdoor and one indoor swimming pool, snooker clubs, skate parks, laser quest, and various arcades, which may have particular relevance for where young people spend their time.

Prior to 2007, there were 13 secondary schools[5] in the study area. In 2007, two new 'academies' replaced five pre-existing schools. These new schools are circled on Figure 4.2,[6] and those they replaced are crossed through. Industrial estates and business parks are located on the south and east outskirts of the built-up area and alongside the main railway line running north to south through the city (see Figure 4.2).

### 4.2.3 Green space

The topography of the wider Peterborough district is notoriously flat and low lying. The wetlands (Fens) to the east of the city are sparsely populated, such that rural villages lie mainly to the north, south, and west. The river Nene runs east to west through the city, passing close to the city centre. A series of country parks bracket the river, especially to the west of the city centre. Other large areas of open space are found throughout the city, such as the 'embankment' in the shadow of the cathedral, Bretton Park just north of Bretton Centre, the smaller Central Park to the north east of the city centre, and the sizeable 'East of England Showground' on the south west corner. However, some parts of the city, especially near the city centre, have less open space than called for by council standards (Peterborough City Council 2005).

### 4.2.4 Transportation

Peterborough occupies a strategic location between the East Midlands and East Anglia and enjoys a robust transportation network of roads and railways. It lies 80 miles north of London, less than one hour by train, and connects to a number of major roadways

---

[5] In addition, there was one special needs school, one independent school, and several programmes and referral units for young people with unique behavioural needs, such as disruptive pupils and young offenders, as well as young mothers.

[6] As is Peterborough Regional College, an educational facility mainly for post-16 education that also runs part- and full-time courses for some under 16s with special needs (for example young mothers, young offenders, etc.).

which provide vehicular access to the rest of the United Kingdom. A network of tree-lined, high-speed, dual carriageways (known as parkways; see Figure 4.2), constructed around the city in the 1970s, ensures that Peterborough has particularly short commute times compared to other cities in the United Kingdom (T. Gibson 2006). Peterborough also has a comprehensive 'Green Wheel' network of footpaths and cycle routes allowing traffic-free access to all areas of the city and surrounding villages.

## 4.3  Residential segregation

One key form of land use is housing. The population of urban areas tends to be highly residentially differentiated along social and economic dimensions (Janson 1980b; Logan and Molotch 1987; Massey and Denton 1993; Schwirian 1974; Timms 1971; W. J. Wilson 1987). Different mixes of people with particular social and economic resources, traditions, and lifestyles populate different residential areas of a city, contributing to the urban spatial variation in local social life and efficacy of informal social controls (Wikström and Sampson 2003).

Urban ecological research into the relationship between residential land use and crime and disorder has typically focused on aspects of population composition and turnover, highlighting three key dimensions: *social disadvantage* (a lack of resources, eg social or financial, also referred to as deprivation; see W. J. Wilson 1987), *residential instability* (the residential population turnover), and *population heterogeneity* (differences between residents' cultures or ethnicity) (eg, Kornhauser 1978: 83; see also, eg, Sampson and Groves 1989; Shaw and McKay [1942] 1969). Social disorganization theory (see section 1.4.1) has attempted to explain the relationship between these variables and crime and disorder through their influence on two key social processes, social cohesion and informal social control. Areas with higher levels of social cohesion and informal social control are assumed to be better able to regulate people's behaviour because residents share beliefs about social conduct and are better poised to intervene when rules of conduct are breached (Kornhauser 1978: 63) (see also Bursik 1988; Sampson and Groves 1989; Shaw and McKay [1942] 1969). However, it has not been possible to test these assumptions until more recently, with the introduction of large-scale community surveys (Sampson and Groves 1989; Sampson et al. 1997; Sampson and Wikström 2008; Wikström and Dolmen 2001).

## 4.3.1 Social disadvantage

Arguably the most prominent structural variable discussed in relation to crime and disorder is social disadvantage: the lack of social and economic resources (Wikström and Sampson 2003; W. J. Wilson 1987). These resources may include material resources, such as financial capital, or more personal resources, such as job skills and educational qualifications (human capital), or resourceful networks of relatives and friends (social capital), and may be lacking at the communal or individual level.

Understanding the role of social disadvantage for human development and action is one of the most important topics for social research; growing up and living in disadvantaged areas has been correlated with a number of negative social outcomes, including teen pregnancy, low intelligence, maltreatment, drug and alcohol abuse, and crime and victimization (see, eg, Brooks-Gunn et al. 1997; Coulton et al. 1995; G. J. Duncan et al. 1994).

Peterborough contains areas characterized by both high and low social disadvantage. The Indices of Multiple Deprivation 2004 (see chapter 2, footnote 58) ranked Peterborough among the most deprived third of local authorities in England,[7] with 22 (16.4 per cent) of its 134 super output areas (SOAs)[8] ranked among the most deprived in England (Head 2004). However, 25 (18.7 per cent) of its SOAs ranked among the *least* deprived, making Peterborough one of three towns (alongside Swindon and Trafford) to receive special mention in a 2004 Office of the Deputy Prime Minister (ODPM) report for presenting extremes of both high and low deprivation.

Across many specific socioeconomic indicators, Peterborough is generally similar to other UK cities. The average household income for the Peterborough Unitary Authority in 2002, when the study began, was £24,800, only slightly lower than the national average of £26,200 (CACI 2002). The percentage of people living in local authority housing in Peterborough is comparable to other UK cities. During the study period, 20.8 per cent of pupils per Peterborough primary school, on average, were eligible for free school meals,[9]

---

[7] Based on income, employment, health deprivation and disability, education skills and training, barriers to housing and services, crime, and the living environment (see Noble et al. 2004).

[8] Super output areas are larger geographical units comprised, on average, of five output areas.

[9] Free school meals are a common marker of family disadvantage as eligibility is determined by financial capital (means tested).

which is on par with the rate for schools in cities of a similar size. However, there was considerable variation across schools, with around 5 per cent of schools having more than 50 per cent of pupils eligible, and 15 per cent of schools having fewer than 5 per cent, echoing the diverse picture suggested by the rates of disadvantage.

To analyse the distribution of social disadvantage across Peterborough, we developed a measure for disadvantage at the output area level comparable to the IMD at the super output area level. We based this measure on census data for area residents' job skills, educational qualifications, employment, and home ownership. We employed principal component analysis to ensure all variables in the index represent one latent factor[10] (see Table 4.2). As expected, all variables loaded on a single factor (eigenvalue 3.3) and all loadings were higher than .50. The output area distribution of disadvantage in Peterborough is shown in Figure 4.3 (for details on how maps in this book are created see technical appendix, section A1.2).

Although early ecological studies in the United States suggested that areas of high disadvantage could be found in a belt around the city centre, known as the 'zone in transition' (eg Park et al. [1925] 1967: 50–8), more recent US research demonstrates the importance of the introduction of public housing, which is generally more widespread (eg Loeber and Wikström 1993: 182; McNulty and Holloway 2000; Sampson 1990; Wikström and Loeber 2000). Earlier studies in the United Kingdom had already shown that in UK cities social housing initiatives led to the clustering of social disadvantage in areas with a high concentration of social housing, not necessarily close to the city centre (Baldwin 1975; Baldwin and Bottoms 1976; Mays 1963: 160). Similar findings regarding the location of disadvantaged areas are also reported for Sweden (Wikström 1991). In Peterborough, there is a high level of disadvantage in parts of the city characterized by a high concentration of

---

[10] The original analysis also included variables relating to (1) the concentration of young people (percentage of area residents under the age of 16), which did not load highly on either factor; and (2) the concentration of ethnic minorities (percentage of area residents who were Asian, black, or had more than one person per room in their household), which clearly constituted a separate factor that we later used to construct an ethnic diversity index (see section 4.3.3). We included these variables because previous research, particularly in the United States where the link between African Americans and disadvantage is so robust, has found it difficult to disentangle the relationship between disadvantage and racial concentration (Morenoff et al. 2001). However, ethnicity and disadvantage are not that highly correlated in Peterborough.

**Table 4.2  Factor scores for social disadvantage (*N* = 518 output areas)**

|  | Factor loadings | Communalities |
|---|---|---|
| Percentage of area residents who are working class[a] | .96 | .86 |
| Percentage of area residents with no/lower educational qualifications[b] | .87 | .72 |
| Percentage of area residents who reside in social housing[c] | .78 | .67 |
| Percentage of area residents who are unemployed | .56 | .48 |
| Percentage of area residents who reside in detached houses | −.53 | .48 |

[a] National Readership Survey (see <www.nrs.co.uk/lifestyle.html>). Social grades are based on the occupation of the head of the household. Working class encompasses grades C2, D, and E: skilled, semi-skilled, and unskilled manual workers; casual or lowest grade workers; pensioners and others who rely on state benefits.
[b] The National Qualifications Framework (<www.direct.gov.uk/en/EducationAndLearning/ QualificationsExplained/DG_10039017>). Includes educational qualifications up to level 2, generally equivalent to those obtained when completing compulsory education (at best GCSEs grades A-C, a Level 2 NVQ, or a Level 2 diploma, for example).
[c] UK social housing is rented from the council or from independent, not-for-profit, private housing associations. Council housing is provided primarily for working class people and families on lower incomes. Housing associations also provide low-cost social housing for older people; people with mental health or learning disabilities; people with substance misuse problems; the formerly homeless; young people; ex-offenders; and women fleeing domestic violence.

rented social housing (eg parts of Dogsthorpe/Welland, Eastfield, Eastgate, Eye, Orton Waterville, Paston, Ravensthorpe, Stanground, and Werrington Local Centre: see Figure 4.1).

### 4.3.2  Residential instability

Residential instability refers to population turnover as people move into or out of an area. Instability may impede the development of local ties and trust between residents and their neighbours or communities, undermining social institutions and hampering the creation of social cohesion and the efficacy of informal social control (Bursik 1988; Kornhauser 1978; Sampson 1987; Sampson et al. 1997; Shaw and McKay [1942] 1969).

To measure residential instability in Peterborough, we used 2001 census data regarding the percentage of residents in an output area who had moved to their current address the previous year. Ideally, such a measure would also take into account the percentage of

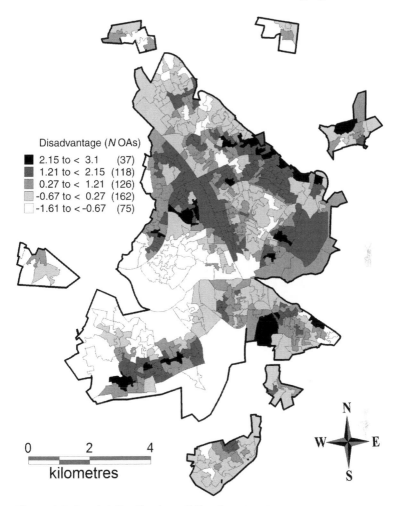

Figure 4.3  Spatial distribution of disadvantage[a]

[a] On chloropleth maps see technical appendix, section A1.2.1.

residents who moved out of an area; unfortunately, this cannot be determined from census data. Areas undergoing recent urban development distort the distribution (appearing as extreme outliers); we identified nine such outliers (four in the Hamptons, three in the north of Yaxley, one in Stanground, one on the outskirts of the Ortons, and one in Woodston). The relationship between residential stability and other variables tended to be stronger when these nine areas were excluded. Very few output areas (aside from these nine) had high residential instability. One of the most unstable areas was the city centre. Other areas with moderate residential instability included those with high rates of socially rented housing.

Consistent with findings from other UK (Sheffield; Baldwin and Bottoms 1976) and European (Stockholm; Wikström 1991) cities, residential instability in Peterborough was not related to area disadvantage ($r = .06$, *n.s.*). However, a weak relationship was obscured by the nine outliers (excluding these outliers, $r = .16$, $p = .000$). Peterborough also showed a positive weak relationship between area instability and ethnic diversity (see further below) ($r = .15$, $p = .000$). However, areas with particularly high ethnic diversity showed only moderate instability. Many of these areas had a large Asian (especially Pakistani) population, which was unrelated to residential instability ($r = .02$, *n.s.*), suggesting that areas with large Asian communities tended to be rather residentially stable.

### 4.3.3 Population heterogeneity

Population heterogeneity is a measure of the mixture of an area's population, commonly analysed in terms of race or ethnicity. Ethnic heterogeneity may influence the social milieu of an area through its potential impact on social cohesion and area rules and their level of enforcement; people with different cultural values may find it difficult to share common goals and may hold different views about some rules of conduct and how they should be regulated (Kornhauser 1978; Shaw and McKay [1942] 1969). For example, parents may be less able to control their children if they have difficulties with the local language or lack knowledge about relevant social and cultural practices.

In the 2001 UK census, 10.3 per cent of people in Peterborough described themselves as non-white, compared to 9.1 per cent in England (and 7.9 per cent in the United Kingdom), far more than the Cambridgeshire rate of 4 per cent. The largest ethnic minority group in Peterborough was Pakistani, accounting for 4.5 per cent of the city's population (compared to 1.4 per cent nationally). Peterborough was also home to a small but significant number of people from other ethnic minority groups, including people of Indian, Irish, Italian, and Caribbean descent. In recent years the city has also seen a dramatic increase in immigrants from eastern European countries such as Poland and the Slovak Republic.

Ethnic heterogeneity can be quantified in various ways, but two common methods are measures of ethnic dissimilarity and

ethnic diversity. Dissimilarity measures are often based on population concentration, ie the proportion of an area's population that
are ethnic minorities (or from a particular ethnic minority group);
a higher concentration means greater dissimilarity. A diversity measure indicates the degree of ethnic mixture in an area; an area is less
ethnically diverse if it contains fewer different groups.[11] This means
that areas with a high concentration of any one group (minority or
not) will have a low diversity score. Diversity scores thus measure
heterogeneity more explicitly than dissimilarity scores, which are
relative to an overarching ethnic majority.

We used both a dissimilarity measure (percentage of the area population that is Asian), and a diversity measure created using Gibbs
and Martin's (1962) method (based on the four largest ethnic groups
in Peterborough: white, Pakistani, Indian, and black). Ethnic diversity had a u-shaped relationship with ethnic dissimilarity: areas with
low and high concentrations of Asian residents have lower ethnic
diversity. At the output area level, we found a dissimilarity index for
white and Asian segregation of 0.59, and for white and black segregation of 0.41. These indices were slightly higher than those reported
in the State of the English Cities report, but this may be a result of the
latter using a larger unit of analysis (Parkinson et al. 2006: 147)
(whites and Asians, 0.55; whites and blacks, 0.29).

The most ethnically diverse areas of Peterborough were concentrated near the city centre and to the east, although areas with
more moderate diversity were spread throughout most of the city.
The diverse areas around the city centre tended to have a high concentration of Asian residents (although those with the highest concentration—up to 83 per cent Asian—were, of course, less diverse).
These findings generally suggest that Asians in Peterborough were
particularly segregated (particularly Pakistanis).

Previous data from Peterborough show a relationship between
ethnic heterogeneity and social disadvantage. For example,
Parkinson et al. (2006) reported an unusually high concentration
of Asian people in disadvantaged areas of Peterborough (compared
with other ethnic minority groups); in fact, Peterborough had
the highest concentration of Asian people in disadvantaged areas

---

[11] The diversity index was proposed by Gibbs and Martin (1962) to capture
the economic diversification of national economies and has more recently been
applied to the study of ethnic mixture at the area level (eg Laurence 2011; Letki
2008).

(at the super output area level, where super output areas represent larger geographical units of five output areas on average) of all UK cities with a non-white population of 6 per cent or higher, and was one of only four cities in which more than five times as many Asians lived in the most disadvantaged super output areas (27.9 per cent) compared to other super output areas (5.2 per cent) (Parkinson et al. 2006: 151).

At the output area level, we found only a weak relationship between ethnic diversity and area disadvantage ($r = .16$, $p = .000$); many areas with considerable diversity were not significantly disadvantaged. This was especially true of areas with a large Asian population. Areas with the highest concentration of Asian residents were also only moderately disadvantaged, and area concentrations of Asian people were not significantly related to area disadvantage ($r = .08$, $p = n.s.$).

### 4.3.4 Collective efficacy

The social disorganization perspective theorizes that structural factors, such as population disadvantage, heterogeneity, and turnover, influence action through their affect on area social cohesion and control. Sampson and colleagues, in the context of the Project on Human Development in Chicago Neighbourhoods (PHDCN: Sampson et al. 1997; Sampson et al. 1999; Sampson 2004, 2006a, 2006b), have forwarded the concept of *collective efficacy* as a measure of the activation of these social processes in a collective willingness of area residents to intervene for the common good (see section 1.4.1). Collective efficacy has subsequently emerged as a key factor within area level crime research reflecting an area's crime-controlling capacity. It shares similarities with other concepts of area level social control (Bellair 1997; Taylor 1996; Warner and Rountree 1997) and has been adopted by scholars both in the United States (eg Cancino 2005; T. E. Duncan et al. 2003; C. L. Gibson et al. 2002; Simons et al. 2005; Xu et al. 2005) and in Europe (Friedrichs and Oberwittler 2007; Lüdemann 2006; Lüdemann and Peter 2007) as well as cross-nationally (eg Sampson and Wikström 2008).

Although some researchers have chosen to study social control and cohesion separately (often focusing on informal social control; see, eg, Oberwittler and Wikström 2009; Silver and Miller 2004; Taylor 2002; Wikström and Dolmen 2001), there is evidence that the two are highly interconnected. Informal social control may be impossible without some degree of trust and shared values, while working towards common goals enhances cohesion (Raudenbush and Sampson 1999: 10). Silver and Miller (2004: 568) found that a considerable portion of area variation in informal social control (76 per cent) resulted from residents' shared beliefs about other residents' willingness to engage in informal social control. Brown (2004) found a very strong correlation between social trust and informal social control in Edinburgh neighbourhoods. Sampson, Raudenbush, and Earls (1997) reported a strong neighbourhood-level bivariate correlation between trust and expectations for action ($r = .80$) and felt justified in conceptualizing these variables as two parts of a unified construct. Across Peterborough's output areas, the corresponding correlation between social cohesion and informal control (both empirical Bayes estimates) was almost identical ($r = .78, p = .000$).

Empirical findings from the Chicago study underline the situational salience of collective efficacy (Sampson 2006a: 157): collective efficacy predicted area violent crime rates but not the prevalence of violence committed by resident adolescents (Kirk 2008; Sampson et al. 2005). In this book we focus on the immediate (situational) action-relevant impact of collective efficacy, using it, within the analytical framework of SAT, as a measure of the moral context— the common rules that apply to a setting and their level of enforcement (see further sections 1.3.4 and 1.4.1).

The idea of collective efficacy relies on two assumptions: (1) that residents' intentions to intervene would generally match their *behaviour*; and (2) that potential offenders can discern residents' intentions to intervene, and this influences their behaviour. To our knowledge, hardly any research has tested these assumptions. However, some support for the assumption that people would intervene when necessary in areas that score high on measures of collective efficacy may be inferred from Sampson's 'lost letter drop' experiment, which showed that an area's collective efficacy was significantly related to actual altruistic behaviour (ie returning a lost letter; Sampson 2012: 225). This provides some support for using collective efficacy as a valid measure of an area's moral context.

The spatial distribution of collective efficacy across the study area is shown in Figure 4.4. Major concentrations of poor collective efficacy were evident in parts of the Ortons, Bretton, and Paston. Output area rates of collective efficacy were largely independent of

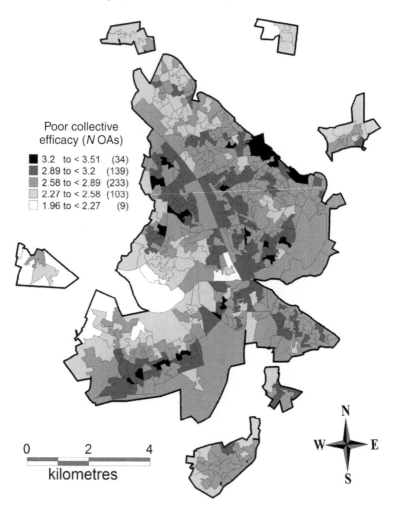

Figure 4.4  Spatial distribution of poor collective efficacy

respondents' sociodemographic characteristics (as shown in section 3.3.2, Table 3.24), which supports the fact that this measure captures real area differences.

Area (poor) collective efficacy was very strongly related to area social disadvantage (Figure 4.5) ($r = .67, p = .000$). Although this is a well-established statistical relationship (eg A. M. Brown 2004; Sampson et al. 1997; Sampson and Wikström 2008), it has yet to be fully theoretically explained. Social disorganization/collective

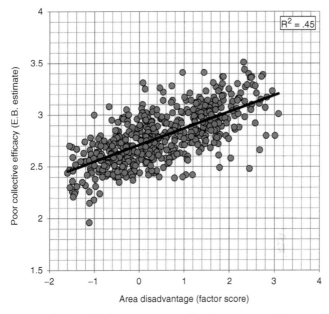

**Figure 4.5** Relationship between area disadvantage and poor collective efficacy

efficacy theory posits that in communities that lack sufficient resources, residents find it more difficult 'to collectively create and uphold effective rules for behaviour (collective efficacy)' (Wikström and Sampson 2003: 129). Disadvantaged areas tend to have more residents with mental health, alcohol, and/or drug problems, and people who are heavily involved in crime, which may lead to a lack of trust between residents, and therefore poor social cohesion (see, eg, G. J. Duncan and Brooks-Gunn 1997; Leventhal and Brooks-Gunn 2000). 'It may also be argued that community rules (weak collective efficacy), in the longer run, may impact upon community resources... through the... selective out-migration by more socially and economically resourceful residents and institutions' (Wikström and Sampson 2003: 129) (see also Sampson and Raudenbush 1999; Skogan 1990; Taub et al. 1984).

Although not as strongly as it was related to disadvantage, area (poor) collective efficacy in Peterborough was also related to residential instability ($r = .25, p = .000$), a relationship that becomes stronger once the nine areas undergoing significant urban development were excluded ($r = .34, p = .000$). Area (poor) collective efficacy was also modestly predicted by ethnic diversity ($r = .31, p = .000$), despite the fact that Asian respondents generally reported stronger collective efficacy than other ethnic groups. Pakistani and Bangladeshi respondents, on average, assessed their areas as half a standard deviation stronger in collective efficacy than their British neighbours (the same relationship held for Indian respondents, but to a lesser degree). Closer examination showed that Asian and British assessments of collective efficacy diverged as area concentrations of Asian residents increased, with British respondents reporting increasingly poorer collective efficacy, and Asian respondents reporting increasingly stronger collective efficacy, until the Asian population became an ethnic majority, at which point British respondents' assessments improved. One possible explanation could be the differential involvement of British and Asian respondents in local social networks and their differential perception of the trustworthiness and readiness for common action of residents of different ethnic background. Recent research on interethnic relations and social capital in segregated communities supports the idea that ethnically heterogeneous communities display lower levels of social capital due to a lack of social interaction between members of different ethnic groups (Laurence 2011; Putnam 2007). Ethnic minorities tend to have strong social ties *within* their ethnic groups which do not extend to other neighbouring residents. This hypothesis is supported by our finding that Asian respondents reported much more social interaction with neighbours in areas with a high Asian concentration compared to British respondents in those same areas, and much less interaction in areas with a low Asian concentration.

### Family disruption

Along with disadvantage, residential instability, and population heterogeneity, which are all seen to influence collective efficacy, Sampson (1987, 1993) has highlighted family disruption as an important area characteristic, for its particular influence on the informal social control of young people. Family disruption refers to the fragmentation of a traditional two-parent household due to separation, divorce, or the absence of a parent. Having fewer adults per household with children reduces the potential for supervision at home as well as in the wider community (Sampson 1987).[12]

---

[12] This effect may be larger for poorer households, as more affluent families may be more able to offset this reduction by, for example, employing child care providers.

In Peterborough in 2001, single-parent families made up one-quarter of all households with dependent children. These families were concentrated in areas that exhibit other important features of segregation. There was a very strong correlation between area concentration of lone parents families and social disadvantage ($r = .72$, $p = .000$). Lone parent families often have less social and financial capital, which feeds into area disadvantage; on the other hand, area disadvantage may increase family conflict and instability, increasing the likelihood of disruption (Loeber and Stouthamer-Loeber 1986; McNulty and Bellair 2003; Sampson 1986, 1987).

Previous research has also found a link between family disruption and ethnicity. For example, McNulty and Bellair (2003) reported that lone-parent families were more common among certain ethnic minority groups (eg African Americans, Hispanic Americans, and Native Americans) than others (eg Asian Americans). Peterborough's ethnic minority population is predominately Asian and, consistent with McNulty and Bellair's findings, the concentration of lone-parent families in Peterborough was only marginally significantly related to area ethnic diversity ($r = .09$, $p = .048$) and not significantly related to Asian concentration ($r = -.07$, $n.s.$).

There was a strong relationship between lone-parent households and (poor) collective efficacy ($r = .59$, $p = .000$), supporting Sampson's argument that this variable is a key predictor. However, this relationship may have been driven in part by the link between lone-parent families and disadvantage. In Figure 4.6, we can see that high concentrations of lone-parent families almost exclusively occurred in areas with greater social disadvantage, and these areas tended also to have poor collective efficacy. Lone-parent families are not included in subsequent models predicting collective efficacy because of the strong correlation with social disadvantage.

### 4.3.5 Structural antecedents of collective efficacy

The basic idea behind the concept of collective efficacy is that it is more difficult to create social cohesion and effective social control in areas where people experience disadvantage (ie have few social and economic resources), ethnic diversity, and residential instability. A multiple OLS model (Table 4.3) shows that the three main area structural features were all significant predictors of area variations in (poor) collective efficacy (together explaining about half the variance).

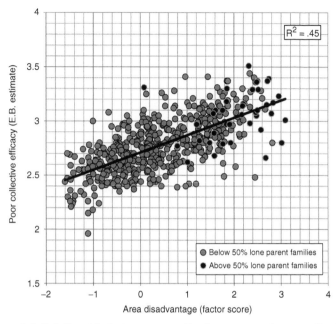

**Figure 4.6  Relationship between area disadvantage and poor collective efficacy showing area concentrations of lone parent families**

**Table 4.3  OLS regression of output area poor collective efficacy[a] predicted by structural characteristics (N = 518 output areas)**

|  | b | t | Beta | Prob. |
|---|---|---|---|---|
| Social disadvantage (factor score) | .16 | 19.6 | .61 | .000 |
| Residential instability (log) | .05 | 6.1 | .19 | .000 |
| Ethnic diversity | .05 | 5.8 | .18 | .000 |
| Multiple R² x 100 = 52.0 | | | | |

[a] Empirical Bayes estimate.

The most important structural factor influencing collective efficacy was area disadvantage. If entered alone into the model, it would explain 45 per cent of the variance between output areas. This finding corroborates those of many other studies which have also found social disadvantage (or deprivation) has the most detrimental effects on collective efficacy or related measures of social capital

(Friedrichs and Oberwittler 2007; Laurence 2011; Ross et al. 2001; Sampson et al. 1997; Sampson and Wikström 2008).

Residential instability, too, had a significant effect on collective efficacy, although it was only one-third as influential as social disadvantage. Output areas in which more residents had lived in the area for less than one year scored lower on collective efficacy. Ethnic diversity had an effect on collective efficacy of roughly the same magnitude as residential instability; the more ethnically mixed an output area, the weaker its collective efficacy. Thus areas with no or very few Asian residents, as well as areas with predominantly Asian residents, scored higher on collective efficacy than areas with ethnically mixed populations.

### 4.3.6 Land use and collective efficacy

We have already considered some of the key structural features of areas dominated by residential land use, such as population disadvantage, turnover, and heterogeneity, which purportedly affect the moral context via their influence on social cohesion and control. It has been suggested that non-residential land use may also have an impact on these social processes (see, eg, Gardiner 1978; Kurtz et al. 1998; Sampson 1987; Taylor 1995; and Wilcox et al. 2004); for example, public venues like schools, shopping or entertainment centres may increase the number of people in an area, which can interfere with monitoring and area cohesion, reducing informal social control. Non-residential land use also potentially contributes more to a criminogenic social context via its impact on what kinds of people it attracts, and the opportunities and frictions it presents. The fact that non-residential land use in Peterborough[13] was barely significantly related to area collective efficacy ($r = .09$, $p = .034$) indicates that poor collective efficacy among residents and non-residential land use (as a marker of the presence of commercial and entertainment activities and their related social consequences) are two largely independent dimensions of social conditions purportedly affecting an area's moral context.

---

[13] Output area level data on non-residential land use, ie the proportion of the built environment which is non-residential, was provided from the Generalised Land Use Database 2005 (compiled by the Office of the Deputy Prime Minister, later the Department for Communities and Local Government), which relied heavily upon Ordinance Survey Mastermap to classify topographic information on every landscape feature (see Department for Communities and Local Government 2007).

## 4.4 Area patterns of crime and disorder

Differences in the organization of urban social life 'are of great importance criminologically' (Bottoms and Wiles 1997: 306). Land use and residential segregation have both been posited as social contextual factors that influence area rates of crime and disorder (see, eg, Baldwin and Bottoms 1976; P. L. Brantingham and Brantingham 1981; Chilton 1964; Pratt and Cullen 2005; Rhodes and Conly 1981; Wikström 1991). Here we consider if these relationships hold true in Peterborough, at the small area (output area) level.

### 4.4.1 Disorder

Disorder refers to a visible deterioration in the physical state of an area and the social behaviour of those within it (for example graffiti, broken windows, litter; aggressive or threatening behaviour, public intoxication, open solicitation) (Sampson and Raudenbush 1999: 604). It serves as an indicator of how an area is used and how effective its residents are at maintaining or improving their environment. Crime and disorder are closely related (Skogan 1990; Wikström and Dolmen 2001). The 'broken windows' hypothesis suggests that disorder attracts crime to an area because it signals a lack of control, eg an unwillingness among residents to confront strangers or intervene in misconduct (Kelling and Coles 1996; J. Q. Wilson and Kelling 1982). An alternate hypothesis is that rather than a cause of crime, disorder is 'part and parcel of crime itself'; both are 'manifestations of the same explanatory process, albeit at different ends of a "seriousness" continuum' (Sampson and Raudenbush 1999: 608; see also Taylor 2001). Like crime, disorder can be seen as actions, or evidence of actions, that break rules of conduct. In fact, levels of disorder could provide a more discernible and reliable measure of the level of rule-breaking than crime itself, which is much more sporadic (Sampson and Raudenbush 1999).

The measures of disorder were derived from a principal component analysis (oblimin rotation) of selected items in the PCS questionnaire (Table 4.4). Respondents were asked (1) whether they thought there was a problem in their neighbourhood with various forms of physical disorder and disorderly behaviour, such as litter, unsupervised children, vandalism, and drug dealing;[14] and (2) the

---

[14] Response categories: No, no problem at all (doesn't exist or is uncommon); Yes, somewhat of a problem (it is quite common); Yes, a big problem (it is very common).

**Table 4.4 Principal component analysis of PCS items related to disorder (N = 518 output areas)**

| | Factor 1 (36.6%): Disorder | Factor 2 (8.2%): Drug dealing and prostitution | Factor 3 (6.4%): Formal social control | Extraction |
|---|---|---|---|---|
| Would you say that in your neighbourhood there is a problem with... | | | | |
| Litter in streets and public places | .63 | | | .38 |
| Run-down buildings and poorly maintained open space | .49 | | | .38 |
| People driving dangerously | .62 | | | .38 |
| Unsupervised children who hang about in streets and parks | .84 | | | .64 |
| Young people who show disrespect to adults | .85 | | | .68 |
| People who cause problems for or disturb their neighbours | .66 | | | .51 |
| People who are drunk and misbehave in public places | .63 | | | .56 |
| People being harassed or attacked in public places | .58 | .38 | | .60 |
| Vandalism | .73 | | | .53 |
| People using narcotic drugs | .49 | .45 | | .62 |
| People carrying weapons | .44 | .49 | | .56 |
| Houses / flats in which drug dealing takes place | .40 | .52 | | .58 |
| Drug dealing that openly occurs in public places | .30 | .62 | | .61 |
| Houses / flats in which females sell sex for money | | .81 | | .63 |
| Females who openly sell sex for money in public places | | .81 | | .61 |

*(continued)*

**Table 4.4** *(Continued)*

|  | Factor 1 (36.6%): Disorder | Factor 2 (8.2%): Drug dealing and prostitution | Factor 3 (6.4%): Formal social control | Extraction |
|---|---|---|---|---|
| When was the last time you saw in your neighbourhood… | | | | |
| Someone driving dangerously | **.56** | | | .37 |
| A group of unsupervised children | **.67** | | | .46 |
| Young persons showing disrespect to an adult | **.74** | | | .60 |
| A drunken person | **.57** | | | .51 |
| Someone harassing or attacking another person | **.50** | | | .50 |
| Someone destroying or damaging property | **.63** | | | .48 |
| Someone carrying a weapon | .32 | **.35** | | .38 |
| Someone dealing drugs | | **.47** | | .45 |
| A prostitute soliciting | | **.64** | | .45 |
| A police car | | | **.63** | .46 |
| A police officer on foot | | | **.73** | .57 |
| A community support officer or street warden | | | **.71** | .53 |
| A private security officer | | | **.53** | .28 |

last time they saw particular signs of disorder or the presence of police or security officers in their neighbourhoods.[15] Three factors were extracted (with an eigenvalue above one) interpreted as (1) disorder, (2) drug dealing and prostitution, and (3) formal social control (the latter of which we do not deal with in this book).

Disorder was concentrated in particular areas of the city (eg Ravensthorpe, Orton Goldhay and Malborne, Millfield and New England, Paston/Welland). There was only a comparably moderate level of disorder in the city centre, which may be explained by the

---

[15] Response categories: Today or yesterday; Last week; Last month; Last year; More than a year ago; Never.

fact that the most defining items of this factor referred mainly to youth-related problems, which residents in the city centre may have been less likely to report, as there is considerable movement of young people (as well as adults) in and out of this setting, the majority of which is unproblematic (see Figure 4.7).

Drug dealing and prostitution, on the other hand, are highly concentrated around the north of the city centre and the city's other key entertainment district to the east, and uncommon elsewhere (although slightly more prevalent in parts of Orton and Ravensthorpe) (Figure 4.7).

### 4.4.2 Crime

Beginning with Shaw and McKay ([1942] 1969), an extensive body of research has evidenced the link between urban area rates of crime and characteristics of segregation and land use across diverse urban environments, from major US cities to European capitals to UK urban centres (see, eg, Baldwin and Bottoms 1976; Chilton 1964; Sampson and Groves 1989; Shaw and McKay [1942] 1969; Wikström 1991; Wikström and Dolmen 2001). Initially, the study of urban crime focused on the concentration of *offenders* in particular urban areas; less attention was paid to the concentration of *offences* (Baldwin and Bottoms 1976; Wikström 1991: 191). In the mid-1970s, however, the offence was 'rediscovered', with subsequent research revealing significant area variations in offence patterns, including rates and types of crime, which differ from offender patterns (see, eg, Baldwin and Bottoms 1976; Boggs 1965; Pyle et al. 1974; Schmid 1960a, 1960b; Wikström 1991). The difference between the distribution of crimes and offenders is addressed in section 5.3.

Contemporary research on crime 'hotspots' evidences the disproportionate geographical distribution of crime, albeit often at a smaller ecological level (see, eg, Sherman et al. 1989; Sherman and Weisburd 1995; Weisburd et al. 2009). For example, hotspots research has demonstrated the extreme concentration of crime at a very small number of locations (Roncek 2000; Weisburd et al. 2004; Weisburd et al. 2009; Wikström 1985). Sherman, Gartin, and Buerger (1989: 37) found that 50.4 per cent of police calls in Minneapolis in 1986 originated from 3.3 per cent of all addresses or intersections. Calls for predatory crimes were especially concentrated (calls for robbery came from 2.2 per cent of all addresses, calls for rape from 1.2 per cent, and calls for car theft from 2.7 per cent)

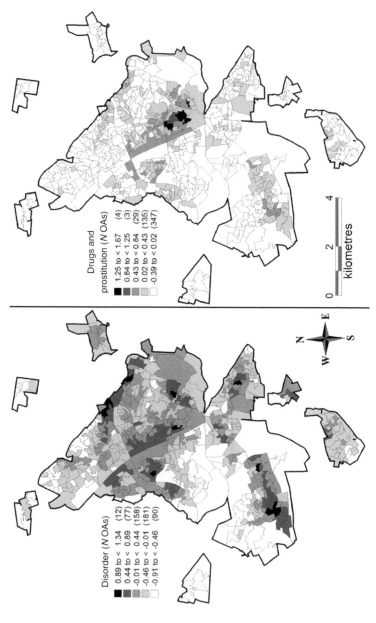

**Figure 4.7　Spatial distribution of disorder (left) and drug dealing and prostitution (right)**

(ibid.: 39). More 'private' crimes were also concentrated, with calls for domestic disturbances originating from 9 per cent of all addresses, calls for assault from 7 per cent of all addresses, and calls for burglary from 11 per cent of all addresses (ibid.: 41).

For a mid-sized, south eastern UK city—characteristics generally associated with a lower rate of crime—Peterborough has an unexpectedly high crime rate (Parkinson et al. 2006: 136). In this chapter we analyse selected crime categories committed by people of all ages (crimes by young people will be specifically analysed in chapter 5) between 2003 and 2007. The included crimes cover violence, vandalism, arson, burglaries, thefts of and from cars, and shoplifting (consistent with those self-reported in the PADS+ questionnaire[16]). There were 93,666 such crimes reported to the police in the study area between 2003 and 2007 (Table 4.5).

As Figure 4.8[17] shows, the majority of crimes in Peterborough were concentrated in several key areas (the Gini coefficient[18] is .46).

**Table 4.5  Police-recorded crimes[a] in the Peterborough study area 2003–07**

| Category | Detail | N |
|---|---|---|
| Vandalism | Residential, non-residential, vehicle, and other criminal damage; arson; arson endangering life | 30,889 |
| Violence | Robbery, grievous bodily harm (GBH), actual bodily harm (ABH), wounding, affray, common assault, violent disorder, possession of weapons | 22,741 |
| Shoplifting | | 7,218 |
| Vehicle crime | Theft of a car, unauthorized taking of a vehicle, theft from a car | 18,101 |
| Burglary | Residential and non-residential | 14,717 |
| Total | | 93,666 |

[a] Of crime types equivalent to those self-reported in PADS+.

[16] Thefts from a person were not included as it was impossible to determine which police-recorded acts of theft matched this self-report category.

[17] For details on how kernel density estimation maps in this book are created see technical appendix, section A1.2.2.

[18] The Gini coefficient ($G$) is a measure of statistical dispersion ranging from 0 to 1, where 0 suggests a completely equal dispersion, and 1 suggests a maximally disparate dispersion. It is calculated as the ratio of the area between the line of perfect equality and the Lorenz curve (a cumulative distribution function of the empirical probability distribution).

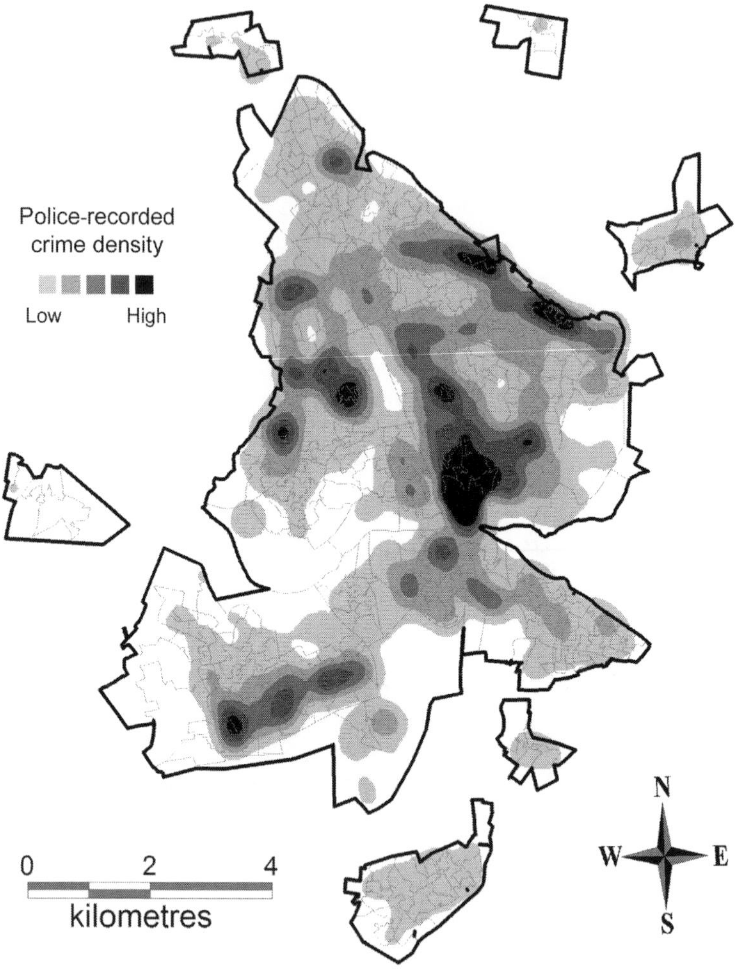

Figure 4.8  **Relative density of police-recorded crimes (N = 93,666)**[a]

[a] On kernel density estimation maps see technical appendix, section A.1.2.2.

The greatest concentration was in and around the city centre. There were also concentrations in three other areas of the city, namely in parts of the Ortons in the south west, Bretton in the midwest, and Paston in the north east. Concentrations could also be seen around local centres, such as Werrington Centre to the north. A comparison of the distribution of crime across the study area for each year (2003–07) revealed no major differences in the locations of the main hotspots (ie places of crime concentrations) (year-to-year rank correlations range from .77 to .87, all $p = .000$). This is consistent with Weisburd et al. (2004) and Groff et al. (2010), who found that most crime hotspots were stable over time.

### 4.4.3 The relationship between crime and disorder

The distribution of crime in Peterborough was strongly related to that of disorder ($r = .54$, $p = .000$) (Figure 4.9), which is consistent with previous research showing a link between the two, including a recent ecological study in Edinburgh (ESYTC, A. M. Brown 2004; see also; Sampson and Raudenbush 1999; Wikström and Dolmen 2001; J. Q. Wilson and Kelling 1982). An analysis of outliers (to three standard deviations) showed that six output areas had considerably more crime than expected based on their level of public disorder. For five it is easy to find an explanation. Three of these areas were in the city centre, one was in the Hampton Centre, and one contained a large entertainment complex (including a pub, theatre, cinema, swimming pool, and leisure centre). The major discrepancy in crime incidents in these areas involved

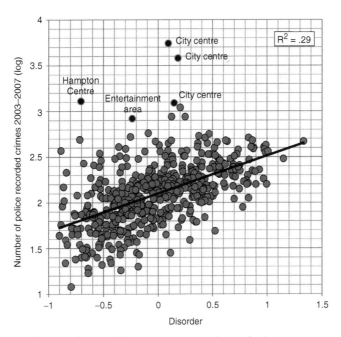

**Figure 4.9 The relationship between disorder and crime**

acts of shoplifting (which is not a form of disorder), which represented 31.3 per cent of crimes in outlier areas, but only 3.9 per cent of crimes in other areas.

### 4.4.4 Residential segregation, disorder, and crime

Disorder and crime have been discussed both as a cause and an outcome of residential structural characteristics (Skogan 1990; Taub et al. 1984). Disorder and crime may, for example, increase fear of crime, leading to withdrawal from community life, which reduces cohesion and control, and potentially residential instability and changes in the population composition as residents emigrate (Skogan 1986). On the other hand, area structural characteristics such as disadvantage, residential instability, and population heterogeneity may also reduce social control and cohesion, leading to a potential increase in rates of crime and disorder (Raudenbush and Sampson 1999; Sampson and Raudenbush 1999).

#### Social disadvantage, disorder, and crime

Sociological and criminological research suggests that areas that suffer from high concentrations of multiple forms of disadvantage also suffer from high concentrations of crime (Sampson et al. 2002: 446; see also A. M. Brown 2004). Vélez (2001: 850), for example, found that areas with high levels of disadvantage had 1.5 to 6 times the victimization rates of areas with low levels of disadvantage (see also Kennedy and Forde 1990; Miethe and McDowall 1993; Miethe and Meier 1994; Sampson and Wooldredge 1987; D. A. Smith and Jarjoura 1989).

There is evidence that the relationship between area disadvantage and crime rates is more robust for more serious crimes, while minor forms of crime are more widely dispersed (Oberwittler 2004: 213). Hipp (2007: 679) found that concentrated disadvantage was related to rates of violent, but not property, crimes. Other studies have evidenced that the quality of violent crimes may differ in disadvantaged neighbourhoods (in, for example, the degree of injury, the presence of a weapon, and the response of the victim; see, eg, Baumer et al. 2003). Disadvantage has also been linked to violent recidivism; Mears et al. (2008: 322) found that the disadvantage of the county into which individuals were released after prison was significantly related to their subsequent violent, but not their property, crime.

In Peterborough, area disadvantage was very strongly related to disorder ($r = .75$, $p = .000$), but not so strongly related to drug dealing and prostitution ($r = .34$, $p = .000$), arguably because this latter kind of disorder was generally concentrated in the city centre, which has low disadvantage. This is comparable to findings for the Edinburgh Community Survey, which found that deprivation was strongly related to a measure of general disorder (A. M. Brown 2004). In Peterborough, disadvantage was also strongly related to crime (logged; $r = .48$, $p = .000$), as was found in Edinburgh (A. M. Brown 2004). Our findings also show that it was most strongly related to rates of violence (logged; $r = .53$, $p = .000$) and vandalism (logged; $r = .59$, $p = .000$), and only moderately related to car crime and burglary ($r = .27$ and $.30$, respectively, $p = .000$) and not related to shoplifting ($r = .06$, n.s.).

### Residential instability, disorder, and crime

Residential instability and low rates of home ownership correlate consistently with problem behaviours (Brooks-Gunn et al. 1997). Osgood and Chambers (2000: 102) found that even in a non-metropolitan sample, residential instability was significantly associated with rape, simple and aggravated assault, weapons violations, and violent crime generally, and Markowitz et al. (2001: 304) found a similar relationship with area rates of disorder. Morenoff and Sampson (1997) found that both crime rates in a given area, and crime rates in adjacent areas, predicted residential instability. Victimization has also been linked to residential instability (J. B. Cullen and Levitt 1999; Liska and Bellair 1995; Sampson and Wooldredge 1987; Taylor 1995; Xie and McDowall 2008), although this effect may differ by crime type. In the Edinburgh Neighbourhood Survey, Brown (2004) found a relationship between residents' neighbourhood satisfaction (a measure of whether they liked their neighbourhood or would like to live elsewhere) was strongly related to area crime rates and very strongly related to area incivilities (a measure of general disorder).

We found that residential instability in Peterborough was weakly related to disorder ($r = .12$, $p = .006$), and drug dealing and prostitution ($r = .18$, $p = .000$), but more strongly related to crime (logged; $r = .33$, $p = .000$). The relationship between residential instability, social disadvantage, and other structural variables in the explanation of area crime rates are modelled in section 4.5.

### Population heterogeneity, disorder, and crime

Population heterogeneity can be measured using indicators of concentration (dissimilarity measures[19]) or composition (diversity measures) at the area level. Both types of measures have been linked to area rates of violent and property crimes (see, eg, Hipp 2007; Markowitz et al. 2001; McNulty and Holloway 2000; Osgood and Chambers 2000). Some studies suggest the relationship between area concentrations of different minority groups and crime and disorder may reflect different social mechanisms (see, eg, Haynie and Payne 2006; McNulty and Bellair 2003; Mears et al. 2008; Parker 2001: 102).

In Peterborough, ethnic diversity was modestly related to disorder ($r = .31$, $p = .000$), and strongly related to drug dealing and prostitution ($r = .49$, $p = .000$), although this latter relationship may be an artefact of the concentration of ethnic minority groups near the city centre, where drug dealing and prostitution were particularly prevalent. Ethnic diversity was also modestly related to crime (logged; $r = .38$, $p = .000$). Ethnic diversity was more strongly related to both crime and disorder than an ethnic dissimilarity measure based on the percentage of Asian residents, which was only moderately related to general disorder ($r = .24$, $p = .000$), although more strongly related to drugs and prostitution ($r = .44$, $p = .000$), and only modestly related to crime (logged; $r = .23$, $p = .000$).

### Lone-parent families, disorder, and crime

Area rates of family disruption have been positively related to area rates of disorder and crime (Markowitz et al. 2001: 304; Osgood and Chambers 2000). Sampson and Groves (1989: 790) found that family disruption had indirect effects on victimization via unsupervised peer groups. Osgood and Chambers (2000: 103) found that family disruption, measured as female-headed households, was a strong predictor of violent crimes (except homicide); a 13 per cent increase in area rates of family disruption predicted twice as many violent crimes. Smith et al. (2001: 507) found that the number of single-parent households was related to an increase in an area's robbery rate. Hipp (2007: 681) found that family disruption was

---

[19] In some countries (eg the United States), the distribution of specific minority groups may be of particular interest, while in others (eg many European countries) factors such as immigrant status may be more relevant (see Sampson and Wikström 2008, eg, on 'outgroups').

linked to rates of all crime types, although the relationship was weakest for murder.

Parker and Johns (2002) found that family 'diversification' (non-married or female-headed households, or households in which children were not living with both parents) was positively related to acquaintance, stranger, and total white homicide rates, and yet negatively related to acquaintance and family-related homicide among African Americans. Although this seems contrary to expectations, the authors argue that family diversification is the urban norm for African Americans, and is supported by extended kinship ties. Similarly, they found that divorce was related to white, but not black, homicide rates. This is similar to Peterson and Krivo's (1993: 1011) finding that marital dissolution is not related to African American homicide rates, but does not accord with Sampson's (1987) finding that black family disruption significantly affected rates of black murder and robbery, especially among young people. Parker (2001: 102–3) found that divorce significantly predicted rates of family homicide among blacks as well as whites.

In Peterborough, area concentrations of lone-parent families were strongly related to disorder ($r = .55, p = .000$), but less strongly related to drug dealing and prostitution ($r = .24, p = .000$). The concentration of lone-parent families was clearly related to crime (logged; $r = .41, p = .000$). Unlike many US studies, in Peterborough the strength of the relationship between the concentration of lone-parent families and area rates of violent crime was not particularly different from that of all crime ($r = .42, p = .000$).

## Collective efficacy, disorder, and crime

There is consistent empirical support that the link between structural characteristics and crime is mediated by social disorganization/collective efficacy. A number of studies utilizing large-scale community surveys support this proposed relationship using various measures of crime and disorder (eg Oberwittler 2004; Sampson and Groves 1989; Sampson et al. 1997; Sampson and Wikström 2008; Wikström et al. 1997; Wikström and Dolmen 2001).

The relationship between collective efficacy and area rates of violent crime seems particularly robust. Sampson, Raudenbush, and Earls (1997) found that collective efficacy was strongly related to violence, largely mediated the link between concentrated disadvantage and residential instability and violence, and fully mediated the link between immigrant concentration and violence. A cross-national comparison by Sampson and Wikström (2008: 112) found that collective efficacy was negatively related to rates of violent crime in both Chicago and Stockholm. Morenoff, Sampson, and Raudenbush (2001) linked area levels of collective efficacy to area levels of police-recorded homicide and homicide victimization. An earlier study by Sampson and Raudenbush (1999) also linked collective efficacy to area rates of homicide, as well as burglary, robbery, and victimization.

In Peterborough, collective efficacy was very strongly related to disorder ($r = .77, p = .000$), and strongly related to drug dealing and prostitution ($r = .43, p = .000$). It was also strongly related to police-recorded crime (logged; $r = .52$, $p = .000$), making it a stronger predictor of disorder and crime than most structural variables. In earlier analyses we showed that structural characteristics (especially social disadvantage) strongly predicted collective efficacy (see Table 4.3). In section 4.5 we look at how collective efficacy mediates the relationship between structural characteristics and crime rates at the output area level. First, we consider the relationship between land use and crime and disorder.

### 4.4.5 Land use, disorder, and crime

Particular routine activities are linked to crime because they bring certain kinds of people into certain kinds of settings and provide different opportunities and frictions, creating situations to which people may respond with acts of crime and disorder. Land use is a marker of routine activities, and therefore one would expect a relationship between particular kinds of land use and crime and disorder. Pratt and Cullen (2005) conducted a meta-analysis on existing studies and found only moderate empirical support for routine activity theory, but as it is generally studied at the aggregate level using inadequate proxies for routine activities (such as demographics; see, for example, Cohen et al. 1980), when it should in fact be tested at the situational level (Eck 1995), it is impossible to draw firm conclusions about its soundness. Some studies, however, have used land use as a proxy for routines, with arguably more validity and success (eg Felson 1987; Rhodes and Conly 1981). In fact, the dynamic aspects of routine activity theory—how societal routines lead to the convergence of offenders and targets (in the absence of) guardianship, and how that convergence leads to crime—have rarely been properly tested (Bursik and Grasmick 1993: 89; but see Wikström et al. 2010).

Empirically, land use has been linked to area rates of crime and disorder. Higher rates of crime are related to areas characterized by commercial businesses (LaGrange 1999; W. R. Smith et al. 2000; Stucky and Ottensmann 2009: 1240), schools (LaGrange 1999), parks and recreational land (E. Groff and McCord 2011; Lockwood 2007; Wilcox et al. 2004), industrial areas (Lockwood 2007; although others have suggested industrial areas are linked to lower rates of crime; see Felson 1987), and dense residential areas (Stucky and Ottensmann 2009: 1240). Regardless of neighbourhoods' sociodemographics, Sampson and Raudenbush (1999: 624) found that those with mixed residential and commercial land use showed higher disorder.

Some argue that non-residential land use interferes with informal social control by increasing the number of people and cars and the presence of strangers, hindering differentiation of residents and 'outsiders' (see, eg, Gardiner 1978; Kurtz et al. 1998; Taylor et al. 1995; Wilcox et al. 2004). Findings in support of this show a relationship between factors such as commercial land use and population density and rates of crime and disorder (eg Peterson and Krivo 1993; Wilcox et al. 2004). However, Wilcox et al. (2004) suggest this relationship may depend on other structural characteristics, such as residential instability.

Stucky and Ottensman (2009: 1237) found that all types of violent crime were highest in commercial areas with high disadvantage, and lowest in non-commercial areas with low disadvantage. Robbery was significantly higher than the mean in commercial areas with low disadvantage, while homicide was significantly higher than the mean in non-commercial areas with high disadvantage, suggesting that the presence of commercial businesses helps to drive robbery, while homicide, which tends to occur between acquaintances, is more strongly related to area disadvantage (ibid.: 1237).

As area disadvantage increases, the effect of dense housing on area violence decreases (Stucky and Ottensmann 2009: 1241). Similarly, as area disadvantage increases, the relationship between the concentration of major roads and violent crime decreases (ibid.: 1247). In areas with high disadvantage, the concentration of commercial land use ceases to have an effect on rates of violence (ibid.: 1245), while the concentration of industrial land use blunts the relationship between disadvantage and violence (ibid.: 1246).

Research has linked 'public entertainment settings' to violence in particular (see, eg, Block and Block 1995; Curtis 1974: 143–5;

Downes 1958: 145; Eisner and Wikström 1999; G. Hughes 2011; McClintock 1963: 40; McClintock and Wikström 1992; Nelson et al. 2001; Roncek and Maier 1991; Wikström 1985, 1991). Smith et al. (2000: 507–8) found that bars, restaurants, gas stations, or hotels in an area increased the rate of robbery. Lockwood (2007) also found a relationship between robbery and 'recreational' land use.

In Peterborough, non-residential land use was not strongly related to disorder ($r = .14$, $p = .001$), and was only slightly more strongly related to drug dealing and prostitution ($r = .24$, $p = .000$), the latter most likely being an effect of drug dealing and prostitution being centred around entertainment settings, such as the city centre. However, non-residential land showed a strong relationship to crime ($r = .57$, $p = .000$). Recall that crime shows a stronger concentration in the city centre than disorder (compare Figures 4.7 and 4.8; and see also Figure 4.9).

## 4.5  Modelling population structure, collective efficacy, land use, and crime events

So far we have considered the relationship between crime and key residential structural characteristics and land use variables separately; we conclude this chapter by modelling their roles in the occurrence of crime events. We specifically test whether residential area population disadvantage, heterogeneity, and turnover predict the level of (poor) collective efficacy, and whether (poor) collective efficacy, in turn, together with the independent influence of non-residential land use (as a marker for commercial and entertainment environments), are the main predictors of area variation in the frequency of crime events.

### 4.5.1  Path modelling technique

To analyse the spatial distribution of police-recorded crimes by all age groups in Peterborough during the study period (2003–07) we computed a series of analogous negative binomial path models for different categories of crime (total crime, violent crime, vandalism including arson, serious property crimes, and shoplifting). These models integrate standard linear regression and non-linear Poisson regression within a single model, making it possible to have both normally distributed continuous variables as well as highly skewed count variables as dependent (endogenous) variables without violating assumptions of classic regression analysis. This feature is available in Mplus 5 (see Muthén and Muthén 2009). To interpret the path coefficients, it is therefore essential to distinguish those that follow the 'normal' metric of a linear regression analysis from those that follow the logistic metric of a Poisson regression. This distinction falls between the part of the models covering path coefficients directed towards the endogenous variable 'poor collective efficacy', and the part of the models covering path coefficients directed towards the crime outcomes. Whereas the former coefficients (directed towards poor collective efficacy) are in standard linear metric and are identical across all output area level path models (in this and subsequent chapters, with the only exception being the path model predicting offender home locations[20]), the latter coefficients (directed towards different crime outcomes) are in logistic metric and are different across models according to different crime outcomes. Table 4.6 summarizes all path models; the linear path coefficients (directed towards poor collective efficacy) are reported in the first column, and subsequent columns report divergent logistic path coefficients for each model with different crime outcomes.

All path coefficients reported are unstandardized. However, because all predictors—including poor collective efficacy—are z-standardized, the linear path coefficients from the exogenous variables directed towards poor collective efficacy are identical to standardized beta coefficients in an OLS regression. For the logistic path coefficients, we additionally report exp(b)—the odds ratio—below the raw coefficients from the Mplus output. Because the crime distribution across output areas is highly skewed, we employ negative binomial regression for the paths directed towards crime accounting for overdispersion (Long and Freese 2006: 372).

Non-significant coefficients ($p > .05$) have been removed from the models, which have been run again without these coefficients to increase the precision of estimates. We did not include any control variables for population or area size, as output areas have been designed to be fairly even in terms of population size; as a result the resident population does not vary dramatically between output areas, and hence cannot account for large differences in crime volumes

[20] There is a marginal difference in the value of these coefficients because all output areas were not included due to a lack of resident young people in some output areas.

(which from our theoretical viewpoint cannot be the case anyway; see technical appendix, section A1.3). For example, it is well known from spatial crime analysis that the resident population cannot represent the much bigger transient population in the city centre (Andresen 2006; Wikström 1991: 194). However, in order to test the robustness of our results, we also ran models with the resident population as a control variable. There were no significant differences in the coefficients. The significance of differences between models without and with population control was measured by computing the lower and upper margins of confidence intervals at $p = .05$ and testing whether there was a lack of overlap between coefficients.

### 4.5.2 Findings from the path analyses

The findings of the path analysis for total crimes show that area poor collective efficacy predicted the frequency of crime events at the output area level, and that a significant part of the effect of the population structural variables (social disadvantage, ethnic diversity, and residential stability) on crime, particularly in regards to area social disadvantage, were mediated through their impact on an area's level of (poor) collective efficacy. The path analysis also demonstrates that non-residential land use had a strong effect on an area's frequency of crime events independent of its level of (poor) collective efficacy (Figure 4.10).

As previously discussed (see section 4.3.4), higher levels of social disadvantage, heterogeneity, and turnover may impede social and moral integration among area residents. For example, it may be difficult to generate social cohesion (ie social and moral integration among residents) in areas in which personal and institutional resources are lacking; significant groups of residents experience personal and social problems (eg mental health, alcohol, and drugs problems) and are more seriously involved in crime; residents come from many different cultural backgrounds; and residents face frequent changes in their neighbours. As a consequence, it may be difficult for residents to learn to trust one another. If there is a lack of trust (and even fear) among residents, this may discourage them from intervening (eg personally or by summoning the police) when confronted with acts of disorder and crime. The relationship between an area's poor collective efficacy and the frequency of crime events is thus likely to reflect variations between residential

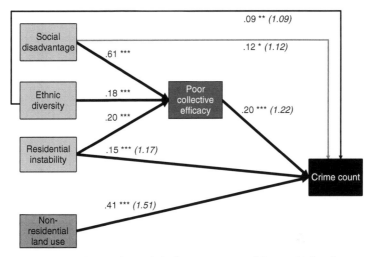

**Figure 4.10 Mplus path model of area structural features, land use, collective efficacy, and crime[a,b]**

[a] Odds ratios in brackets; paths to poor collective efficacy in metric scale; paths to crime in logarithmic scale.
[b] Significance level: *** $p < .001$, ** $p < .01$, * $p < .05$.

areas in the efficacy of informal social control as a consequence of residents' degree of social and moral integration (ie social cohesion). Residential areas with poor collective efficacy may be seen as environments whose moral context may entice (or fail to deter) people from responding to temptations and provocations with acts of crime.

Non-residential land use was a strong predictor of the frequency of crime events. As crime was highly concentrated in the city centre (and to a lesser degree in local centres), where commercial and recreational land use were concentrated, this finding does not come as a surprise, because this is essentially what our measure of non-residential land use captures. Areas of commerce and entertainment are likely (at least at particular times of the day and week) to produce particularly high levels of temptations (in the case of commercial areas) and provocations (in the case of entertainment areas) in moral contexts that may be particularly criminogenic. Commercial and entertainment centres generally attract a large number of temporary visitors who are mostly strangers and, particularly for larger centres that draw people from a wider area, may bring together people of different social and cultural backgrounds. Entertainment activities (such as those that take place in pubs and clubs) often involve those under the influence of alcohol and drugs under circumstances that at times may be particularly liable to cause friction. It is a reasonable assumption that the social and moral integration among people in such public environments may be rather low and that this may affect their willingness to exercise informal social control when confronted with acts of disorder and crime.[21]

Different subcategories of crime displayed somewhat different patterns of association with structural conditions (see Table 4.6). The only significant predictor of *shoplifting* was non-residential land use. The particular strength of this relationship compared to other crime types reflects the dependence of shoplifting on the extremely skewed distribution of shops within the city. However, this finding obscured the fact that shoplifting outside the city centre tended to occur in areas with poor collective efficacy (see section 5.1.1). A 'technical' reason for this is that the extreme concentration of commercial establishments in the city centre, coupled with the fact that most output areas outside the city centre, regardless of their level of collective efficacy, lacked shops, means that any stronger relationship between output area levels of (poor) collective efficacy and incidents of shoplifting are not to be expected.[22]

For all other crime types (violence, vandalism, and serious theft) both levels of non-residential land use and poor collective efficacy were significant predictors of the frequency of crime events. What differed among these crime categories was the extent to which the population structural variables, in addition to the effects mediated by poor collective efficacy, also directly predicted the frequency of crime events. For vandalism none of the population structural variables were significantly related to the frequency of crime events. For serious theft (burglaries and car crime) the frequency of crime events were significantly predicted by ethnic diversity and residential instability, but not social disadvantage. Finally all population structural variables significantly predicted the frequency of acts of violent crime. It is possible that the remaining (direct) effects of

---

[21] However, a group that may have a higher motivation to intervene in crime and disorder in centre areas are people who are employed in commercial and entertainment establishments.

[22] The same reasoning also applies to the lack of relationship between population structural variables and shoplifting (ie most areas lacked shops).

**Table 4.6 Mplus path models predicting counts of crime[a] per output area by crime type**

| | | Poor collective efficacy | All crimes[b] | Violent crime | Vandalism | Serious theft | Shoplifting |
|---|---|---|---|---|---|---|---|
| **Structural (exogenous)** | | | | | | | |
| Social disadvantage | Coefficient[c] | 0.61*** | 0.12* | 0.23*** | n.s. | n.s | n.s. |
| | Odds ratio | | 1.12 | 1.25 | | | |
| Ethnic diversity | Coefficient[c] | 0.18 *** | 0.09** | 0.14** | n.s. | 0.11** | n.s. |
| | Odds ratio | | 1.09 | 1.15 | | 1.11 | |
| Residential instability | Coefficient[c] | 0.20*** | 0.15*** | 0.16*** | n.s. | 0.16*** | n.s. |
| | Odds ratio | | 1.17 | 1.17 | | 1.17 | |
| Non-residential land use | Coefficient[c] | n.s. | 0.41*** | 0.55*** | 0.53*** | 0.33*** | 1.57*** |
| | Odds ratio | | 1.51 | 1.73 | 1.70 | 1.39 | 4.80 |
| **Mediating (endogenous)** | | | | | | | |
| Poor collective efficacy | Coefficient[c] | | 0.20*** | 0.20*** | 0.24* | 0.12*** | n.s. |
| | Odds ratio | | 1.22 | 1.22 | 1.27 | 1.12 | |

[a] Offences in Peterborough between January 2003 and December 2007.
[b] Police-recorded crime types equivalent to those self-reported in PADS+.
[c] Significance level: *** $p < .001$, ** $p < .01$, * $p < .05$.

the population variables (those not mediated by poor collective efficacy) partly reflect who spends time in different areas, eg the impact of the local supply of crime prone people.

All in all, the findings show that, overall:

(1)  areas with concentrations of commercial and entertainment settings, and
(2)  residential areas with poor collective efficacy

are the most criminogenic urban environments. The suggested explanation for this is that these environments (especially at particular times of the day and week) provide the kinds of moral contexts that may encourage crime prone people to break the law (or fail to discourage them from doing so) in response to particular temptations and provocations. The findings also clearly demonstrate

(3)  the dependency of area poor collective efficacy on population structural features, particularly social disadvantage.

Although these analyses clearly show the importance of the role of environmental features for predicting variation in and concentrations of crime events, we have yet to introduce another key component of the SAT model: the kinds of people present. Recall that Situational Action Theory predicts that different kinds of people will react differently to different kinds of environments (eg some people are vulnerable while others are resistant to criminogenic influences of their environments) and, therefore, that crime concentrations are most likely to occur at locations where the number of intersections between crime prone people and criminogenic settings is high. Hence we expect that taking into consideration who spends time in certain settings will help to further explain and specify the relationship between environmental features and the frequency of crime events.

## 4.6  Summary and conclusion

In this chapter we have introduced the research site of Peterborough, its history in brief, its main patterns of land use, and its patterns of residential segregation (according to social disadvantage, ethnic heterogeneity, and residential instability). Analysis of this urban structure suggests that the patterns of residential segregation in Peterborough are consistent with those observed elsewhere in the United Kingdom.

We then explored area variations in poor collective efficacy (one of our main measures of settings' moral contexts) and demonstrated that it was strongly related to area variations in disadvantage and family disruption (ie single-parent households). A multiple regression model showed that 52 per cent of the variance in poor collective efficacy was (statistically) explained by population structural variables (social disadvantage alone explained 45 per cent of the statistical variance in poor collective efficacy).

Next we introduced our area measures of disorder and police-recorded crime, which were strongly correlated, and illustrated their spatial distributions and concentrations. The role of the city centre as the main crime hot spot was clearly evident, although other dense concentrations appeared in residential areas with poor collective efficacy and local centres of Peterborough. The relationships between the area distributions of crime and disorder and the population structural variables, land use, and poor collective efficacy were largely as expected from previous social ecological research into crime and disorder. Crime and disorder were more common in areas with higher levels of population disadvantage, poor collective efficacy, and higher proportions of non-residential land use.

This chapter concluded with a structural equation model showing that non-residential land use (a marker for the presence of commercial enterprises and public entertainment) and poor collective efficacy (in that rank order) were the strongest predictors of the spatial variation in the overall levels of crime, and that the effects on crime of population structural variables (particularly the effect of social disadvantage) appeared to be mediated, to a large extent, through their influence on poor collective efficacy.

All in all, the findings indicate that crime events tend to be most frequent in areas in which the (law-relevant) moral context is the weakest, that is in areas where residents lack trust and, therefore, are reluctant to intervene when they observe breaches of common rules of conduct, and in areas of commerce and entertainment that bring together large numbers of strangers from different social backgrounds in circumstances that promote temptation (commercial enterprises) and provocation (entertainment activities) in moral contexts that may encourage (or fail to prevent) acts of crime.

Criminogenic environments affect people differently and the presence of people with different levels of crime propensity in a particular environment is likely to be of importance for its level of crime. In this analysis we have focused solely on how area variations in environmental characteristics relate to variations in crime. The basic patterns (and the processes they implicate) seem to be largely the same as demonstrated in previous US and European social ecological research into urban crime, although we used (for theoretical reasons) a small area unit of analysis (the output area, which is much smaller than the units commonly used; see section 2.8.2). In subsequent chapters (chapters 5 and 6) we will expand the analyses presented in this chapter by exploring the importance of the distribution of offenders' home location and people's activity fields for the explanation of urban crime patterns.

# 5

# Young Offenders and Their Crimes in the Urban Environment

Having introduced Peterborough (the research site), its key dimensions of residential segregation, how these relate to variations in area (poor) collective efficacy and, in turn, in conjunction with non-residential land use, predict variations in the levels of disorder and crime in Peterborough's urban environments (see chapter 4), we now return to the main topic of the book: young people, their crime involvement, and its explanation. The findings presented in chapter 4 provide the context against which we can analyse patterns of young people's urban crime in greater depth.

The key aims of this chapter are to:

(1) explore young people's urban crime patterns and statistically model the factors that predict area variation in and concentrations of young people's crime;

(2) explore area variation in and concentrations of young offenders' home locations (for both police-recorded and self-reported offenders) and assess to what extent this reflects area variations in the number of resident crime prone young people (ie young people with a weak law-relevant morality and poor ability to exercise self-control);

(3) statistically model what features of residential areas predict area variations in resident young offenders;

(4) investigate the relationship between young offenders' home locations and the locations of their acts of crime (generally referred to as the study of crime and distance).

We start by exploring (1) whether young people's crime patterns are similar to those of all offenders (see section 4.4.2 and Figure 4.8), and (2) whether a model predicting area variation in young people's crime frequency is similar to that predicting area variation in the crime frequency for all offenders (see section 4.5.2). There is no major reason to expect that the distribution of young people's crime, and its relationship to population structural and land use variables, would be very different from that for crime by all offenders. Any differences that may occur most likely stem from differences between young people's routine activities and those of older people (we specifically investigate young people's activity patterns and their relation to young people's patterns of crime in chapter 6).[1] One source of such differences is that with increasing age people's crimes (particularly crimes such as violence and vandalism) occur to a higher degree in private and domestic circumstances and, therefore, may show a stronger association with area population characteristics than young people's crimes (particularly cases of violence and vandalism), which are more likely to occur in public and semi-public spaces and, therefore, are more affected by public area features such as the level of (poor) collective efficacy.

Once we have described area patterns of young people's crime, we turn to exploring area patterns of resident young offenders and the extent to which they mirror the area distribution of crime prone young people (as measured by weak law-relevant morality and poor ability to exercise self-control). We have already demonstrated (see section 3.2.4) that young people with a higher crime propensity commit more acts of crime; therefore we would expect to find a relationship between area levels of crime prone young people and young offenders, particularly frequent and serious young offenders. In other words, we anticipate that the reason why some areas have more resident young offenders is they have more resident young people with a weaker law-relevant morality and a poor ability to exercise self-control.

Next we employ the same model we used to predict area variation in the frequency of crime events (see section 5.2) to predict variation in resident young offenders. We expect this model to show some significant differences from the model predicting the locations of crime events. There are good reasons, based on the findings from previous social ecological and human development studies, to assume that area population social disadvantage would be a particularly important predictor of the number of resident young offenders because of the close link between family and neighbourhood disadvantage and unfavourable conditions for the development of personal characteristics relevant to young people's crime

---

[1] Please note that young people's crimes are included in crimes by all offenders, and that differences when comparing the two would likely be greater if the comparison was made between young people's and other people's crime.

propensity (eg Brooks-Gunn et al. 1997; Coulton et al. 1995; G. J. Duncan et al. 1994).

The chapter concludes with analyses of the relationship between young offenders' home locations and the locations of their crime events (generally referred to as the study of crime and distance). The crucial question here is how important the local supply of offenders is for the frequency of crimes that occur in an area and neighbouring areas. The extent to which young offenders commit their crimes locally is the extent to which their pattern of home locations (segregation) will parallel the pattern of their crime locations in the urban area.

## 5.1  Area patterns of young people's crime

Young people are responsible for a large proportion of all acts of crime practically universally (see, eg, Hirschi and Gottfredson 1983). In England and Wales it has been reported that 10- to 17-year-olds are responsible for around one-fifth of all crimes cautioned or convicted annually (Budd et al. 2005), although in 2001 they represented only around one-tenth of the population over the age of legal responsibility (see section 2.1.2). Self-report data suggests these caution and conviction rates may actually underestimate the proportion of all crimes for which young people are responsible, as many crimes by young people (especially minor ones) are not officially recorded, either because they are undetected or, when they are, charges are not pressed (by victims or the police; see section 3.1.2).

Between April 2004 and December 2007 (see section 2.6), the police linked 2,555 acts of crime in Peterborough (the study area) that matched the crime types targeted by PADS+ to young offenders aged 13 to 17 (Table 5.1).[2] As with crimes by all offenders (see section 4.4.2), these crimes clustered in certain areas, and this clustering was reasonably stable over time, even at the small area level.[3] Other studies have also reported stability in the distribution of

---

[2] Only acts of crime for which the offender is known to the police can be included in this analysis; any crimes by young people that went undetected (or unrecorded) by the police are therefore excluded.

[3] At the output area level, the distribution of young people's crime correlated strongly year to year (mean $r = .51$, $p = .000$), and even more strongly when excluding 2007 (mean $r = .69$, $p = .000$).

**Table 5.1  Police-recorded crime in the Peterborough study area by 13- to 17-year-olds between 2004 and 2007 by crime type and spatial concentration**

| Offence type | | |
|---|---|---|
| Comprising | *N* | Gini[a] |
| *All* | *2,555* | *0.66* |
| *Vandalism* | *450* | *0.77* |
| Criminal damage (residential, non-residential, vehicle, other) | 434 | |
| Arson (including endangering life) | 16 | |
| *Violence* | *826* | *0.74* |
| Assault (actual/grievous bodily harm, wounding, affray, common assault, violent disorder) | 762 | |
| Robbery (personal) | 64 | |
| *Shoplifting* | *587* | *0.99* |
| *Theft from a person* | *10* | *0.98* |
| *Vehicle crime* | *421* | *0.69* |
| Theft of a vehicle (including unauthorized taking) | 257 | |
| Theft from a car | 164 | |
| *Burglary* | *261* | *0.78* |
| Residential | 155 | |
| Non-residential | 106 | |

[a] At the output area level.

young people's crime, in some cases also at the small area level (E. Groff et al. 2009; Weisburd et al. 2009).

Figure 5.1 shows that the most concentrated area of police-recorded young people's crime[4] in Peterborough during the study period was the city centre, where more than one-fifth of young people's crimes clustered in just two output areas.[5] There were also smaller concentrations in local centres (Orton Centre and Hampton Centre in particular), and certain residential areas of the city (Ortons Malborne and Goldhay, Ravensthorpe, and an area running through

---

[4] See section 2.6 for details about police-recorded crime data.

[5] For details on how kernel density estimation maps in this book are created see technical appendix, section A1.2.2.

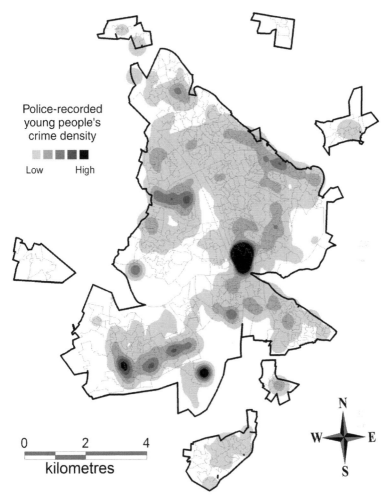

**Figure 5.1 Relative density of police-recorded crimes committed by offenders aged 13–17 (N = 2,555)**

Welland, Dogsthorpe, and Paston). At the same time, no incidents were reported in one-fifth of all output areas (eg in the villages of Newborough, Ailsworth, and Castor; large parts of Werrington, Longthorpe, and Woodston; and some parts of Park Farm, and Ortons Wistow and Brimbles) (G = .66; see Table 5.1).

The dispersion of young people's crime was similar to that of police-recorded crime in Peterborough by all age groups (see

Figure 4.8[6]); in fact, at the output area level, counts of crime by young people and counts of crime by all offenders were closely correlated ($r = .92, p = .000$[7]). This is not surprising as a large proportion of unsolved police-recorded crimes will have been committed by young people, consistent with the fact that a disproportionate number of solved crimes have been linked to young people. There were, however, some interesting, if slight, differences. Young people's crimes were more concentrated in the city centre. A large concentration was also apparent in the Serpentine Green Shopping Centre, which was not evident for all offenders.

### 5.1.1 Area patterns of young people's crime by crime type

Crime types differ in their patterns of variation between areas of the city and in their level of concentration in certain areas. Situational Action Theory (SAT) predicts that these patterns are a consequence of the social processes and personal preferences that select certain kinds of people, ie those with a high crime propensity, into certain kinds of settings, ie criminogenic settings (see section 1.4.2). Different social environments will be associated with different kinds of person–setting intersections, and different kinds of interactions may promote different types of crime. The types of crime, the circumstances of crime events (ie timing, ongoing activity, functional place), and potentially the kinds of young people involved, thus vary across social environments, but in potentially explicable ways. Table 5.1 shows that the concentration of crime in Peterborough varied at the output area level by crime type. To explore these nuances, we need to look more closely at these patterns of crime and the small areas in which crime clustered (or, alternatively, was unusually sparse).

### Area patterns of shoplifting

Opportunities for shoplifting are spatially determined by the location of shops, particularly major retail outlets. Hence young people's shoplifting, despite being one of the most common police-recorded

---

[6] Because Figures 4.8 and 5.1 are relative density maps (see technical appendix section A1.2.2), it is not possible to compare the volume of crime.

[7] Crimes by known young offenders and crimes by all offenders represent separate datasets. For reasons of confidentiality, they have no common identifier; therefore crimes by known young offenders cannot be excluded from crimes by all offenders. However, the impact of the 2,555 crimes by known young offenders on the distribution of the 93,666 crimes by all offenders is minimal.

offences during Phase 1, was extremely spatially concentrated ($G = .99$; see Table 5.1), with 84.8 per cent of such acts taking place in fewer than 1 per cent of all output areas ($N = 5$) (and all such acts taking place in fewer than 10 per cent of all output areas; $N = 45$).

Not surprisingly, most acts of shoplifting took place in the city centre, with more than two-thirds of acts of shoplifting by young offenders occurring in the two city centre output areas that contain the Queensgate Shopping Centre, a number of smaller shopping arcades, and main retail streets. A second concentration (8.7 per cent) was apparent at the Serpentine Green Shopping Centre in the Hamptons, which also draws young people from across the study area, being relatively new and offering attractive shopping facilities. A further 7.3 per cent of shoplifting occurred at other local centres (Orton, Bretton, and Werrington Centres; see Figure 4.2).

In addition to the city and local centres, concentrations of shoplifting also appeared in areas containing what we refer to as 'residential shops': smaller clusters of shops within otherwise residential areas. These concentrations were not evident at the site of all residential shops, however, but rather only at those in areas characterized by poor collective efficacy and a high offender concentration (see section 5.3.1), eg Dogsthorpe, Parnwell, Ravensthorpe, and Orton Malborne. Analyses also show that young people who stole from residential shops and smaller local centres were more local than those who shoplifted in larger local centres or the city centre (Table 5.2).

**Table 5.2  Distance from young offender's home to shoplifting location[a]**

| Shoplifting location | N | % < 500 m | % 500 m to 1 km | % > 1 km | Mean km | SD |
|---|---|---|---|---|---|---|
| All | 481 | 5.8 | 12.7 | 81.5 | 2.92 | 1.97 |
| City centre | 318 | 0.9 | 7.5 | 91.5 | 3.13 | 1.63 |
| Hampton Centre | 35 | 8.6 | 2.9 | 88.6 | 2.81 | 1.87 |
| Smaller local centres | 43 | 11.6 | 46.5 | 41.9 | 2.46 | 3.14 |
| Residential shops | 85 | 20.0 | 18.8 | 61.1 | 2.43 | 2.31 |

[a] For offences where both the offender's home and the crime location fell within the study area. See technical appendix section A1.1 on calculating distance.

Clearly, although commercial land use significantly constrained shoplifting in space, features of residential segregation and the social environment, eg collective efficacy, were also influential. In chapter 4 we highlighted settings characterized by commercial centres (local and city centres) and poor collective efficacy as examples of particularly criminogenic settings; both are purportedly characterized by weak moral contexts (a lack of cohesive moral rules and weak enforcement), in the case of the former because of the constant traffic of users in and out of settings, which weakens social cohesion and control, and in the case of the latter because residents lack the social and moral integration to assert clear rules or intervene effectively when rules are broken.

## Area patterns of violent crime

Unlike shoplifting, which is limited by definition to particular settings, violent crime can occur in any setting where people are present and able to cause interpersonal friction. Consequently, police-recorded violent crime was less spatially concentrated than shoplifting ($G = .74$), although still strongly clustered. Around one-eighth of police-recorded violent crimes by young people took place in two city centre output areas, while concentrations were also apparent in more residential areas in the southern Ortons, Bretton, Ravensthorpe, Welland, Paston, and to the north and north east of the city centre.

Previous research has found public violence to be disproportionately concentrated in, and en route to, public entertainment settings, such as those characterized by restaurants, bars, and nightclubs. Public entertainment settings are likely to create frequent circumstances that may instigate violence (J. G. Fox and Sobol 2000; Graham et al. 2006; Graham and Homel 2008; K. Hughes et al. 2011; Roncek and Maier 1991; Tomsen et al. 1991; Treno et al. 2007; Wikström 1985, 1995) by bringing people from different backgrounds together (eg male strangers from different social strata or cultural heritage) during unstructured leisure activities that may fuel interpersonal frictions, especially when drugs and alcohol increase sensitivity and reduce reasoning and self-control.

Violent crime is concentrated temporally as well as spatially; for example, a considerable amount of violent crime occurs the hour after pubs and bars close (Hope 1986; P. Marsh and Fox-Kibby 1992; Tuck 1989) when people, many of whom will be under the influence of alcohol, converge in the streets. Although young people may have less access to pubs and nightclubs (the legal drinking age in the United Kingdom is 18), this does not always stop them from drinking, and the city centre remains for them a key entertainment setting, especially for late night public activities. Consequently, their violent crime is still concentrated in these settings, especially on Friday and Saturday evenings, when they may converge with those who do have access, adding to the potential for interpersonal frictions that may provoke violence.

Adults and young people differ in the settings in which they spend time and the activities in which they take part; these differences need to be taken into account when considering the distribution of young people's crime in space and time. Young people do not have the same mobility as adults and therefore tend to congregate in their own and friends' homes, or seek settings close to their homes that they can reach by foot or bicycle. Outdoor spaces such as streets and parks are particularly accessible and allow young people to congregate away from adults, who use more purpose-built settings, and younger children, who have less independence. Importantly, some of these settings will share important characteristics with the entertainment venues that appear to generate violent crime among adults (eg under-controlled settings in which strangers converge under the influence of drugs and alcohol).

Despite these differences, there was considerable correspondence between the number of violent offences by young people and offenders of all ages at the output area level ($r = .65$, $p = .000$), driven mainly by the fact that both clustered in the city centre. However, young people's violent crimes were more widespread across other parts of the city. Detailed assessment of the location of young people's violent crime outside the city centre revealed clusters around local centres, schools, residential shops (but only in socially disadvantaged output areas), Thorpe Wood Police Station, and parks and open green spaces (again, only in socially disadvantaged areas). In addition, sites of supported accommodation for young people also showed higher concentrations of violent crime, which may arguably be driven by the concentration of young people who may be prone to violent crime and/or vulnerable to violent victimization.

Some of the smaller concentrations of young people's violent crime occurred in residential areas, such as particular parks and streets that serve as local youth hangouts. These emerged almost exclusively in areas characterized by poor collective efficacy, where crime prone young people may be self and socially selected into under-controlled settings. In areas with higher collective efficacy (and fewer resident young offenders), similar kinds of settings (eg other school and shopping venues) did not exhibit concentrations of violent crime, which is consistent with our finding that young people spend little time congregating in these settings (see section 6.2.3). Young people are typically the targets of other young people's violence (Wikström 1985; Wikström and Butterworth 2006: 40); therefore, young people's violence is most likely to occur in settings where young people congregate in circumstances liable to cause friction. Recall (as shown in section 3.1.1) that most victims of young people's violence are known to them (and many are pupils at the offender's school). Only as they grow older does the frequency of strangers as victims increase, most likely reflecting changes in leisure time routine activities (eg higher levels of participation in public entertainment activities). Why they congregate in areas with poor collective efficacy undoubtedly has to do with social selection (eg more young people live in areas with poor collective efficacy) and self selection (as young people choose to congregate in areas where they are less likely to be monitored).

### Area patterns of vandalism and arson/fire-setting

Vandalism (including arson/fire-setting) may be even more opportune, across more settings, than violence or shoplifting, as it may target practically anything in the physical environment, from man-made objects to natural features, and requires only the presence of the offender. This is reflected in its broad distribution: unlike other crime types, vandalism was as concentrated in locations around the city as it was in the city centre. Interestingly, vandalism still clustered in certain areas ($G = .77$, see Table 5.1), and almost one in three acts took place in just 3 per cent of all output areas. In the city centre, vandalism was more concentrated in the northern sector, which contains a park, the job centre, the Youth Offending Service, and many night time entertainment venues (eg restaurants, pubs, and nightclubs). Vandalism also clustered in certain local centres (Bretton and Werrington Centres) and a number of parks and residential areas (Dogsthorpe, Paston, Eastgate, Eastfield, Stanground, Ravensthorpe, South Bretton, New and Old Fletton, Orton Goldhay, and Orton Brimbles). One concentration was driven entirely by the Thorpe Wood Police Station, where, for example, young people vandalized cells or police cars while in custody.

Area patterns of serious theft

Burglary clustered predominantly in residential areas. Residential burglary clearly requires a residential setting; however, most non-residential burglaries by young people also took place in residential areas, as these typically involved outbuildings (eg sheds and garages), rather than industrial or commercial buildings. Burglary was generally more common in areas with greater social disadvantage (see Table 5.14). Car crimes also clustered predominantly in residential areas, and not in commercial areas, such as the city centre, presumably because in the latter parking facilities are generally more closely monitored and secured.

## 5.2 Modelling the distribution of young people's crime

The following models integrate standard linear regression and non-linear Poisson regression within a single model; linear regression is used to predict poor collective efficacy while negative binomial regression is used to predict the count of crime incidents per output area (see section 4.5.1 for details of the statistical technique employed). These models include the same predictors as those presented in section 4.5, except these models explain variation in the concentration of young people's police-recorded crime (not police recorded crime by all offenders). These models do not control for population or area size because variation in these dimensions among output areas is, by definition, generally small. However, to ensure this decision did not affect the findings, all models were also tested with logged resident population as a control variable, which did not change the coefficients significantly.

Figure 5.2 presents the findings for total crimes by young people. Non-residential land use had the strongest effect (OR = 1.75) in the model predicting all crime counts. Poor collective efficacy also had a strong effect, with an odds ratio of 1.45; one standard deviation drop in collective efficacy was associated with a 45 per cent increase in young people's crime. Social disadvantage did not have a direct effect on crime counts, being fully mediated by poor collective efficacy. Greater residential instability was associated with more crime (OR = 1.24) while greater ethnic diversity was associated with less (OR = 0.87). Greater ethnic diversity indirectly increased young people's crime by increasing poor collective efficacy, but decreased it directly. Looking to the breakdown by crime type (Table 5.3),

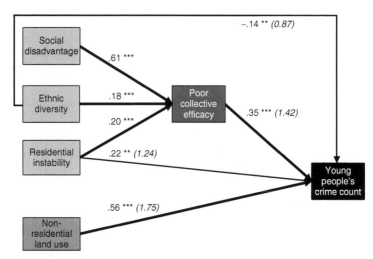

**Figure 5.2 Mplus path model of area structural features, land use, collective efficacy, and young people's police-recorded crime**[a,b]

[a] Odds ratios in brackets; paths to poor collective efficacy in metric scale; paths to crime in logarithmic scale.
[b] Significance level: *** $p < .001$, ** $p < .01$, * $p < .05$.

however, we see that the association between ethnic diversity and young people's crime was only significant for shoplifting, which may be related to the concentration of Asian residents near the city centre. Non-residential land use was the strongest predictor for most crime types. Its coefficient was exceptionally high for shoplifting, reflecting the obvious link between the spatial concentration of shops and theft from shops. Social disadvantage had a direct effect only on serious property offences.

Comparing the model explaining young people's total crime with that explaining all offenders' total crime, there are similarities but also noteworthy differences. Non-residential land use (OR = 1.75 vs. 1.51) and poor collective efficacy (OR = 1.42 vs. 1.22) were stronger predictors of young people's crime counts, while social disadvantage was not a significant predictor of young people's crime counts (*n.s.* vs. 1.12), and ethnic diversity predicted fewer crime counts for young people, but more for all people (OR = 0.87 vs. 1.09). Importantly, the findings for young people's crime counts, even to a higher degree than those for all crime counts, support the assertion that areas of commerce and entertainment and

**Table 5.3  Mplus path models predicting counts of young people's crime[a] per output area by crime type**

| | | Poor collective efficacy | All crimes[b] | Violent crime | Vandalism | Serious theft | Shoplifting[c] |
|---|---|---|---|---|---|---|---|
| **Structural (exogenous)** | | | | | | | |
| Social disadvantage | Coefficient[d] | 0.61*** | n.s. | n.s. | n.s. | 0.33*** | n.s. |
| | Odds ratio | | | | | 1.38 | |
| Ethnic diversity | Coefficient[d] | 0.18*** | −0.14** | n.s. | n.s. | n.s. | −0.53** |
| | Odds ratio | | 0.87 | | | | 0.59 |
| Residential instability | Coefficient[d] | 0.20*** | 0.22** | n.s. | n.s. | 0.19** | n.s. |
| | Odds ratio | | 1.24 | | | 1.21 | |
| Non-residential land use | Coefficient[d] | n.s. | 0.56*** | 0.60*** | 0.53*** | 0.19* | 1.98*** |
| | Odds ratio | | 1.75 | 1.82 | 1.70 | 1.21 | 7.24 |
| **Mediating (endogenous)** | | | | | | | |
| Poor collective efficacy | Coefficient[d] | | 0.35*** | 0.33*** | 0.24* | 0.15* | n.s. |
| | Odds ratio | | 1.42 | 1.39 | 1.27 | 1.17 | |

[a] Known young offenders aged 13–17 who offended between April 2004 and December 2007.
[b] Police-recorded crimes types equivalent to those self-reported in PADS+.
[c] Model did not converge in Mplus 5 and was computed in STATA 11.
[d] Significance level: *** $p < .001$, ** $p < .01$, * $p < .05$.

residential areas with poor collective efficacy are the most crimino-genic urban areas.

## 5.3 Offender home locations

Just as the concentration of crime varies across the urban area so do the locations of offenders' homes. The extent to which the two distributions overlap depends on the extent to which offenders tend to commit their crimes locally. Even if research shows that many crimes are committed near the offender's home, the distribution of crime events and offender home locations are far from identical (eg Baldwin and Bottoms 1976; Wikström 1991; Wiles and Costello 2000; see P. J. Brantingham and Brantingham 1984: 291–331; and Rossmo 2000 for overviews). Before analysing the topic of crime and distance we will investigate in some detail the offender home distribution and its relationship to the distribution of crime prone young people.

### 5.3.1 Police-recorded offender home locations

The number of police-recorded young offenders living in an output area during the study period was derived from the number of home addresses of offenders aged 13–17 who lived and offended[9] within the study area between April 2004 and December 2007.[10] A total of 1,162 offenders were identified living at 1,269 unique addresses across the 518 output areas.[11]

Generally, there were very few young offenders per output area: one-quarter of output areas (126) had no resident police-recorded young offenders, while another quarter (135) had only one resident young offender. The main concentrations appeared in east Paston

---

[9] Offences include only those equivalent to crime types covered by the self-report questionnaire; see section 3.1.

[10] This count can only be seen as a proxy for the actual number of resident young offenders, as it excludes any who only offended outside the study area during the study period (but see the discussion on crime and distance in section 5.5.1) and of course any who were not caught by the police (which we can begin to address by analysing self-report data; see section 5.3.2).

[11] For different offenders (eg, siblings) living at the same address, that address counted once for each. For offenders who moved house between offences, and therefore had multiple home locations, additional home locations were counted only if their addresses were in different output areas.

(in the Crabtree area), a large area in the Ravensthorpe/Westwood area, a number of areas in the Ortons (around Goldhay, Waterville, and Malborne), and an area in Millfield to the north of the city centre. There were also some smaller concentrations, for example, in north Bretton, New England, the Welland estate, south Bretton, and Eastgate.

There was some overlap with areas that contained a high percentage of social housing. This applied particularly to sites of supported accommodation for young people,[12] all of which lie to the north and west of the city centre. Interestingly, clusters of resident young offenders only appeared over sites housing older adolescents and young adults, and not sites solely catering to children and young adolescents, which may differ in the services they offer, and therefore the kinds of young people they accommodate. Secure units were not represented because offender home locations were measured at the time of the offence.

The homes of more frequent police-recorded offenders were more clustered than those of all offenders (Table 5.4); the more police-recorded offences young people had, the more concentrated their home locations. This is largely consistent with previous findings (Oberwittler 2004; Wikström 1991).

**Table 5.4 Distribution of the homes of various types of police-recorded offenders**

|  |  | All offenders | Frequent offenders[a] | | |
|---|---|---|---|---|---|
|  |  |  | 3 or more crimes | 5 or more crimes | 10 or more crimes |
| Total | Offenders | 1,162 | 226 | 91 | 20 |
|  | Homes | 1,269 | 315 | 149 | 47 |
| Homes per OA | Mean | 2.5 | 0.6 | 0.3 | 0.1 |
|  | SD | 2.8 | 1.1 | 0.7 | 0.3 |
|  | Max | 18 | 9 | 4 | 3 |
| Concentration | Gini | .56 | .76 | .84 | .93 |

[a] Groups are not mutually exclusive.

[12] Supported accommodation (such as that offered by the YMCA) provides vulnerable and/or homeless young people with safe accommodation and access to a range of personal, social, and educational services.

## 5.3.2 Self-reported offender home locations

As 70.4 per cent of the sample reported an act of crime during Phase 1,[13] and their homes were well spread across the city, self-reported offender homes were also well spread across the study area. As with police-recorded offenders, however, more frequent self-reported offenders showed more definitive concentrations, as did more serious theft offenders. Frequent offenders were defined as those who self-reported 50 or more crimes (11.1 per cent) and 75 or more crimes (6.8 per cent) over the five studied years (see section 3.1.1). Serious theft offenders were defined as those who self-reported acts of burglary (residential and non-residential) and car crime (theft of or from a car).[14] As can be seen in Table 5.5, the concentration of offenders' home locations increased with the seriousness and frequency of young people's self-reported offences, in line with the pattern seen for young people's police-recorded offences (eg the Gini coefficient ($G$) for all offenders is 0.58 compared to 0.94 when restricted to serious theft offenders having committed 10 or more serious theft crimes).

**Table 5.5  Distribution of the homes of various groups of self-reported offenders[a]**

|  | All offenders | Frequent offenders | | Serious theft offenders | | |
| --- | --- | --- | --- | --- | --- | --- |
|  | All crimes | 50 or more crimes | 75 or more crimes | Any serious thefts | 5 or more serious thefts | 10 or more serious thefts |
| N offenders | 488 | 77 | 47 | 93 | 35 | 22 |
| N homes | 549 | 90 | 60 | 107 | 50 | 37 |
| G | .58 | .87 | .91 | .84 | .92 | .94 |

[a] Groups are not mutually exclusive.

[13] Only the 693 young people who completed the self-reported crime section of the questionnaire in all five waves were included in these particular analyses.

[14] Wikström (1995) discusses strategic offences that are particularly indicative of young offenders' future crime involvement; Svensson (2002) found that such offences include serious acts of theft (such as robbery and car crime) but not minor acts (such as shoplifting). We have chosen not to include robbery as a serious crime as our self-report instrument does not differentiate between serious and more minor acts of violence (see Table 3.1).

Figure 5.3 shows the distribution of home locations for the 107 young people who reported serious thefts during Phase 1. The greatest concentrations occurred on the Welland estate, in an area in north Dogsthorpe and east Paston, a large area in the Ravensthorpe and Westwood area, and a number of areas in the Ortons (Malborne, Goldhay, and Waterville), areas that overlapped considerably with the concentration of frequent offenders' home locations.

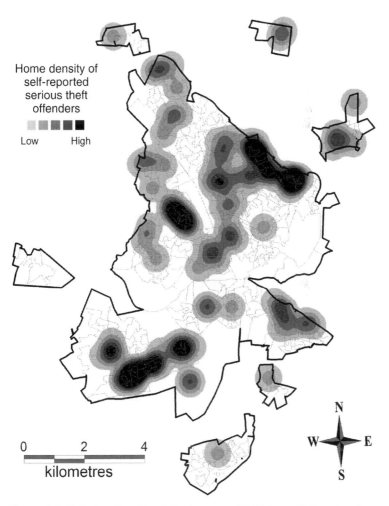

**Figure 5.3 Relative density of the homes of PADS+ participants who self-reported serious thefts in Phase 1 (*N* = 107)**

Despite the specificity of the analysis, the small number of (police-recorded or self-reported) young offenders' homes per output area, and the wide dispersion of self-reported young offenders across the study area, the number of self-reported offenders' homes correlated significantly with that of police-recorded offenders' homes at the output area level ($r = .28, p = .000$). Even for the self-reported serious theft offenders' home locations, the correlation with police-recorded young offenders' home locations remained robust ($r = .24, p = .000$), despite the fact there were fewer serious theft offenders and their home locations were more concentrated. The greater concurrence between the distribution of police-recorded offenders' home locations and those of frequent and/or serious theft versus all self-reported offenders is apparent by visual inspection of their relative density maps; this is consistent with the finding that more frequent and/or serious theft offenders are more likely to become known to the police (see section 3.1.2). The key areas of concentration are the same, although there is a notable divergence to the north and north east of the city centre, where there is a heavier concentration of police-recorded offenders' homes. This is an artefact of one site of supported accommodation, which caters to young people who have particularly serious personal problems and, in many cases, high levels of crime involvement, and are subsequently known to the police.

Part of the shared variance between these counts of offender home locations can almost certainly be attributed to the number of resident young people per output area. It is possible to use the number of resident PADS+ participants as a proxy for 13–17-year-olds (see technical appendix, section A1.3, on problems with using 2001 census data to estimate the population of young people per output area); as a random sample, the distribution of PADS+ participants should reflect that of young people within their age cohort across the study area. To align this with the rolling count of young offenders requires the assumption that this distribution reflects that of all adolescents between 13 and 17 years old, an assumption supported by 2001 census data. However, the number living in any given output area was very small; the most participants living in any output area was six, no participants lived in 35.7 per cent of all output areas, and 92.7 per cent of output areas contained three or fewer participants. To combat the random error inherent at this level of analysis, we decided to aggregate up to groups of output areas, creating a larger pool of young people and young offenders to examine, while capturing larger geographical units that may represent unified areas.

In order to analyse key differences between output areas with high and low offender counts, we isolated output area aggregates that consistently displayed the densest or sparsest concentrations of offenders' homes, respectively, across analyses of *both* self-reported and police -recorded offenders at the output area level. Only output area aggregates that showed a high (or low) concentration of offenders' homes for all groups of offenders (including serious theft and/or frequent offenders) were considered consistent. Natural boundaries, such as roads and green space, were taken into account in characterizing output area aggregate borders, and output areas containing major geographical features, such as a large country park or golf course, were excluded. Such features also formed the boundary between several aggregates (eg Ferry Meadows Country Park formed the boundary between the Longthorpe and Orton Longueville aggregates; see below).

Three output area aggregates with a consistently high concentration of police-recorded and self-reported offenders' homes emerged: one along the south of the Ortons (Orton Malborne and Orton Goldhay); one which covered most of the Westwood area; and one along the eastern edge of the city encompassing parts of the Welland estate, north Dogsthorpe, and eastern parts of Paston (see Figure 5.4).

Output area aggregates with a consistently low offender concentration emerged in North Gunthorpe, Orton Longueville, and Longthorpe (Figure 5.4). Although they did not differ significantly in geographical size, these low offender concentration aggregates had about one-third the number of total residents as high offender concentrations aggregates, and only one-fifth the number of young people.

In high offender concentration aggregates, 82 per cent of resident PADS+ participants reported at least one act of crime, compared to just 28 per cent in low offender concentration aggregates. Differences between these areas were even more marked for more frequent and serious theft offenders (Table 5.6). More than one in four PADS+ participants living in high offender concentration aggregates reported more than 50 crimes during Phase 1 (ie during the five studied years). In contrast, five out of the seven offenders living in low offender concentration aggregates reported fewer than five acts of crime, and the most any offender reported was 37.

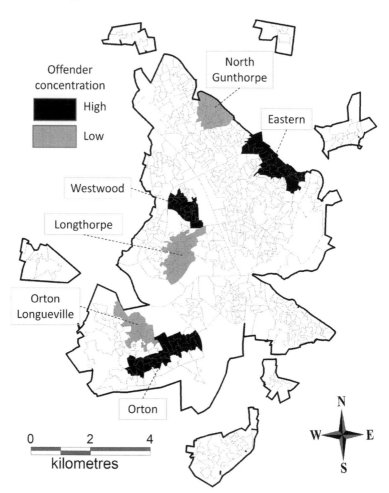

**Figure 5.4 Output area aggregates with consistently high or low offender concentrations**

Two-fifths of the offenders living in high offender concentration aggregates reported at least one serious theft during Phase 1 (and nearly one in 10 more than 10 serious thefts), while no young people living in low offender concentration aggregates reported a single serious theft (Table 5.6).

Table 5.7 reports statistics for selected significance tests, which confirm that young people in high offender concentration aggregates were significantly more likely than those living in low offender

**Table 5.6 Self-reported offender percentages for output area aggregates**

| Output area aggregate | Participants | | Offenders | | | | |
|---|---|---|---|---|---|---|---|
| | $N^a$ | Percentage offenders | Percentage self-reporting 50 or more crimes | Percentage self-reporting 75 or more crimes | Percentage self-reporting serious thefts | Percentage self-reporting 5 or more serious thefts | Percentage self-reporting 10 or more serious thefts |
| All young people | 693 | 70.4 | 15.8 | 9.6 | 19.1 | 7.2 | 4.5 |
| High offender concentration aggregates | 118 | 82.2 | 26.8 | 18.6 | 38.1 | 15.5 | 11.3 |
| Orton | 53 | 79.2 | 23.8 | 16.7 | 40.5 | 11.9 | 7.1 |
| Westwood | 25 | 92.0 | 30.4 | 30.4 | 30.4 | 21.7 | 21.7 |
| Eastern | 39 | 79.5 | 29.0 | 12.9 | 41.9 | 16.1 | 9.7 |
| Low offender concentration aggregates | 25 | 28.0 | 0.0 | 0.0 | 0.0 | 0.0 | 0.0 |
| Longthorpe | 8 | 12.5 | 0.0 | 0.0 | 0.0 | 0.0 | 0.0 |
| North Gunthorpe | 11 | 36.4 | 0.0 | 0.0 | 0.0 | 0.0 | 0.0 |
| Orton Longueville | 6 | 33.3 | 0.0 | 0.0 | 0.0 | 0.0 | 0.0 |
| Other output areas | 498 | 70.1 | 12.9 | 7.2 | 15.2 | 5.4 | 2.9 |

[a] Refers to the number of young people who lived in an output area aggregate for at least three years during Phase 1

**Table 5.7  Differences in self-reported and police-recorded prevalence of young people living in low and high offender output area aggregates**

| | Prevalence | Odds ratio | Chi² | Cramer's V | Prob. | High vs. low offender concentration aggregates | | |
|---|---|---|---|---|---|---|---|---|
| | | | | | | Chi² | Phi | Prob. |
| *Self-reported offenders* | | | | | | | | |
| Low offender concentration aggregates | 28.0 | 0.4 | | | | | | |
| High offender concentration aggregates | 82.2 | 2.3 | 29.62 | 0.22 | .000 | 30.56 | −.46 | .000 |
| Other output areas | 70.1 | 4.6 | | | | | | |
| *PNC offenders* | | | | | | | | |
| Low offender concentration aggregates | 0.0 | 0.0 | | | | | | |
| High offender concentration aggregates | 18.6 | 0.1 | 28.20 | 0.21 | .000 | 30.56 | −.20 | .020 |
| Other output areas | 5.0 | 0.2 | | | | | | |

concentration aggregates to self-report acts of crime, and to have a police record for offending. Young people in high offender concentration aggregates were also significantly more likely to self-report frequent acts of crime and/or serious thefts (analyses not shown).

High and low concentration aggregates differed in their numbers of resident offenders; at the same time, however, their resident offenders self-reported significantly different levels of crime involvement (Table 5.8). Offenders living in high offender concentration aggregates self-reported significantly more acts of crime, than those living in other output areas ($p = .001$). Clearly, these output area aggregates differed substantially in not only the count of resident young offenders, but also in those offenders' per capita rate of crime and serious theft.

**Table 5.8 Self-reported crime frequency of young people living in low and high concentration aggregates**

| | Self-reported crime frequency | |
| --- | --- | --- |
| | Mean | SD |
| High offender concentration aggregates | 57.5 | 96.1 |
| Other output areas | 25.4 | 64.7 |
| Low offender concentration aggregates | 2.9 | 8.8 |

These aggregates also differed in key social environmental features. Output areas in aggregates with a high offender concentration were significantly more disadvantaged and had significantly poorer collective efficacy than other output areas, while those in aggregates with a low offender concentration were significantly less disadvantaged and had significantly stronger collective efficacy (Table 5.9).

Both collective efficacy and social disadvantage were related to the prevalence and quality of resident offenders at the output area level (Table 5.10). Characterizing output areas by both factors, we find that disadvantaged areas with poor collective efficacy had significantly more self-reported offenders than advantaged areas with strong collective efficacy ($\chi^2 = 13.6, p = .000$; odds ratio = 2.93), and significantly more police-recorded offenders than advantaged areas with strong collective efficacy. No PADS+ participants living in advantaged areas with strong collective efficacy had police records, compared to nearly 15 per cent of those living in disadvantaged

**Table 5.9 Mean social disadvantage and collective efficacy for output areas in aggregates and other output areas**

| Output areas | N | Social disadvantage (mean)[a] | Collective efficacy (mean)[a] |
| --- | --- | --- | --- |
| All | 518 | 0.51 | 2.79 |
| High offender concentration aggregates | 62 | 1.80 | 3.08 |
| Other output areas | 433 | 0.40 | 2.76 |
| Low offender concentration aggregates | 23 | −0.90 | 2.55 |

[a] Means for high and low offender concentration aggregates and other output areas were all significantly different at the .000 level.

**Table 5.10  Prevalence and frequency of PADS+ offenders living in disadvantaged areas with poor collective efficacy versus advantaged areas with strong collective efficacy**

| Disadvantage/ collective efficacy | Resident partici- pants[a] | Percent of sample | Self-reported crime | | Police-recorded crime | |
|---|---|---|---|---|---|---|
| | | | Preva- lence | Mean frequency[b] | Preva- lence | Mean frequency[b] |
| Disadvantaged areas with poor collective efficacy | 130 | 19.2 | 80.2 | 46.6 | 14.3 | 2.5 |
| Other areas | 443 | 65.4 | 72.0 | 32.4 | 8.4 | 1.9 |
| Advantaged areas with strong collective efficacy | 104 | 15.4 | 58.0 | 16.9 | 0.0 | 0.0 |

[a] Those living in the study area during the parents' interviews (2003) $N = 677$.
[b] Offenders only.

areas with poor collective efficacy (versus 8 per cent in other areas).

Self-reported PADS+ offenders living in disadvantaged areas with poor collective efficacy also reported, on average, nearly 50 crimes during Phase 1, while self-reported offenders living in advantaged areas with strong collective efficacy reported fewer than 20 (a difference that was significant at the $p < .01$ level). Police-recorded PADS+ offenders from the former areas also, on average, had multiple warnings, reprimands or convictions. Clearly, young people living in these particularly difficult environments were more likely to be involved in crime and, when they were involved in crime, to be much more involved than young people living in other settings, while young people living in particularly privileged environments were very unlikely to be involved in crime, and, when they were, only to a minor degree.

### 5.3.3  Spatial distribution of crime prone and crime averse young people

Since we already know (see section 3.2.4) that young people who are crime prone (have weak morality and a poor ability to exercise self-control) are significantly more likely to be offenders, we would expect to find a relationship between area rates of resident crime prone young people and resident young offenders. Many studies have looked at the spatial distribution of offenders, but there are none that we know of that have looked in detail at the spatial distribution of people with varying crime propensities.

Crime propensity, described in section 3.2, is measured across Phase 1; hence only young people who took part in all five waves are included in these analyses.[15] Their home locations[16] were well spread across 325 (63 per cent) of the 518 output areas, although those with high and low crime propensities tended to cluster in different areas. Some areas (eg North Werrington, Newark, Longthorpe, and the northern Ortons) exhibited a denser concentration of resident young people with a low crime propensity, while others (eg parts of Dogsthorpe and Ravensthorpe, and the southern Ortons) exhibited a denser concentration of young people with a high crime propensity.

At the output area level we found that the distribution of young people with a high crime propensity predicted counts of self-reported and police-recorded offenders; the more young people with a high crime propensity, the more self-reported and police-recorded offenders (see Figure 5.5).[17]

The number of resident young people with high, medium, and low crime propensity predicted the number of self-reported offenders per output area, but only the number of young people with a high and medium crime propensity predicted the number of offenders self-reporting a high crime frequency and the number self-reporting serious thefts. The number of young people with a medium or high crime propensity also predicted the count of police-recorded offender homes per output area (Table 5.11).

At a larger area level, a quarter of PADS+ participants living in aggregates with a high offender concentration had a high crime propensity, and only a tenth had a low crime propensity (Table 5.12). In these areas the mean crime propensity score was 0.68 (Table 5.13). Output area aggregates with a low concentration of young offender

---

[15] Of these 693 participants, 38 lived outside the study area during the parents' interview and are therefore excluded. Of those living outside the study area, a greater proportion had a low crime propensity (mean = −0.60).

[16] Measured at the time of the parents' interview.

[17] The reason the resident number of police-recorded offenders is higher than the resident number of self-reported offenders is because the sample of police-recorded offenders is much larger than the PADS+ sample.

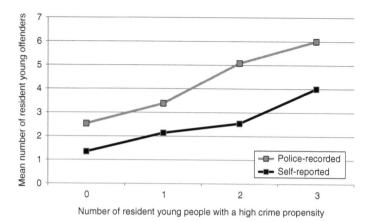

Figure 5.5  **Mean number of resident young offenders living in output areas with differing numbers of resident young people from the PADS+ sample with a high crime propensity**

Table 5.11  Counts of resident young people with high, medium, and low crime propensity predicting area counts of resident offenders[a]

| Propensity | Self-reported offenders | | | | | | | | | Police-recorded | | |
|---|---|---|---|---|---|---|---|---|---|---|---|---|
| | All | | | High frequency (50+) | | | Serious theft | | | | | |
| | b | Beta | Prob. | b | Beta | Prob. | b | Beta | Prob. | b | Beta | Prob. |
| Low | .24 | .11 | .006 | .03 | .03 | n.s. | .04 | .04 | n.s. | −.02 | −.00 | n.s. |
| Medium | .78 | .68 | .000 | .11 | .22 | .000 | .14 | .26 | .000 | .42 | .16 | .000 |
| High | .95 | .46 | .000 | .46 | .50 | .000 | .44 | .46 | .000 | 1.2 | .21 | .000 |
| Multiple $R^2$ x 100 | | 55.6 | | | 26.5 | | | 23.5 | | | 7.2 | |

[a] For models predicting self-reported crimes, only output areas with resident PADS+ participants are included.

homes did not house large numbers of young people with a high crime propensity.[18] Across all low offender concentration aggregates, the mean crime propensity score was −1.09 (Table 5.13); only one-tenth

[18] In North Gunthorpe three resident young people did display a high crime propensity. However, all three had crime propensity scores at the very bottom of the high propensity range, and two moved out of the area early in the study period; the mean crime propensity score for this aggregate was −0.70, more than one-third of a standard deviation below the mean.

**Table 5.12 Aggregate residents by crime propensity group[a]**

|  | Valid N | Percentage in crime propensity group | | |
|---|---|---|---|---|
|  |  | Low | Med | High |
| High concentration aggregates | 131 | 8 | 64 | 28 |
| Orton | 60 | 7 | 63 | 30 |
| Westwood | 30 | 13 | 57 | 30 |
| Eastern | 41 | 7 | 71 | 22 |
| Low concentration aggregates | 26 | 46 | 42 | 12 |
| Longthorpe | 8 | 50 | 50 | 0 |
| North Gunthorpe | 12 | 42 | 33 | 25 |
| Orton Longueville | 6 | 50 | 50 | 0 |
| Other output areas | 487 | 15 | 72 | 13 |
| Total study area | 644 | 15 | 69 | 16 |

[a] Total participants living in the study area with a crime propensity score (N = 644). Participants' homes are defined as their home at the time of the parent's interview for the purpose of this analysis.

**Table 5.13 Aggregate residents' mean crime propensity**

|  | Crime propensity score | | | | |
|---|---|---|---|---|---|
|  | N | Min | Max | Mean | SD |
| All participants | 682 | −5.23 | 7.08 | −0.00 | 1.73 |
| High concentration aggregates | 131 | −3.11 | 5.31 | 0.68 | 1.91 |
| Orton | 60 | −2.96 | 5.30 | 0.66 | 1.76 |
| Westwood | 30 | −3.11 | 5.31 | 0.71 | 2.15 |
| Eastern | 41 | −2.96 | 5.11 | 0.71 | 1.98 |
| Low concentration aggregates | 26 | −4.58 | 1.99 | −1.09 | 1.77 |
| Longthorpe | 8 | −2.05 | 1.10 | −1.27 | 1.08 |
| North Gunthorpe | 12 | −4.58 | 1.99 | −0.70 | 2.25 |
| Orton Longueville | 6 | −3.48 | 0.68 | −1.64 | 1.45 |
| Other areas | 487 | −5.23 | 7.08 | −0.08 | 1.64 |
| Home outside study area | 38 | −2.99 | 3.19 | −0.68 | 1.42 |

of participants in low offender concentration aggregates had a high crime propensity, and more than a third had a low crime propensity (Table 5.12). The mean crime propensity score in high offender concentration aggregates was significantly higher than that in low offender concentration aggregates ($p = .000$), and both differed significantly from the mean crime propensity of participants living in other output areas (although the difference was slightly less significant for low offender concentration aggregates, $p = .018$, than high offender concentration aggregates, $p = .000$).

Both high and low offender concentration aggregates housed young people with very low crime propensities, but *only* high offender concentration aggregates housed young people with very high crime propensities. In the low offender concentration aggregates the highest crime propensities of resident young people were around one standard deviation above the mean, just falling into the high crime propensity category, while in all high offender concentration aggregates there were participants whose crime propensity scores fell around three standard deviations above the mean (Table 5.13).

Across the study area, we found associations at the output area level between the number of young people with a high crime propensity in the PADS+ sample and the number of resident offenders, both self-reported ($r = .35$, $p = .000$) and police-recorded ($r = .18$, $p = .001$). These relationships were even stronger for frequent self-reported offenders (for those reporting more than 50 crimes ($r = .43$, $p = .000$) and for young people self-reporting acts of serious theft ($r = .38$, $p = .000$).

Hence we are able to conclude that areas with more police-recorded and self-reported offenders (especially those self-reporting a high crime frequency and/or serious thefts) are also characterized by larger populations of young people with a high crime propensity (ie young people with weaker law-relevant morality and ability to exercise self-control), a finding that is consistent with arguments forwarded by SAT and not surprising given the strong individual-level relationship between crime propensity and crime involvement demonstrated in section 3.2.4.

## 5.4 Modelling the distribution of young offenders

So far we have established that areas that have more young offenders also have more crime prone young people (ie young people with a weak law-relevant morality and poor ability to exercise self-control). We have also shown that the frequency and (per capita) rate of young offenders (particularly those reporting frequent crimes and serious thefts) tends to be highest in disadvantaged areas. In this section we test whether the same area factors that predicted area variations in the number of young people's police-recorded crimes (see section 5.2) also predict area variations in resident police-recorded young offenders (Figure 5.6).

Because the number of resident young offenders may just be a consequence of the number of resident young people, we included the resident adolescent population using the number of resident young people aged 9 to 13 in 2001 per output area as a control variable in negative binomial regression models[19] (see section 4.5.1 for details of the statistical technique used, and the technical appendix, section A1.3, on problems relating to this variable). Comparisons between models with and without this population control variable showed it had a strong effect on the estimation of the coefficients. Area disadvantage was particularly attenuated by introducing the population of young people as a control variable. This is to be expected as output areas with greater social disadvantage tended to have more adolescent residents (ie more resident families with adolescent children). Thus not controlling for the number of adolescents would introduce a bias into the models and, therefore, the shown models do control for the adolescent population.

Sensitivity analyses revealed three outlying areas with very high counts of resident adolescent offenders that attenuated the coefficients, especially for collective efficacy and area disadvantage on offender rates. Extreme growth during the period 2004–07 in one output area containing the new Hampton development to the south of the city was not reflected in the population as counted by the census in 2001, whereas offenders moving into new homes in the area were captured by police data covering the period 2004–07. This means that the number of offenders resident in this area appears unduly high when controlling for resident young people.[20] The two other areas each contained a supported accommodation unit that

[19] Technically, the natural log is used in Poisson regression analysis (Long and Freese 2006: 370).

[20] As reported elsewhere in this book, this output area was often an outlier in analyses due to its large size, a consequence of its low population density at the beginning of the study, and extreme growth during the study period.

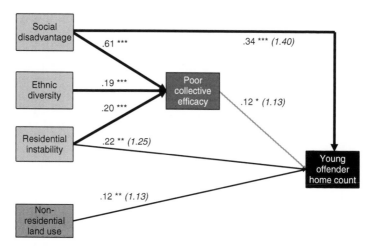

**Figure 5.6  Mplus path model of area population structural features, land use, collective efficacy, and police-recorded young offender[a] home locations (N = 499[b])[c,d]**

[a] Known young offenders aged 13–17 who offended between April 2004 and December 2007, controlling for resident population of 9–13-year-olds in 2001.
[b] 16 output areas with no resident young people aged 9–13 in 2001 are excluded, as are the three outliers (this explains some slight differences in coefficients between population structure variables and poor collective efficacy presented for previous models).
[c] Odds ratios in brackets; paths to poor collective efficacy in metric scale; paths to crime in logarithmic scale.
[d] Significance level: *** $p < .001$, ** $p < .01$, * $p < .05$.

houses vulnerable and/or homeless young people who have been taken into the care of the social authorities. The prevalence of offending is often higher among young people experiencing social difficulty and/or housing problems and, coupled with high resident turnover in such units, the offender count in these areas was very high. The final regression model therefore excluded these three outliers.

Area social disadvantage and residential instability were the strongest predictors of young offenders' home locations (Figure 5.6). One standard deviation increase in social disadvantage was associated with an approximately 40 per cent increase in the number of offenders, while a similar increase in residential instability was associated with a 25 per cent increase. In contrast to the model predicting crime events (see section 5.2), in which non-residential land use and poor collective efficacy (in that order) were the strongest predictors, in this model non-residential land use and poor collective efficacy were relatively weak predictors of resident young offenders. Moreover, ethnic diversity did not show a significant direct association with the distribution of young offenders. Thus the model shows that young offenders tended to live in disadvantaged and residentially unstable areas.

The fact that poor collective efficacy appears to be a considerably stronger predictor of where people commit crimes than where offenders live is consistent with recent findings from US research (Kirk 2008; Sampson et al. 2005). It is possible that other aspects of collective efficacy, such as the collective efficacy of families (their social cohesion and informal social control of their children), are more important than collective efficacy among neighbours in relation to the development of young people's crime propensity. Using Phase 1 data, Wikström (2011b) showed that poor family collective efficacy was a much stronger predictor of young people's crime propensity (ie law-relevant morality and ability to exercise self-control) than either their school or neighbourhood collective efficacy (although both of the latter were also significant predictors). The fact that area population social disadvantage was a particularly important predictor of the number of resident young offenders may depend on the close link between family and neighbourhood disadvantage and unfavourable conditions (such as poor family collective efficacy) for the development of personal characteristics and experiences relevant to young people's development of a higher crime propensity. Although social disadvantage and its influence on the efficacy of key social institutions such as the family and school are clearly implicated in the understanding of why some young people develop a stronger crime propensity, this is not the topic of this book (but one we will return to and analyse in future publications).

## 5.5  Crime and distance

To what extent does the home location of young offenders affect an area's level of crime? That is, to what extent do young people commit acts of crime in and around the places where they live? Measuring the distance between where offenders live and where they commit acts of crime is one way of capturing the relationship between offender and offence concentrations (Wikström 1991: 213; for an overview of relevant research see Costanzo et al. 1986; McIver 1981; Phillips 1980). Generally, studies find there is a distance-decay function: the number of crimes tends to decrease with distance from the offender's home. A significant proportion of offenders' crimes are committed close to home, with this relationship holding particularly true for young offenders (see, for example, Baldwin and Bottoms 1976; Rhodes and Conly 1981; Wikström 1985: 212–32; 1991: 213–25). Young offenders have less mobility than their adult counterparts and therefore more restricted activity fields that revolve around key locations (eg home, school, friends' homes), of which the home forms the core (see Wikström and Butterworth 2006). This appears to hold true for their illicit as well as their legitimate activities.

To analyse the distance young people in Peterborough offended from home, we calculated the straight-line distance between police-recorded young offenders' homes and the locations of their crimes when both fell within the study area.[21,22] For offences committed by multiple offenders, this distance was included for each offender. Figure 5.7 shows a clear distance-decay relationship between offenders' home and crime locations: fewer crimes occurred further from offenders' areas of residence. Figure 5.8 shows this relationship held true for both violent and property crimes,[23] but was particularly strong for violent crime and vandalism. Pyle et al. (1974) and Wikström (1991) also found the distance-decay relationship to be particularly strong for violent crimes.

The mean distance between an offender's home and offence location was 2.1 kilometres (Table 5.15), only about a 20-minute walk, which is consistent with the contention that people tend to operate where they are familiar, such as the area close to their home.

[21] Overall, 16.6 per cent of offences were excluded. Most were excluded because the offender lived outside the study area (the further offenders lived from the study area, the less accurate or complete the police-recorded data). For most crime types this meant a loss of between 5 and 7 per cent of offences, but for shoplifting nearly 36 per cent were excluded (accounting for more than half of all excluded offences). A small proportion (3 per cent) of excluded offences were due to missing data on the offender's home location (eg, if the offender was homeless).

[22] Offender home locations were recorded at the output area level and assigned the coordinates of the output area's population centre (see technical appendix, section A1.1). For smaller, more populated output areas this would, at most, make a difference of a few hundred metres. In larger, rural output areas it could make a greater difference, but is likely to be more accurate than the geographic centre.

[23] Recall that the distance from offender's home to shoplifting locations may be considerably underestimated, considering a large proportion of acts of shoplifting occurred outside the study area.

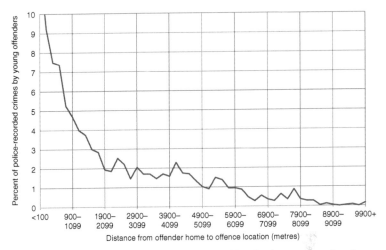

**Figure 5.7 Distance decay of offence to offender home location for police-recorded offences by 13- to 17-year-olds**

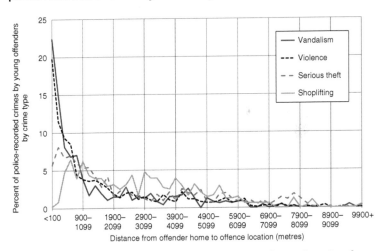

**Figure 5.8 Distance decay of offence to offender home location for police-recorded offences by 13- to 17-year-olds by crime type**

Car crimes and shoplifting tended to occur furthest from young people's homes. The latter was undoubtedly strongly influenced by the location of shopping venues.[24] For some crime types there was

---

[24] Indeed, the distance travelled to shoplift may be significantly underestimated as more than one-third of such acts either took place, or were committed by those who lived, outside the study area.

**Table 5.14 Distance police-recorded acts of residential and non-residential burglary by 13- to 17-year-olds occurred from offenders' homes by social disadvantage[a]**

| Offence location | Mean distance from offender's home (km) | N burglaries |
|---|---|---|
| All output areas | 1.9 | 289 |
| 25% most advantaged output areas | 2.8 | 44 |
| 50% average advantaged output areas | 2.1 | 143 |
| 25% most disadvantaged output areas | 1.3 | 102 |

[a] For offences committed within the study area by young offenders living within the study area.

a link between environmental features and the distance of crimes from offenders' homes. For example, burglary in disadvantaged areas was more likely to be committed by local young offenders, while burglary in more advantaged areas was more likely to be committed by offenders who lived further away (Table 5.14).

Crimes of a more expressive nature occurred closer to home than more instrumental crimes: acts of vandalism and violence were committed, on average, only a kilometre and a half from the offender's home. In fact, nearly half of young people's violence and vandalism occurred within half a kilometre of their homes (compared to only one-fifth of their acts of serious theft).

Despite the clear distance-decay relationship, many crimes took place outside the immediate area around offenders' homes (Table 5.15), consistent with studies that have also found that despite the concentration of crimes near offenders' homes, the majority of crimes occur further away (Tita and Griffiths 2005; Wikström 1985; 1991: 220). That many crimes are committed outside offenders' areas of residence, and different crime types tend to occur different distances from offenders' homes, was highlighted by some of the earliest social ecological research (eg see Burgess [1925] 1967). It is our contention that the same mechanism explains crime concentrations and the distance-decay relationship: crimes occur where potential offenders (ie people with a high crime propensity) spend time (under certain circumstances), and potential offenders, like everyone else, spend much of their time at or near their homes (and are therefore more likely to encounter certain circumstances closer to, rather than further from, home).

**Table 5.15 Distance between offenders' home and crime locations[a]**

| Crime type | N | Distance in km | | Percentage crime within distance from home | | | Percentage crime in other place in study area |
|---|---|---|---|---|---|---|---|
| | | Mean | SD | 100 m | 100–500 m | 500–1000 m | |
| Car crime | 428 | 3.0 | 2.6 | 4.4 | 10.5 | 16.1 | 68.9 |
| Shoplifting | 481 | 2.9 | 2.0 | 0.2 | 5.6 | 12.7 | 81.5 |
| Burglary | 289 | 1.9 | 1.8 | 7.6 | 21.1 | 15.9 | 55.4 |
| Violence | 861 | 1.6 | 1.9 | 19.7 | 20.8 | 15.2 | 44.3 |
| Vandalism | 469 | 1.5 | 1.9 | 22.4 | 23.0 | 16.6 | 38.0 |
| Theft from a person | 9 | 1.3 | 1.7 | 11.1 | 33.3 | 11.1 | 44.4 |
| Serious theft | 717 | 2.6 | 2.4 | 5.7 | 14.8 | 16.0 | 63.5 |
| Violence and vandalism | 1330 | 1.6 | 1.9 | 20.7 | 21.6 | 15.7 | 42.0 |
| All | 2537 | 2.1 | 2.1 | 12.5 | 16.7 | 15.2 | 55.6 |

[a] Police-recorded crimes of selected crime types by 13–17-year-olds.

### 5.5.1 Crime and distance in action

Consistent with the argument that a large portion of an offender's crimes are committed locally, we found that the number of resident police-recorded young offenders correlated significantly with the count of young people's crime at the output area level (Table 5.16). Across all output areas this correlation was significant: more young offenders lived in output areas where there were more crimes by young people. This relationship held true for all crime types except shoplifting (which is to be expected considering the nature of shoplifting and its spatial distribution; see section 5.1.1), and was particularly strong for expressive crimes such as violence and vandalism.

The city and local centres, however, were substantial outliers. The city centre was especially extreme; although the vast majority of young people's crime was concentrated in the city centre, especially in the two main city centre output areas, it had few resident offenders. In fact, the two main output areas had only six resident young people each in 2001 (aged 9–13) and no resident police- or self-recorded young offenders during the study period. Excluding these commercial centres strengthened the relationship between the number of resident young offenders and crimes by young people for all crimes and all crime types, except shoplifting (already described as a special case) and serious theft, which remained unaffected (as these are rarer events that typically took place in residential settings—see section 5.1.1— the local and city centres were not such extreme outliers). All in all, these findings suggest that young people's crime mainly tends to occur in and around their place of residence and at key locations they are attracted to (such as the city and local centres).

Early research on urbanization and crime has linked urban centres (areas close to the central business district) with high offender concentrations (eg US: Lander 1954; Schmid 1960b: 660; UK: Burt 1944; Castle and Gittus 1961: 420; Morris 1957: 21; Wallis and Maliphant 1967). Subsequent research, however, has found that this relationship may hold only in cities with a particular urban structure (ie similar to that of Chicago as Shaw and McKay found it in the 1920s) (see, eg, Baldwin 1975; Baldwin and Bottoms 1976; Bottoms and Wiles 1997: 331; Bursik 1986; Harries 1974: 74–5; Herbert 1972: 217; Mays 1963: 160; Taub et al. 1984). In the United Kingdom the relocation of people from slum areas to housing estates shifted the concentration of offenders from inner-city areas to the outskirts of the city (Baldwin 1975; Baldwin and Bottoms 1976; Herbert 1978; Mays 1963: 160). Contemporary UK city centres, including Peterborough's, have fewer residents, and are

**Table 5.16 Zero-order correlations[a] between the number of all resident police-recorded young offenders (logged) and number of police-recorded crimes (logged) committed by young people (by crime type) at the output area level**

| Crime type | All output areas | Output areas outside the local and city centres |
|---|---|---|
| All crime | .41 | .47 |
| Vandalism | .32 | .36 |
| Violence | .38 | .43 |
| Shoplifting | n.s. | n.s. |
| Car crime | .24 | .24 |
| Burglary | .19 | .18 |
| Serious theft (burglary and car crime) | .28 | .29 |
| Violence and vandalism | .43 | .48 |

[a] All correlations significant at the .000 level.

generally 'populated' by non-residents moving in and out of the centre following the ebb and flow of daily activities.

Three of the four output areas that make up Peterborough city centre had few resident young people, and all had a low rate of young offenders, whether police-recorded or self-reported (see Figure 5.3 and Table 5.17). Most of the land in these output areas is devoted to commercial and public use and characterized by shopping centres and streets, transport stations, commercial buildings, and green space, rather than housing; therefore these population characteristics are unsurprising. Output areas containing local centres, however, were more residential (despite containing shops and local services such as libraries, doctors' surgeries, and schools) and alternatively did not vary from the mean in terms of resident young people. They were however, home to nearly three times the rate of police-recorded young offenders (but only a slightly higher rate of self-reported young offenders)[25] (Table 5.17).

**Table 5.17  Resident young people and offenders in city and local centre output areas**

| Output areas (OAs) | Resident young people (9–13 in 2001) | Police-recorded young offenders | Self-reported young offenders |
| --- | --- | --- | --- |
| All | | | |
| Mean | 21.2 | 2.4 | 2.5 |
| City centre (4 OAs) | 56 | 6 | 2 |
| Mean per OA | 14.0 | 1.5 | 0.5 |
| Local centre (6 OAs) | 112 | 39 | 10 |
| Hampton Centre | 25 | 17 | 5 |
| Bretton Centre | 18 | 3 | 1 |
| Werrington Centre (2 OAs) | 27 | 3 | 2 |
| Orton Centre (2 OAs) | 42 | 16 | 2 |
| Mean per OA | 19.3 | 6.5 | 1.7 |

[25] There was a slight effect of urban development in the output area containing the Hampton Centre, which means the rate of resident young offenders was artificially close to the number of young residents, as the population of young people in 2001 did not reflect the largely increased population during Phase 1. However, even when this local centre was excluded, the mean rate of young offenders in areas with local centres was still twice that of all output areas.

This point was clearly supported by the finding that young offenders living in different output area aggregates offended in different parts of the city: predominantly near their home aggregate, but also in key locations like nearby local centres. Young people from all areas, however, also offended in the city centre. To illustrate this, Figure 5.9 shows that acts of violence and vandalism by young offenders living in the Orton output area aggregate clustered in or around the aggregate, with additional concentrations in the city centre, Thorpe Wood Police Station, Orton Longueville School,[26] and Hampton Centre.[27] Serious thefts, consistent with earlier discussions, were slightly more spread out, although the main clusters remained near the aggregate and in the city centre. Even shoplifting, the spatial distribution of which was driven significantly by the location of shops, was reasonably localized, occurring mainly in the city centre and nearby local centres (ie Orton and Hampton Centres), rather than more distant retail centres.

Similar patterns held for all other output area aggregates with a high young offender concentration, with the majority of crimes being committed close to home or in the city centre (Figure 5.10).

Clearly, offender home locations strongly influence crime locations (as we have argued, because routine activities, against a backdrop of social environmental factors that lead to the emergence of crime prone people and crime-conducive settings, bring crime prone young people into contact with crime-conducive settings). For some crimes, we can go even further, to look at the impact of particular offenders, from particular home locations, and their particular acts of crime, on the overall spatial patterns. Upon closer inspection, we found that the distribution of serious thefts by young people in Peterborough during the study period was driven by a very select group of offenders: one-third of all police-recorded burglaries by known young offenders between 2004 and 2007 were committed by three young offenders (2 per cent of all young burglars), while more than two-fifths (41.6 per cent) of all thefts of or from a vehicle were committed by just four young offenders (4.8 per cent of all offenders committing vehicle-related thefts). Other crime types did not demonstrate anything like this kind of concentration at the level of individual offenders.

---

[26] Orton Longueville School and Bushfield Community College both serve the Orton output area aggregate; the latter, however, is located within the aggregate.

[27] Because Figures 5.9 and 5.10 show relative density maps (see technical appendix, section A1.2.2), it is not possible to compare the volume of crime.

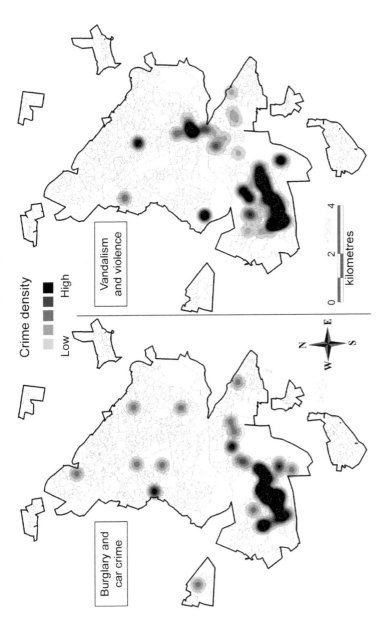

**Figure 5.9 Relative density of crime locations by police-recorded young offenders living within the Orton output area aggregate**

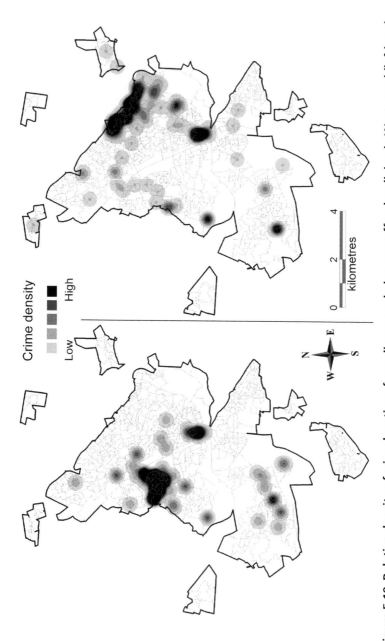

**Figure 5.10  Relative density of crime locations for police-recorded young offenders living in Westwood (left) and Eastern (right) output area aggregates**

The fact that offenders tend to offend near their homes means that the location of these young offenders' homes significantly influenced the distribution of burglary and car crime across the study area. For example, the top two police-recorded young burglars, both of whom lived in the Ortons, were responsible for one-fifth of all 261 burglaries by a known young offender; only one of their 54 burglaries (45 of which were of residential buildings) took place outside the Ortons, leading to a heavy concentration of burglaries in the Ortons (ie Orton Malborne, Orton Goldhay, and Orton Waterville; see Figure 5.11).

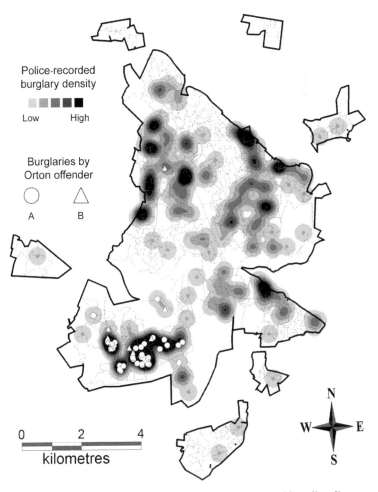

Figure 5.11 Relative density of burglaries committed by all police-recorded young offenders, and burglaries by the two most prolific (*N* = 261)

## 5.6 Summary and conclusion

In this chapter we analysed the spatial concentration of young people's crime events and its key area predictors, the spatial concentration of young offender's home locations and its key area predictors, and the relationship between offenders' home locations and the location of their crime events (generally referred to as the study of crime and distance).

Generally, the patterns of young people's crime were similar to those of the total population, which is not surprising as young people make up a large proportion of all offenders. Young people's crimes were concentrated in the city and local centres and in residential areas with poor collective efficacy, which we have highlighted as the two most criminogenic kinds of urban environments.

We showed that the home locations of police-recorded offenders were concentrated in certain areas, which tended to overlap with areas where offenders self-reporting a high crime frequency and/or serious thefts tended to live, which were also the same areas where crime prone young people tended to live. These findings thus imply that young offenders are concentrated in particular areas because crime prone young people are concentrated in those areas. In other words, areas that have more resident young people who have weaker law-relevant morality and a poor ability to exercise self-control have more resident young people who are frequently involved in crime. These areas tended to have greater disadvantage, and, although young people tended to live in areas with greater disadvantage, we showed that differences between areas where offenders were concentrated and areas where they were not were greater than what we would expect taking rates of resident young people into account.

We showed that young people often, but not exclusively, offend close to home. Distance-decay (and hence the residential segregation of crime prone young people) is apparently *one* important factor that determines the locations of young people's crime. However, significant portions of young people's crime are also committed at a distance from their homes (particularly those crimes that occur in the city centre).

While the residential segregation of crime prone young people, coupled with the distance-decay function, goes some way to explaining the locations of young people's crime, this is far from the whole story. People's criminogenic exposure is not only a function of where they live but also where they spend time more generally (as a consequence of self and social selection processes). Therefore, to explain their urban crime patterns we need to more comprehensively analyse how young people's social lives (activity fields) relate to criminogenic exposure.

# 6

# Young People, Their Activities, and Criminogenic Exposure

To understand the role of the environment for young people's crime we need to understand their social lives. We can do so by studying their activity patterns—what they do, and where and under what circumstances they do it. These activity patterns can be quantified as their *activity fields*—the configuration of settings, and their circumstances, to which a person is exposed during a particular period of time. It is through these settings that the environment exerts its influence on people's behaviour. Situational Action Theory (SAT) proposes that criminogenic exposure is a key explanatory variable in young people's crime involvement, because it is when crime prone people intersect with such settings that crime may occur.

The main aims of this chapter are to:

(1) present young people's general activity patterns across time and space, classify them according to orientation, and then explore differences in rates of crime by orientation category;

(2) focus on the most criminogenic activity category—peer-oriented time—and discuss and analyse the criminogenic potential of two key circumstances: a lack of supervision and a lack of structure;

(3) analyse why young people vary in their exposure to criminogenic settings, as a function of their levels of supervision and home locations; and, finally

(4) statistically test the explanation that area variations in the concentration of young people's crime are a consequence of the convergence of crime prone young people and criminogenic social environments.

## 6.1 Young people's activity patterns

In their daily lives, young people are involved in many different kinds of activities across many different settings, from basic necessities (eg eating and personal care), to education, employment, and innumerable pastimes. A host of factors may be linked to what activities certain young people take part in in which settings, including personal factors (eg sex, age), family factors (eg resources, family structure), cultural factors (eg religion, customs), legal factors (eg education and employment laws), and area factors (eg resources, residential segregation, land use). However, the general constraints on young people's time use (such as their greater dependence on and therefore supervision by adults, the demands of compulsory education, and limitations on their mobility), mean that young people's activity patterns may vary less than those of adults, both in the kinds of activities that young people take part in and when and where those activities take place. This means that space–time budget methods may be particularly useful for studying young people and capturing and characterizing their activity patterns across space and time.

Young people's activities patterns can (and have been) characterized in many different ways. Within criminology, activity patterns are often discussed using the concept of *routines* (eg Cohen and Felson 1979; Wikström and Sampson 2003) or *lifestyles* (eg Hindelang et al. 1978; Riley 1987; West and Farrington 1977). However, there are few methodologies that can operationalize these concepts effectively. A common approach has been simply to measure what young people do (or, eg, where they go), and for how long (or, in some cases, how often), often using stylized questionnaires. The space–time budget methodology (see section 2.5) is capable of going much further in characterizing complete activity fields, as well as the circumstances of action that are key to understanding young people's exposure and the role of the social environment. In the following section we use data from the space–time budget to describe the typical daily routines of Peterborough youths aged 13 to 17 and their general lifestyles.[1] We consider the major social influences on young people and their time use and begin to hone in on elements of that time use that are most criminogenic.

### 6.1.1 Young people's general time use

At certain times of day, on certain days of the week, young people's patterns of activity converge. How young people spend their time

---

[1] See technical appendix, section A1.4, for details on how time use was quantified.

during convergent hours is predominantly determined by social selection (influences such as the school calendar, working days, etc.). When their time diverges, self selection effects (preferences) and personal differences (eg resources, which may limit access) play a more significant role in what settings they take part in, and therefore their activity fields and exposure.

In Figure 6.1 we show how participation in key activities varies over a typical day for 13- to 17-year-olds in Peterborough. This and similar analyses (see, eg, Copperman and Bhat 2007; Wikström and Butterworth 2006) show us that young people's weekly life follows a general pattern. Figure 6.2 shows how this participation changes by age (for example, time spent in family activities declines while time with peers increases).

Particularly divergent time for young people occurs in the early evenings after school, and on the weekends, especially in the middle of the day. Most young people in the PADS+ sample spent their discretionary time at home with their families, although some converged towards peer-related activities, especially on weekends.

For most young people aged 13 to 17, weekdays were dominated by the school day; therefore most young people had a similar activity pattern between 06:00 and 16:00. They tended to wake up between 07:00 and 08:00 (sleeping in longer as they got older), spend about an hour getting ready for school, head to school between 08:00 and 09:00 and leave school between 14:30 and 15:30. They spent between five and a half and six and a half hours at school. They also reported, on average, two to three and a half hours of spare time, most of which was spent travelling to and from school and socializing or playing sports and games during the school lunch hour.

After school, most young people had, on average, five to six hours of spare time. One to two and a half of these hours were often spent with peers, generally immediately after school, often on the way home. Most of this time, however, was spent at home with family members (typically with adult guardians present), generally in unstructured activities, including around two hours watching television and up to an hour and a half socializing with parents, siblings, and/or peers, as well as personal care (eg bathing, eating). Most 13- to 17-year-olds were in bed by 22:00 or 23:00 on weekday evenings, although they stayed up later as they got older. Their sleeping patterns were consistent with those reported in other studies of adolescents' time use (see, eg, Larson and Verma 1999;

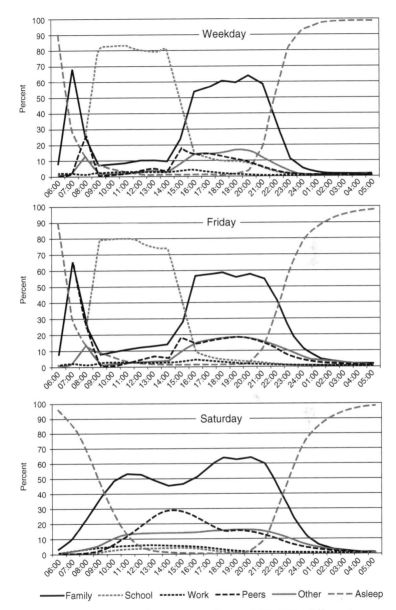

**Figure 6.1  Percentage of young people aged 13–17 in different activity categories[a] over time by day of the week (Phase 1)**

[a] For how these categories are defined, see Table 6.3.

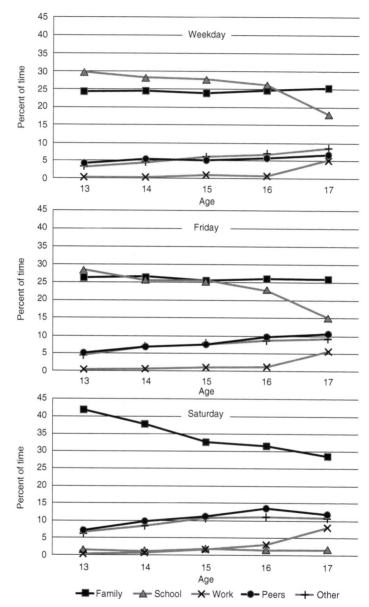

**Figure 6.2  Percentage of time young people spent in activity categories by age**

Olds et al. 2009); they slept, on average, around nine hours per weekday and 10 hours per Saturday[2] across Phase 1 (with total sleep falling slightly with age, especially on the weekends).[3]

Unlike weekdays, weekend days were dominated by spare time, much of which young people spent at home and/or with their families doing unstructured activities such as watching television and socializing. They tended to wake up between 09:00 and 10:00 and spent some time in the city centre (one hour, generally between 12:00 and 16:00) and with their peers (one and a half hours), with this time often overlapping, and unsupervised.

Most young people spent most of their weekend evenings at home with their families (four to five hours), although many also spent free time with their peers (two to four hours), generally supervised and at one another's homes. Weekend evenings were generally devoted to unstructured leisure. Watching television and socializing remained key activities, with young people watching around two and a half hours of television and socializing for one to two and a half hours. They went to bed later on Saturday nights than weeknights and Friday nights, though most were asleep at 23:00 or 24:00.

These general weekly patterns characterized most school weeks. PADS+ space–time budget data was collected primarily during the first quarter of the year, so can be seen to characterize the middle term of the school year. We would expect considerable variation during school holidays, as well as some variation across different seasons (for example differences in daylight hours and temperature will affect outdoor activities).

---

[2] Time slept per day does not reflect continuous hours of sleep over a particular night (see technical appendix, section A1.4). While we feel that hours slept between 06:00 on one weekday and 06:00 the next (eg between 06:00 Wednesday and 06:00 Thursday) will accurately capture hours slept on weekday nights, and hours slept between 06:00 Saturday and 06:00 Sunday will generally capture sleeping patterns on weekend nights, Friday is excluded from this analysis as sleep between Friday morning (a weekday morning) and 06:00 Saturday cannot be taken to reflect sleep either on a weekend or a weekday night.

[3] While sleep is important for physical and mental health, time spent asleep is not particularly interesting in the study of young people's exposure and the role of the social environment, as it cannot be rationally quantified as exposure to any particular social setting when a setting is defined as the external features one can access with one's senses. Hence we focus our analyses on the 205,885 (of 329,952 total) hours which PADS+ participants spent awake during the study period.

## 6.1.2  Young people's general spatial dynamics

As their general time use shows, young people spend a large proportion of their time at home, and much of their remaining time at school; because their schools are typically near their homes, their activity fields are highly localized in space. Peterborough's urban design of insular townships also means young people have access to local centres, with shops and services, also near their homes, although they also gravitate towards the main city centre.

The average distance young people travelled from their home to any outside activity was around 2.5 (SD = 3) km.[4, 5] There were clear changes with age; young people's activities moved further afield as they got older, with a significant jump at age 17, when young people's activities took place on average 3.7 km from home (SD = 5 km) (see Figure 6.9). This jump is most likely accounted for by the fact that at 17 some young people's activity fields were not as constrained in their routine activities—they had left school and many held jobs further from home (such as in the city centre)—and some young people (or their peers) had acquired their driving licences and therefore had access to personal motor transport (see, eg, Bichler et al. 2011). As they got older, young people also gravitated more towards the city centre, where they spent an increasing amount of time with their peers, much of it unsupervised, and working (Table 6.1).

Although young people's activity fields widened as they grew older, most of their activities during the study period remained constrained around certain key locations, including their homes, schools, places of work, friends' homes, nearest local centre, and the city centre.

Certain kinds of activities tend naturally to cluster at certain locations; for example school activities generally clustered in output areas containing schools (as illustrated by the high Gini coefficient: $G = .94$), although 9.3 per cent of school-related activities

---

[4] We geocoded many locations where young people spent time that lay outside the study area, but limited this to within a 50-mile radius of the city centre. Therefore we will always underestimate the average distance young people travel to their activities. However, as we were able to calculate distance from home for 97.1 per cent of all hours that young people spent awake, this underestimation will be minimal.

[5] Straight-line distances; see technical appendix, section A1.1, for how these are calculated.

**Table 6.1  Hours spent in the city centre by age**

| Age | Total hours | With peers | Unsupervised with peers | Paid work |
|---|---|---|---|---|
| | Hours (% *time awake*) | Hours (% *time in city centre*) | Hours (% *time in city centre*) | Hours (% *time in city centre*) |
| 13 | 859 (*2.1*) | 462 (*53.8*) | 329 (*38.3*) | 0 (*0.0*) |
| 14 | 924 (*2.2*) | 559 (*60.5*) | 487 (*52.7*) | 11 (*1.2*) |
| 15 | 1,142 (*2.8*) | 839 (*73.5*) | 688 (*60.2*) | 9 (*0.8*) |
| 16 | 1,529 (*3.7*) | 1,079 (*70.6*) | 853 (*55.8*) | 135 (*8.9*) |
| 17 | 2,972 (*7.5*) | 2,150 (*72.3*) | 1,287 (*43.3*) | 728 (*24.5*) |

took place in other settings (92.2 per cent of these hours were devoted to homework and 98.9 per cent of homework hours were spent at home or in another's home). Similarly, work-related activities also naturally concentrated in workplaces, although the changing nature of young people's work as they aged meant the spatial distribution of their working hours also changed; during early adolescence (ages 13 and 14) the majority of young people's paid work involved paper delivery rounds (64 per cent),[6] and was therefore concentrated in residential areas ($G = .94$), while in later adolescence their work was increasingly concentrated in more commercial areas (especially the city centre) and industrial areas ($G = .94$).

Family activities, as expected, tended to cluster in young people's homes, which were widely distributed around the study area. Much of young people's discretionary time was also spent in the home, but also spread to nearby public spaces and key entertainment settings, such as nearby local centres or the city centre.

Regardless of the activity, young people's time was considerably localized around these key locations. To illustrate this, Figure 6.3 shows the spatial distribution of discretionary time spent by young people who lived in the Orton output area aggregate.[7] As was the case for all young people, these young people spent much of their

---

[6] Although paper delivery rounds accounted for only 5.6 per cent of the total working hours in Phase 1.

[7] As defined in section 5.3.2. For details on how chloropleth maps are created see technical appendix, section A1.2.1.

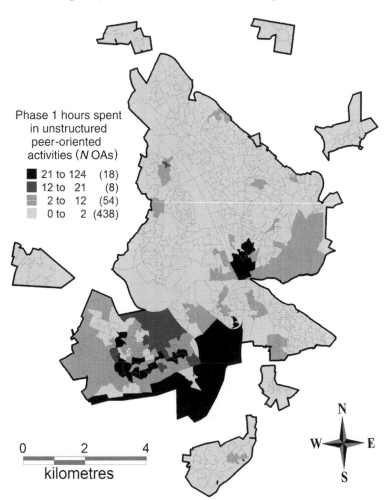

Figure 6.3 Spatial distribution of young people from the Orton area's discretionary time (unstructured peer-oriented activities: see section 6.2.2)

time at home and local schools, but it is clear that even in their more discretionary time they spent very little of it outside their local areas, except in the city centre and a few key locations, such as the large Serpentine Green Shopping Centre in the Hamptons.

Across Phase 1, 92.2 per cent of all hours the young people spent awake occurred within 500 metres of their home, school, three best

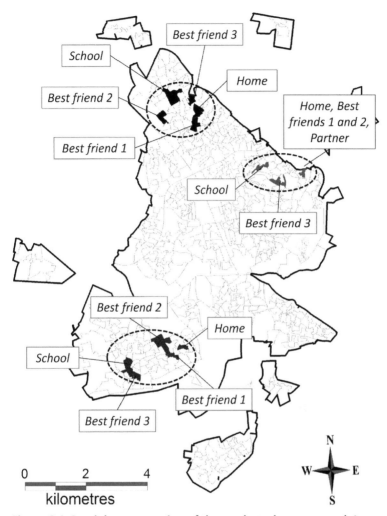

**Figure 6.4 Spatial concentration of three selected young people's key locations**

friends' homes, nearest local centre, and the city centre.[8] This illustrates the extreme degree to which their activities were spatially constrained. Figure 6.4 shows the spatial distribution of three young people's key locations (excluding the city and local centres, which can

[8] Distances represent metres between the population centres of the output areas containing each key location (see technical appendix, section A1.1).

**Table 6.2  Distribution of time spent awake
within 500 m of key locations by age**

| Age | Percentage hours awake |
|-----|------------------------|
| 13–17 | 92.2 |
| 13 | 94.4 |
| 14 | 94.2 |
| 15 | 93.0 |
| 16 | 92.2 |
| 17 | 86.9 |

be seen in Figure 4.2) to demonstrate what this localization means in terms of geographic area, which helps to further explain patterns of time use such as those illustrated in Figure 6.3).

As they aged young people did spend less time in such close proximity to these key locations (Table 6.2), demonstrating their greater mobility and increasing discretionary time.

### 6.1.3  Young people's general activities

The concentration of young people's activities around key locations highlights several activity domains that may be seen to characterize the majority of young people's time use: family, school, work, and peers. These domains, representing key social institutions, exert different but significant influences on young people, both developmentally and situationally, and, in general, some (eg peers) may be more conducive to crime than others (eg family, school, and work; see Table 6.9).

To characterize time use across these domains, we drew upon several dimensions of space–time budget data, including information about the main activity, functional setting, and people present. Bringing together these circumstantial factors creates a very specific portrayal of different contexts of action (ie settings and circumstances; see Stafford 2009: 23 on complex constructions). For example, although the main activity is the same, an hour spent socializing with peers is contextually very different from an hour spent socializing with family members. Similarly, although the activity and people present are the same, socializing with peers at school during the lunch break is contextually very different from socializing with peers on a street corner late at night. Our detailed space–time budget methodology provides us with multimodal circumstantial data with which we can differentiate between contexts specifically and conceptually, allowing for much more complex, and particular, data manipulation and analysis, far beyond what is typically feasible.

We divided young people's time use by its *orientation*, ie whether it was oriented towards family, school, work, or peer domains. Table 6.3 shows the conceptualization of key orientation variables

**Table 6.3  Conceptualization and definition of key activity categories**

| Orientation | | Definition |
|---|---|---|
| Work | Time spent doing activities related to paid work | Paid work anywhere (including paper rounds and babysitting) or any activity in one's workplace |
| School | Time spent doing activities related to one's education or school | Educational activities (eg attending classes, serving detention, doing homework) anywhere, or any activities at school |
| | | *Exceptions*: activities in a workplace or paid work in a school |
| Family | Time spent with one's family, or time spent at home doing personal activities | Any activity at home or any activity outside the home with an adult family member[a] present |
| | | *Exceptions*: activities that are unsupervised with peers, educational activities or paid work (not including chores), or socializing electronically |
| Peers | Time spent unsupervised with peers or young family members | Any unsupervised activity with peers, partners, and/or young family members |
| | | *Exceptions*: educational activities or paid work, or activities with young family members only |
| Other | Time spent in activities that are not work, school, family, or peer-oriented | Includes activities spent outside school, work, and home contexts and centred on people other than family and peers, such as socializing electronically (during hours that are not school, work, or peer-oriented), time spent alone (outside the home), and time spent in other people's homes |
| Asleep | Time spent sleeping | Sleeping anywhere |

[a]The concept of family members includes the extended family, eg grandparents and cousins.

and precisely how they are defined.[9] Data was categorized primarily in accordance with our conceptual framework and the nature of the space–time budget data, as well as knowledge about the young people and their activities gained through one-to-one interviews.

## Family-oriented activities

There is no question that the family is a key context in which young people develop and act throughout childhood and adolescence; consequently, much research into the role of the environment in that development and action has focused on the home (or the surrounding neighbourhood; see, for example, Brooks-Gunn et al. 1993).[10] Although the home is a key setting for family-oriented activities, not all family-oriented activities take place at home, and not all time at home is family-oriented. Conceptually, family-oriented activities (like peer-oriented activities) depend more on who a young person is with than where a young person is or what he or she is doing. For example, time at home spent unsupervised with peers can be seen as oriented towards those peers, rather than the family. At the same time, playing football with parents and siblings outside the home is oriented towards the family. We were able to capture these intricacies by defining any activities in or outside the home that were supervised by parents or other family adults as family-oriented. Domestic activities in the home were also defined as family-oriented, as they entail care of the home and the self, which are a part of family life. However, when there was overlap between family and work or school domains, the latter two were taken to dominate, as the presence of family adults during school or work activities, or in school or work settings, is likely to be less central to the context (eg when a parent comes to their child's school, the focus of both the parent and child typically remains on school activities). Thus a young person doing homework at home was involved in a school, not a family, oriented activity, even if his or her parents were present.

[9] We refer to an hour's orientation as its activity category. However, the orientation of a particular hour is defined not only by the ongoing activity, but also by the circumstances, including the functional place and who is present (just as an activity field refers to what young people do, where, and with whom).

[10] While the fact that young people spend more time at home than in any other context vouches for the value of this research, young people spend more time awake outside the home environment than in it, hence it is important to take into account the role of other environments.

Of the 15 hours they spent awake on average per day during Phase 1, PADS+ participants spent more than six and a half hours at home.[11] Most of this time was family-oriented, although as they aged young people spent an increasing amount of time at home in other activities (from 8.2 per cent of their time at home at age 13 to 18.3 per cent at age 17), including steady increases in the time they spent unsupervised with their peers and doing homework. Most family-oriented time was spent watching television and DVDs (39.4 per cent), playing on consoles or computers or browsing the internet (9.6 per cent), and socializing face to face (4.2 per cent).

## School-oriented activities

In most westernized countries, education is compulsory until mid to late adolescence, meaning that time in school-oriented activities significantly shapes young people's activity patterns. School activities are generally highly structured, with specific goals (typically directed towards cognitive and social development), schedules, codes of conduct, and high levels of monitoring and supervision. For this reason they are highly significant as developmental contexts, and may play a critical role in the acquisition of young people's personal morality and ability to exercise self-control (hence their crime propensity). However, the relevance of the school context for young people's lifestyles changes dramatically, at least for some young people, once they reach the age where they can leave compulsory education, depending on the decisions they make about continuing their education or entering the workforce, and different groups of young people emerge leading significantly different lifestyles.

To capture school-oriented activities, we defined any activity in a school setting as school-oriented, unless the activity was paid work, and any school-related activity in any other setting as school-oriented, unless it took place in a workplace, as doing paid work in a school is more likely to be an occupational than an educational activity, while classes in a workplace are likely to be vocational, and therefore work-oriented.

Up to the age of 15, very few of the sample (1 per cent) were not in education; in the United Kingdom young people are only able to

---

[11] Unless otherwise specified, 'home' refers to the young person's main home and any alternative home where he or she may live part of the time (eg where he or she spends more than a couple of days every fortnight on a regular basis), for example if his or her parents are divorced.

leave compulsory education when they turn 16. PADS+ participants turned 16 during Wave 4, but 96.2 per cent of participants
remained in education (over 90 per cent full time), until Wave 5.
However, when participants were 17, the number of young people
not in education (23.8 per cent) was more significant.[12]

School provides an important context for socialization, which
may be particularly important for young people who lack effective
influences at home; the fact that young people spend around 30 per
cent of their time awake at school, especially early in adolescence
(an important developmental window, eg for agency, self-regula-
tion, and moral reasoning), suggests school can be an important
conduit for influencing that development (for example, via moral
education). Participants spent around six hours at school per weekday during Phase 1,[13] which included one to two hours when they
were not in classes (eg lunch and other breaks). Most crime reported
during school-oriented activities took place outside the classroom,
which suggests that even within the school day social settings vary
significantly, including in their criminogeneity.

The most common school-oriented activity that takes place outside
the school setting is homework. Most PADS+ participants spent very
little time on homework (on average less than half an hour throughout Phase 1), although there was a significant increase at 17 for those
remaining in full-time education (to more than one hour), which is
consistent with findings from other research (eg Olds et al. 2009).

### Work-oriented activities

Because UK employment law restricts the amount, time, and type of
employment, for young people under 16 (and these restrictions are
particularly tight for children under 14), in order to protect young
people's health, safety, and development, as well as safeguard attendance and performance at school, work is not a key activity, and
workplaces are not a key setting, for most young people between the
ages of 13 and 17. Compulsory school attendance also restricts
young people's employment options. PADS+ participants spent very
little time working until later adolescence; only 2.8 per cent of their

[12] This is consistent with data from the Department for Education for young
people in the same year group across the Peterborough local education authority.

[13] The length of time that students spend at school on a typical school day varies
cross-nationally, from between six to seven and half hours in most European countries and the United States (Alsaker and Flammer 1999; Fuligni and Stevenson
1995; Hofferth and Sandberg 2001), to between eight and a half to more than
nine hours in some east Asian countries (Fuligni and Stevenson 1995).

time awake during Phase 1 was work-oriented, and 64.5 per cent of those hours occurred during Wave 5 when they were 17, at which point nearly half the sample reported some kind of paid work.

Due to these restrictions on young people's employment, delivering newspapers by foot or bike[14] was the most common job young people held under the age of 16. These paper delivery rounds typically lasted for one hour and were completed before or after school on weekdays, or on Saturday mornings. To capture this time, work-oriented activities included not only time spent in a workplace, but also paid work anywhere else. Even when participants were 17, work-oriented activity accounted for only 9.3 per cent of their time awake. This indicates that workplaces may only become a key location in people's activity fields as they complete the transition into adulthood, at which time most people's activity patterns are dominated by employment.[15]

## Peer-oriented activities

Commitments to school (and later work) and dependence on the family instil a degree of conformity in how young people spend their time, much more so than the dynamics of adult life, significantly influencing their activity patterns and hence their exposure to different contexts of action. The time young people spend outside these key contexts is therefore of particular interest in understanding individual differences in criminogenic exposure. Family, school, and work-oriented contexts tend to constrain the kinds of activities that take place within them, being associated with stricter expectations for conduct (moral rules) and greater supervision (enforcement), be it by parents, teachers, or employers. During Phase 1 young people spent 22.9 per cent of their time awake in other settings that may have less stringent moral rules and weaker enforcement (and in which their reported rates of crime were significantly higher; see Table 6.9). More than half of this

[14] There is no specific space–time budget code for 'paper round'. Instead, paper rounds would have been coded as paid work in the streets or moving around by foot or bike; few other occupations would warrant this combination of codes. We chose to include only hours that young people spent this way alone as paper rounds, although some young people completed their paper rounds with friends, siblings, and even in some instances their parents, to avoid overestimating paper rounds by including other forms of work. Hence the estimates for paper rounds are conservative.

[15] Work-oriented activities have therefore taken a more central role in the design of data collection measures in Phase 2.

time was peer-oriented (spent unsupervised with peers outside of school or work contexts).

Peer-oriented activities capture the time that young people spend only in the presence of their peers.[16] This is a conservative approach, which maintains peers as the central social influence. Young people spent most of their peer-oriented time in settings outside their and others' homes. More than a quarter of this time was spent in streets or parks (see section 6.2.3). Young people also spent a considerable amount of peer-oriented time in shopping locales, although they spent only half of that time actually shopping. Other peer-oriented activities included sports and media. However, the vast majority of peer-oriented time was spent moving around (for example walking to and from school, but also around areas of the city)[17] and socializing face to face (Table 6.4 and Table 6.6).

The amount of time young people spent socializing face to face during peer-oriented activities increased substantially in later adolescence, likely in line with their increasing independence (see

**Table 6.4  Key places and activities for 13- to 17-year-olds' peer-oriented time**

| Activity | Percentage of peer-oriented time | Functional place | Percentage of peer-oriented time |
|---|---|---|---|
| Socializing | 36.3 | Streets or parks | 25.8 |
| Moving around | 21.5 | Moving around | 24.1 |
| Sport | 9.9 | Shopping locales | 15.8 |
| Shopping | 8.2 | Other's home | 13.7 |
| Media | 7.7 | Home | 5.2 |
| Other (eg hobbies, personal care) | 16.4 | Other (eg sports venue, leisure centre) | 15.4 |

[16] Young family members were counted as peers when they were in a setting where peers were also present. When a young person spent time alone with only young family members we abstained from quantifying this time, as it conceptually falls somewhere between family and peer-oriented time in regards to its influence on the moral context. Such time therefore is included in the other orientation category (although, all in all, only 1.8 per cent of all hours awake in Phase 1 were spent with young family members only).

[17] See section 6.2.3 on young people's time spent moving around, and some methodological considerations.

Table 6.5), although this tapered slightly at age 17 when educational and occupational demands increased.

Unlike school, work, and (to a lesser degree) family-oriented activities, peer-oriented activities experience little spatial constraints aside from those that generally affect young people's activities, as they are defined solely by who is present. Figure 6.5 shows the spatial distribution of time spent in peer-oriented activities during Phase 1. Although much of this time was concentrated in or near the city centre (17 per cent of all peer-oriented hours within the study area), as well as other local centres and shopping areas (such

**Table 6.5  Average time[18] spent socializing face to face during peer-oriented hours per day by age**

| Age | Peer-oriented socializing face to face | | |
|---|---|---|---|
| | Hrs:Mins per day | Hours | Percentage peer-oriented time |
| 13 | 0:17 | 809 | 23.7 |
| 14 | 0:19 | 881 | 19.6 |
| 15 | 0:38 | 1770 | 37.1 |
| 16 | 0:51 | 2299 | 40.9 |
| 17 | 0:46 | 2020 | 36.2 |
| Phase 1 | 0:34 | 7779 | 32.6 |

**Table 6.6  Average time[18] spent socializing face to face during peer-oriented hours by time and day of the week**

| Day | Time[a] | Peer-oriented socializing | |
|---|---|---|---|
| | | Hrs:Mins per day | Percentage of peer-oriented time |
| Weekday | Day | 0:05 | 13.7 |
| | Evening | 0:16 | 39.2 |
| Weekend | Day | 0:20 | 27.0 |
| | Evening | 0:34 | 44.9 |

[a]Daytime refers to the hours between 06:00 and 16:00, while evening refers to the hours between 16:00 and 06:00 the following morning (see technical appendix, section A1.4).

[18] Hours and minutes a young person would be expected to spend, on average, per day, doing the given activity. For more detail on how this is calculated, see technical appendix, section A1.4.

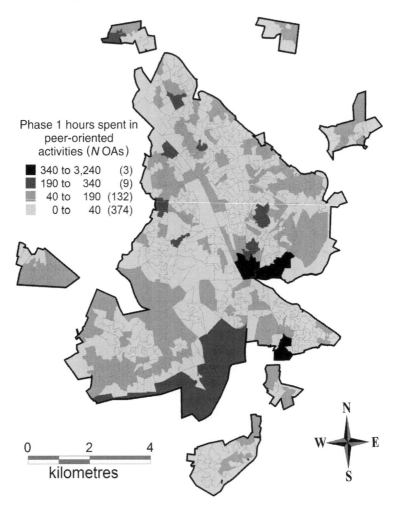

**Figure 6.5  Spatial distribution of peer-oriented activities by 13- to 17-year-olds**

as the Hampton Centre; 6 per cent), it was also distributed across residential areas, where young people were involved in peer-oriented activities in one another's homes (13.7 per cent), or in outdoor spaces such as streets (11.8 per cent), parks (14 per cent), or moving around (24.1 per cent). There was also a concentration of peer-oriented time in key entertainment locations, such as the output areas that house the ice rink (0.9 per cent) and Powerleague (a facility for five-a-side football) (2.1 per cent).

There was a considerable difference between this distribution and that of time spent merely unsupervised with peers. Time spent unsupervised with peers was concentrated in the city centre, but also in areas containing schools (see Figure 4.2), as young people spent time each school day with their peers (for example during the lunch hour and immediately after school) when they were not directly supervised. Because most young people are at school every weekday, these unsupervised hours come to dominate the time young people spend unsupervised with their peers, obscuring their more self selected time. When peer-oriented activities were defined more explicitly (excluding such time spent in school and work-related contexts), most output areas with schools dropped out as key areas (although some did remain, as they are familiar and accessible meeting points for young people, and often include popular recreational settings such as playing fields).

### Other activities

Activities that did not qualify as work, school, family, or peer-oriented were defined as 'other' activities. Only 11.3 per cent of all hours the young people spent awake in Phase 1 lacked an orientation (Table 6.9). Nearly one-third of these activities occurred in other people's homes, for example, at friends' houses with their parents present, which fell conceptually somewhere between family and peer-oriented time. Nearly another third was spent socializing electronically (eg over the internet or phone), which could be characterized either with regards to who was physically present (eg family while socializing electronically at home), or with whom the young person was socializing (eg peers who were not present). A large proportion (13.4 per cent) was spent alone (outside of school, work, and home environments).

### Summary

Nearly 90 per cent of young people's time awake was captured within the four orientation categories (family, school, work, and peers), three-quarters in family or school-oriented activities alone (which is comparable to earlier findings from Peterborough; see Wikström and Butterworth 2006: 213). However, as they grew older, young people spent less time, on average, in family and school-oriented activities, and more time in work and peer-oriented, as well as other, activities (see Figure 6.2 and Table 6.7).

Tables 6.7 and 6.8 show the average time, per day, young people spent doing activities in each activity category, by age and by day

**Table 6.7 Average time spent in key activities per day and percentage of all time awake by age**

| Age | Family | | School | | Work | | Peer | | Other | | Sleep |
|---|---|---|---|---|---|---|---|---|---|---|---|
| | Percentage of time awake | Hrs:Mins per day | Percentage of time awake | Hrs:Mins per day | Percentage of time awake | Hrs:Mins per day | Percentage of time awake | Hrs:Mins per day | Percentage of time awake | Hrs:Mins per day | Hrs:Mins per day |
| 13 | 47.7 | 6:58 | 36.4 | 5:19 | 0.5 | 0:04 | 8.2 | 1:12 | 7.1 | 1:33 | 9:24 |
| 14 | 45.2 | 6:44 | 33.3 | 4:58 | 0.8 | 0:07 | 10.8 | 1:37 | 9.9 | 2:17 | 9:06 |
| 15 | 42.0 | 6:18 | 32.9 | 4:55 | 1.5 | 0:14 | 11.5 | 1:44 | 12.0 | 3:02 | 9:01 |
| 16 | 41.6 | 6:23 | 29.8 | 4:35 | 2.1 | 0:20 | 13.5 | 2:04 | 13.0 | 3:10 | 8:39 |
| 17 | 41.5 | 6:16 | 20.8 | 3:08 | 9.3 | 1:24 | 14.0 | 2:07 | 14.4 | 3:14 | 8:55 |
| Phase 1 | 43.6 | 6:32 | 30.7 | 4:36 | 2.8 | 0:25 | 11.6 | 1:44 | 11.3 | 2:39 | 9:01 |

**Table 6.8 Average time spent in key activities and percentage of all time awake by time and day of the week**

| Age | | Family | | School | | Work | | Peer | | Other | | Sleep |
|---|---|---|---|---|---|---|---|---|---|---|---|---|
| | | Percentage of time awake | Hrs:Mins per day | Percentage of time awake | Hrs:Mins per day | Percentage of time awake | Hrs:Mins per day | Percentage of time awake | Hrs:Mins per day | Percentage of time awake | Hrs:Mins per day | Hrs:Mins per day |
| Weekday | Day | 21.4 | 1:49 | 64.7 | 5:30 | 2.4 | 0:12 | 7.0 | 0:35 | 4.5 | 0:23 | 1:30 |
| | Evening | 62.4 | 4:05 | 9.4 | 0:37 | 1.8 | 0:07 | 10.7 | 0:42 | 15.7 | 1:01 | 7:28 |
| Weekend | Day | 56.4 | 3:40 | 3.7 | 0:15 | 6.9 | 0:27 | 18.9 | 1:14 | 14.0 | 0:55 | 3:30 |
| | Evening | 59.6 | 4:25 | 3.0 | 0:13 | 2.4 | 0:11 | 17.1 | 1:16 | 17.8 | 1:19 | 6:35 |

and time, respectively. Although, as we see below, there was considerable variation in these activity patterns between young people, this provides a general overview of a typical young person's activity pattern by age and across a typical school week.

### 6.1.4  Variation in young people's general activities

There is significant variation in young people's activity patterns (Figure 6.6), and this variation plays a role in how certain kinds of young people intersect with certain kinds of settings. In subsequent sections we look at this variation in detail and analyse how it can explain differences in young people's crime involvement.

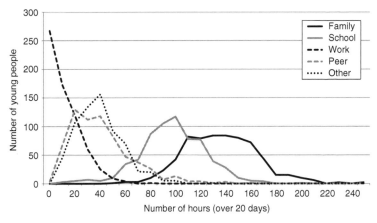

**Figure 6.6  Variation in the time young people aged 13–17 spent in activity categories (Phase 1[a])**

[a] For the 657 participants who completed space–time budgets in all five waves.

### 6.1.5  Young people's activities and crime

Certain kinds of time use may be more or less related to young people's crime involvement. We found distinct differences in young people's reported rates of crime (in the space–time budget) during activities falling under each life domain. Table 6.9 shows the rate of space–time budget crimes reported per 1,000 hours[19] participants

---

[19] Crimes per 1,000 hours provides a rate that accounts for the differing amounts of time participants spent in different kinds of settings, such that settings in which

**Table 6.9  Space–time budget crime rate for hours spent awake in different kinds of activities**

| Activity orientation | Percentage hours awake | Percentage space–time budget crimes (N) | Crimes/1,000 hours |
|---|---|---|---|
| Family | 43.6 | 9.9 (14) | 0.2 |
| School | 30.7 | 14.2 (20) | 0.3 |
| Work | 2.8 | 0.7  (1) | 0.2 |
| Peers | 11.6 | 62.4 (88) | 3.7 |
| Other | 11.3 | 12.8 (18) | 0.8 |
| All hours | 100.0 | 100.0 (141) | 0.7 |

spent doing activities in each domain. Crime was considerably rare during any activities, but it was most common during peer-oriented activities.

Table 6.9 shows that the rate of crime during family-oriented activities was the lowest of any life domain. Although young people spent the majority of their time awake in family-oriented activities, they rarely offended at these times. Generally, the family setting is not conducive to crime. In the main, parents (as well as other family members) represent prosocial influences, and report prosocial attitudes towards their children's behaviour. As Table 6.10 shows, 99.7 per cent of parents of PADS+ participants agreed that it was

**Table 6.10  Percentage of parents[a] reporting prosocial attitudes towards their children's behaviour**

| It is very important to me that my child... | Strongly disagree | Disagree | Neither agree nor disagree | Agree | Strongly agree |
|---|---|---|---|---|---|
| ...stays out of trouble with the law | 0 | 0 | 0.3 | 6.7 | 93.0 |
| ...is well behaved, helpful, and nice to other people | 0 | 0 | 0.6 | 9.8 | 89.7 |

[a] Items from the parents' interview (see section 2.3), N = 716.

they spent little time but committed relatively many crimes are not overshadowed by settings in which they spent a great deal of their time and committed many, but proportionately fewer, crimes. See section 7.2 for more on this rate and space-time budget crimes.

very important that their children stay out of trouble with the law, and 99.5 per cent agreed that it was very important that their children were well behaved (the slight differences between responses to the items may reflect the fact that a small proportion of parents were slightly more concerned about their children getting in trouble for misbehaving, than misbehaving in the first place). Hence, the vast majority of parents can be presumed to represent prosocial influences,[20] and many will exert that influence by supervising their children's behaviour.

Only one crime occurred during work-oriented time; hence the rate of crime during work-oriented activities was as low as during family-oriented activities.

School-oriented activities were only slightly more conducive to crime than family and work-oriented activities. However, as in the family setting, although the *rate* of crime was low, a significant proportion of space–time budget crimes did occur in the school setting; most involved fights with other young people (this is consistent with earlier findings from Peterborough: see Wikström and Butterworth 2006; and Cardiff: see Boxford 2006). Generally, family, school, and work-oriented time is more rule-guided, with stronger enforcement, than more discretionary time use.

Peer-oriented activities, of all the key activity categories, are the most criminogenic. In fact, peer-oriented hours were more than five times more criminogenic than hours spent under any other circumstances (and more than fifteen times more criminogenic than hours spent in family, school, or work-oriented activities).[21] Much of the remainder of this chapter is spent exploring why spending time unsupervised with peers may increase young people's likelihood of

[20] There will be exceptions, meaning that for some young people the family context may be more conducive to rule-breaking and, as a consequence, their development of a high crime propensity, as well as their exposure to criminogenic settings (see section 6.3 on individual differences in family settings).

[21] Family, school, and work-oriented activities clearly have a strong (dampening) effect on young people's crime involvement. They also have a significant developmental effect (especially family and school activities) as they may significantly influence the development of young people's morality and ability to exercise self-control (ie their crime propensity), which interacts with their exposure to crime-conducive settings. Peers, on the other hand, may exert the majority of their influence situationally, through their immediate effects on the social and moral context (although peers will arguably also exert at least some developmental pressure; see, for example, Harris 1995, 1998).

seeing and choosing crime as an alternative, and its link to area crime rates.

## 6.2  Settings and circumstances of criminogenic exposure

Certain settings and circumstantial features may be particularly conducive for young people's crime. Below we consider how activities that lack adult supervision or structure may constitute particularly criminogenic circumstances. We also look at how these circumstances interact with key criminogenic settings (eg areas with poor collective efficacy, and the city and local centres) and explore how they relate to young people's use of time and space.

### 6.2.1  Supervision

Supervision (the presence of an adult guardian) is a dimension of young people's activities that is highly relevant to their social behaviour, as it plays a critical role developmentally in their socialization, and situationally in their rule-breaking. An adult guardian is typically responsible for monitoring behaviour and enforcing rules, and in some circumstances asserting those rules, and therefore generally strengthens the moral context (although guardians will differ in the degree of and efficacy with which they monitor behaviour and enforce rules of conduct). Much of adolescents' time is spent with key supervisory figures such as parents and teachers, and later work supervisors (see Table 6.11 and also findings from Wikström and Butterworth 2006: 207–37).

During most of the school day, young people in the PADS+ sample were supervised by teachers and other staff members. At other times they were generally supervised by family adults, although this declined with age, especially on the weekends (Table 6.11 and Table 6.12; see also Larson and Verma 1999). This reflects their increasing independence and mobility as they aged through adolescence, expressed through their discretionary time use (although they were still supervised for most of their time awake at any age). A decrease in their supervised time on Saturdays (from 10 hours at age 13 to seven hours at age 17) was mirrored by an increase in peer-oriented time (from four hours at age 13 to seven hours at age 17); there was less change on weekdays, as young people had less discretionary time, mainly because of school. This 'reorientation' from spending time with family

**Table 6.11  Average time per day and percentage of time awake spent supervised, unsupervised, and unsupervised with peers by age**

| Age | Supervised | | Unsupervised | | Unsupervised with peers | |
|---|---|---|---|---|---|---|
| | Percentage of time awake | Hrs:Mins per day | Percentage of time awake | Hrs:Mins per day | Percentage of time awake | Hrs:Mins per day |
| 13 | 83.6 | 12:12 | 16.4 | 2:24 | 12.8 | 1:52 |
| 14 | 80.5 | 12:00 | 19.5 | 2:54 | 14.6 | 2:10 |
| 15 | 77.7 | 11:39 | 22.3 | 3:20 | 16.6 | 2:29 |
| 16 | 76.2 | 11:41 | 23.8 | 3:39 | 16.4 | 2:31 |
| 17 | 72.5 | 10:57 | 27.5 | 4:09 | 16.3 | 2:28 |
| Phase 1 | 78.1 | 11:42 | 21.9 | 3:16 | 15.3 | 2:18 |

**Table 6.12  Average time per day and percentage of time awake spent supervised, unsupervised, and unsupervised with peers by day and time of the week**

| Day | Time | Supervised | | Unsupervised | | Unsupervised with peers | |
|---|---|---|---|---|---|---|---|
| | | Percent-age of time awake | Hrs:Mins per day | Percent-age of time awake | Hrs:Mins per day | Percent-age of time awake | Hrs:Mins per day |
| Weekday | Day | 77.4 | 6:34 | 22.6 | 1:55 | 16.4 | 1:24 |
| | Evening | 82.5 | 5:23 | 17.5 | 1:09 | 10.3 | 0:41 |
| Weekend | Day | 74.1 | 4:50 | 25.9 | 1:41 | 18.0 | 1:10 |
| | Evening | 77.4 | 5:44 | 22.6 | 1:41 | 16.5 | 1:14 |

adults, in particular, to spending time with peers is a key feature of adolescence and one that may go a long way towards explaining the social dynamics of adolescent life (Crosnoe and Trinitapoli 2008; Eccles et al. 1993; Furstenberg 2000; Steinberg 2001).

Most of the young people's time with their peers was supervised, as much of it took place at school, in the presence of teachers and other educational staff, and at home (or a friend's home) where parents were present. As they grew older, however, more of their time with their peers was unsupervised (from 26.9 per cent at age

13 to 36.3 per cent at age 17). Although few, these hours may be particularly important for young people's crime involvement as they may be the hours that young people spend in the weakest moral contexts (when guardians are not present to temper negative peer influences).

In quantifying supervision, we have treated the presence of any adult guardian in a setting as a supervisory figure. This may overestimate the actual degree of monitoring and enforcement an adult guardian represents (thereby underestimating the actual impact of supervision), as not all adults may act as direct supervisors. For example, parents are often at home with their children, and therefore counted as adult guardians, even though they may not be engaged in the same activity as the young person, or even in the same room (eg they may be upstairs asleep while the young person is downstairs with his or her peers). Similarly, adult guardians are almost always present during school activities, yet may not be directly monitoring a particular young person, or group of young people's, behaviour. In these cases, the adults present (ie parents, teachers) are clearly responsible for monitoring and enforcing rules of conduct; the young person is aware of that authority and the potential for formal social control; hence we expect the presence of such a guardian will still, however indirectly, actively influence the moral context of the setting. In other settings where adults are likely to be present, such as at the cinema or on public transport, but do not play an active supervisory role, we would expect them to have much less impact on the moral context (or for that impact to be captured more fully through social background characteristics, such as collective efficacy); such adults, therefore, were not coded as adult guardians.

Another consideration in analysing data on supervision is that in the space–time budget supervisory figures were included as present in a setting during an hour if they were present for the majority of that hour. It may be the case that for some hours a guardian was not present for the entire hour, and rule-breaking may have occurred when they were not in the setting. If anything, this would also lead us to underestimate the role of supervision.

The rate of crimes per 1,000 hours spent unsupervised was 2.4, more than 10 times higher than the rate during supervised hours (0.2 crimes per 1,000 hours). In fact, more than three-quarters of all space–time budget crimes were committed during unsupervised hours (see further section 7.2.1). The relationship between young people's experience of supervision and their exposure to criminogenic settings is further explored in section 6.3.

## 6.2.2 Structure

Structure—the degree to which an activity is organized and directed towards a particular end—can, like orientation, be used to characterize, and categorize, activities. *Structured activities* place restrictions on how time is spent, as they are typically organized and supervised by adults and take place, often according to a fixed schedule, at specific times and places (often in relatively public settings) (see, eg, Lareau and Weininger 2008; Osgood et al. 2005); in other words, they tend to present many rules and expectations for conduct that are consistently monitored and enforced. They generally have a particular agenda or objective (eg practising a musical instrument, learning a craft, or playing sport). As a consequence, they preoccupy goal-directed attention, providing less opportunity for participants to become motivated towards secondary activities, including crime, or to perceive them as an option for action. *Unstructured activities*, on the other hand, often lack specific aims and direction, are much less likely to be organized or supervised or to hold particular (or formal) expectations, and therefore may be more conducive for secondary activities such as crime.

Participation in structured activities is generally seen as developmentally positive, for example fostering initiative, achievement, and socio-emotional competence (Dearing et al. 2009; Denault and Poulin 2009; Eccles and Barber 1999; Larson 2000; H. W. Marsh and Kleitman 2002; Simpkins et al. 2005). However, participation in these activities has been shown to decline with age across most populations (eg Canadian: see Denault and Poulin 2009; Australian: see Olds et al. 2009).

Although time spent at school or work may also be seen as structured (comprising set tasks at set times in set places), we defined structure in relation to leisure time only, as our aim was to differentiate structured and unstructured discretionary time (see Table 6.13). By our strict criteria, participants spent very little of their leisure time in structured activities, with a large proportion (40.8 per cent) reporting no leisure time in structured activities during Phase 1 (Figure 6.7), and 91.4 per cent of those who did reporting fewer than 15 hours over all five years. Although participants reported somewhat fewer structured leisure activities in later adolescence, there was no clear pattern of decline across the data waves[22] (Table 6.14).

---

[22] That the decline in structured activities by age found in other studies (see above) was not found to the same degree in PADS+ data is most likely because many studies include what we isolate as semi-structured activities, which did decline, within their conceptualization of structured activities (see below).

**Table 6.13 Definitions of structural categories and relative leisure time spent in each**

| Leisure activity category | Percentage of all time awake | Percentage of all leisure time | Percentage of leisure time in activity category |
|---|---|---|---|
| Structured | 1.6 | 3.3 | |
|   Meetings of drama/dance/music groups[a] | | | 33.7 |
|   Sports in a sports venue[a] | | | 31.3 |
|   Meetings of other clubs and societies[a] | | | 14.5 |
|   Religious activities in a religious setting | | | 14.1 |
|   Music lessons[a] | | | 6.5 |
|   *All structured activities* | | | *100.0* |
| Semi-structured | 7.7 | 15.7 | |
|   Sports[b] | | | 35.9 |
|   Shopping | | | 26.2 |
|   Selected hobbies and games (eg board games, snooker, arts and crafts, fishing) | | | 22.9 |
|   Cultural activities (eg museum, watching a sports event, live entertainment) | | | 6.2 |
|   Playing a musical instrument[c] | | | 3.1 |
|   Watching a movie at the cinema | | | 2.6 |
|   Meetings of clubs and societies[c] | | | 2.1 |
|   Religious activities not in a religious setting | | | 1.1 |
|   *All semi-structured activities* | | | *100.0* |
| Unstructured | 39.8 | 80.9 | |
|   Media consumption (eg watching television, playing computer or console games, reading) | | | 59.8 |
|   Socializing (including electronic socializing and sexual activity) | | | 39.2 |
|   Inactive | | | 1.0 |
|   *All unstructured activities* | | | *100.0* |

[a] Supervised by a non-family adult.[23]
[b] If in a sports venue, not supervised by a non-family adult.
[c] Not supervised by a non-family adult.

[23] The decision to focus on non-family adults was made so that the many cases where a parent was present during their child's activity but not actively involved were legitimately excluded. This means that legitimate cases where parents were coaching their child's structured activity were also excluded, but we expect there would have been few such cases.

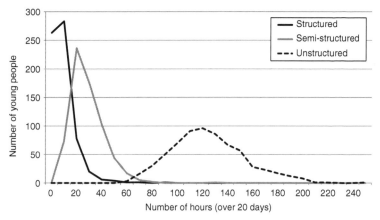

**Figure 6.7 Variation in the time young people aged 13–17 spent in structured, semi-structured, and unstructured leisure activities (Phase 1[a])**

[a] For the 657 participants who completed space–time budgets in all five waves.

The rate of crime during structured leisure activities was very low (0.3 crimes per 1,000 hours; see Table 6.15) and similar to that for family, work, and school-oriented activities.

We created an intermediate category of semi-structured leisure activities to help differentiate leisure activities with some degree of structure and organization from highly organized structured leisure activities and entirely unorganized unstructured leisure activities (Table 6.13). These leisure activities are less constrained and closely supervised than structured leisure activities (as defined above), so they provide some opportunity for divergent activities and, potentially, rule-breaking. At the same time, however, they also provide some direction to, and some restrictions on, young people's behaviour.

PADS+ participants spent more of their leisure time in semi-structured than structured activities (Table 6.14): just under an hour on weekdays (including Fridays), and two hours on Saturdays. Such participation declined across all five waves, slightly on weekdays, but from two and three-quarter hours to an hour and a half on Saturdays.

The rate of crime during semi-structured leisure activities (1.4 crimes per 1,000 hours; Table 6.15) was considerably higher than during structured leisure activities. Most of these crimes occurred when participants were playing sports (63.6 per cent, 36.4 per cent while playing football), when frictions may be common, and/or in outdoor spaces (54.5 per cent), where young people tended to spend unsupervised leisure time with peers.

Unstructured leisure activities, during which young people's behaviour is the least constrained by supervision and competing demands on how time is spent, may be more conducive to divergent activities and rule-breaking. The largest categories of unstructured leisure activities are media consumption (eg watching TV, listening to music, playing on the computer) and socializing. Media consumption is not highly associated with crime.[24] Generally, less passive interpersonal activities, such as more active socializing, are more closely related to crime (at least situationally). Socializing was particularly common on Fridays and Saturdays and, consistent with other findings, increased as the young people grew older.

Overall, PADS+ participants spent much more leisure time in unstructured than structured or semi-structured activities (Table 6.14): five hours on average per weekday, six hours on Fridays and seven and a half hours on Saturdays. There was a notable increase in unstructured leisure activities across Phase 1 on weekdays, reflecting changes in how often young people socialized (and the increase in their peer-oriented time). This trend was less noticeable on Saturdays.

Crimes were also more common during unstructured leisure time than structured leisure time (Table 6.15). The rate was slightly lower than that during semi-structured leisure activities, although when we focus on peer-oriented time, the rate of crimes is much higher during unstructured hours (13.6 per cent of crimes during semi-structured leisure activities occurred during school-oriented time, and 22.7 per cent during other time).

---

[24] There is much discussion about the negative (but also positive) impact of media content (for example, on young people's development of crime propensity); of particular interest criminologically is the suggestion that violent content may be related to violent behaviour, although the evidence for this remains controversial (C. A. Anderson et al. 2003; C. A. Anderson 2004; Berkowitz 1984; Browne and Hamilton-Giachritsis 2005). Although PADS+ data does not record media content, and therefore cannot analyse these effects, this is the kind of research question to which time budget data would certainly lend itself. Media content can be seen as part of the social setting; therefore this kind of analysis would fit within the SAT framework.

**Table 6.14  Average time and percentage of all time awake spent in structured, semi-structured and unstructured leisure activities per day by age**

| Age | Structured activities | | Semi-structured activities | | Unstructured activities | |
|---|---|---|---|---|---|---|
| | Percentage of time awake | Hrs:Mins per day | Percentage of time awake | Hrs:Mins per day | Percentage of time awake | Hrs:Mins per day |
| 13 | 2.1 | 0:18 | 9.9 | 1:27 | 36.1 | 5:17 |
| 14 | 1.7 | 0:15 | 8.5 | 1:16 | 36.6 | 5:27 |
| 15 | 1.9 | 0:17 | 7.2 | 1:05 | 41.0 | 6:09 |
| 16 | 1.5 | 0:13 | 6.6 | 1:00 | 42.6 | 6:32 |
| 17 | 1.1 | 0:10 | 6.5 | 0:58 | 42.7 | 6:27 |
| Phase 1 | 1.6 | 0:15 | 7.7 | 1:09 | 39.8 | 5:58 |

**Table 6.15  Crimes per 1,000 hours during leisure activities by structure**

| Leisure activity | All leisure hours | Peer-oriented leisure hours |
|---|---|---|
| Structured | 0.3 | 0.0 |
| Semi-structured | 1.4 | 2.1 |
| Unstructured | 1.0 | 5.7 |

Below we focus on unstructured peer-oriented time, as we can see this time is of particular interest in relation to young people's crime. Of all their hours awake, young people spent only 5.3 per cent in unstructured peer-oriented activities, yet during this time they reported 42.6 per cent of all space–time budget crimes.

### Unstructured peer-oriented time[25]

We previously highlighted peer-oriented time as particularly criminogenic. Nearly half of young people's peer-oriented time was

---

[25] Unstructured peer-oriented time refers only to peer-oriented activities during leisure time. Three-quarters of peer-oriented time occurred during leisure time (and of that which did not, 20 per cent was spent doing domestic and personal activities, such as chores or eating, and 80 per cent was spent moving around).

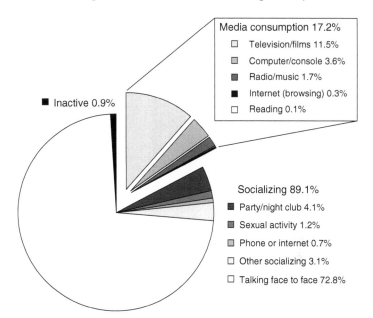

**Figure 6.8  Time spent unsupervised in unstructured activities with peers**

unstructured, while only about one-quarter was semi-structured.[26] As Figure 6.8 shows, the vast majority of unstructured peer-oriented time was spent socializing, generally face to face. As young people move from childhood to adolescence, socializing typically replaces unstructured play (Larson and Verma 1999), increasing significantly during adolescence but then declining after early adulthood (Meeks and Mauldin 1990; Olds et al. 2009).

Unstructured, unsupervised activities with peers have been identified, theoretically and empirically, as particularly conducive to young people's crime involvement (see, eg, Mahoney and Stattin 2000; Osgood et al. 1996; Osgood and Anderson 2004; Osgood et al. 2005; Riley 1987; Sampson and Groves 1989; West and Farrington 1977; Wikström and Butterworth 2006).

[26] Structured activities, except for religious activities in a religious setting, are by definition supervised, and therefore excluded from peer-oriented activities. Very few hours in Phase 1 (88) were spent unsupervised with peers and young family members in religious activities in religious settings, and most involved participants attending religious services with their siblings or young cousins, which also did not qualify as peer-oriented.

**Table 6.16  Unstructured peer-oriented time in domestic and non-domestic settings**

| Setting | Percentage of unstructured peer-oriented time |
|---|---|
| *Domestic* | *32.9* |
|    Home | 7.4 |
|    Other's home | 25.5 |
| *Non-domestic* | *67.1* |
|    *Public indoor* | *25.0* |
|       Shopping locales | 15.2 |
|       Pubs, clubs, restaurants | 7.3 |
|       Other | 2.5 |
|    *Public outdoor* | *42.1* |
|       Streets | 20.0 |
|       Parks | 16.2 |
|       Moving around | 5.2 |
|       Other | 0.7 |

Most of the time young people in the PADS+ sample spent in unstructured peer-oriented activities occurred in non-residential settings, such as shopping locales and public outdoor places, usually streets and parks (Table 6.16).

Despite the fact that most unstructured peer-oriented time occurred outside domestic settings, young people still spent this time, on average, closer to home than most other activities, although the distance increased significantly as they grew older, from 1.38 kilometres (SD = 2.30) at age 13 to 3.49 kilometres (SD = 4.24) at age 17 (Figure 6.9).[27]

Unstructured peer-oriented time took place predominantly on Fridays and Saturdays, particularly in the evenings, when young people had more discretionary time (Table 6.17).

Previously (Figure 6.5) we showed the spatial distribution of peer-oriented time, and discussed the difference between this distribution and that of all time unsupervised with peers (which, by the nature of young people's lifestyles, was significantly skewed towards

---

[27] Straight-line distances; see technical appendix, section A1.1, for how these are calculated.

**Table 6.17  Average time spent in peer-oriented activities by time and day of the week**

|  |  | Peer-oriented activities | Unstructured peer-oriented activities |
|---|---|---|---|
| Weekday | Monday-Thursday | 1:17 | 0:28 |
|  | Friday | 1:51 | 0:53 |
|  | Day | 0:35 | 0:07 |
|  | Evening | 0:42 | 0:22 |
| Weekend |  | 2:32 | 1:14 |
|  | Day | 1:14 | 0:25 |
|  | Evening | 1:16 | 0:47 |

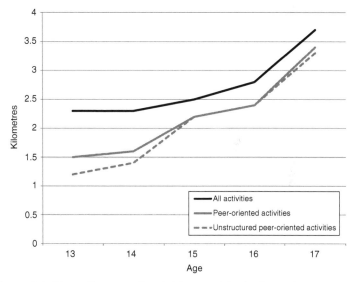

Figure 6.9  Mean distance of activities outside the home by age

time spent at school). Schools were not the only settings that drove the concentration of unsupervised hours with peers into select settings. Popular recreational settings for young people that offer more structured activities, such as the ice rink, Powerleague, bowling alleys, and the cinema, also created a clustering of unsupervised time with peers. Activities in these settings may be less conducive to crime as they tend to be focused on constructive or leisure activities in contexts where at least some level of rules will apply, and some level of monitoring and enforcement exist, for example by those who own and run sports and leisure facilities, as well as young people who support their intended use (as well as other young people's parents who may be present to monitor their own children's behaviour). Focusing purely on unstructured activities creates a distinctly different distribution of peer-oriented time (Figure 6.10).

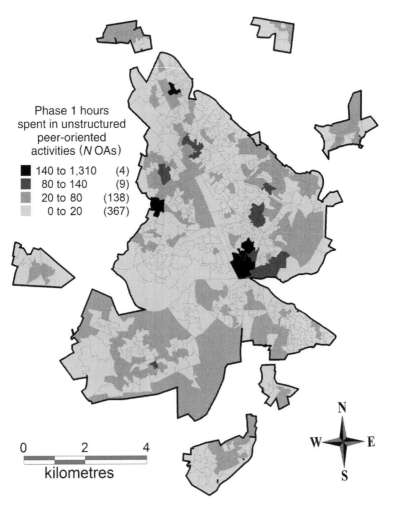

Figure 6.10  Spatial distribution of young people's unstructured peer-oriented activities

As expected, the significance of schools and key entertainment venues reduces dramatically. Related to this is a slight reduction in the proportion of time spent in the city centre, and a slight increase in the proportion of time spent in local centres that are closer to young people's homes and therefore more convenient places to hang around. There is an increase in the proportion of time spent in streets (20 per cent) and parks (15.6 per cent) and in domestic settings (one's home and other's homes; 32.9 per cent). Young people spent a greater proportion of their unstructured peer-oriented time in areas with poor collective efficacy, and a smaller proportion in areas with strong collective efficacy, which has implications for informal social control (see sections 3.3.2 and 6.2.3); in fact, the greater the proportion of peer-oriented time spent in unstructured activities in a given output area, the poorer its collective efficacy $(r = .29, p = .001)$.[28]

To look more closely at the kinds of areas in which young people spend unstructured peer-oriented time, we identified 26 key output areas where young people spent the greatest portion of this time, both in separate waves and across all waves[29] (see Figure 6.11). These output areas were spread across the city and unstructured peer-oriented time was fairly evenly distributed between them except in four output areas of the city centre, where young people

[28] Because of the small number of peer-oriented hours spent in some output areas, this analysis was run using the 128 output areas in the PCS study area where young people spent more than the mean number of peer-oriented hours (46 hours), excluding five outliers with residuals more than two standard deviations above the mean. These outliers included settings such as local centres in areas with high collective efficacy where young people tended to spend unstructured peer-oriented time, as well as entertainment settings in areas with poor collective efficacy such as the ice rink where young people spent more semi-structured peer-oriented time.

[29] Three criteria were used to identify key areas: (1) if the number of hours spent in unstructured peer-oriented activities in the area during Phase 1 was two or more standard deviations above the mean; (2) if the area scored six or more points when given one point for every wave in which the number of hours spent in that area was between one and two standard deviations above the mean, and two points for every wave in which it was two or more standard deviations above the mean; and/or (3) if the area scored five points according to criteria (2) and the number of hours spent in the area was two or more standard deviations above the mean in two or more waves. This allowed us to identify areas that were consistently popular places for young people to spend unstructured unsupervised time with their peers, and those that gained (and lost) popularity with certain age groups in certain years.

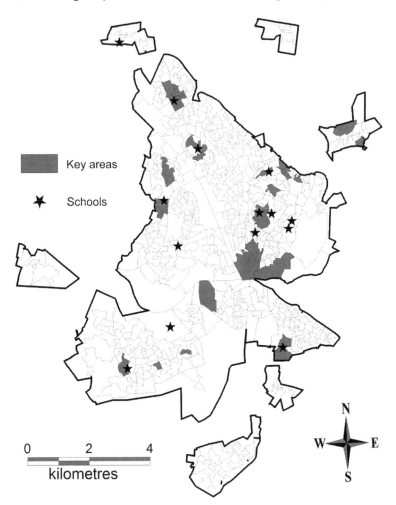

**Figure 6.11 Twenty-six key output areas where young people spent time in unstructured peer-oriented activities during Phase 1**

spent almost half (49.6 per cent) of all their unstructured peer-oriented time in these 26 output areas during Phase 1. These areas were dominated by entertainment settings such as shopping centres, restaurants, a cinema, pubs, and nightclubs. Time in these areas increased significantly with age—nearly one-third (31.3 per cent) of unstructured peer-oriented hours spent in these four output areas occurred when young people were 17 (and only 5 per cent when they were 13)—indicating significant changes in the settings young people self selected into and/or had access to, reflecting changes in their mobility and independence. Nearly all unstructured peer-oriented time in the city centre was spent socializing (96 per cent) and occurred during discretionary time; in the main city centre output area, this took place in shopping areas (76 per cent), predominantly during the day on Saturdays, and into the early evening. However, in the two output areas to the north east of the main city centre most of this time (occurring in latter waves, particularly when young people were 17) was spent in pubs, bars, and nightclubs (78 per cent) in the evenings (94 per cent), especially on Friday and Saturday nights (78 per cent). In the large output area to the east of the main city centre, unstructured peer-oriented time was split between the cinema (37.8 per cent), restaurants (8.9 per cent), and open spaces such as streets and parks (43.3 per cent).

Outside the city centre, key areas were characterized by local centres;[30] residential areas containing local shops, parks, and in some cases sports facilities; and schools (generally also featuring green spaces or sports facilities). These 26 areas did not vary significantly from other output areas in their proportion of resident young people, but they did have a slightly lower population density, most likely because they were characterized by less residential land use, including more green space and commercial tracts such as shopping locales. They were also significantly more disadvantaged than other areas and had a higher proportion of socially rented housing and a lower proportion of owner-occupied residences. As a consequence, they may have lacked resources or investment by residents to exert informal social control. Experiencing strong informal social control is something that some young people may actively avoid (valuing their independence). At the same time, these areas were characterized by significantly more lone-parent households than other output areas, meaning there may have been fewer adults around to monitor young people's behaviour (although this lack of monitoring may also feed into young residents spending more of their time unsupervised).

---

[30] Only one area with a local centre (Hampton Centre) did not qualify as a key area. Hampton Centre is situated on the outskirts of Peterborough and less accessible to young people; hence most of the time young people spent there was supervised by their parents, who drove them there.

Certain features of settings may attract young people, such as shopping centres and entertainment locales, as well as open spaces, such as streets and parks, where they can congregate freely and detach themselves from parents and other adults. Young people may spend time in certain places because those places are conveniently situated, such as areas around their homes and schools, or easily accessed, such as the city centre, which is supplied by public transport. For example, when they are 17 years old, young people may spend more time unsupervised with their peers in the city centre because (1) they have more access to the city centre and self select to be there, and (2) they go to the city centre for other reasons (eg work) and hence are socially selected into it and surrounding settings. Spatial analyses can be particularly useful for exploring these selective processes. How young people are selected into environments—ie how they come to be exposed to certain settings—may be important for prevention or intervention efforts.

Different kinds of activities take place with different frequencies in different places and at different times of the week. Unstructured peer-oriented activities also varied by place over time. On weekday days domestic settings were the dominant venues for such time use; in general, however, young people spent little time (while not at school) unsupervised with their peers in unstructured activities on weekday days. On weekday evenings, however, outdoor public spaces such as streets and parks, as well as moving around, were more popular settings where young people spent close to half of all their unstructured peer-oriented hours (mostly within 1 kilometre of home). On weekend days unstructured peer-oriented activities clustered in the city centre, although outdoor public spaces remained popular, as they did on weekend evenings, when young people moved away from shopping locales to more residential areas (Table 6.18).

These analyses highlight key settings where young people tend to spend unstructured peer-oriented time (eg entertainment settings, outdoor public spaces, and residential areas with poor collective efficacy). These areas also present a number of criminogenic features that may make them particularly conducive to crime during unstructured peer-oriented activities, at least for the situationally vulnerable. Below we look at these settings in closer detail, and their relationship to peer-oriented time and young people's crime involvement.

**Table 6.18 Percentage of unstructured peer-oriented time spent in key settings at different times of the week[a]**

| Activity orientation | Day/time of day | Key settings | | | | | | | | |
| | | Private indoor | | Public indoor | | | | Public outdoor | | |
| | | Home | Others' home | School | Workplace | Shopping locale | Pubs and nightclubs | Streets | Parks | Moving around |
|---|---|---|---|---|---|---|---|---|---|---|
| Unstructured peer-oriented | | 7.4 | 25.5 | 0 | 0 | 15.2 | 5.9 | 20.0 | 15.6 | 5.2 |
| | Weekday day | 1.4 | 2.8 | 0 | 0 | 2.3 | 0.1 | 1.7 | 1.0 | 0.8 |
| | Weekday evening | 1.6 | 5.6 | 0 | 0 | 2.8 | 1.0 | 6.0 | 4.2 | 1.8 |
| | Weekend day | 0.5 | 2.3 | 0 | 0 | 5.5 | 0.1 | 2.2 | 1.9 | 0.3 |
| | Weekend evening | 3.9 | 14.7 | 0 | 0 | 4.6 | 4.7 | 10.1 | 8.5 | 2.3 |

[a] For example, 20 per cent of all time spent in unstructured peer-oriented activities in Phase 1 took place in the streets, and 10.1 per cent took place in the streets on weekend evenings.

## 6.2.3 Criminogenic settings

We defined and operationalized criminogenic exposure in section 3.3.2 as unstructured peer-oriented time spent in areas with poor collective efficacy, or in the city and local centres (in which measures of residents' reported experiences of collective efficacy may not be representative of the level experienced by others moving in and out of these high traffic areas). In the following section, applying the discussion developed above regarding young people's activity patterns, we look more closely at these settings and the circumstances under which young people tend to encounter them.

### Collective efficacy

Collective efficacy is a concept we have used to provide a measure of the moral context (see section 3.3.2). Because (as measured by the PCS) it quantifies residents' willingness to enforce collective rules of conduct, it is perhaps most appropriate when applied to residential settings. In commercial areas, for example, residents' collective efficacy may have less of an influence on the moral context than factors such as human traffic, which is why we look at the city and local centres as a special case. Even in residential settings, collective efficacy may not be uniformly influential; for example, residents may be less willing and/or able to intervene in misbehaviour in parks near their homes than local streets, partly because of where their routine activity patterns take them (not all residents will visit the local park regularly, whereas they may walk down the same street several times a day) and partly because of factors relating to ownership or guardianship (residents may not see a public green space as their responsibility to safeguard, compared to the area immediately around their homes and neighbours' homes); we therefore also look at these settings as a special case below.

**Table 6.19  Crimes per 1,000 hours in areas outside the city and local centres by collective efficacy**

| Activity | Collective efficacy | | |
|---|---|---|---|
| | Poor | Medium | Strong |
| All | 1.0 | 0.6 | 0.5 |
| Peer-oriented | 4.3 | 3.8 | 1.8 |
| Unstructured peer-oriented | 4.6 | 6.7 | 2.0 |

Consistent with the argument that areas with poor collective efficacy present a weak moral context, and therefore will be more conducive to crime, we found that outside the city and local centres, as collective efficacy fell young people's reports of acts of crime increased, especially during peer-oriented activities (Table 6.19). The relationship between area collective efficacy and young people's crime is discussed in greater detail in chapter 7.

## City and local centres

We have argued that in recreational settings—ie areas that attract people for activities such as shopping, eating out, consuming alcohol, and other pastimes (eg going to the cinema, bowling, ice skating)—such as those found in most city and local centres, which are often conducive to crime (see, eg Block and Block 1995; Curtis 1974; Downes 1958; G. Hughes 2011; Lockwood 2007; McClintock 1963; Miethe and Meier 1994; Nelson et al. 2001; Roncek and Maier 1991; D. J. Smith et al. 2001; Wikström 1991), residents' collective efficacy may not provide an adequate measure of the social dynamics. Such settings are generally accessible to most people, and appeal to many as they provide desired services in a centralized setting; as a consequence, they experience heavy traffic by non-residents, especially at certain times of the day, making it difficult for behaviour to be monitored. At the same time, there is less collective cohesion between users of the setting about rules of conduct, how they should be enforced, and who should enforce them, which weakens informal social control and people's willingness to intervene if they witness rule-breaking.

Recreational settings also offer more motivators to offend. For example, there are many potential temptations that could motivate young people to steal (eg in shopping locales), and more people who may cause greater interpersonal friction, which may provoke violence. In settings where alcohol is consumed, these frictions may be especially likely to result in violence, as users' sensitivity increases and their ability to exercise self-control declines with intoxication.

We have previously captured the additional effects of these settings through area levels of non-residential land use. Here we focus on young people's time use in entertainment settings, namely Peterborough's city and local centres. Young people's experience of these settings differs from that of adults. Young people do not have the same degree of access to some settings, eg because of their age (pubs, nightclubs, games arcades), their lack of mobility, or their lack of financial capital. Young people also exhibit different preferences in their activities than adults, for example they spend more time playing sports, games, and pursuing hobbies (in part because they have more leisure time; see Denault and Poulin 2009; Olds et al. 2009). As a result, while the city and local centres are key recreational settings for young people, leisure venues like the cinema, the ice rink, the bowling alley, etc., are also implicated (although compared to the city and local centres, young people spend relatively little time in the latter leisure settings). Pubs and nightclubs (which tend to cluster in city and local centres, forming part of the 'entertainment district') only become relevant for young people's activity fields in later adolescence. Young people spend much of their time in these settings congregating for the purpose of socialization, rather than to take direct part in the setting (for example, in the PADS+ sample young people spent less than two-thirds of their total time awake in shopping locales actually shopping, and more than a quarter socializing).

Young people in the PADS+ sample spent a large proportion of their peer-oriented time in the city and local centres (22.9 per cent), and much of this time was unstructured (43.6 per cent). In fact, half of all the time young people spent awake in the city centre was peer-oriented (of which 43 per cent was unstructured). We have argued that city and local centres are particularly criminogenic (see section 3.3.2), as are unstructured peer-oriented activities (section 6.2.2); hence it is not surprising that city and local centres were also a common setting for young people's crime (see Table 6.20 and section 7.2).

Table 6.20  Crimes per 1,000 hours in outdoor
public spaces by activity

| Activity | City centre | Local centres |
|---|---|---|
| All | 1.6 | 1.0 |
| Peer-oriented | 2.0 | 8.2 |
| Unstructured peer-oriented | 4.9 | 15.0 |

## Outdoor public spaces

Outdoor public spaces may serve a similar purpose for young people as some entertainment settings do for adults. Young people tend to congregate and socialize in places such as streets and parks, rather than in more commercial settings (eg pubs or restaurants). In the PADS+ sample, young people spent considerably more of their time awake (10.6 per cent) in outdoor public spaces (including outdoor sports venues, streets, parks, and recreation grounds) than recreational settings (including indoor sports and leisure centres, youth clubs, and community centres; 3.1 per cent), including 41.5 per cent of their unstructured peer-oriented time. Young people spent comparably little time in sports and recreation grounds (7.1 per cent of all their time in outdoor public spaces) compared to the time they spent in streets and on street corners (16.9 per cent) and in parks (including most public green space that is not devoted to sports fields; 20.3 per cent).

As settings, streets are designed for transportation, whether vehicular or bipedal, yet young people find them popular places to socialize with their peers. They are accessible on foot, especially in an urban environment like Peterborough, which is designed to encourage foot traffic, eg with many walking and cycle routes linking key locations and heavy road traffic deflected around the city on various bypasses. Streets will not typically present a strong moral context; movement in and out of the setting means that monitoring and enforcing rules will be difficult and responsibility diffused. There will be little collective energy behind rules of conduct by those who use the setting only temporarily, and often only in passing between other settings. Streets are often unpopulated, especially in quiet residential areas, adding to the lack of monitoring and reducing deterrence. In the evenings, lighting may be dim, creating a further obstacle to effective monitoring.

Parks differ from streets in that they may feature large open spaces, which are difficult to monitor and control for their sheer size. By design, parks may also be situated away from areas of heavy human traffic, meaning there may be few people present to monitor and enforce rule-following. Like streets, parks are accessible to young people; efforts have been made in planning the development of the city to provide green spaces, and to separate them from commercial and industrial areas. Many residential areas have local green spaces, even if these are rather small, which may attract young people living in those areas.

Most of the time young people spent in outdoor public spaces was spent moving around, eg walking, cycling, and travelling in cars. This means they were moving from setting to setting, which makes monitoring and enforcing rules difficult. Generally, young

**Table 6.21   Crimes per 1,000 hours in outdoor public spaces by activity**

| Activity | Outdoor public setting | | |
|---|---|---|---|
| | Streets | Parks | Moving around |
| All | 7.8 | 4.0 | 1.4 |
| Peer-oriented | 8.9 | 4.8 | 1.9 |
| Unstructured peer-oriented | 9.5 | 8.5 | 0.0 |

people had limited access to vehicular transport, hence a large proportion (22 per cent) of the time they spent moving around was on foot, for example between their home, school, and friends' houses.[31] Two-thirds of the time young people spent moving around unsupervised with their peers occurred between 08:00 and 09:00 and 15:00 and 16:00, when many were travelling to and from school. Quite a lot of this time was also spent on the bus (13.8 per cent), namely as a result of many young people riding the school bus on a daily basis.

As in other recreational settings (eg the city and local centres), the rate of crime during time spent in parks, streets, and moving around was particularly high, especially during unstructured peer-oriented time (except in the case of moving around, as very few hours were unstructured) (Table 6.21). In streets and parks the crime rate approached one crime every 100 hours, making them some of the most criminogenic settings.

### 6.2.4   Conclusions about young people's activity patterns

In section 6.1 we illustrated the spread of young people's general activities across different days of the week, and how the distribution of their key activities changes as they age from 13 to 17. In subsequent sections we have looked at how young people spend their time, concluding that the vast majority of their time, including their discretionary time, is spent in family and school-oriented activities, but that peer-oriented time may be of particular interest as it may take place in settings with moral contexts most conducive

---

[31] The overlap between their moving around and socializing as main activities complicated the coding of this time use.

to crime, especially when it is unstructured. We have looked at where young people spend their time, particularly during their discretionary time and outside key settings such as home and school; entertainment settings such as the city and local centres proved popular venues, especially for peer-oriented time, but so did outdoor public spaces such as streets and parks. We have looked at when young people are involved in different kinds of activities, honing in on their discretionary time in the evenings and on the weekends. Finally, we have brought all these analyses together to explore when young people spend time in certain kinds of activities in specific settings, to highlight that their peer-oriented activities cluster during their discretionary time on evenings and weekends in places such as the city and local centres, streets, and parks, which may be especially conducive to crime involvement.

Table 6.22 summarizes these findings by presenting the percentage of time spent in key kinds of activities in key settings at key times on different days of the week. This provides a snapshot of at least a portion of young people's activity fields. In the following section we consider the role of personal differences in how young people spend their time, and in chapter 7 we link time use to crime involvement to analyse whether or not crimes are indeed clustering in the settings we have identified as particularly criminogenic.

## 6.3  Social sources of young people's criminogenic exposure

Young people vary in the degree to which they are exposed to different kinds of settings and the circumstances under which they take part in those settings. According to SAT, differential exposure to particular kinds of settings (such as criminogenic settings) is largely an outcome of processes of social and self selection (see section 1.4.2), which, in turn, have particular social and personal sources.

This section of chapter 6 addresses the topic of the social sources of young people's exposure to criminogenic settings. Adult supervision is proposed and investigated as one key cause of young people's differential exposure to criminogenic settings. Some families will have more extensive and effective supervision than others. The relationship between young people's social situation (ie the social rules that apply and the resources available), as indicated by their sex, ethnicity, and family socioeconomic resources, and the levels of adult supervision they experience are explored (Figure 6.12). Finally, the impact of

**Table 6.22** Percentage of time awake (by orientation of activity) spent in key settings at different times of the week[a]

| Activity orientation | Day/time of day | Key settings | | | | | | | | | |
| | | Private indoor | | Public indoor | | | | Public outdoor | | | |
| | | Home | Others' home | School | Workplace | Shopping locale | Pubs and nightclubs | Streets | Parks | Moving around |
| --- | --- | --- | --- | --- | --- | --- | --- | --- | --- | --- |
| Family | Weekday day | 86.8 | 5.0 | 0 | 0 | 2.1 | 0.4 | 0.1 | 0.4 | 2.8 |
| | Weekday evening | 18.4 | 0.5 | 0 | 0 | 0.3 | 0 | 0 | 0 | 1.4 |
| | Weekday evening | 29.0 | 1.0 | 0 | 0 | 0.4 | 0 | 0 | 0 | 0.3 |
| | Weekend day | 10.5 | 1.0 | 0 | 0 | 1.1 | 0 | 0 | 0.2 | 0.5 |
| | Weekend evening | 28.9 | 2.5 | 0 | 0 | 0.3 | 0.3 | 0 | 0.1 | 0.6 |
| School | Weekday day | 8.6 | 0.2 | 90.7 | 0 | 0 | 0 | 0 | 0 | 0.2 |
| | Weekday day | 0.9 | 0 | 88.4 | 0 | 0 | 0 | 0 | 0 | 0.1 |
| | Weekday evening | 4.9 | 0.1 | 1.6 | 0 | 0 | 0 | 0 | 0 | 0 |
| | Weekend day | 0.9 | 0 | 0.3 | 0 | 0 | 0 | 0 | 0 | 0 |
| | Weekend evening | 1.9 | 0.1 | 0.4 | 0 | 0 | 0 | 0 | 0 | 0 |
| Work | Weekday day | 0 | 0 | 0 | 100.0[b] | 0 | 0 | 0 | 0 | 0 |
| | Weekday evening | 0 | 0 | 0 | 37.2 | 0 | 0 | 0 | 0 | 0 |
| | Weekday evening | 0 | 0 | 0 | 14.2 | 0 | 0 | 0 | 0 | 0 |
| | Weekend day | 0 | 0 | 0 | 26.8 | 0 | 0 | 0 | 0 | 0 |
| | Weekend evening | 0 | 0 | 0 | 21.8 | 0 | 0 | 0 | 0 | 0 |

| | | | | | | | | | |
|---|---|---|---|---|---|---|---|---|---|
| **Peer** | 5.2 | 13.7 | 0 | 0 | 15.8 | 3.2 | 11.8 | 14.0 | 24.1 |
| Weekday day | 1.1 | 1.6 | 0 | 0 | 2.6 | 0.1 | 1.0 | 1.0 | 17.1 |
| Weekday evening | 1.2 | 3.0 | 0 | 0 | 2.3 | 0.6 | 3.7 | 4.0 | 2.7 |
| Weekend day | 0.5 | 1.5 | 0 | 0 | 7.1 | 0.1 | 1.6 | 3.1 | 1.2 |
| Weekend evening | 2.4 | 7.7 | 0 | 0 | 3.8 | 2.5 | 5.4 | 6.0 | 3.2 |
| **Other** | 26.3 | 36.3 | 0 | 0 | 2.1 | 1.2 | 1.3 | 2.3 | 14.6 |
| Weekday day | 1.7 | 2.5 | 0 | 0 | 0.6 | 0 | 0.3 | 0.3 | 9.4 |
| Weekday evening | 12.7 | 8.4 | 0 | 0 | 0.4 | 0.2 | 0.4 | 0.5 | 1.8 |
| Weekend day | 1.6 | 5.3 | 0 | 0 | 0.8 | 0.1 | 0.2 | 0.9 | 1.2 |
| Weekend evening | 10.3 | 20.2 | 0 | 0 | 0.4 | 0.9 | 0.5 | 0.6 | 2.1 |

[a] For example, during Phase 1 young people spent 86.8 per cent of their time awake in family-oriented activities in their own home, and 18.4 per cent of their time awake in family-oriented activities in their own home on weekday days.

[b] Not all places where work-oriented hours were spent are coded in the space–time budget as workplaces, despite the fact that all such places functioned as work-places. Hence they are treated as workplaces here.

**Figure 6.12  Proposed relationship between young people's social situation, adult supervision, and exposure to criminogenic settings**

home location (residential segregation) is considered as an additional factor in young people's exposure to criminogenic settings.

Young people vary in their social situations in terms of the social rules (eg traditions, conventions) they encounter relevant to their taking part in different kinds of settings (for example differing expectations, depending on their gender and/or ethnic culture, about how they should spend their time), and the social and financial resources available to them relevant to their access to and motivation to take part in different kinds of settings. More importantly, their social situation may also relate to the efficacy of their guardians, eg parents and teachers, to supervise and influence the kinds of setting in which they take part.

Criminogenic exposure, the outcome of interest, is measured as the number of hours, over the 20 days covered by space–time budget interviews during Phase 1 (four days each year from ages 13 to 17),[32] a young person spent in *unstructured peer-oriented activities* (1) *in local and city centres* and (2) *in areas with poor collective efficacy* (see section 3.3 regarding the rationale for choosing these settings and circumstances as criminogenic and how the measures are constructed). The combined time spent in either of these two settings provides an overall measure of criminogenic exposure (correcting for the overlap[33] due to some city and local centre output areas having poor collective efficacy).

To measure young people's social situation, dummy variables are included for sex and ethnicity. Ethnicity refers to whether or not a participant is of Asian origin (Asians being by far the dominant ethnic minority in Peterborough[34]). Data on the highest occupational

---

[32] See section 2.5.1.

[33] 1,575 of 4,638 hours.

[34] There are obviously other ethnic minorities in Peterborough but for these analyses they have been grouped together with the ethnic majority (non-Asian) group. These other minority groups represent only very small proportions of the

social class[35] and highest educational level of a participant's parents, as well as their household income, was collected during the parents' interviews (see section 2.3) and refers to the parents' situation when the participant was aged 12. These markers of young people's social situation are arguably rough and their validity depends on the extent to which they are (as we assume) correlated with variations in relevant social rules and social and economic resources affecting young people's access to and preferences for particular activities in particular settings (arguably, more direct measures would have been preferable but were not available).

Parental monitoring and school truancy are measured using indexes for the Phase 1 period constructed using the same technique as described in section 3.2.3 to measure crime propensity. The items for parental monitoring asked the young person whether his or her parents typically knew where he or she was (place), with whom, and doing what, when he or she was out by himself or herself or with friends.[36] The item for truancy asked how many times a young person had skipped school without an excuse during the previous year (coded into the categories never, one time, two to four times, five to eight times, or 10 or more times[37]). The extent of parental knowledge about a young person's whereabouts and the extent of truancy by that young person are assumed to reflect the efficacy of parents' and teachers' ability to monitor and influence his or her whereabouts; this, in turn, is assumed to have some effect on the degree to which he or she is exposed to criminogenic settings (the city and local centres and areas with poor collective efficacy) under circumstances (during unstructured peer-oriented

population of Peterborough (in total fewer than 2 per cent according to the 2001 census, and fewer than 1.5 per cent of the PADS+ sample) and are, therefore, not statistically feasible to analyse as markers of particular 'cultural influences'.

[35] Occupational social class is a four-class scale divided into lower working (unskilled workers), working (skilled workers and low ranking white collar employees), lower middle (officials and small-scale entrepreneurs), and upper middle and upper class (large-scale entrepreneurs, high-ranking officials, and high-ranking white collar employees).

[36] We feel that this measure of parental knowledge of activities and associations is a sufficient measure of parental monitoring (for discussion, see Dishion and McMahon 1998; Stanton et al. 2000; Stattin and Kerr 2000).

[37] Truancy will be underestimated because (1) the variable is capped; (2) some young people who left school illegitimately may not have reported their lack of attendance as truanting; and (3) it does not account for the fact that many young people left school in Wave 5.

activities) that may be conducive to law-breaking (for those who are crime prone).

### 6.3.1 Zero-order correlations

Table 6.23 shows the zero-order correlations between the social situation, adult supervision, and criminogenic exposure variables. The analyses in this chapter exclude participants who did not take part in all five waves (ages 13 to 17) of the space–time budget. The following observations can be made.

Whether or not the participant was male or female was largely unrelated to other social situation variables, monitoring, or exposure. Particularly noteworthy was the lack of any significant sex differences in levels of parental monitoring. There was a barely significant difference between males and females in terms of truanting, in that females truanted more frequently than males.[38] Accordingly, there were no significant sex differences in exposure to criminogenic settings. The negligible sex differences in parental monitoring and criminogenic exposure most likely reflect the convergence of the social circumstances of young males' and females' lives in recent times.

The three indicators of family socioeconomic resources and status were, as expected, strongly correlated, particularly occupational social class and income.[39] Somewhat surprisingly, the level of parental monitoring was not related to parents' occupational social class, income, or education.[40] However, it was related to parents' ethnicity; Asian parents reported higher levels of parental monitoring than parents in general, and their children had lower levels of truancy, although Asian families tended, on average, to have a lower income and level of education.

---

[38] This little difference may be partly related to a higher fear of bullying among females, which leads them to avoid going to school. In the cross-sectional Peterborough Youth Study (Wikström and Butterworth 2006: 161) 15.7 per cent of the females and 9.8 per cent of the males at age 16 reported that they stayed away from school because they were afraid of being beaten up or bullied.

[39] However, tests show that these correlations are not strong enough to cause any problems with multicollinearity.

[40] Results from other studies are mixed (see, eg, Borawski et al. 2003; Crouter et al. 1999; Laird et al. 2003; Larzelere and Patterson 1990; Loeber and Stouthamer-Loeber 1986; Pettit et al. 2001; Sampson and Laub 1994; Smetana and Daddis 2002), most likely due to inconsistent conceptualization and measurement of both parental monitoring/knowledge and various aspects of socioeconomic status.

**Table 6.23  Zero-order correlations for social situation, adult supervision, and criminogenic exposure variables[a,b]**

|  | Female | Asian | Class[c] | Income[c] | Education[c] | Parental monitoring | Truancy | Exposure I (log)[d] | Exposure II (log)[d] |
|---|---|---|---|---|---|---|---|---|---|
| Female | 1.0 | | | | | | | | |
| Asian | .03 | 1.0 | | | | | | | |
| Class[c] | .02 | -.08 | 1.0 | | | | | | |
| Income[c] | -.01 | -.13* | .74* | 1.0 | | | | | |
| Education[c] | .02 | -.13* | .57* | .51* | 1.0 | | | | |
| Parental monitoring | .05 | .22* | .05 | .05 | .04 | 1.0 | | | |
| Truancy | .10* | -.12* | -.16* | -.16* | -.11* | -.47* | 1.0 | | |
| Exposure I (log)[d] | .03 | -.04 | -.06 | -.11* | -.01 | -.34* | .35* | 1.0 | |
| Exposure II (log)[d] | .03 | -.09 | -.25* | -.25* | -.13* | -.39* | .42* | .69* | 1.0 |

[a] Significance level: * $p < .01$ (or better).
[b] Only those who took part in the space–time budget in all five waves are included; N varies between 657 and 636 depending on the variable combination.
[c] Parents' highest occupational social class, highest level of education, or household income from parents' interview (2003).
[d] Unstructured peer-oriented activities in (Exposure I) the city or local centres or (Exposure II) areas with poor collective efficacy. Being highly skewed, both exposure variables are logged.

Truancy was related to parents' occupational social class, income, and education. Young people whose parents had a higher occupational class, level of education, and household income, truanted less frequently (which may reflect socioeconomic differences in educational culture), except in Asian families, as noted above.

The variables that most strongly predicted criminogenic exposure were parental monitoring (which predicted less exposure) and truancy from school (which predicted more exposure); these two variables were also strongly correlated ($r = -.47$). However, there were clear differences between the exposure variables: the time a young person spent in unstructured peer-oriented activities in areas with poor collective efficacy, but not in the city or local centres, was related to his or her parents' class, income, and education. Young people whose parents reported a lower occupational social class, income, and level of education tended to spend more time in unstructured peer-oriented activities in areas with poor collective efficacy. This is most likely explained by the strong relationship between area disadvantage and poor collective efficacy (as demonstrated in sections 4.3.4 and 4.3.5): disadvantaged families were more likely to live in disadvantaged areas, which generally had a poorer collective efficacy (the zero-order correlation between family and home output area disadvantage was .56, $p = .000$). The same relationship did not hold for the time young people spent in unstructured peer-oriented activities in the city or local centres: the correlations with parents' class and education were non-significant and the correlation with household income only barely significant.

The two separate measures of criminogenic exposure were very strongly correlated ($r = .69$).

### 6.3.2  Trends in adult supervision and exposure to criminogenic settings

Exploring age-related changes in adult supervision and exposure to criminogenic settings reveals a distinctive pattern. While adult supervision decreased with age (parental monitoring decreased and school truancy increased), criminogenic exposure increased (Figure 6.13). In other words, the decrease in adult supervision was mirrored by an increase in exposure to criminogenic settings.

### 6.3.3  Multiple regressions

Young people's social situations explained 8 per cent of the variance in their exposure to criminogenic settings (Table 6.24,

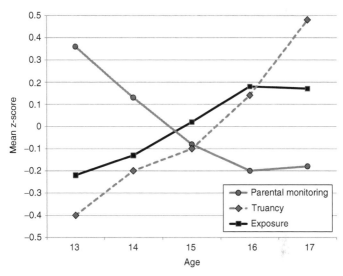

**Figure 6.13 Phase 1 trends in parental monitoring, school truancy, and criminogenic exposure (z-scores)**

Model 1), with being Asian and of a higher occupational social class and income predicting less criminogenic exposure. All in all, young people's social situation appeared to have a modest influence on their exposure to criminogenic settings.

Introducing the two adult supervision variables (Model 2)[41] resulted in all social situation variables (except household income) becoming non-significant, which may be interpreted as demonstrating that their modest influence on criminogenic exposure was mediated through their impact on levels of adult supervision. Moreover, and crucially, the variance explained increased significantly to 29.0 per cent. Young people who experienced poor parental controls, and truanted more frequently from school, tended to spend more time in criminogenic settings.

It is plausible that the location of young people's homes also plays an important role in their exposure to criminogenic settings (due to the common distance-decay function of human activities); for example, young people who live in areas with poor collective efficacy are likely to spend more time in such areas than those who

---

[41] There is a lower *N* for Model 2 which is mainly due to internal non-responses for answers to questions regarding parental monitoring or truancy.

**Table 6.24 Multiple regressions predicting time spent in criminogenic settings**[a]

|  | Model 1 | | Model 2 | | Model 3 | |
|---|---|---|---|---|---|---|
|  | Beta | Prob. | Beta | Prob. | Beta | Prob. |
| Female | .03 | *n.s.* | −.01 | *n.s.* | −.01 | *n.s.* |
| Asian | −.14 | .000 | −.03 | *n.s.* | −.03 | *n.s.* |
| Class[b] | −.13 | .030 | −.10 | *n.s.* | −.07 | *n.s.* |
| Income[b] | −.16 | .004 | −.11 | .039 | −.02 | *n.s.* |
| Education[b] | .02 | *n.s.* | .03 | *n.s.* | .04 | *n.s.* |
| Parental monitoring | | | −.26 | .000 | −.28 | .000 |
| Truancy | | | .30 | .000 | .26 | .000 |
| Home output area poor collective efficacy index | | | | | .23 | .000 |
| Multiple R² x 100 | 8.0% | | 29.0% | | 33.3% | |

[a] Hours spent in unstructured peer-oriented activities in the city or local centres or areas with poor collective efficacy; being highly skewed, the exposure variable is logged.
[b] Parents' highest class, highest level of education, and household income from parents' interview (2003).

do not. Hence, the collective efficacy of a young person's home output area was taken into account (Model 3). This score represented the added collective efficacy scores of a young person's home output area across all five waves.[42]

As expected, living in an area with poor collective efficacy had a significant influence on the time young people spent in criminogenic settings, although there was far from any one-to-one relationship (Table 6.25). Even young people who lived in areas with the poorest collective efficacy showed a substantial variation in the time they spent awake in areas with poor collective efficacy (ranging from fewer than 20 per cent to 99 per cent of their time awake during Phase 1; see Table 6.25).

---

[42] By taking into account a young person's home output area in each of the five waves, this score captures any changes in young people's exposure due to their moving home.

**Table 6.25** Descriptives for hours spent during Phase 1 in areas with poor collective efficacy[a] by collective efficacy score of participants' home output areas

| Home output area collective efficacy | Mean | SD | Min | Max | N residents |
|---|---|---|---|---|---|
| Strong | 19.0 | 24.1 | 0 | 151 | 163 |
| Medium | 41.3 | 43.2 | 0 | 232 | 299 |
| Poor | 189.4 | 46.4 | 50 | 305 | 135 |

[a] Areas with poor collective efficacy defined as the 25 per cent of all output areas with the highest scores of poor collective efficacy.

Table 6.26 shows that young people spent most of their time awake in output areas with the same level of collective efficacy as their home output areas, which is to be expected as young people spend much of their time awake at home.

Table 6.27 shows that the distribution of time spent in output areas with different levels of collective efficacy was different for unstructured peer-oriented hours than for hours awake. Although young people still spend most of their unstructured peer-oriented time in areas with the same level of collective efficacy as their home output areas, the distribution was skewed towards areas with poorer collective efficacy. Even young people who lived in areas with strong collective efficacy still spent more than a quarter of their unstructured peer-oriented time in areas with poor collective

**Table 6.26** Percentage of time young people living in output areas with different levels of collective efficacy spent awake in output areas with different levels of collective efficacy

| Home output area collective efficacy | Percentage time awake | | | |
|---|---|---|---|---|
| | Output area collective efficacy | | | All |
| | Strong | Medium | Poor | |
| Strong | 75.9 | 17.2 | 7.0 | 100.0 |
| Medium | 12.6 | 75.4 | 12.2 | 100.0 |
| Poor | 12.9 | 18.9 | 64.4 | 100.0 |
| All | 30.2 | 45.8 | 24.0 | 100.0 |

**Table 6.27  Percentage of time young people living in output areas with different levels of collective efficacy spent in unstructured peer-oriented activities in output areas with different levels of collective efficacy**

| Home output area collective efficacy | Percentage unstructured peer-oriented time | | | |
|---|---|---|---|---|
| | Output area collective efficacy | | | All |
| | Strong | Medium | Poor | |
| Strong | 45.5 | 27.9 | 26.6 | 100.0 |
| Medium | 13.0 | 53.7 | 33.3 | 100.0 |
| Poor | 7.4 | 31.2 | 61.4 | 100.0 |
| All | 17.8 | 41.7 | 40.5 | 100.0 |

efficacy, although they spent less than one-tenth of their time awake in such settings. Across all time spent in unstructured peer-oriented activities in Phase 1, more than 40 per cent was spent in areas with poor collective efficacy.

The introduction of home location collective efficacy did not substantially affect the influence of adult supervision (Model 3, Table 6.24),[43, 44] but rendered parents' occupational social class non-significant. It is plausible that the significant relationships between parents' (low) occupational social class and (low) income (in Model 1), and (low) household income (in Models 1 and 2), and criminogenic exposure was just a consequence of the residential segregation of these families in more disadvantaged areas (which also generally had poorer collective efficacy). This assertion is supported by the fact that the zero-order correlation between poor collective efficacy and disadvantage[45] in the young people's home location was very strong ($r = .74, p = .000, N = 596$).

[43] There is a lower $N$ for Model 3 which mainly reflects the loss of participants who moved outside the study area during Phase 1 and therefore had no home location collective efficacy score in some data collection waves.

[44] However, a special analysis (not shown) demonstrated a significant interaction between home area collective efficacy and parental monitoring in predicting exposure to criminogenic settings. Poor parental monitoring had, on average, a greater impact on young people's exposure to criminogenic settings for those who lived in areas with the poorest collective efficacy.

[45] Calculated using the same method as home location poor collective efficacy.

All in all, the findings from these analyses suggest that

(1)  home location (residential segregation) and
(2)  levels of adult supervision

are key social sources of variation in young people's exposure to criminogenic settings. Young people who lived in areas with poor collective efficacy and/or who experienced less adult supervision tended to spend more time in criminogenic settings.

As reported in section 3.3.4, exposure to criminogenic settings predicted crime involvement but this was far from a one-to-one relationship. This is to be expected on theoretical grounds. Recall that SAT proposes that the influence of criminogenic exposure on a person's acts of crime depends on his or her crime propensity (section 1.3.4).

## 6.4  Differential effects of criminogenic exposure by young people's crime propensity

The central proposition of SAT is that crime involvement is explained by the interaction between crime prone people and criminogenic settings. This means that the criminogenic nature of settings is only relevant for those who are situationally vulnerable—ie those with a high crime propensity. Hence we would predict that the time young people spend in criminogenic settings is related to their crime involvement, but only for those with a high crime propensity.

If we analyse this relationship at the output area level, we find that area rates of police-recorded crime by young people aged 13–17 in the study area during Phase 1 (logged), correlated significantly with the amount of unstructured peer-oriented time all young people in the PADS+ sample spent in each output area ($r = .38, p = .000$, $N = 518$), despite the fact that in many output areas this amounted to very few hours. Regression analysis shows that this relationship, as predicted, was driven purely by the unstructured peer-oriented time spent by high propensity young people (Table 6.28). It did not appear to matter to the rate of police-recorded crime where young people with a lower crime propensity spent time under these more criminogenic circumstances.

Further underlining the significance of this finding is the fact that young people with a high crime propensity also spent significantly more time in unstructured peer-oriented activities, and more time in such activities in more criminogenic settings, than young people

**Table 6.28  Regression predicting police-recorded crime (logged) by young people in Peterborough (aged 13–17, 2004–07) at the output area level by time spent in unstructured peer-oriented activities by PADS+ participants (aged 13–17, 2004–08) with varying crime propensities[a]**

| Unstructured peer-oriented time | b | Beta | Prob. |
|---|---|---|---|
| (constant) | .49 | | .000 |
| Low crime propensity | –.01 | –.04 | n.s. |
| Medium crime propensity | .00 | .07 | n.s. |
| High crime propensity | .01 | .36 | .000 |
| Multiple $R^2$ x 100 | 15.5% | | |

[a] 34 participants had no Phase 1 crime propensity score; therefore their hours are not included in this analysis.

**Table 6.29  Percentage of time awake in unstructured peer-oriented activities by crime propensity**

| Crime propensity | Unstructured peer-oriented activities | Unstructured peer-oriented activities in the city and local centres and areas with poor collective efficacy |
|---|---|---|
| Low | 1.4 | 0.4 |
| Medium | 4.4 | 1.9 |
| High | 11.6 | 5.9 |

with a medium crime propensity, who spent considerably more time in such settings, under such conditions, than young people with a low crime propensity (Table 6.29; all group differences were significant to the $p = .000$ level).

## 6.5  Explaining the variation in area concentrations of young people's crime

SAT proposes that acts of crime are essentially an outcome of the interaction between a person's crime propensity and criminogenic exposure (see section 1.3). On that basis the theory predicts that spatial concentrations of crime will occur at places where crime prone people and criminogenic settings regularly converge (see section 1.5). We have already demonstrated, using a structural equation model, that setting characteristics assumed to represent weaker moral contexts (city and local centres and areas with poor collective efficacy) predicted higher levels of crime by young people (see section 5.2). However, what was still missing was the importance of what kinds of people are present under what circumstances in the setting. To test this we have added to the model three variables measuring unstructured peer-oriented time spent outside of domestic settings by young people with low, medium, and high crime propensities (for definition of crime propensity categories see section 3.2.3, Table 3.22).

As with similar structural equation models presented in sections 4.5 and 5.2, the following models use negative binomial regression to predict the outcome (ie the count of crime incidents), and do not use any controls like population or area size. However, to ensure this decision did not affect the findings, all models were tested using logged resident population as a control variable, which had no significant effect on the coefficients (for details of the statistical techniques employed, see section 4.5.1). In contrast to previous models, the models presented here make use of space–time budget data to represent the amount of time young people with differing levels of crime propensity spent in unstructured peer-oriented activities per output area. We specifically included only unstructured peer-oriented activities outside domestic settings, as this time is particularly criminogenic (see section 6.2.2). Our aim is to discover whether area rates of young people's (police-recorded) crime can be predicted by the presence of young people with different crime propensities under certain criminogenic circumstances.

Space–time budget time use variables (time spent in unstructured peer-oriented activities outside domestic settings) for the different propensity groups were log-transformed because their distribution was extremely skewed. All other predictor variables were z-transformed, while the dependent variable—crime counts—remains untransformed. For interpretation, a one-unit change in the area predictor variables (disadvantage, ethnic diversity, residential instability, non-residential land use, and poor collective efficacy) represents a change of one standard deviation, while a one-unit change in time use variables represents a proportional increase of hours spent in unstructured peer-oriented activities. As the dependent variable was modelled in a logarithmic scale within the negative binomial (Poisson) framework, we are in any case looking at proportional increases in crime, which can be expressed as odds ratios. Thus the odds ratios reported in Table 6.30 and Figure 6.14 express proportional changes in crime associated with standard deviation increases of area characteristics, and likewise proportional changes in crime associated with a proportional increase of hours recorded in the space-time budget.[46]

Table 6.30 (the path model for which is illustrated in Figure 6.14) supports the assertion that the presence of certain kinds of young people in certain kinds of settings was associated with area rates of young people's crime. An increase of 100 per cent in the time spent by young people with a high crime propensity in unstructured peer-oriented time outside domestic settings in a given output area predicted a 31 per cent increase in the rate of police-recorded young people's crime (as the predictor variable is the logarithm of a count of hours). In fact, time spent by young people with a high crime propensity significantly predicted area crime rates for total crime counts, and all crime types. On the other hand, no measurement of time spent in an output area by young people with a low crime propensity had any significant effect on area crime rates. Time spent by young people with a medium crime propensity (the largest propensity group) was associated with total crime counts and rates of violent crime and shoplifting. An increase of 100 per cent in unstructured peer-oriented activities outside domestic settings by young people with a medium crime propensity led to a 14 per cent increase in total crime, a 24 per cent increase in violent crime, and a 48 per cent increase in shoplifting.

Shoplifting showed the strongest association with time spent in unstructured peer-oriented activities outside domestic settings by young people with a high crime propensity (a 100 per cent increase in time use led to a 99 per cent increase in shoplifting). For all crime, and all crime types, time spent by the high crime propensity group was associated with a greater increase in crime compared to time spent by the medium crime propensity group (though only marginally so in the case of violence).

The path model also contains information about which structural features of output areas influenced the amount of time spent there by the three crime propensity groups. Two major effects were

---

[46] The interpretation of the effect of log-transformed predictors (hours) on a log-scaled outcome follows the econometric approach of 'elasticities' (of prices, demand, etc.).

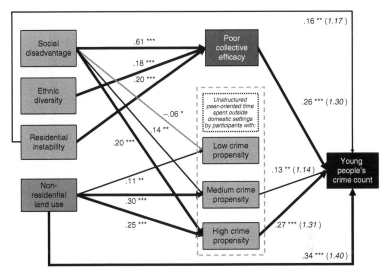

**Figure 6.14 Mplus path model of area structural variables, land use, and young people's time use (by propensity) predicting young people's police-recorded crime[a,b]**

[a] Odds ratios in brackets; paths to poor collective efficacy in metric scale; paths to crime in logarithmic scale.
[b] Significance levels: *** $p < .001$, ** $p < .01$, * $p < .05$.

at work. First, all three crime propensity groups had a tendency to spend more peer-oriented time in output areas with greater non-residential land use, eg commercial and entertainment buildings (particularly when that peer-oriented time occurred outside domestic settings). Second, young people with a low crime propensity spent less time in areas with greater disadvantage (coefficient = -.06), whereas young people with medium and particularly high crime propensities spent more time (coefficient = .17 and .35, respectively). Thus, there was a differential effect of social disadvantage on the presence of young people according to their crime propensity. One reason for this is that areas with greater disadvantage tend to have a higher frequency of crime prone people among their residents (see section 5.3.3).

The introduction of the measurement of time use into the explanation of police-recorded young people's crime had a dramatic effect on the relevance of non-residential land use. Table 6.31 shows that a relevant part of the effect of non-residential land use on

Table 6.30 **Mplus path models using space–time budget unstructured peer-oriented hours outside domestic settings[a] by young people with different crime propensities and structural variables to predict counts of young people's crime[b] per output area by crime type**

| | | Poor collective efficacy | Exposure of crime propensity groups | | | All crimes[c] | Crime types | | | |
| --- | --- | --- | --- | --- | --- | --- | --- | --- | --- | --- |
| | | | Low | Medium | High | | Violent crime | Vandalism | Serious theft | Shoplifting[d] |
| Structural (exogenous) | | | | | | | | | | |
| Social disadvantage | Coefficient[e] | 0.61*** | −0.06** | 0.14** | 0.20*** | n.s. | n.s. | n.s. | 0.31*** | n.s. |
| | Odds ratio | | | | | | | | 1.36 | |
| Ethnic diversity | Coefficient[e] | 0.18*** | n.s. | n.s. | n.s. | n.s. | n.s. | n.s. | n.s. | n.s. |
| | Odds ratio | | | | | | | | | |
| Residential instability | Coefficient[e] | 0.20*** | n.s. | n.s. | n.s. | 0.16** | n.s. | n.s. | 0.18** | n.s. |
| | Odds ratio | | | | | 1.17 | | | 1.20 | |
| Non-residential land use | Coefficient[e] | n.s. | 0.11** | 0.30*** | 0.25*** | 0.34*** | 0.36*** | 0.42*** | 0.16* | 0.97*** |
| | Odds ratio | | | | | 1.40 | 1.44 | 1.52 | 1.18 | 2.63 |

Mediating (endogenous)

| | | | | | |
|---|---|---|---|---|---|
| **Poor collective efficacy** | Coefficient[e] | 0.26*** | 0.28*** | n.s. | 0.15* | n.s. |
| | Odds ratio | 1.30 | 1.32 | | 1.17 | |
| **Unstructured peer-oriented activities outside domestic settings** | | | | | | |
| Low propensity | Coefficient[e] | n.s. | n.s. | n.s. | n.s. | n.s. |
| | Odds ratio | | | | | |
| Medium propensity | Coefficient[e] | 0.13** | 0.22*** | n.s. | n.s. | 0.40* |
| | Odds ratio | 1.14 | 1.24 | | | 1.48 |
| High propensity | Coefficient[e] | 0.27*** | 0.23*** | 0.29*** | 0.11* | 0.69* |
| | Odds ratio | 1.31 | 1.26 | 1.34 | 1.12 | 1.99 |

[a] Unstructured peer-oriented hours outside domestic settings log-transformed.
[b] Known young offenders aged 13–17 who offended between April 2004 and December 2007.
[c] Police-recorded crime types equivalent to those self-reported in PADS+.
[d] Model did not converge in Mplus; computed in STATA 11.
[e] Significance levels: *** $p < .001$, ** $p < .01$, * $p < .05$.

**Table 6.31** **Comparison of odds ratios[a] for models predicting area counts of young people's crime including and excluding time use variables by propensity groups**

| | Non-residential land use | | | Poor collective efficacy | | |
|---|---|---|---|---|---|---|
| | Model excluding time use variables by propensity groups[b] | Model including time use variables by propensity groups[c] | Percent-age reduction in odds ratio | Model excluding time use variables by propensity groups[b] | Model including time use variables by propensity groups[c] | Percent-age reduction in odds ratio |
| All crime | 1.75*** | 1.40*** | 20.0 | 1.42*** | 1.30*** | 8.5 |
| Violence | 1.82*** | 1.44*** | 20.9 | 1.39*** | 1.32*** | 5.0 |
| Vandalism | 1.70*** | 1.52*** | 10.6 | 1.27* | n.s. | |
| Serious property | 1.21** | 1.18* | 2.5 | 1.17* | 1.17* | 0.0 |
| Shoplifting | 7.24*** | 2.63** | 63.7 | n.s. | n.s. | |

[a] Significance levels: ***$p < .001$, **$p < .01$, *$p < .05$.
[b] See Figure 5.2 and Table 5.3.
[c] See Figure 6.14 and Table 6.30.

young people's crime was spurious in the sense that it was mediated by the presence of people who were potential offenders. This was particularly obvious in the case of shoplifting. Output areas in which shoplifting was the most prevalent (eg shopping locales) were also areas where many young people spent a lot of time. When this time use was measured and accounted for in the model, the effect of non-residential land use fell precipitously (from an odds ratio of 7.3 to 2.6, a reduction of 64 per cent).

This dramatic decrease of coefficients was limited to non-residential land use. In contrast, the coefficients of collective efficacy were attenuated to a much lesser extent. One can conclude that using information on the spatial distribution of particular kinds of time use (eg peer-oriented activities, and variants thereof) by young people can help to clarify the role of non-residential land use in crime causation, and stress the importance of what kinds of young people (with what crime propensities) spend time in what kinds of settings.

The analyses presented in Figure 6.14 and Table 6.30 support the assertion of SAT that acts of crime are an outcome of the intersection of crime prone people (ie those with a weak law-relevant morality and ability to exercise self-control) and criminogenic settings (eg areas of commerce and entertainment and residential areas with poor collective efficacy) and, particularly, that concentrations (hot spots) of young people's crime tend to occur at locations where crime prone young people spend a lot of time in unstructured peer-oriented activities in moral contexts that encourage (or fail to discourage) acts that break rules of conduct (stated in law).

## 6.6  Summary and conclusion

In this chapter we have demonstrated how young people's activities vary by time, space, and content. We established that crimes are more closely linked to certain kinds of activities than others (ie unsupervised activities with peers outside the school and work setting). We then developed this further to highlight the importance of a lack of supervision or structure, particularly during these more criminogenic activities. As expected, we found that the rate of crime is particularly high during unstructured peer-oriented activities. We also showed a link to particular settings highlighted in earlier chapters, ie areas with poor collective efficacy and city and local centres.

Having established the kinds of activities that are the most criminogenic, and individual differences in young people's involvement in these activities, we turned to the question of explaining these differences. We investigated the importance of the level of adult supervision and home location and found both predicted differences in young people's exposure to criminogenic settings. However, as SAT predicts, criminogenic exposure is only relevant to crime prone people. We subsequently established that this was the case, and that crime prone young people also spend more time in criminogenic settings than less situationally vulnerable young people.

We then brought together in one model insights about the importance of environmental conditions for young people's crime involvement (identified in chapters 4 and 5) with insights about young people's time use and crime propensity. This model showed that area concentrations of young people's crime are highly dependent on the interplay between features of the settings and time spent in an area by crime prone young people. In part 3 we analyse this interplay at the situational level.

# PART 3

# The Situational Dynamics of Young People's Crime

Chapter 7 uses space–time budget data to explore the convergence of crime prone young people with criminogenic settings, and which intersections (of which young people with which settings) lead to crime. Chapter 8 then delves into the perception–choice process by analysing violent behavioural intentions of young people with varying crime propensities to scenarios varying in levels of provocation and deterrence, and relating this to actual violent behaviour.

# 7

# The Crime Convergence: Kinds of People in Kinds of Settings

## 7.1 Studying the intersection of people and settings

At the core of Situational Action Theory (SAT) lies the argument that crime is an outcome of the interaction between crime prone people and crime-conducive settings. When crime prone people are exposed to criminogenic settings, they may perceive crime as an alternative for action because their own morality and the moral context of the setting promote the breaking of rules of conduct (stated in law), and they may choose to commit an act of crime because they lack the ability to exercise self-control and there is nothing in the setting that deters them. As many studies have previously demonstrated, crimes tend to be committed by certain kinds of people, and to be concentrated in certain kinds of places. In this chapter we bring together data on settings (from the space–time budget and community survey; see sections 2.5.1 and 2.8, respectively), exposure to settings (from the space–time budget), and people (from the young people's questionnaire; see section 2.4.1) to investigate the intersection of people and settings in a way no other study, as far as we are aware, has done before—by analysing what happens when people who differ in their crime propensity take part in settings that differ in their criminogeneity. Our findings show that it is indeed the intersection between crime prone people and crime conducive settings that is key to understanding the causes of acts of crime.

## 7.2 Distribution of space–time budget crimes

Crime is a rare event in most young people's lives (see section 3.1.1). In fact, during the 205,885 space–time budget hours the 710 PADS+ participants spent awake during the 13,964 studied days (four days per person per year),[1] 74 young people reported a total of 141 crimes (between the ages of 13 and 17). Over half of these were acts of violence, and nearly a third were acts of vandalism; the remainder were acts of theft, shoplifting, and driving offences (Table 7.1). This amounted to, on average, 0.7 crimes per 1,000 hours the sample spent awake, or, more pointedly, 6.5 crimes per 1,000 hours the 74 offenders spent awake. This means the 74 offenders committed, on average (taking into account the hours they spent asleep) one crime every tenth day (a mean of 180 crimes per offender over the five studied years).[2]

Extrapolating space–time budget crimes to estimate the number of crimes young people would have reported across Phase 1, had we interviewed them every day, it becomes apparent that even

### Table 7.1  Space–time budget crime types

| Crime type | N | % |
| --- | --- | --- |
| Violence | 72 | 51.1 |
| Vandalism | 44 | 31.2 |
| Theft from a person | 10 | 7.1 |
| Shoplifting | 9 | 6.4 |
| Driving offences | 6 | 4.3[a] |
| Total | 141 | 100.1 |

[a] All six driving offences were reported by one young person on one day.

[1] Not all 710 young people completed space–time budget interviews in all five waves (see section 2.5.1). 657 took part in all five waves (12 young people completed only one interview, six only two, 12 only three, and 23 only four).

[2] A figure that is largely consistent with what we found analysing crimes self-reported in the questionnaire (see section 3.3.1) where the most active self-reported offenders (those who self-reported 100 or more crimes over the five studied years) were responsible, on average, for about one crime per week. Since the space–time budget only covers four days per person per year it is likely that space–time budget crimes over represent high frequency offenders (ie those who offend with some regularity). This is supported by the fact that those self-reporting a space–time budget crime self-reported on average 110 crimes in the questionnaire over the study period, compared to 32.7 crimes self-reported on average by all offenders who self-reported crimes in the questionnaire over the study period. Moreover, the four days covered by the space–time budget over represent Fridays and Saturdays, when crime is more common (see Table 7.10), thereby overestimating the rate of crime by approximately 15 per cent.

though crime, on a personal level, is a rare event, it is a significant problem among adolescents that clearly deserves attention: the young people in our sample alone would have committed over 11,500 crimes between the ages of 13 and 17.[3]

There is considerable correspondence between the rates and distribution of space–time budget crimes and that of the sample's self-reported and official crimes. For example, the extrapolated 11,500 crimes is of a similar magnitude to the 16,000 crimes the same young people self-reported on the questionnaire between the ages of 12 and 16 (see section 3.1.1). There is a strong correlation between the frequency of crime participants self-reported in the space–time budget and questionnaire ($r = .57$, $p = .000$, $N = 657$), and those who reported space–time budget crimes were also more likely to have a police record of a reprimand, warning, or conviction ($\varphi = .20$, $p = .000$, $N = 657$) than those who did not report space–time budget crimes.

A unique aspect of the space–time budget is that the participants reported the exact time and place their crimes occurred, which means that (in contrast to self-reported crimes on the questionnaire, which do not include such information) the temporal and spatial distribution of space–time budget crimes can be compared with that of police-recorded crimes for young offenders across Peterborough. The distribution of crimes reported in the space–time budget is consistent in space (Figure 7.1) and time

---

[3] To extrapolate space–time budget crimes over Phase 1 we first calculated the average number of crimes reported on weekdays, Fridays, and Saturdays for each year, multiplied these averages by the number of weekdays, Fridays, and Saturdays there were in each year (respectively), and summed the results to provide an estimate of the average number of space–time budget crimes one would expect to be reported by a single participant if he or she was interviewed every day of the given year. We then multiplied the estimate for each year by the number of participants taking part that year to estimate how many crimes we would expect the sample to have reported if they provided space–time budget data for every day, and summed these estimates to achieve the final estimate (11,502) of the number of crimes the entire sample would have reported in Phase 1. We treated Sunday as a weekday as there is evidence that it resembles a weekday in some regards more than a weekend day (see section 2.5.1). By doing so, if anything, we will have *under*estimated the total number of crimes that would have been reported in Phase 1. As young people predominantly reported their time use in the first quarter of the year, during the second school term, we can also expect variation in rates of offending to be apparent at other times of the year (eg summer holidays; see section 2.5.1) that we cannot take into account.

(Figure 7.2) with corresponding police data on young people's crime in Peterborough.[4] The correlation at the output area level between police-recorded and space–time budget crimes is rather

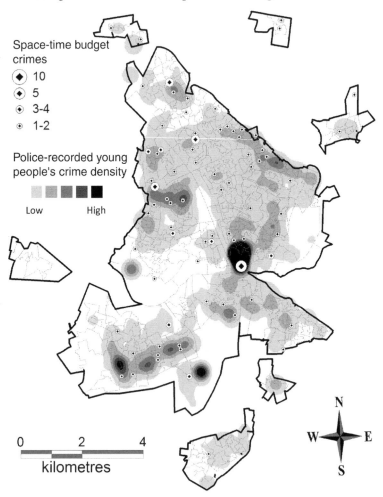

**Figure 7.1 Relative density of police-recorded crime by young people and distribution of Phase 1 space–time budget crimes**[a]

[a] This kernel density estimation map uses coordinate-level police data, while the overlaid space–time budget crime points are assigned the coordinates of the population centre of the output areas within which they occurred (see technical appendix, section A1.2.2, for discussion).

[4] The spatial comparison (Figure 7.1) incorporates acts from all nine key crime types, while the temporal comparison (Figure 7.2) is limited to acts of violence because police-recorded data on when crimes take place is generally more reliable for crimes against other people than for crimes against property.

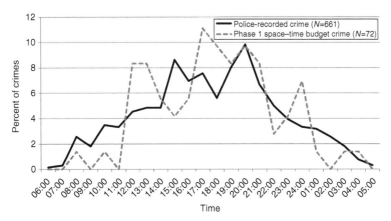

**Figure 7.2 Temporal distribution of young people's violent crime[a]**

[a] Police-recorded assaults by offenders aged 13–17 within the PCS area from April 2004 to December 2007 (see section 2.6); Phase 1 space–time budget self-reported violent offences 2004–08.

strong ($r = .56$, $p = .000$). Given the small number of crimes captured in the four days covered (annually) by the space–time budget, and the small size of output areas as an environmental unit, the space–time correspondence between the two measures is impressive. It is improbable that participants could or would recreate these spatial and temporal patterns by, for example, generally making up information.

## 7.2.1 Circumstances of space–time budget crimes

SAT argues that crimes occur in settings that have a moral context that encourages the breaking of rules of conduct (stated in law), eg that are characterized by incentives to offend, weak law-relevant moral norms, and weak enforcement of the law. To compare levels of crime across a variety of settings under differing circumstances, both criminogenic and not, we calculated the rates of crime per 1,000 hours young people spent (awake) in those settings under those particular circumstances. By calculating crimes per *person-hours*, we controlled for differential exposure and ensured that settings in which young people spent little time and reported few, albeit frequent, acts of crime, were not overshadowed by settings in which young people spent a considerable amount of time and reported many acts of crime, albeit infrequently. These crimes per 1,000 hours can be seen as the crimes per unit exposure to the given setting (for simplicity, we will subsequently, in this chapter, refer to the rate of crimes per 1,000 person-hours awake as the *crime rate*). A setting's rate of crimes per 1,000 person-hours may be regarded as a test of its criminogeneity. However, it is important to bear in mind that this test is only partial because, according to SAT, it is the interaction between crime prone people and criminogenic settings that is of key importance to a setting's level of crime. We therefore expect to find that the rate of crime in criminogenic settings and circumstances per person-hour will be much higher for crime prone people and much lower for crime averse people when we (from section 7.3 onward) introduce young people's differential crime propensity into our analyses.

## Key factors in young people's crime involvement: Presence of peers

We assume that peers, when present, exert an active moral influence upon an actor and his or her actions (ie crime prone peers will encourage and crime averse peers will discourage acts of crime). However, the space–time budget does not measure the involvement of peers in the ongoing action. A young person on the school bus, for example, is in the presence of peers, but he or she is not necessarily interacting with those peers. It is reasonable to assume those peers still exert some influence upon the young person and his or her actions; however, that influence may not be as significant as that of peers with whom he or she is directly engaged. In characterizing these sorts of settings, we have taken the decision to record the presence of peers, even if the young person is not directly interacting with them; thus, if anything, we risk underestimating the importance of peers' influence on young people's crime involvement.

In chapter 6 we paid particular attention to the importance of peers for the moral context. One limitation of traditional peer delinquency research that the space–time budget is able to address is the inability to place peers in the setting at the time of the crime event. Although space–time budget data provides details about peers in the setting, eg their numbers and gender, it does not provide details about potentially important factors such as their crime propensity or previous crime involvement. However, data about participants' peers and their crime involvement was collected in the questionnaire, at the individual level, and is analysed in section 7.3.4 (see also section 3.3.5). Both questionnaire and space–time budget data confirm the importance of peers for young people's

**Table 7.2 Percentage of self-reported crimes committed in the presence of peers**

| Crime type | Percentage of young people who were with friends during the last incident reported in the questionnaire | Percentage of space–time budget crimes with peers present |
|---|---|---|
| Arson | 96 | — |
| Vandalism | 80 | 91 |
| Violence | 72 | 86 |
| Shoplifting | 81 | 78 |
| Theft from person | 60 | 90 |
| Residential burglary | 100 | — |
| Non-residential burglary | 100 | — |
| Theft from a car | 100 | — |
| Theft of a car | 93 | — |
| Driving offences | — | 50[a] |

[a] Three driving offences were committed with peers only and three with young family members only (eg cousins). It is not unreasonable to presume that young family members, such as cousins, of a similar age may have a similar effect upon rule-breaking as peers.

crime involvement. At age 16 (Wave 4), an overwhelming majority of young people reported in the questionnaire they were with friends the last time they committed a particular type of crime. This varied by crime type, but in only two crime categories (theft from a person and violent crime) did fewer than 80 per cent of offenders report they committed their last such offence with their peers (see Table 7.2). For rare but serious offences (residential burglary, non-residential burglary, and theft of a car) all offenders reported committing their last offence with their peers. A similar pattern emerged from the space–time budget crimes: 85.8 per cent of space–time budget crimes occurred in the presence of peers.

The 14.2 per cent of space–time budget crimes in which peers did not feature occurred predominately in the home (60 per cent) and/or in the presence of family members (75 per cent). In keeping with the general patterns of crime, most were violent offences.

### Key factors in young people's crime involvement: Supervision

We assume that an adult guardian exerts an active moral influence upon an actor and his or her actions; however, in some settings, an adult guardian may be present but his or her involvement with and therefore influence upon the young person and his or her actions may be minimal, such as a bus driver on the school bus, or a parent who is at home but in another room. Again, we have taken the decision that the presence of the guardian, in any capacity, qualitatively changes the moral context (in this case, strengthens it). If anything, then, we underestimate the influence of direct supervision by including cases where supervision is actually quite minimal.

Most space–time budget crimes (76 per cent) occurred when young people were unsupervised. For crimes that did occur while young people were supervised, most still took place in the presence of peers (62 per cent), suggesting peers exerted a criminogenic influence even in settings where young people's behaviour was being monitored. Two-thirds of these supervised crimes were acts of violence and nearly half took place at school. It is possible that many occurred in settings where an adult was present but not directly involved, such as a teacher on lunch duty who was far from the scene of a schoolground fight, and therefore the role of supervision was overestimated.

### Key factors in young people's crime involvement: Activities

Table 7.3 shows the comparable rates of crime across different types of time use, using the orientation classification introduced in section 6.1.3 (see Table 6.3). The rate of crimes was significantly higher during peer-oriented activities than any other activities. During family-oriented activities, a crime was reported approximately

**Table 7.3 Space-time budget crime rate for hours spent in different kinds of activities**

| Activity orientation | Percentage space-time budget crimes (N) | | Percentage hours awake | Crimes/ 1,000 hours |
|---|---|---|---|---|
| Family | 9.9 | (14) | 43.6 | 0.2 |
| School | 14.2 | (20) | 30.7 | 0.3 |
| Work | 0.7 | (1) | 2.8 | 0.2 |
| Peers | 62.4 | (88) | 11.6 | 3.7 |
| Other | 12.8 | (18) | 11.3 | 0.8 |
| All hours | 100.0 | (141) | 100.0 | 0.7 |

once every 5,000 hours[5]; as the young people spent, on average, six and a half hours in family-oriented activities per day, at this rate a given young person would offend during family-oriented activities approximately once every two years. During school-oriented activities, a crime was reported once every 3,330 hours. Considering the time they spent in school-oriented activities per weekday, however, an even greater span of time is implied between school-related than family-oriented crimes: more than 100 school weeks, or two years and nine months (of course, because this is an average, we would expect some young people to offend more frequently and others less). Hence, although nearly a quarter of all space–time budget crimes were reported under family and school-oriented circumstances, they are clearly not very criminogenic. Compare this to crimes under peer-oriented circumstances in which a crime was reported every 270 hours: despite the fact that young people spent considerably less time per day in peer-oriented activities (less than two hours), at this rate a given young person would report an offence during peer-oriented time approximately once every five months.

The rate of crime was particularly high during unstructured peer-oriented activities, during which rules of conduct may be less enforced and motivation potentially directed towards breaking them. Young people were almost 2.7 times more likely to report an act of crime during their unstructured peer-oriented activities than other peer-oriented activities. Interestingly, this ratio differed by crime type; young people were even more likely to report an act of violence, but no more likely to report an act of shoplifting (Table 7.4).

**Table 7.4  Crimes per 1,000 hours in peer-oriented activities**

| Crime type | Unstructured peer-oriented activities | Other peer-oriented activities |
| --- | --- | --- |
| All | 5.7 | 2.1 |
| Violence | 3.0 | 0.3 |
| Vandalism | 2.1 | 0.8 |
| Theft | 0.4 | 0.1 |
| Shoplifting | 0.3 | 0.3 |

[5] Recall that hours spent asleep were assigned their own orientation category (Table 6.3), therefore hours spent in family, school, work, and peer-oriented activities refer only to hours spent awake.

**Table 7.5 Summary of the crime rate for peer-oriented hours**

| Setting | Crimes (%) | Hours (%) | Crimes/1,000 hours |
|---|---|---|---|
| All | 141 (100) | 205,838 (100) | 0.7 |
| Peer-oriented activity | 88 (62) | 23,864 (12) | 3.7 |
| Unstructured peer-oriented activity | 60 (43) | 10,487 (5) | 5.7 |

This is because the vast majority of violent crimes were reported while young people were socializing face to face, compared to other crime types that were more broadly distributed across activities (eg moving around), while shoplifting tended to occur when young people were involved in more structured activities in or near shopping venues.

Focusing on hours spent in unstructured peer-oriented activities, we account for nearly 43 per cent of all space–time budget crimes within only 5 per cent of the time young people spent awake (Table 7.5), a clear indication that such time use is uniquely criminogenic.

### 7.2.2 Spatial distribution of space–time budget crimes

Not only what young people are doing (activities) but also the setting and circumstances in which those activities take place are of importance for their likelihood of becoming involved in crime. For example, socializing with a group of friends outside of school while waiting for your parents to pick you up may be less conducive to offending than socializing with a group of acquaintances in a local park when your parents do not know where you are.

#### Distance to crime

The home is perhaps the most central location in any person's activity field, and therefore it is a good anchor point for studying the relationship between a person's activity field and the locations of his or her crimes. The average distance from a young person's home[6] to the scene of a space–time budget crime in Phase 1 was

---

[6] For distance-to-crime analyses we refer only to the young person's main home at the time of the crime. These analyses do not take into account the output areas of young people's alternative homes (where four space–time budget crimes

2.2 kilometres,[7] although there was considerable variation (with young people reporting acts of crime up to 14 kilometres from home). Interestingly, this was slightly closer to home than the average distance young people travelled to any activity (2.5 kilometres; see section 6.1.2) and exactly the distance they travelled on average to unstructured peer-oriented activities. For all crime types except driving offences (which were all committed by one young person on one day less than 0.5 kilometres from his or her home) the average distance travelled from home in Phase 1 was between 2.0 and 2.3 kilometres.

There was a clear distance-decay effect for space–time budget crimes (Figure 7.3).[8] As is typically the case (see section 5.5), young people tended to commit more crimes closer to home. Just under 10 per cent of space–time budget crimes were reported in the output area where the young person lived (of which 57.1 per cent occurred during family-oriented activities), and more than 20 per cent were reported within 300 metres of the young person's home, thus likely no further than a neighbouring output area. Half of all crimes were reported within one kilometre of home.

## Key locations and crime

The home is not the only key location in people's activity fields. For young people, other key locations include their school, three best friends' homes, nearby local centres, and the city centre, as demonstrated in section 6.1.2. Young people spent most of their time (92.2 per cent), and reported most of their space–time budget crimes (76.5 per cent), within 500 metres of these key locations. This supports Brantingham and Brantingham's (1993) crime pattern theory, which aims to explain why crimes occur at certain places. Their theory argues that people's movement patterns are determined by their individual routine activities (clustering around key geographical locations) and that people offend in relation to their activity space.

---

took place), which, if anything, leads us to overestimate the distance between where young people live and where they offend.

[7] This distance is calculated from the population centre of the young person's home output area to the population centre of the output area in which he or she reported a crime (see technical appendix, section A1.1).

[8] Measured as straight-line distances from the population centre of the offender's home output area to the population centre of the output area in which the crime took place (see technical appendix, section A1.1, for how this is calculated).

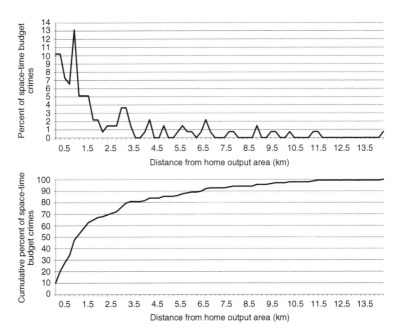

**Figure 7.3 Distance-decay of space–time budget crimes from the offender's home output area, and cumulative percent of space–time budget crimes by distance from home output area**

Crime is not randomly distributed in time and space. It is clustered, but the shape of the clustering is greatly influenced by where people live within a city, how and why they travel or move about a city, and how networks of people who know each other spend their time.

(P. J. Brantingham and Brantingham 2008: 91)

As far we are aware, PADS+ is the first study that has properly tested these assumptions.

### Criminogenic settings

We have argued that, because they imply weak moral contexts, certain environmental features, such as poor collective efficacy, and certain land use characteristics, such as the presence of recreational and entertainment venues, may be particularly criminogenic (see section 6.2.3). Consistent with this, the rate of space–time budget crimes across all hours was particularly high in recreational and entertainment settings such as the city and local centres, and in residential areas with poor collective efficacy (Table 7.6).

**Table 7.6  Crimes per 1,000 hours in settings with particular environmental features**

| Setting | All hours | Peer-oriented activities | Peer-oriented activities outside domestic settings | Unstructured peer-oriented activities outside domestic settings |
|---|---|---|---|---|
| City centre | 1.6 | 2.9 | 2.9 | 5.0 |
| Local centres | 1.0 | 8.2 | 9.1 | 17.6 |
| Other areas with poor collective efficacy | 1.0 | 4.3 | 5.4 | 6.6 |
| Other areas with medium collective efficacy | 0.6 | 3.8 | 4.6 | 10.6 |
| Other areas with strong collective efficacy | 0.5 | 1.8 | 2.0 | 3.4 |

During peer-oriented hours, the city centre, while still boasting a high rate of crime, paled in criminogeneity next to local centres and residential areas with poor and even medium collective efficacy, namely because the city centre was such a popular setting for peer-oriented activities, including those that did not lead to crime. Residential areas with strong collective efficacy, reflecting a stronger moral context, had the lowest rate of crime involvement during peer-oriented hours (see Table 7.6). The same pattern holds, although crime rates are higher, when the focus is narrowed to peer-oriented hours spent outside domestic settings. However, the pattern shifts when the focus is placed on unstructured peer-oriented time, when the crime rate in areas with medium collective efficacy surpassed that in areas with poor collective efficacy. Part of this is likely a result of the fact that the number of hours, and crime hours, becomes smaller and therefore more sensitive to random variation. Another part, however, appears to be a result of differences in how young people spend their time in areas with poor versus medium collective efficacy, and the circumstances under which they offend. In areas with poor collective efficacy, young people reported more offences during semi-structured activities, such as violence during impromptu football games.

Geographically, space–time budget crimes were highly concentrated in the 10 output areas that form the city centre or contain key local centres. Young people spent a disproportionate amount of their time awake in these areas, during most of which they were involved in legitimate activities, such as shopping, working, dining out, etc., often in the company of their parents or other adult guardians.

Nearly all crime reported in the city centre (92 per cent) and all crimes reported in local centres occurred during peer-oriented activities, and three-quarters of crimes in both settings occurred during unstructured peer-oriented activities. City and local centres were popular places for peer-oriented activities by 13- to 17-year-olds, accommodating more than one-fifth of all peer-oriented time in Phase 1. In fact, half of all the time young people spent in the city centre was peer-oriented (compared to only 20 per cent of the time they spent in local centres[9]). This concentration of peer-oriented time reflects the fact that the city centre attracted young people from across the city, while local centres mainly attracted young people from nearby residential areas and local schools.

Young people tended to congregate in groups both in the city and local centres. However they were more likely to do so in local centres, where they were also more likely to offend in groups: while fewer than half (42 per cent) of the space–time budget crimes reported in the city centre were committed in groups of three or more young people, all such crimes reported in local centres were committed in groups of three or more young people.

Although many crimes occurred in shopping locales (39.1 per cent), young people were also likely to offend with their peers in outdoor spaces in the city and local centres, such as streets (21.7 per cent), car parks (4.3 per cent), and bus stops (4.3 per cent). Young people reported a crime every 40 hours they spent in peer-oriented activities in streets in the city centre, and a crime every 100 hours they spent in peer-oriented activities in streets in local centres (Table 7.7).

In fact, the rate of crime in streets and other outdoor public spaces was high during peer-oriented activities in any setting; for example, during time spent in unstructured peer-oriented activities the rate in streets and parks reached nearly one crime every 100 hours (see Table 7.8). More than a quarter of all space–time budget crimes took place during unstructured peer-oriented activities in streets and parks, although young people spent less than 2 per cent of their time awake in these settings.

---

[9] 57 per cent of the time they spent in local centres was in schools located in local centres.

**Table 7.7  Crimes per 1,000 hours in outdoor public spaces**

| Setting | Time | Parks | Streets | Moving around |
|---|---|---|---|---|
| City centre | Other | 0 | 0 | 0 |
| | *Peer-oriented* | *0* | *25.2* | *8.3* |
| Local centres | Other | 0 | 0 | 0 |
| | *Peer-oriented* | *0* | *10.5* | *0* |
| Other areas with poor collective efficacy | Other | 0 | 14.9 | 1.1 |
| | *Peer-oriented* | *3.1* | *7.7* | *3.6* |
| Other areas with medium collective efficacy | Other | 0 | 0 | 1.9 |
| | *Peer-oriented* | *6.9* | *7.4* | *1.7* |
| Other areas with strong collective efficacy | Other | 0 | 4.3 | 0.8 |
| | *Peer-oriented* | *4.6* | *7.1* | *0* |

In areas outside the city and local centres, streets and parks were also important settings for crimes. More than a third of all crimes outside the city and local centres took place in streets or parks, and nearly three-quarters of those crimes were reported when young people were engaged in unstructured peer-oriented activities. Interestingly, streets were a more popular setting for crimes in areas with poor collective efficacy, while parks were a more popular setting in areas with stronger collective efficacy. However, the rate of crime was higher in streets than parks across all settings (Table 7.7).

The rate of crime in streets during peer-oriented activities did not vary by an area's level of collective efficacy. However, the rate of crime in parks during peer-oriented activities was highest in areas with medium collective efficacy, and lowest in areas with poor collective efficacy. Young people spent slightly less time in parks in areas with poor collective efficacy than areas with medium and strong collective efficacy, but a much larger proportion of their time in the streets (most likely because areas with poor collective efficacy encompassed less green space). They also reported more crimes in outdoor spaces such as football pitches, which may say something about the kinds of outdoor spaces present in areas with poor collective efficacy (eg that there is less parkland or woodland). It is likely also the case that area residents' collective efficacy does not have the same impact on the social environment of green spaces than it does in the more residential parts of an output area, as residents may be less capable of observing what happens in areas such as parks and playgrounds (see section 6.2.3).

Young people also reported high rates of crimes during time in which their main activity was moving around in outdoor spaces, for example walking, driving, or cycling around their neighbourhoods or their friends' neighbourhoods (see section 6.2.3), especially when they were with their peers (Table 7.8). This proved a frequent pastime for young people during their discretionary time; they spent nearly one-quarter of their peer-oriented time moving around. It is difficult to qualify the settings they were exposed to when involved in such transient activities, but rule-following during such activities may be difficult for residents to effectively monitor and enforce. Consistent with this, more than one-tenth of all crimes were reported when young people were moving around.

To summarize, crime rates were highest in the city and local centres and areas with poorer collective efficacy,[10] and when young people were engaged in peer-oriented activities (Table 7.9). The poorer an area's collective efficacy, the greater the proportion of time young people spent in that setting in peer-oriented activities,[11] and the higher the rate of crimes they reported during that time. Most crime was reported when young people were in groups of peers, rather than with a single peer (or alone). These findings support the contention that outdoor settings in recreational and entertainment areas and areas with poor collective efficacy are particularly criminogenic, especially when young people are engaged in peer-oriented activities in groups. Such settings are expected to present weak moral contexts in which the impetus and ability of potential guardians to monitor and enforce rule-following is impaired, while the motivation to offend may be promoted by the presence of temptations or frictions and peers who encourage rule-breaking, all of which change the situational dynamics of the setting so that crime is more likely to be perceived and chosen as an alternative for action.

---

[10] Except during work-oriented activities, during which only one crime was reported in an area with strong collective efficacy.

[11] Ironically, the same is true of family-oriented activities, namely because more young people live in areas with poorer collective efficacy.

**Table 7.8 Crimes per 1,000 hours by activity and key settings**

| Orientation of activity | Key settings | | | | | | | | |
| --- | --- | --- | --- | --- | --- | --- | --- | --- | --- |
| | Private indoor | | Public indoor | | | | Public outdoor | | |
| | Home | Others' home | School | Workplace | Shopping locale | Pubs and nightclubs | Streets | Parks | Moving around |
| Family | 0.2 | 0.2 | 0 | 0 | 0 | 3.2 | 0 | 0 | 0 |
| School | 0 | 0 | 0.3 | 0 | 0 | 0 | 0 | 0 | 0 |
| Work | 0 | 0 | 0 | 0.2 | 0 | 0 | 0 | 0 | 0 |
| Peer | 0 | 1.5 | 0 | 0 | 4.0 | 6.5 | 8.9 | 4.8 | 1.9 |
| Other | 0 | 0.4 | 0 | 0 | 0 | 3.6 | 12.8 | 1.9 | 1.8 |
| Unstructured peer-oriented | 0 | 1.1 | 0 | 0 | 8.1 | 8.1 | 9.5 | 8.5 | 0 |

**Table 7.9  Crimes per 1,000 hours in key social environments**

| Orientation of activity | Social environment | | | | |
| --- | --- | --- | --- | --- | --- |
| | City centre | Local centres | Other areas with strong collective efficacy | Other areas with medium collective efficacy | Other areas with poor collective efficacy |
| Family | 0 | 0 | 0.2 | 0.1 | 0.2 |
| School | 0 | 0 | 0.4 | 0.2 | 0.8 |
| Work | 0 | 0 | 0.7 | 0 | 0 |
| Peer | 2.9 | 8.2 | 1.8 | 3.8 | 4.3 |
| Other | 1.1 | 0 | 0.4 | 0.7 | 1.5 |
| Unstructured peer-oriented | 4.9 | 15.0 | 2.0 | 6.7 | 4.6 |

## 7.2.3 Temporal distribution of space–time budget crimes

Although some settings have higher levels of crime than others, this does not apply equally across time for a particular setting. Some times of the day and week may be more or less conducive to crime, because of temporal variations in the efficacy of moral contextual factors, such as levels of adult supervision, as well as young people's activity patterns, which influence when they spend discretionary time in the setting and engage in peer-oriented activities.

Across all settings, crime rates were low during the daytime,[12] even on weekends, and higher in the evenings, especially on Fridays and Saturdays (Table 7.10).

**Table 7.10  Crimes per 1,000 hours by day and time**

| Day | Daytime (06:00–16:00) | Evening (16:00–05:00) |
| --- | --- | --- |
| Monday–Thursday | 0.3 | 0.8 |
| Friday | 0.3 | 1.5 |
| Saturday | 0.5 | 1.2 |

[12] See technical appendix, section A1.4, on the operationalization of daytime and evening time.

**Table 7.11  Crimes per 1,000 hours by day, time, and activity**

| Activity | Daytime | | Evening | | Total |
|---|---|---|---|---|---|
| | Weekday | Weekend | Weekday | Weekend | |
| Family | 0.1 | 0.1 | 0.2 | 0.2 | 0.2 |
| School | 0.3 | 0 | 0.2 | 0 | 0.3 |
| Work | 0 | 0 | 1.2[a] | 0 | 0.2 |
| Peer | 0.7 | 2.1 | 5.0 | 5.8 | 3.7 |
| Other | 0.3 | 0.3 | 0.7 | 1.2 | 0.8 |
| All | 0.3 | 0.5 | 0.8 | 1.3 | 0.7 |

[a] Because there are so few work-oriented hours, the one work-related crime yields a high crime rate.

However, these rates varied considerably depending on the orientation of young people's activities. Rates of crime during family, school, and work-oriented activities were generally lower than during other activities, regardless of the time or day. They were, for obvious reasons, highest on weekdays for school-oriented activities, as the few school-oriented activities that took place outside school hours typically constituted doing homework, often in a supervised family setting. During school hours, however, young people were often with their peers, at times unsupervised, and occasionally this fed into their involvement in acts of crime (acts of violence and vandalism in particular). Crime rates during family- and work-oriented activities were higher during the evenings. However, the rate of offending during peer-oriented activities, which was particularly high in the evenings, was still higher on weekday days than the rates during family, work, or school-oriented activities (Table 7.11).

### 7.2.4  Activity fields and space–time budget crimes

As we have shown, some activities are generally more conducive to crime, as are certain settings, and certain times of the day and week, all because they have features that weaken the moral context's efficacy in promoting law-abiding behaviour. For example, some activities are less supervised and take place in the presence of those who are less likely to enforce rule-following and who may even encourage rule-breaking, and at some times monitoring and enforcement may be more reduced as a result of natural factors, such as darkness, or routine activities, such as others' sleeping. When these activities overlap with these settings at these times, the moral context may be especially weak in encouraging law-abiding behaviour, and, therefore, their effect on people's behaviour may be especially criminogenic.

Most space–time budget crimes were reported during peer-oriented activities outside domestic settings (ie outside one's home and others' homes) in the evening. Under these circumstances, the crime rate was consistently high, regardless of the setting, although it was considerably lower in areas with strong collective efficacy (Table 7.12). On weekday evenings, the crime rate was particularly high in city and local centres and areas with poor collective efficacy.

Streets and parks boasted high crime rates during peer-oriented hours, especially in the evenings, and especially during unstructured activities (see Tables 7.13 and 7.14). On weekday evenings, crimes were particularly frequent when young people spent unstructured time with their peers in the streets. Young people reported one crime every 70 hours spent in these settings.

Few crimes were reported in any setting on weekday days. Crime rates were also low in most settings on weekend days, even settings like the city centre, and even during peer-oriented time. Many young people congregated in the city centre on weekend days (see section 6.2.3), and most were involved in activities that did not

**Table 7.12  Crimes per 1,000 hours in peer-oriented activities outside domestic settings**

| Setting | Weekday day | Weekday evening | Weekend day | Weekend evening |
|---|---|---|---|---|
| City centre | 0 | 8.4 | 0.6 | 5.1 |
| Local centres | 0 | 12.9 | 10.9 | 12.0 |
| Other areas with poor collective efficacy | 0 | 8.5 | 8.0 | 7.1 |
| Other areas with medium collective efficacy | 1.4 | 5.5 | 0 | 8.5 |
| Other areas with strong collective efficacy | 0 | 1.9 | 4.8 | 3.7 |
| Total | 0.6 | 6.7 | 2.3 | 7.1 |

Table 7.13 Crimes per 1,000 hours spent in different activities in key settings at certain times of the day and week[a][b]

| | Key settings | | | | | | | | | | | | | |
| | Private indoor | | Public indoor | | | | Public outdoor | | | Social environment | | | | |
| Activity Time | Home | Others' home | School | Workplace | Shopping locale | Pubs and nightclubs | Streets | Parks | Moving around | City centre | Local centres | Other areas with strong CE[c] | Other areas with medium CE[c] | Other areas with poor CE[c] |
|---|---|---|---|---|---|---|---|---|---|---|---|---|---|---|
| Family | 0.2 | 0.2 | 0 | 0 | 0 | 3.2 | 0 | 0 | 0 | 0 | 0 | 0.2 | 0.1 | 0.2 |
| Weekday day | 0.1 | 0 | 0 | 0 | 0 | 0 | 0 | 0 | 0 | 0 | 0 | 0.5 | 0 | 0 |
| Weekday evening | 0.2 | 1.1 | 0 | 0 | 0 | 0 | 0 | 0 | 0 | 0 | 0 | 0.4 | 0.1 | 0.2 |
| Weekend day | 0.1 | 0 | 0 | 0 | 0 | 0 | 0 | 0 | 0 | 0 | 0 | | 0 | 0.4 |
| Weekend evening | 0.2 | 0 | 0 | 0 | 0 | 4.2 | 0 | 0 | 0 | 0 | 0 | 0 | 0.2 | 0.3 |
| School | 0 | 0 | 0 | 0 | 0 | 0 | 0 | 0 | 0 | 0 | 0 | 0.4 | 0.2 | 0.8 |
| Weekday day | 0 | 0 | 0.3 | 0 | 0 | 0 | 0 | 0 | 0 | 0 | 0 | 0.4 | 0.2 | 0.9 |
| Weekday evening | 0 | 0 | 0.3 | 0 | 0 | 0 | 0 | 0 | 0 | 0 | 0 | 0.7 | 0 | 0 |
| Weekend day | 0 | 0 | 1.0 | 0 | 0 | 0 | 0 | 0 | 0 | 0 | 0 | 0 | 0 | 0 |
| Weekend evening | 0 | 0 | 0 | 0 | 0 | 0 | 0 | 0 | 0 | 0 | 0 | 0 | 0 | 0 |

(continued)

**Table 7.13** (Continued)

| | | Key settings | | | | | | Public outdoor | | | Social environment | | | | |
|---|---|---|---|---|---|---|---|---|---|---|---|---|---|---|---|
| | | Private indoor | | Public indoor | | | | | | | | | | | |
| Activity | Time | Home | Others' home | School | Workplace | Shopping locale | Pubs and nightclubs | Streets | Parks | Moving around | City centre | Local centres | Other areas with strong CE[c] | Other areas with medium poor CE[c] | Other areas with poor CE[c] |
| Work | | 0 | 0 | 0 | 0.2 | 0 | 0 | 0 | 0 | 0 | 0 | 0 | 0.7 | 0 | 0 |
| | Weekday day | 0 | 0 | 0 | 0 | 0 | 0 | 0 | 0 | 0 | 0 | 0 | 0 | 0 | 0 |
| | Weekday evening | 0 | 0 | 0 | 1.8 | 0 | 0 | 0 | 0 | 0 | 0 | 0 | 4.6 | 0 | 0 |
| | Weekend day | 0 | 0 | 0 | 0 | 0 | 0 | 0 | 0 | 0 | 0 | 0 | 0 | 0 | 0 |
| | Weekend evening | 0 | 0 | 0 | 0 | 0 | 0 | 0 | 0 | 0 | 0 | 0 | 0 | 0 | 0 |
| Peer | | 0 | 1.5 | 0 | 0 | 4.0 | 6.5 | 8.9 | 4.8 | 1.9 | 2.9 | 8.2 | 1.8 | 3.8 | 4.3 |
| | Weekday day | 0 | 0 | 0 | 0 | 1.6 | 0 | 4.2 | 0 | 0.5 | 0 | 0 | 0 | 1.2 | 0 |
| | Weekday evening | 0 | 0 | 0 | 0 | 9.3 | 0 | 12.3 | 3.1 | 3.1 | 8.3 | 11.9 | 1.4 | 4.3 | 6.2 |
| | Weekend day | 0 | 2.8 | 0 | 0 | 0.6 | 0 | 2.6 | 2.7 | 7.0 | 0.6 | 10.0 | 4.1 | 1.0 | 6.0 |
| | Weekend evening | 0 | 2.2 | 0 | 0 | 8.9 | 8.4 | 9.3 | 7.7 | 6.6 | 5.1 | 10.5 | 3.2 | 6.3 | 5.6 |

| | | | | | | | | | | | | | |
|---|---|---|---|---|---|---|---|---|---|---|---|---|---|
| Other | 0 | 0.4 | 0 | 0 | 3.6 | 12.8 | 1.9 | 1.8 | 1.1 | 0 | 0.4 | 0.7 | 1.5 |
| Weekday day | 0 | 0 | 0 | 0 | 0 | 0 | 0 | 0.5 | 0 | 0 | 1.3 | 0 | 0 |
| Weekday evening | 0 | 0.5 | 0 | 0 | 21.3 | 30.6 | 0 | 0 | 6.4 | 0 | 0.7 | 0 | 1.4 |
| Weekend day | 0 | 0 | 0 | 0 | 0 | 0 | 4.9 | 0 | 0 | 0 | 0 | 0 | 0 |
| Weekend evening | 0 | 0.4 | 0 | 0 | 0 | 9.5 | 0 | 10.2 | 0 | 0 | 0 | 1.6 | 2.8 |

[a] For example, participants reported 8.9 crimes per 1,000 hours spent in peer-oriented activities in the streets, but 12.3 crimes per 1,000 hours spent in peer-oriented activities in the streets on weekday evenings.

[b] The division of key settings by their private and public nature is mutually exclusive, as is the division of social environments.

[c] Collective efficacy.

**Table 7.14 Crimes per 1,000 hours spent in unstructured peer-oriented activities in key settings at certain times of the day and week[a,b]**

| Activity | Time | Key settings | | | | | | | | | | | | | |
| | | Private indoor | | Public indoor | | | | Public outdoor | | | Social environment | | | | |
| | | Home | Others' home | School | Workplace | Shopping locale | Pubs and nightclubs | Streets | Parks | Moving around | City centre | Local centres | Other areas with strong CE[c] | Other areas with medium CE[c] | Other areas with poor CE[c] |
|---|---|---|---|---|---|---|---|---|---|---|---|---|---|---|---|
| Unstructured peer-oriented | | 0 | 1.1 | 0 | 0 | 8.1 | 8.1 | 9.5 | 8.5 | 0 | 4.9 | 15.0 | 2.0 | 6.7 | 4.6 |
| | Weekday day | 0 | 0 | 0 | 0 | 0 | 0 | 0 | 0 | 0 | 0 | 0 | 0 | 0 | 0 |
| | Weekday evening | 0 | 0 | 0 | 0 | 17.2 | 0 | 14.3 | 4.6 | 0 | 13.2 | 25.5 | 0 | 7.6 | 5.6 |
| | Weekend day | 0 | 0 | 0 | 0 | 0 | 0 | 4.4 | 9.9 | 0 | 0 | 0 | 13.5 | 0 | 5.5 |
| | Weekend evening | 0 | 1.9 | 0 | 0 | 16.6 | 10.1 | 9.4 | 11.2 | 0 | 7.5 | 17.5 | 1.2 | 8.9 | 4.9 |

[a] For example, participants reported 9.5 crimes per 1,000 hours spent in unstructured peer-oriented activities in the streets, but 14.3 crimes per 1,000 hours spent in unstructured peer-oriented activities in the streets on weekday evenings.

[b] The division of key settings by their private and public nature is mutually exclusive, as is the division of social environments.

[c] Collective efficacy.

involve crime; hence the crime rate (ie crimes per 1,000 person-hours) was low. In local centres, however, the crime rate on weekend days remained very high. Local centres appear to be a particularly popular place for young people to meet to socialize with their peers, whereas in the city centre they spend a greater proportion of their time in activities that are structured and often supervised, such as shopping and eating out (see section 6.2.3).

In areas with strong collective efficacy the rate of crime was also relatively high on weekend days. However, this reflects only two acts of crime (one act of vandalism and one act of theft, both while socializing with male peers in a park). All in all, young people spent relatively few peer-oriented hours outside domestic settings on weekend days—less, in fact, than they spent on weekday evenings—and the vast majority of this time was in the city centre.

Both weekday and weekend evenings boasted particularly high rates of space–time budget crimes (Table 7.10). Young people's rate of offending was high in recreational settings, for example, in the city and local centres, on weekday and weekend evenings. At these times, young people also offended at a high rate in residential areas with medium and poor collective efficacy. Offending in outdoor public spaces such as streets and parks was particularly prevalent.

These findings, summarized in Tables 7.13 and 7.14, show that young people rarely offend in the strong moral contexts that characterize family, school, and work-related activities at any time of the week. Rather, it is during their discretionary time with their peers, especially in the evenings, in settings outside the home in which supervision is minimal, that they report significant frequencies of crime. These settings present much weaker moral contexts, making it more likely that young people will see, and even choose, crime as an alternative for action.

## 7.3 Exposure to criminogenic settings and crime involvement by crime propensity

There is a clear concentration of crimes in particular kinds of settings. However, so far we have not taken into consideration the fact that people vary in their crime propensity, and hence their vulnerability to criminogenic influences. According to SAT, crimes are likely to be committed only by certain kinds of people—those who are situationally vulnerable to criminogenic settings. The key factors that make people situationally vulnerable and confer upon them a high crime propensity are weak morality and an inability to exercise self-control (see section 1.3.4). The measure of crime propensity used in the analyses below is a composite score derived from measures of PADS+ participants' morality and ability to exercise self-control across all five data waves (see section 3.2). For illustrative purposes, we divide the participants into high, medium, and low crime propensity categories defined by standard deviations (see section 3.2.3).

### 7.3.1 Crime propensity and criminogenic exposure: Key activities

We have demonstrated that young people with a high crime propensity self-report more crime than others (see section 3.2.4), and, therefore, we would expect that young people with a high crime propensity would also report more space–time budget crimes. This is indeed the case. Only one young person with a low crime propensity reported an act of crime in the space–time budget (at age 13)— an act of violence just after school on a Friday afternoon. A small percentage of young people with a medium crime propensity (fewer than one in 10) reported a space–time budget crime. However, nearly one in three young people with a high crime propensity (32 per cent) reported a space–time budget crime. Young people with a high crime propensity were also more likely to report more than one space–time budget crime: nearly half of the young people with a high crime propensity who reported a crime reported more than one, and 15 per cent reported five or more (to a maximum of nine), while only one-third of young people with a medium crime propensity who reported a crime reported more than one, and only one (0.9 per cent) reported more than three (he or she reported five crimes).

In Table 6.29 we showed that young people with a high crime propensity spent more time in criminogenic settings than young people with lower crime propensities. By measuring rates of crime by person-hours, we control for these differences in exposure, hence differing rates of crime between propensity groups reflect the interaction between young people's crime propensity and exposure to criminogenic settings. Young people with a high crime propensity were responsible for the majority of crimes in any setting during any activity, and they demonstrated particularly high rates during peer-oriented activities (see Table 7.15).

**Table 7.15  Crimes per 1,000 hours by activity and crime propensity**

| Activity orientation | Crime propensity | | |
|---|---|---|---|
| | Low | Medium | High |
| Family | 0.0 | 0.1 | 0.4 |
| School | 0.0 | 0.3 | 0.8 |
| Work | 0.0 | 0.0 | 1.0 |
| Peers | 0.0 | 1.9 | 9.0 |
| Other | 0.4 | 0.3 | 2.5 |
| All hours | 0.0 | 0.4 | 2.5 |

Young people with a low crime propensity reported virtually no crimes during any activity, while young people with either medium or high crime propensities reported most of their crimes during peer-oriented activities. Those with a high crime propensity reported nearly one crime every 100 hours they spent in peer-oriented activities. Young people with a high crime propensity appear particularly vulnerable to seeing and choosing crime as an alternative during unstructured peer-oriented activities, especially when these take place outside the home (circumstances we have identified as particularly criminogenic). In fact, nearly a quarter of all space–time budget crimes occurred within the 1.2 per cent of all hours awake that the 15 per cent of the sample with a high crime propensity spent in peer-oriented activities. At the same time, young people with a low crime propensity still reported no crime involvement even in these very criminogenic circumstances, consistent with the concept of situational resistance (Table 7.16).

Peer-oriented time increased fairly steadily for all young people between ages 13 and 17, but young people with a high crime propensity already spent more time in peer-oriented activities when they were 13 years old than other young people did when they were 17 years old (see Table 7.17).

### 7.3.2  Crime propensity and criminogenic exposure: Key settings

The crime rate (ie crimes per 1,000 person-hours) was highest when young people were engaged in peer-oriented activities in local

**Table 7.16  Crimes per 1,000 hours by crime propensity and peer-oriented activities**

| Activity | Crime propensity | | | All |
|---|---|---|---|---|
| | Low | Medium | High | |
| Peer-oriented | 0.0 | 1.9 | 9.0 | 3.7 |
| Unstructured peer-oriented | 0.0 | 3.3 | 10.1 | 5.7 |
| Unstructured peer-oriented, outside domestic settings | 0.0 | 4.8 | 13.9 | 8.1 |

**Table 7.17  Mean time (hours:minutes) spent in peer-oriented activities by crime propensity and percentage of time (within parentheses) by wave (four days)**

| Wave | Age | Crime propensity | | |
|---|---|---|---|---|
| | | Low | Medium | High |
| 1 | 13 | 2:11 (3.8) | 4:38  (7.8) | 8:32 (14.3) |
| 2 | 14 | 4:09 (7.1) | 6:12 (10.4) | 10:09 (16.8) |
| 3 | 15 | 2:48 (4.7) | 6:33 (10.9) | 12:33 (20.8) |
| 4 | 16 | 3:39 (6.0) | 7:48 (12.7) | 14:57 (24.3) |
| 5 | 17 | 4:53 (8.0) | 8:21 (13.8) | 12:38 (21.3) |
| Phase 1 | 13–17 | 17:08 (5.9) | 32:44 (11.1) | 57:40 (19.5) |

centres, residential areas with poorer collective efficacy, and the city centre (in that order; Table 7.18). Supporting the key assumptions of SAT, young people with a high crime propensity had the highest rate of crime, and those with a low crime propensity the lowest rate of crime, across all settings when engaged in peer-oriented activities (Table 7.18). It is particularly noteworthy that young people with a low crime propensity committed virtually no crimes in any setting.[13] We can thus conclude that when young people with a medium, and particularly those with a high, crime propensity take part in a crim-inogenic setting, their rate of crime increases markedly, while the

[13] The only exception being one young person with a low crime propensity who reported one violent crime during an activity that was not peer-oriented in an area with medium collective efficacy.

**Table 7.18  Crimes per 1,000 hours in key settings and circumstances by crime propensity**

| Setting | Hours | Crime propensity | | | All |
|---|---|---|---|---|---|
| | | Low | Medium | High | |
| City centre | Other | 0 | 0.4 | 0 | 0.3 |
| | *Peer-oriented* | *0* | *1.2* | *9.6* | *2.9* |
| Local centres | Other | 0 | 0 | 0 | 0 |
| | *Peer-oriented* | *0* | *5.2* | *18.3* | *8.2* |
| Other areas with poor collective efficacy | Other | 0 | 0.2 | 2.1 | 0.5 |
| | *Peer-oriented* | *0* | *2.0* | *12.3* | *4.3* |
| Other areas with medium collective efficacy | Other | 0.1 | 0.2 | 0.5 | 0.2 |
| | *Peer-oriented* | *0* | *2.9* | *10.2* | *3.8* |
| Other areas with strong collective efficacy | Other | 0 | 0.3 | 1.0 | 0.3 |
| | *Peer-oriented* | *0* | *1.4* | *5.7* | *1.8* |
| Total | Other | 0 | 0.2 | 1.0 | 0.3 |
| | *Peer-oriented* | *0* | *2.3* | *10.8* | *3.7* |

features of a setting have little to no effect on the offending of young people with a low crime propensity.

Figure 7.4 illustrates this interaction very clearly. Young people with a high crime propensity offended at a dramatically higher rate when exposed to criminogenic settings and circumstances than they did in less crime-conducive settings, while young people with a lower crime propensity rarely offended regardless of the criminogenic nature of the setting or circumstances in which they took part. The basic interaction also holds when specifically considering crimes in outdoor public spaces such as streets and parks (Table 7.19).

### 7.3.3  Crime propensity and criminogenic exposure: Key times

Young people with a high crime propensity offended at a significantly higher rate than other young people regardless of the time or day; in fact, on weekday days, when their crime rate was at its lowest, they still offended at a higher rate than other young people

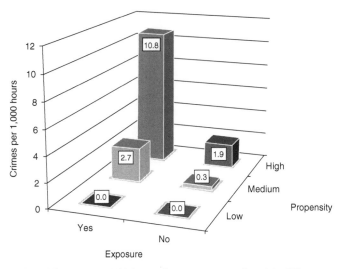

**Figure 7.4 Crimes per 1,000 hours by young people with different crime propensities when exposed to areas with poor collective efficacy or city or local centres during unstructured peer-oriented activities**

**Table 7.19 Crimes per 1,000 hours in outdoor public settings by crime propensity**

| Outdoor public setting | Hours | Crime propensity | | | All |
|---|---|---|---|---|---|
| | | Low | Medium | High | |
| Streets | Other | 0 | 0 | 24.4 | 4.5 |
| | *Peer-oriented* | *0* | *4.1* | *18.8* | *9.1* |
| Parks | Other | 0 | 0 | 0 | 0 |
| | *Peer-oriented* | *0* | *2.4* | *10.5* | *4.6* |
| Moving around | Other | 1.3 | 0.2 | 4.4 | 1.0 |
| | *Peer-oriented* | *0* | *0.8* | *6.6* | *1.8* |

did on weekend evenings, when their crime rate was at its highest (Table 7.20).

Bringing space, time, and young people together, we find that the most reported crimes occurred when young people with a high crime propensity spent discretionary time in the city and local centres and, to a lesser degree, areas with poor collective efficacy,

Table 7.20  Crimes per 1,000 hours by time of the day and week and crime propensity

| Time | Crime propensity | | | Total |
|---|---|---|---|---|
| | Low | Medium | High | |
| Weekday day | 0 | 0.3 | 0.7 | 0.3 |
| Weekday evening | 0 | 0.5 | 2.7 | 0.8 |
| Weekend day | 0 | 0.1 | 2.3 | 0.4 |
| Weekend evening | 0.1 | 0.6 | 4.9 | 1.3 |
| Total | 0 | 0.4 | 2.5 | 0.7 |

especially if they spent that time in peer-oriented activities. Crime involvement by young people with a low crime propensity remained negligible, while that of young people with a medium crime propensity differed significantly in degree, and somewhat over time and place, from that of young people with a high crime propensity (Table 7.21).

Offending in the city and local centres was predominantly reported by young people with a high crime propensity and clustered during evenings in the city centre and weekends in local centres. For young people with a medium crime propensity, local centres on weekday evenings appeared to be particularly criminogenic during peer-oriented activities.

Young people with a high crime propensity offended at high rates in areas with poor collective efficacy during much of their discretionary time, while young people with a medium crime propensity only did so on weekend evenings. In other settings (eg those with strong collective efficacy), young people with a high crime propensity reported their highest rates of offending on weekend days, but when interpreting this rate one has to bear in mind that they spent very little time in such settings on weekend days.

Young people with a high crime propensity were also responsible for most acts of crime in outdoor public spaces. They reported crimes in the streets at high rates across all time periods, but especially in the evenings. Young people with a medium crime propensity also reported high rates of offending in the streets, but only in the evenings. Parks were a more common setting for offending by young people with high and medium crime propensity on the weekends, especially in the evenings (Table 7.22).

**Table 7.21  Crimes per 1,000 hours by key setting, time of the day and week, and crime propensity**

| Setting | Time | Crime propensity | | | | | |
|---|---|---|---|---|---|---|---|
| | | Low | | Medium | | High | |
| | | Other | *Peers* | Other | *Peers* | Other | *Peers* |
| City centre | Weekday day | 0 | *0* | 0 | *0* | 0 | *0* |
| | Weekday evening | 0 | *0* | 2.7 | *0* | 0 | *38.5* |
| | Weekend day | 0 | *0* | 0 | *0.9* | 0 | *0* |
| | Weekend evening | 0 | *0* | 0 | *2.5* | 0 | *13.9* |
| Local centre | Weekday day | 0 | *0* | 0 | *0* | 0 | *0* |
| | Weekday evening | 0 | *0* | 0 | *13.5* | 0 | *9.8* |
| | Weekend day | 0 | *0* | 0 | *0* | 0 | *25.6* |
| | Weekend evening | 0 | *0* | 0 | *3.2* | 0 | *27.4* |
| Other areas with poor collective efficacy | Weekday day | 0 | *0* | 0.3 | *0* | 1.9 | *0* |
| | Weekday evening | 0 | *0* | 0.2 | *0* | 1.3 | *14.9* |
| | Weekend day | 0 | *0* | 0 | *0* | 0 | *16.9* |
| | Weekend evening | 0 | *0* | 0.2 | *3.9* | 3.9 | *7.2* |
| Other areas with medium collective efficacy | Weekday day | 0 | *0* | 0.2 | *0.6* | 0 | *3.8* |
| | Weekday evening | 0 | *0* | 0 | *4.1* | 0.4 | *2.0* |
| | Weekend day | 0 | *0* | 0 | *0* | 0 | *4.2* |
| | Weekend evening | 0.3 | *0* | 0.4 | *3.1* | 1.5 | *15.9* |
| Other areas with strong collective efficacy | Weekday day | 0 | *0* | 0.5 | *0* | 0.7 | *0* |
| | Weekday evening | 0 | *0* | 0.3 | *2.0* | 3.3 | *0* |
| | Weekend day | 0 | *0* | 0 | *2.8* | 0 | *13.0* |
| | Weekend evening | 0 | *0* | 0 | *2.2* | 0 | *7.7* |

These analyses show that the criminogenic settings and circumstances highlighted in chapters 6 and the early part of chapter 7 uniquely exert their effects on young people with a higher crime propensity. They are not criminogenic for young people with a low crime propensity. In other words, settings are not inherently crimiongenic for all young people, but only for those who are crime prone.

**Table 7.22  Crimes per 1,000 hours in outdoor public spaces by time of the day and week and crime propensity**

| Setting | Time | Crime propensity | | | | | |
|---------|------|------|------|------|------|------|------|
| | | Low | | Medium | | High | |
| | | Other | *Peers* | Other | *Peers* | Other | *Peers* |
| Streets | Weekday day | 0 | *0* | 0 | *0* | 0 | *8.7* |
| | Weekday evening | 0 | *0* | 0 | *9.1* | 76.9 | *20.8* |
| | Weekend day | 0 | *0* | 0 | *0* | 0 | *10.5* |
| | Weekend evening | 0 | *0* | 0 | *2.6* | 19.6 | *21.7* |
| Parks | Weekday day | 0 | *0* | 0 | *0* | 0 | *0* |
| | Weekday evening | 0 | *0* | 0 | *1.6* | 0 | *3.9* |
| | Weekend day | 0 | *0* | 0 | *2.3* | 0 | *5.5* |
| | Weekend evening | 0 | *0* | 0 | *3.4* | 0 | *19.0* |
| Moving around | Weekday day | 0 | *0* | 0.4 | *0.4* | 0 | *1.7* |
| | Weekday evening | 0 | *0* | 0 | *0* | 0 | *5.7* |
| | Weekend day | 0 | *0* | 0 | *0* | 0 | *27.0* |
| | Weekend evening | 8.1 | *0* | 0 | *4.2* | 21.5 | *13.7* |

## 7.3.4  Crime propensity and criminogenic exposure: Peer crime involvement

It is apparent in our analyses thus far that the presence of peers is highly significant in young people's crime involvement. We have suggested that the presence of peers may weaken the moral context, and this will be particularly true if those peers are willing to break rules themselves when responding to temptations and provocations. We measured participants' peers' crime involvement in the questionnaire (see section 3.3.5).

Young people with a higher crime propensity had peers who were more heavily involved in crime ($r_s$ = .68, $p$ = .000). In fact, no young people with a low crime propensity had peers who were frequently involved in crime (more than one standard deviation above the mean), and more than a third had peers who were rarely, if ever, involved in crime (more than one standard deviation below the mean). By contrast, only one young person with a high crime propensity had peers who were only rarely involved in crime,

**Table 7.23 Percentage of young people's peers' crime involvement by crime propensity**

| Peer crime involvement | Crime propensity | | |
|---|---|---|---|
| | Low | Medium | High |
| Rare (if ever) | 34.0 | 7.9 | 1.0 |
| Occasional | 66.0 | 82.4 | 38.1 |
| Frequent | 0.0 | 9.7 | 61.0 |

and nearly two-thirds had peers who were frequently involved (Table 7.23).

Most young people reported that their peers were occasionally involved in crime, which is consistent with the fact that most young people in the sample self-reported some crime involvement (see section 3.1.1). Having peers who were frequently involved in crime strongly predicted crime involvement for young people with a high or medium crime propensity. For young people with a low crime propensity, their peers' crime involvement made no significant difference to their offending. This pattern also held for both the rate (Table 7.24) and number (Table 7.25) of space–time budget crimes young people with different crime propensities reported, as well as the number of crimes they reported in the questionnaire (Table 7.25), and their police-recorded crimes (Table 7.25). The interaction of participants' crime propensity and the crime involvement of their peers predicted young people's level of crime involvement for all measures of crime (Table 7.25; Figure 7.5).

**Table 7.24 Crimes per 1,000 hours by crime propensity and peer crime involvement**

| Peer crime involvement | Crime propensity | | | | | |
|---|---|---|---|---|---|---|
| | Low | | Medium | | High | |
| | Other hours | *Peer-oriented* | Other hours | *Peer-oriented* | Other hours | *Peer-oriented* |
| Rare (if ever) | 0 | *0* | 0 | *0* | 0 | *0* |
| Occasional | 0.1 | *0* | 0.1 | *1.3* | 0.8 | *5.2* |
| Frequent | — | — | 0.5 | *6.0* | 1.0 | *10.9* |

**Table 7.25  Multiple regression of young people's self-reported crime, crime propensity, and peer crime involvement**

| Number of space–time budget crimes | b | Beta | Prob. | Multiple R² x 100 |
|---|---|---|---|---|
| 1. Propensity | .10 | .24 | .000 | |
| 2. Peer crime involvement | .01 | .04 | *n.s.* | |
| 3. Propensity x Peer crime involvement | .02 | .27 | .000 | |
| | | | | 19.9% |

| Phase 1 self-reported crime frequency | b | Beta | Prob. | Multiple R² x 100 |
|---|---|---|---|---|
| 1. Propensity | 9.57 | .26 | .000 | |
| 2. Peer crime involvement | 2.36 | .14 | .004 | |
| 3. Propensity x Peer crime involvement | 2.32 | .31 | .000 | |
| | | | | 32.5% |

| Phase 1 PNC crime frequency | b | Beta | Prob. | Multiple R² x 100 |
|---|---|---|---|---|
| 1. Propensity | .07 | .18 | .001 | |
| 2. Peer crime involvement | .01 | .07 | *n.s.* | |
| 3. Propensity x Peer crime involvement | .01 | .14 | .001 | |
| | | | | 9.4% |

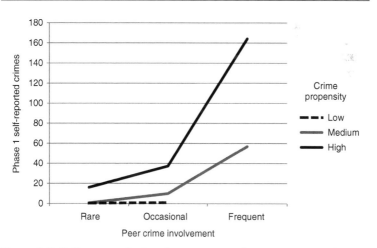

**Figure 7.5  Self-reported crime frequency on the young person's questionnaire[a] by crime propensity and peer crime involvement**

[a] Similar patterns were also observed for space–time budget and police-recorded crime frequencies.

Peer-oriented activities have proven the most criminogenic, particularly during young people's discretionary time in the evenings and, to a lesser degree, on weekend days. Splitting these analyses by participants' peer crime involvement, we see that it is young people with a high crime propensity, especially those whose peers are frequently involved in crime, who are responsible for the concentration of crimes at certain times of the week (Table 7.26).

Young people who had a high crime propensity and peers who were frequently involved in crime were also responsible for the clustering of crimes in the city and local centres (ie in recreational and entertainment settings) and areas with poor collective efficacy. For example, young people who had a medium or high crime propensity

**Table 7.26  Crimes per 1,000 hours by day and time, crime propensity, and peer crime involvement**

| Time  Peer crime involvement | Crime propensity | | | | | |
|---|---|---|---|---|---|---|
| | Low | | Medium | | High | |
| | Other | *Peers* | Other | *Peers* | Other | *Peers* |
| Weekday day | | | | | | |
| Rare | 0 | *0* | 0 | *0* | 0 | *0* |
| Occasional | 0 | *0* | 0.2 | *0.3* | 0.5 | *0* |
| Frequent | — | — | 0.8 | *0* | 0.6 | *3.5* |
| Weekday evening | | | | | | |
| Rare | 0 | *0* | 0 | *0* | 0 | *0* |
| Occasional | 0 | *0* | 0.1 | *2.5* | 1.4 | *2.3* |
| Frequent | — | — | 0.4 | *6.8* | 1.1 | *12.4* |
| Weekend day | | | | | | |
| Rare | 0 | *0* | 0 | *0* | 0 | *0* |
| Occasional | 0 | *0* | 0 | *0.4* | 0 | *9.1* |
| Frequent | — | — | 0 | *2.9* | 0 | *6.3* |
| Weekend evening | | | | | | |
| Rare | 0 | *0* | 0 | *0* | 0 | *0* |
| Occasional | 0.2 | *0* | 0 | *1.8* | 1.3 | *8.1* |
| Frequent | — | — | 0.4 | *9.2* | 1.9 | *15.7* |

and peers who were frequently involved in crime reported one crime every 50 hours they spent in peer-oriented activities in local centres (Table 7.27).

When analysed by time as well as setting (Table 7.28), it becomes even more apparent that there are only certain groups of people who are responsible for acts of crime, and they only commit those crimes in certain places, at certain times, during certain activities. For example, offending by young people in local centres was

**Table 7.27  Crimes per 1,000 hours in key settings by crime propensity and peer crime involvement**

| Setting | Peer crime involvement | Crime propensity | | | | | |
|---|---|---|---|---|---|---|---|
| | | Low | | Medium | | High | |
| | | Other | *Peers* | Other | *Peers* | Other | *Peers* |
| City centre | | | | | | | |
| | Rare | 0 | *0* | 0 | *0* | 0 | *0* |
| | Occasional | 0 | *0* | 0.5 | *0.5* | 0 | *4.6* |
| | Frequent | — | — | 0 | *5.5* | 0 | *11.3* |
| Local centres | | | | | | | |
| | Rare | 0 | *0* | 0 | *0* | 0 | *0* |
| | Occasional | 0 | *0* | 0 | *1.6* | 0 | *7.7* |
| | Frequent | — | — | 0 | *20.1* | 0 | *19.9* |
| Other areas with poor collective efficacy | | | | | | | |
| | Rare | 0 | *0* | 0 | *0* | — | — |
| | Occasional | 0 | *0* | 0.1 | *0.5* | 1.5 | *4.9* |
| | Frequent | — | — | 1.3 | *6.5* | 2.6 | *10.7* |
| Other areas with medium collective efficacy | | | | | | | |
| | Rare | 0 | *0* | 0 | *0* | 0 | — |
| | Occasional | 0.1 | *0* | 0.1 | *2.0* | 0.6 | *5.5* |
| | Frequent | — | — | 0.2 | *5.1* | 0.5 | *9.9* |
| Other areas with strong collective efficacy | | | | | | | |
| | Rare | 0 | *0* | 0 | *0* | 0 | *0* |
| | Occasional | 0 | *0* | 0.3 | *1.4* | 1.1 | *7.8* |
| | Frequent | — | — | 0.6 | *3.3* | 1.1 | *2.5* |

**Table 7.28  Crimes per 1,000 hours in key settings by day and time, crime propensity, and peer crime involvement**

| Setting | | Crime propensity | | | | | |
|---|---|---|---|---|---|---|---|
| | Time | Low | | Medium | | High | |
| | Peer crime involvement | Other | *Peers* | Other | *Peers* | Other | *Peers* |
| City centre | | | | | | | |
| | Weekday day | | | | | | |
| | Rare | 0 | *0* | 0 | *0* | — | *0* |
| | Occasional | 0 | *0* | 0 | *0* | 0 | *0* |
| | Frequent | — | — | 0 | *0* | 0 | *0* |
| | Weekday evening | | | | | | |
| | Rare | 0 | *0* | 0 | *0* | 0 | — |
| | Occasional | 0 | *0* | 3.4 | *0* | 0 | *41.7* |
| | Frequent | — | — | 0 | *0* | 0 | *37.5* |
| | Weekend day | | | | | | |
| | Rare | 0 | *0* | 0 | *0* | — | — |
| | Occasional | 0 | *0* | 0 | *0* | 0 | *0* |
| | Frequent | — | — | 0 | *5.7* | 0 | *0* |
| | Weekend evening | | | | | | |
| | Rare | 0 | *0* | 0 | *0* | — | *0* |
| | Occasional | 0 | *0* | 0 | *1.6* | 0 | *0* |
| | Frequent | — | — | 0 | *8.1* | 0 | *18.3* |
| Local centre | | | | | | | |
| | Weekday day | | | | | | |
| | Rare | 0 | — | 0 | *0* | 0 | *0* |
| | Occasional | 0 | *0* | 0 | *0* | 0 | *0* |
| | Frequent | — | — | 0 | *0* | 0 | *0* |
| | Weekday evening | | | | | | |
| | Rare | 0 | *0* | 0 | *0* | 0 | — |
| | Occasional | 0 | *0* | 0 | *0* | 0 | *0* |
| | Frequent | — | — | 0 | *76.9* | 0 | *16.7* |

| | | | | | | |
|---|---|---|---|---|---|---|
| **Weekend day** | | | | | | |
| Rare | 0 | *0* | 0 | *0* | — | — |
| Occasional | 0 | *0* | 0 | *0* | 0 | *38.5* |
| Frequent | — | — | 0 | *0* | 0 | *20.0* |
| **Weekend evening** | | | | | | |
| Rare | 0 | *0* | 0 | *0* | — | — |
| Occasional | 0 | *0* | 0 | *4.5* | 0 | *0* |
| Frequent | — | — | 0 | *0* | 0 | *36.0* |
| **Other areas with poor collective efficacy** | | | | | | |
| Weekday day | | | | | | |
| Rare | 0 | *0* | 0 | *0* | — | — |
| Occasional | 0 | *0* | 0 | *0* | 0 | *0* |
| Frequent | — | — | 2.6 | *0* | 3.1 | *0* |
| Weekday evening | | | | | | |
| Rare | 0 | *0* | 0 | *0* | — | — |
| Occasional | 0 | *0* | 0.2 | *0* | 3.7 | *0* |
| Frequent | — | — | 0 | *0* | 0 | *19.8* |
| Weekend day | | | | | | |
| Rare | 0 | *0* | 0 | *0* | — | — |
| Occasional | 0 | *0* | 0 | *0* | 0 | *44.4* |
| Frequent | — | — | 0 | *0* | 0 | *8.1* |
| Weekend evening | | | | | | |
| Rare | 0 | *0* | 0 | *0* | — | — |
| Occasional | 0 | *0* | 0 | *1.3* | 1.8 | *0* |
| Frequent | — | — | 1.5 | *15.3* | 5.3 | *10.3* |
| **Other areas with medium collective efficacy** | | | | | | |
| Weekday day | | | | | | |
| Rare | 0 | *0* | 0 | *0* | 0 | — |
| Occasional | 0 | *0* | 0.2 | *0.8* | 0 | *0* |
| Frequent | — | — | 0.6 | *0* | 0 | *5.9* |
| Weekday evening | | | | | | |
| Rare | 0 | *0* | 0 | *0* | 0 | — |
| Occasional | 0.5 | *0* | 0 | *5.0* | 0 | *0* |
| Frequent | — | — | 0 | *0* | 6.1 | *3.0* |

*(continued)*

**Table 7.28** *(Continued)*

| Setting | Crime propensity | | | | | | |
|---|---|---|---|---|---|---|---|
| | Time | Low | | Medium | | High | |
| | Peer crime involvement | Other | *Peers* | Other | *Peers* | Other | *Peers* |
| | Weekend day | | | | | | |
| | Rare | 0 | *0* | 0 | *0* | 0 | — |
| | Occasional | 0 | *0* | 0 | *0* | 0 | *0* |
| | Frequent | — | — | 0 | *0* | 0 | *6.8* |
| | Weekend evening | | | | | | |
| | Rare | 0 | *0* | 0 | *0* | 0 | — |
| | Occasional | 0 | *0* | 0.1 | *1.7* | 2.3 | *14.1* |
| | Frequent | — | — | 0 | *10.2* | 1.1 | *16.7* |
| Other areas with strong collective efficacy | | | | | | | |
| | Weekday day | | | | | | |
| | Rare | 0 | *0* | 0 | *0* | 0 | — |
| | Occasional | 0 | *0* | 0.5 | *0* | 1.4 | *0* |
| | Frequent | — | — | 0.5 | *0* | 0 | *0* |
| | Weekday evening | | | | | | |
| | Rare | 0 | *0* | 0 | *0* | 0 | *0* |
| | Occasional | 0 | *0* | 0 | *2.5* | 1.8 | *0* |
| | Frequent | — | — | 1.7 | *0* | 5.0 | *0* |
| | Weekend day | | | | | | |
| | Rare | 0 | *0* | 0 | *0* | 0 | *0* |
| | Occasional | 0 | *0* | 0 | *3.4* | 0 | *0* |
| | Frequent | — | — | 0 | *0* | 0 | *26.3* |
| | Weekend evening | | | | | | |
| | Rare | 0 | *0* | 0 | *0* | 0 | — |
| | Occasional | 0 | *0* | 0 | *1.4* | 0 | *20.2* |
| | Frequent | — | — | 0 | *8.1* | 0 | *0* |

particularly frequent on weekday evenings, but only by young people who had a higher crime propensity and peers who were frequently involved in crime. These young people report a crime approximately every 25 hours they spent unsupervised with their peers in local centres on weekday evenings.

## 7.4  Summary and conclusions

In this chapter we have shown that young people's rate of crime (crimes per 1,000 person-hours awake) was highest in the kinds of settings under the kinds of circumstances predicted by SAT to be criminogenic, ie settings with a weak law-relevant moral context. The rate of crimes per 1,000 person-hours was highest when young people spent time in unsupervised, peer-oriented activities in settings such as the city and local centres and outdoor public spaces in residential areas with poor collective efficacy, especially during their discretionary time on evenings and weekends and when those activities were unstructured. We then showed that, as predicted by SAT, crime only occurred when crime prone young people spent time in these settings; young people with a low crime propensity did not offend under practically any circumstances. We also brought in the role of peers' crime involvement to show that crimes were particularly common when crime prone young people with peers who had a high level of crime involvement took part in criminogenic settings under criminogenic circumstances.

Our analyses demonstrate clearly the importance of using the crime rate per person-hours as a measure of a setting's criminogeneity. A good illustration involves crime in the school setting; the criminogeneity of school settings for young people may be overestimated if the amount of time young people spend in school is not taken into account. Our analyses also show the importance of taking into consideration the fact that young people vary in their crime propensity. The number of crimes young people commit in a criminogenic setting is not primarily affected by the amount of time all young people spend in that setting, but rather by the amount of time crime prone young people spend in that setting. Criminogenic settings are not criminogenic for all young people.

# 8

# Choosing Crime as an Alternative: Crime Propensity, The Perception–Choice Process, and Crime

PADS+ data presented throughout this book provides evidence for the nature of the social and situational dynamics of crime. Evidence concerning the convergence of criminogenic features of settings and crime propensity in the crime event has been presented in earlier chapters. The question of how individuals in settings come to perceive an act of crime as an action alternative and choose to carry it out (the perception–choice process) remains unaddressed. The analyses presented in this chapter provide a test of this situational process, using data collected when participants were aged 13 and 15, capturing their hypothetical judgements as to whether they would act violently in response to particular (experimentally manipulated) settings and circumstances presented in written scenarios. Violent acts were chosen to test this process because it is a crime type familiar to young people and, as our data attests, common among them.

The situational model outlines the perception–choice process, a two-step process leading to action whereby individuals in settings perceive action alternatives and choose which to carry out (for further detail see section 1.3.5). In the case of violence, provocations may create the motivation to reduce friction,[1] for which some people may see violence as a possible solution (for a review, see Wikström and Treiber 2009a). Whether or not a person perceives violence as an action alternative is determined by the moral filter (moral rule-induced selective perception of action alternatives; see

---

[1] Although people may have different sensitivities to friction we assume that, for all people, higher levels of friction in a setting will result in the experience of higher provocation.

section 1.3.7), which emerges from the interaction of the person's own moral rules, and the moral rules of the setting in which he or she is operating (the moral context). This means that, even in the same setting, people will vary in whether an act of violence is among the action alternatives they perceive when provoked. If they perceive violence as an action alternative, they may choose to act violently out of habit, or after deliberation (see section 1.3.6). If there is conflicting rule-guidance between the rules of the setting and a person's morality regarding acts of violence, a person may deliberate, in which case internal and external controls (self-control and deterrence, respectively) may play a role in whether he or she chooses to act violently (see section 1.3.7).

It is difficult to test this proposed situational mechanism because we cannot peer inside the minds of our participants to understand which action alternatives they perceive and how they deliberate. Directly asking participants to consider the principles behind their perceptions and choices (for example, by using generalized survey questions) is problematic because people usually lack explicit awareness of these processes (see, eg, Greenwald and Banaji 1995), and consciously considering them almost inevitably alters them. For example, when people are asked to consciously consider alternatives for action in a given situation, they often think of alternatives they would never actually think about if they encountered and responded to that situation in real life. At the same time, although generalized survey questions that ask respondents directly about the impact of particular situational factors on their decision-making process can capture individual differences (see, eg, Fishbein and Ajzen 1975: 99–105), they cannot untangle how these factors interact, and often lack the kinds of concrete contextual detail that may be crucial to the judgement of intended action (Alexander and Becker 1978; Rossi and Anderson 1982; Wallander 2008).

We may not be able to measure perception and choice processes directly, but it is possible to devise an experiment whereby we introduce individuals who differ in their crime propensity to settings that differ in their criminogeneity, and observe how they interact. By experimentally manipulating key features of the setting that are causally relevant to the perception–choice process, we can observe the outcome (whether violence occurs), which can help us start to understand factors (personal and environmental) that lead people to perceive and choose violence as an alternative, and how they interact. Clearly, it is not ethical, practical, or safe to subject our participants (or researchers) to real-life experiments where participants are provoked to act violently. We can however, present our participants with a hypothetical situation (scenario) containing a description of controlled and manipulated causally relevant features of the setting, and ask them how they would hypothetically respond (measuring their behavioural intention).

This chapter specifically uses data on participants' violent responses to randomized scenarios that varied in terms of their level of monitoring and provocation. We would expect these factors to interact with participants' crime propensity in determining whether or not they see and choose violence as an alternative. Across all participants, we would expect greater provocations and lower monitoring to increase their tendency to perceive and choose violence as an alternative. Likewise, we would expect greater crime propensity would increase participants' likelihood to perceive and choose violence as an alternative. However, participants with a lower crime propensity, especially those with weak law-relevant personal morality, may be unlikely to see violence as an alternative in any setting, and those with strong self-control may be less likely to choose violence as an alternative, except in extreme situations (for example when their own life, or that of a loved one, is threatened) when provocation is high enough, and external controls low enough. Thus we expect that the threshold for seeing and choosing violence as an alternative will lower (in relation to the levels of provocation and monitoring) as crime propensity increases (and indeed are able to show this in our results).

The situational model suggests that controls only play a role in some action decisions, and only subsequent to the motivation to act (see section 1.3.7). This is consistent with previous research on action decision making that has found that motivation may be more salient to the choice process than consequences (and hence external controls; see, eg, Dhami and Mandel 2011; Parsons et al. 1997; Siegel et al. 1994). Hence we expect (and indeed find) that provocation is generally more influential to the perception–choice process, although we would also expect relative levels to matter (eg extreme levels of monitoring may override the effects of provocation).

In either the hypothetical or real world, behavioural intentions do not always equate to behavioural outcomes. However, we are able to show in the final section of this chapter that people who reported violent behavioural intentions in response to our scenarios were also more likely to self-report acts of violence and to have been convicted of violent or aggressive crimes. This confirms that findings from these hypothetical scenarios have real-world validity and value.

## 8.1 Capturing the perception–choice process: A factorial survey approach

this [scenario] approach is an appropriate one in the study of human choices when the alternatives are complex bundles that vary in many ways.

(Rossi and Nock 1982: 9–10)

In PADS+, we aimed to tap into the perception–choice process via participants' behavioural intentions (ie how they would act in a given situation). Participants were asked to consider how they would act if they were the protagonist in specific hypothetical scenarios (see section 8.2). Randomized scenarios[2] provide a way of integrating the benefits of experimentation with social surveys in the examination of shared features of settings and idiosyncratic features of actors in human choice processes (see Rossi and Nock 1982: 9–10). Participants are asked how they would respond were they the actors in fictional situations that contain experimentally manipulated combinations and levels of key features (dimensions) considered causally relevant to the choice of interest. The scenarios detailed in this chapter presented a situation in which violence could be a possible action alternative, randomly varying the level of provocation and monitoring characterizing the fictional setting.

Randomized scenarios build on the advantages of experimental design by allowing the level of each of the key dimensions to vary independently, making it possible to investigate the relative impact of dimensions that are often very highly correlated (Rossi and Anderson 1982; Wallander 2008). Typically, participants judge only a randomized sample (one, in the case of PADS+) of the possible range of combinations of levels and dimensions (the scenario universe). When presented to a large number of participants, this factorial survey design therefore provides randomized experimental data from people with different personal characteristics in settings with varying environmental characteristics (the 'treatment' groups),

---

[2] Also known as vignettes and factorial objects.

making it possible to study the effects of changing levels of key variables and their interaction.

In short, from the experimental tradition, the factorial survey borrows and adapts the concept of factor orthogonality and from the survey tradition it borrows the greater richness of detail and complexity that characterises real-life circumstances.

(Rossi and Anderson 1982: 16)

This methodology is well suited to tapping into the perception–choice process firstly because the process remains implicit and is therefore not altered by explicit consideration. The systematic manipulation of factors involved in randomized scenarios is far better suited to studying the relevant features of a context that affect judgements than studies that measure judgements using direct methods (Wallander 2008). Secondly, the method measures behavioural intentions, rather than people's reasoning about their behaviour. It has been shown that people are better at making choices under controlled and varied conditions (as required in a factorial survey) than they are at detailing the reasons behind them (as required by general survey questions aimed at ascertaining the relative importance of dimensions) (Alexander and Becker 1978).

Causally relevant personal characteristics (eg crime propensity), unlike features of the fictional situation, cannot be 'assigned' to people and are therefore measured using other methods and then introduced in the analysis of scenario data. In this way, randomized scenarios can capture the differential impact of scenario dimensions on different people, or groups of people, with particular personal characteristics (see also Rossi and Anderson 1982).

Despite its usefulness and potential applications, the factorial survey approach is still relatively infrequently used in the social sciences, particularly outside the United States, although it may be more widely used in criminological research (Wallander 2009). Factorial surveys have been used to study public attitudes, for example in regards to punishment preferences or crime and/or offender types, as well as the decision making of professional members of the criminal justice system (eg judges, police officers). Of specific relevance to this chapter are studies that have investigated and tested factors that influence people's choices of action (specifically, of course, those that break the law or other moral rules). Many of these studies explore the in- and inter-dependent explanatory contributions of motivation and controls (eg temptations, provocations, self-control, deterrence), namely from a rational choice perspective that focuses on the trade off between expected benefits and perceived costs (see, eg Bachman et al. 1992; Elis and Simpson 1995; Klepper and Nagin 1989a, 1989b; Leeper Piquero et al. 2005; Leeper Piquero and Piquero 2006; Nagin and Paternoster 1993). However, there are many limitations to this model of human action decision making (including the emphasis it places on the role of controls and the lack of attention it pays to differential motivation; see further section 1.3.6). SAT presents an alternative model which identifies key causal factors in the moral decision-making process that can be directly tested using the factorial survey method.

## 8.2 PADS+ randomized scenarios

According to Situational Action Theory (SAT), motivators (in the scenarios analysed in this chapter, provocations in particular) and deterrents (the presence of monitors) are the causally relevant features of settings crucial to the perception–choice process and, therefore, the action outcome (in this case, violence). Therefore, these causal dimensions were experimentally and independently varied in PADS+ scenarios; for each scenario, each participant responded to one randomized permutation out of four, which differed in their levels of motivators and deterrence. These scenarios formed only a very small part of the young persons' questionnaire.[3]

### 8.2.1 Detail and dimensions

In this chapter we analyse scenarios that sought to capture participants' tendency to respond violently to different levels of provocation in the presence or absence of monitoring. Only these features of the setting were experimentally manipulated because they are causally relevant to the perception–choice process (according to SAT). Some factorial surveys aim to explain as much of the variance in people's responses as possible by manipulating a large number of dimensions across various levels, but this is not necessary because

---

[3] Scenarios constitute at least the majority of the data collection in most factorial survey studies, and although some studies employ only a short factorial survey, most respondents are asked to judge a large number of scenarios (for a review, see Wallander 2009). The presentation of many permutations of the same scenario increases the risk that participants become aware of the manipulations.

consideration of the nature of the decision-making process can highlight factors that may and may not be of particular importance. Although the scenarios focused on these key dimensions, details that were essential for setting the scene were included and held constant across all permutations (eg where the situation took place). This results in a better informed response, as scenarios that are too vague or abstract may encourage participants to add their own embellishments (see Wallander 2008), meaning they may respond to essentially different situations.

The PADS+ scenarios did not provide detailed information about all the aspects of a real-world setting that may influence the perception–choice process. While a certain amount of detail is important to ensure the realism of the scenario, a large amount of contextual detail is often unnecessary.[4] The inclusion of a large number of dimensions (for experimental manipulation or control purposes) may in fact be detrimental, as longer scenarios may tax participants' attention and information-processing abilities (Rossi and Anderson 1982), potentially leading them to neglect the more important details (Batista-Foguet et al. 1990). As people differ from one another and across settings in their attention to detail, it is impossible to present a realistic level of detail for all participants; consequently it may be more important that scenarios are clear and accessible and the key factors of interest are unambiguous. Concise scenarios were also particularly desirable for PADS+ considering participants' age and variable attention spans and reading abilities. As Rossi and Anderson (1982: 16) note, 'while there may be a seemingly infinite number of ways in which one [setting] differs from another... there are a relatively small number of characteristics of objects to which persons pay attention in making judgements about those objects.' However, they go on to suggest 'it may well be the case that levels can be extended indefinitely but that dimensions are limited by the information processing abilities of respondents' (ibid.: 59).

---

[4] For example, Olafsson (2004) undertook a scenario study relating levels of provocation to violent response using video clips. Although video clips provide considerably more contextual detail than written scenarios, thereby controlling for many more factors, the pattern of relationship between key factors remained the same in these video scenarios as found in the written scenarios described in this chapter.

## 8.2.2 Realism and familiarity

Fundamental to the efficacy of the factorial survey methodology is the assumption that judgements made in hypothetical scenarios are a valid measure of judgements that would be made in real-world situations; in other words how someone reports they would act in response to the hypothetical situation is (more or less) how they would act in the same (or similar) real-world situation. Of course, many factors can influence whether or not a person carries out an intention to act (see section 1.3.5), but it is logical to assume a relationship between behavioural intentions and action; indeed, in the final part of this chapter we are able to validate findings from our scenarios with participants' real-world behaviours.

In order to maximize external validity and ensure scenario findings are generalizable to real-world settings, situations described in scenarios should be set in reasonably familiar, realistic settings (see eg Fishbein and Ajzen 1975; Goudriaan and Nieuwbeerta 2007; Leeper Piquero and Piquero 2006; Rossi and Anderson 1982). However, due to the necessary specificity of the scenario method, many of the participants will not have direct experience of the exact scenarios they are asked to judge, but may have experienced elements of them in different settings. A scenario does not have to be directly within the realms of a participant's experience in order for him or her to be able to accurately judge how he or she would respond; it is plausible for participants to form judgements about how they would act in situations they have never encountered by applying attitudes to, and past experiences of, similar situations. As Thurman et al. (1993: 251) highlight, respondents can still make 'credible judgments' because they have 'made similar decisions before, and are familiar with the consequences of their actions, and thus, have some experiential basis from which to judge what they might do in future'.

Although the factorial survey approach avoids selection bias by 'placing' all participants in the same scenario (albeit different permutations), in reality, certain situations or places may be more common to some individuals than others, therefore it is important that realism and familiarity extend to all participants as far as possible. PADS+ scenarios were designed to present situations that would be both familiar and realistic to young people growing up in the United Kingdom, which were easy for them to imagine, and in which the participant could readily identify with the protagonist. For this reason, the protagonist was a young person of the same gender as the participant. Space–time budget data shows that adolescent violence also tends to occur between same-sex actors (see section 7.2.1), therefore the potential victim was also matched to the participant's (and the protagonist's) gender. Table 8.1 shows the male version of the 2004 violence scenario and Table 8.2 shows the female version of the 2006 violence scenario. By matching the sex of both the potential aggressor and the potential victim in the

**Table 8.1  2004 violence scenario content and design (male version)**

| INTRODUCTION | | It is break between two lessons. David is standing in the school corridor together with a group of other pupils. |
|---|---|---|
| DIMENSION | LEVEL | WORDING |
| Provocation | False accusation | Steve comes up to David and falsely accuses him of having stolen some money. |
| | False accusation and push | Steve comes up to David and falsely accuses him of having stolen some money and pushes him to the ground so that he hurts his back. |
| Monitoring | Teachers | There are several teachers around who can see what is going on. |
| | No teachers | There are no teachers or other adults around who can see what is going on. |
| OUTCOME | Violence | What would you do if you were David? Would you hit Steve? |
| JUDGEMENT | | Yes, I would hit Steve |
| | | No, I would just tell Steve he is an idiot |
| | | No, I would tell a teacher about it |
| | | No, I would do nothing |

| Scenario Universe | | Monitoring | |
|---|---|---|---|
| | | Teachers | No teachers |
| Provocation | False accusation | A | B |
| | False accusation and push | C | D |

scenarios, we also avoided potential bias in reports of violence against the opposite sex.[5]

## 8.2.3 Structure and content

When administering the scenario part of the questionnaire to participants, the questionnaire supervisor first introduced the scenario section to make sure participants understood that they were being asked to place themselves in the story and answer the question as if they were the protagonist. Below is the text of one permutation (high monitoring, high provocation; female version) of the violence scenario given to a randomly selected sample of participants in 2006. The manipulated parts of the scenario are underlined for illustration, but were not marked in any way in the questionnaire. The construction of the different permutations of the violence scenarios are shown in Tables 8.1 and 8.2 and described below.

*Louise is waiting for the bus at a bus stop. She is listening to her iPod. Suddenly a girl who walks by pushes her so she drops her iPod to the ground and it breaks. When Louise asks her why she pushed her, the girl pushes her once again. There are two police officers walking on the other side of the street.*

*If you were Louise, how likely do you think it is that you would hit or push the girl that pushed you?*

- *Very likely*
- *Likely*
- *Unlikely*
- *Very unlikely*

The content and tone of the scenarios allowed and encouraged participants to assume the protagonist was the same age as themselves.

---

[5] Space–time budget data on violent offences during Phase 1 showed that, on the whole, males were violent towards male victims only, whereas females, although they reported more violent acts against other females, also reported a considerable number of violent acts against males. Studies of self-reported partner violence have also shown proportionally fewer acts of violence by males against females than by females against males (Magdol et al. 1997; Moffitt and Caspi 1999). Although this may actually reflect the nature of male violence, it has been suggested that males may underreport, minimize, or deny aggression towards females (Carlson 1990; LeJeune and Follette 1994). It is also possible that females perceive violence against males as more acceptable than males perceive violence against females (Jezl et al. 1996).

**Table 8.2  2006 violence scenario content and design (female version)**

| INTRODUCTION | Louise is waiting for the bus at a bus stop. She is listening to her iPod. | | |
|---|---|---|---|
| DIMENSION | LEVEL | WORDING | |
| Provocation | Pushed and ignored | Suddenly a girl who walks by pushes her. When Louise asks her why she pushed her the girl just ignores her. | |
| | Pushed twice and iPod broken | Suddenly a girl who walks by pushes her so she drops her iPod to the ground and it breaks. When Louise asks her why she pushed her the girl pushes her once again. | |
| Monitoring | Police officers | There are two police officers walking on the other side of the street. | |
| | None | There are no other people at the bus stop. | |
| OUTCOME | Violence | If you were Louise, how likely do you think it is that you would hit or push the girl that pushed you? | |
| JUDGEMENT | | Very likely | |
| | | Likely | |
| | | Very unlikely | |
| | | Unlikely | |
| Scenario Universe | | Monitoring | |
| | | Police officers | No One |
| Provocation | Pushed and ignored | A | B |
| | Pushed twice and iPod broken | C | D |

The first part of the text sets the scene of the scenario (see Tables 8.1 and 8.2). In the scenarios featured in this chapter, the protagonist is either in a school corridor with other pupils, or at a bus stop. Space–time budget data shows that virtually all participants had a great deal of experience of the school setting, and often spent time in streets (including waiting for the bus; many young people commuted to and from school by bus, and/or used the public transport system). Other simple ways to increase realism and familiarity without adding lengthy detail included using the names of specific products (eg iPod) to make the scene easier to imagine, or the name of other characters to indicate they are known to the protagonist.

## Provocation

The first manipulated criminogenic feature (dimension) of the setting was provocation. A provocation occurs when an unwanted external interference (friction) causes a person to experience negative emotions (eg anger or annoyance; see section 1.3.7). The provocations presented in both violence scenarios were chosen to be realistic and plausible in that participants could encounter them and they could lead to a violent response. Personal harm by an aggressor (eg injury, norm violation, damage to property, injustice) creates considerable friction, which some people may see violence as a means of alleviating. Our data also validates that most young people had experienced or witnessed some degree of friction similar to that in the scenarios, and that violent crime was a particularly common crime type among young people (more than half of the sample reported an act of violence during Phase 1; see section 3.1.1).

Selecting appropriate comparative levels of key dimensions is crucial to understanding how they influence the outcome of interest. Different levels should reveal any significant differences in patterns of responses across a population, while still demonstrating variation between people (levels that are too low or too high may predetermine violent or non-violent responses).

Low provocation in the 2004 violence scenario presented a form of injustice (false accusation), whereas high provocation included an additional violent act (push) resulting in injury to the protagonist (see Table 8.1). In the 2006 violence scenario, low provocation involved the protagonist being pushed for no reason and then ignored. In the high provocation permutation, the push was followed by another push that broke the protagonist's property (see Table 8.2).

## Monitoring

The other causally relevant manipulated feature of the setting was deterrence, in the form of monitoring. In the scenarios, the low and high monitoring levels were respectively reflected by the absence or presence of effective monitors (capable guardians or rule enforcers who may deter violence). In the 2004 scenario, although pupils were present in the school corridor in all permutations, teachers were also present in the high monitoring permutations (see Table 8.1). In the 2006 scenario, there were no other people at the bus stop in the low monitoring permutations, while police officers were nearby in the high monitoring permutations (see Table 8.2). These particular guardians were chosen because young people are familiar with the presence (and absence) of both teachers and police officers.[6]

### Scenario permutations and the scenario universe

Having two levels of two causally relevant setting features resulted in four scenario permutations (the scenario universe, shown in the matrix in Table 8.3). The two levels of each of the manipulated setting features (dimensions) were coded into categories so that low provocation and the presence of monitors were assigned a value of 0 (less criminogenic), and high provocation and the absence of monitors were assigned a value of 1 (more criminogenic). One benefit of such a small scenario universe, which results from a limited number of dimensions and levels, is that participants need only judge one permutation of each scenario to result in enough responses to each permutation to enable meaningful statistical analyses.

Based on the principles of SAT, the scenario permutations (A, B, C, and D) can be transformed into a criminogeneity scale, whereby the presence of criminogenic features mean that the setting is more conducive to violence (Table 8.4). Remember that SAT argues that motivation is more fundamental to action decisions than controls,

**Table 8.3 The scenario universe**

| Provocation | Monitoring | |
| --- | --- | --- |
| | Monitored (high) | Not monitored (low) |
| Low | A | B |
| High | C | D |

---

[6] Monitors in scenarios were chosen to be generic to reduce the varied experiential information participants add to the scenario. Thus variance in the effectiveness of parents as monitors (due to, for example, varied parenting styles, family relationships, and monitoring capabilities) meant that parents were not chosen as monitors.

**Table 8.4  Scenario permutation, levels of dimensions, and criminogeneity**

| Scenario permutation | A | B | C | D |
|---|---|---|---|---|
| Levels of dimensions | High monitoring Low provocation | Low monitoring Low provocation | High monitoring High provocation | Low monitoring High provocation |
| Criminogeneity | Low | Medium low | Medium high | High |
| Criminogeneity scale | 0 | 1 | 2 | 3 |

as controls only play a role in deliberate decision making, subsequent to motivation. Thus provocations could be seen as more primary to the conduciveness of a setting than deterrence (eg monitoring); police may be present but if a person is not provoked this is irrelevant to whether or not that person sees and chooses violence as an action alternative.

### 8.2.4  Crime propensity and randomization

Although in many analyses in this book we utilize participants' Phase 1 crime propensity scores, in this chapter we match their crime propensity scores to their scenario responses by year.[7] The scores for each wave are standardized, and divided into crime propensity groups using the same method as the Phase 1 crime propensity score (see section 3.2.3).[8] As with the Phase 1 crime propensity score, the medium propensity group is much larger than the high and low propensity groups, as the low and high groups capture scores that are less than and more than one standard deviation, respectively, from the mean (Table 8.5). Due to internal missing

[7] The overall results in this chapter are the same when the Phase 1 crime propensity score and groups are used. However, as propensity slightly increased over the Phase (due to a slight decline in morality, see section 3.2), we decided to use the yearly scores to avoid overestimating participants' propensity at the time of their responses to the scenarios.

[8] This is actually done by standardizing the morality and self-control scores for the year separately and then summing them. The means of the standardized propensity scores for each year are very close to zero, so are not standardized again.

**Table 8.5 Crime propensity groups by year**

| | Crime propensity category | | | | | | |
| --- | --- | --- | --- | --- | --- | --- | --- |
| | Low | | Medium | | High | |
| Year | Percentage sample | N | Percentage sample | N | Percentage sample | N |
| 2004 | 15.5 | 109 | 70.4 | 495 | 14.1 | 99 |
| 2006 | 16.4 | 115 | 66.9 | 470 | 16.8 | 118 |

data, crime propensity scores could not be calculated for seven participants in 2004.[9]

Participants were randomly assigned scenario permutation A, B, C, or D before the data-collection period each year. A key feature of the randomized scenario method is that the scenarios are characterized by factor orthogonality (perfect non-association between dimensions) and approximate symmetry (all the levels of a particular dimension are equally represented) (Rossi and Anderson 1982; Wallander 2008). As a result of randomization (and few missing data) a similar number of participants responded to each permutation, and each permutation was well spread among the crime propensity groups (Table 8.6).

### 8.2.5 Judgements of behavioural intention

After reading the scenario, participants were asked to state what they would do if they were the protagonist in the story. Rather than present a range of alternatives (which we could not do comprehensively) or ask participants to report possible alternatives (leading to more conscious and creative consideration of alternatives than may be realistic) we focused on the alternative of violent response and asked participants to answer whether or not they would see and choose violence as an alternative (2004, at age 13), or how likely they were to do so (2006, at age 15). As the response items were presented after the participant read the scenario and was asked how he or she would respond, we assume responses reflect whether or not a participant perceived violence as an action alternative and

---

[9] Missing values were imputed for the morality and self-control scales, but only if participants missed fewer than two items (see section 2.7.3).

**Table 8.6  Randomization of scenario permutations (percentage of participants responding to each permutation by crime propensity)**

| Scenario | Crime propensity[a] | | | | | | | |
| | 2004 | | | | 2006 | | | |
| Permutation | *All* | Low | Med | High | *All* | Low | Med | High |
|---|---|---|---|---|---|---|---|---|
| A | *24.4* | 25.7 | 22.4 | 32.0 | *25.0* | 22.6 | 24.7 | 28.8 |
| B | *24.4* | 30.3 | 23.6 | 21.6 | *25.2* | 22.6 | 25.3 | 27.1 |
| C | *25.0* | 22.0 | 26.7 | 19.6 | *25.2* | 26.1 | 25.3 | 23.7 |
| D | *26.1* | 22.0 | 27.3 | 26.8 | *24.6* | 28.7 | 24.7 | 20.3 |
| Sample *N*[b] | *704* | 109 | 491 | 97 | *703* | 115 | 470 | 118 |

[a] Groups based on crime propensity scores for the relevant year.
[b] In 2004, six participants of 710 did not complete the scenario (0.8 per cent), and of those who did, seven did not have crime propensity scores. All participants completed the scenario and all had crime propensity scores in 2006 (703).

intended to choose it, eg we assume participants who would not perceive violence as an action alternative in the real world would not state that they would respond violently to the scenario just because the violent action alternative was presented to them.

Some factorial surveys use magnitude estimation methods to capture scenario response;[10] however, a rating task with a small number of categories was considered more appropriate for young participants, and was also consistent with the types of rating tasks used throughout the young persons' questionnaire.

In 2004, the response options included one violent response (eg 'Yes, I would hit Steve [Helen]') and three other (non-violent) action alternatives (not analysed in this book); in 2006 participants were asked how likely (very unlikely, unlikely, likely, very likely) they thought it was they would 'hit or push the boy [girl] that pushed you'[11] (see Tables 8.1 and 8.2). When the likelihood responses to the 2006 scenario were recoded into a dichotomous

---

[10] For example, continuous outcome measures such as percent likelihoods (see, eg, Thurman et al. 1993) and line production (see, eg, Batista-Foguet et al. 1990); see further Rossi and Anderson (1982) and Fishbein and Ajzen (1975).

[11] Ordered categories like those used in 2006 are the most common rating task employed by factorial surveys (Wallander 2009).

variable, responses were considered violent if participants judged that it was 'very likely' that they would act violently, because the proportion of participants responding that it is 'likely' they would respond violently stayed constant across all permutations of the scenario, regardless of levels of provocation and monitoring. Therefore, of the likely violent responses, only the 'very likely' category was sensitive to the scenario permutations (Figure 8.2).

The scenarios differed in terms of the seriousness of violent response presented. Although participants could report that they would hit the aggressor in response to both scenarios, a less serious option of pushing the aggressor was included in the 2006 scenario. In 2004, participants were also presented with alternative (non-violent) response options. This means that the findings from these scenarios cannot be directly compared longitudinally. These differences should be borne in mind when comparing their results. Results are shown for both years, and, in the case of the 2006 scenario, sometimes for both the likelihood of violent response as well as for the dichotomous violent/non-violent response categories.

## 8.3  Scenario findings

### 8.3.1  Shared criminogenic features of settings

Respondents' responses to the scenarios showed considerable agreement as to which settings were the most conducive to violent responses. This was consistent with observations by Rossi and Anderson (1982: 17) that 'there is more or less agreement among persons on how much weight should be given to relevant characteristics'. The different permutations of both the 2004 and 2006 scenarios elicited significantly different responses from the sample as a whole (Figure 8.1 and Table 8.7), implying that there was general agreement across the sample regarding how the levels of provocation and monitoring in a setting influenced the participants' decision to respond violently.

Figure 8.1 and Table 8.7 show that the 2006 scenario was more conducive to violent responses in general than the 2004 scenario. Differences between the stories, levels of provocation and monitoring, and outcomes in the two scenarios are likely to account for some and maybe all of these differences.[12] Thus we should not

---

[12] Remember that the violent response option for the 2006 scenario was less serious than for the 2004 scenario, hence it is plausible that participants were

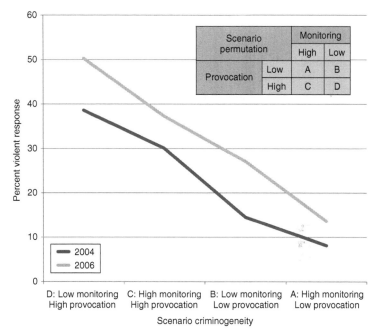

**Figure 8.1 Violent responses to scenarios by scenario permutation**

**Table 8.7 Prevalence of violent responses to scenarios by permutation**

| Scenario | N | Percentage violent response by permutation | | | | Chi² | Cramer's V | Prob. |
|----------|-----|------|------|------|------|-------|------|------|
| | | A | B | C | D | | | |
| 2004 | 710 | 8.1 | 14.5 | 30.1 | 38.6 | 58.40 | .29 | .000 |
| 2006 | 703 | 13.6 | 27.1 | 37.3 | 50.3 | 58.08 | .29 | .000 |

willing to consider the violent option at lower levels of provocation and monitoring. At the same time, monitoring had less of an impact on violent responses in 2004 than 2006 relative to the impact of provocation, which may reflect the differing nature and effectiveness of the specific monitors (teachers in 2004 versus police officers in 2006) (Table 8.9). However, direct comparisons of these two scenarios cannot be conclusive, particularly because participants' responses were measured differently. Instead, findings from the two scenarios should be used to independently analyse the perception–choice process.

assume, based on direct longitudinal comparison of these scenarios, that the sample became more violent between 2004 and 2006, especially as this contradicts the finding that their self-reported assault prevalence fell from 45 per cent to 40 per cent between 2004 and 2006, as part of a trend in declining violence over Phase 1.

Participants' responses indicated that in both scenarios the most criminogenic permutation (D) contained high provocation and low monitoring; this permutation was most conducive to violent responses, while permutation A, which contained low provocation and high monitoring, was the least conducive to violent responses. Of the remaining permutations, those characterized by high provocation (permutation C) were more conducive to violent responses in both years (see Figure 8.1 and Table 8.7). In line with SAT, this suggests that the level of provocation was more fundamental to participants' choice to act violently than the level of monitoring.

Logistic regression models confirm that scenario criminogeneity (higher provocations and, to a lesser extent, an absence of monitoring; see Table 8.4) significantly predicted violent response to scenarios in both years (Table 8.8).

Analysis of the 2006 scenario shows that the most criminogenic permutation (D) resulted in more participants reporting they would be 'very likely' to respond violently, and fewer reporting they would be 'unlikely' or 'very unlikely' to respond violently, while the least criminogenic permutation (A) resulted in more participants reporting they would be 'unlikely' or 'very unlikely' to respond violently and less reporting they would be 'very likely' to do so (Figure 8.2). Indeed, the likelihood of participants' reporting a violent response

**Table 8.8  Predicting violent response using scenario conduciveness (logistic regression[13])**

| Scenario | Predictor[a] | Nagelkerke $R^2$ x 100 | b | SE | Odds ratio | Prob. |
|----------|-----------|------------------------|-----|-----|------------|-------|
| 2004 | Criminogeneity | 12.3 | .74 | .10 | 2.09 | .000 |
| 2006 | Criminogeneity | 11.4 | .65 | .09 | 1.92 | .000 |

[a] The conduciveness scale is standardized.

[13] The logistic regression results for each model in this chapter show good model fit (as indicated by significant Chi2 and non-significant Hosmer and Lemeshow statistics) unless stated.

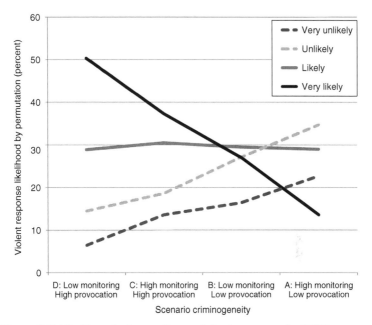

**Figure 8.2  Likelihood of reporting a violent response by 2006 scenario permutation**

was moderately and significantly related to the permutation's criminogeneity ($r_s = .32, p = .000, N = 703$).

One of the main advantages of the randomized scenario method is that the independent experimental manipulation of the levels of provocation and monitoring (dimensions) in the scenario permutations allows analysis of their independent impact on participants' selection of violent responses. Logistic regression models confirm that the level of provocation in a scenario significantly predicted participants' choice of violent responses, as did the level of monitoring, albeit to a lesser degree, in both scenarios (Table 8.9).[14] Participants broadly agreed about which criminogenic features of the scenarios were most conducive to violence: higher levels of provocation and, to a lesser extent, lower levels of monitoring,

[14] Results from a linear regression model predicting participants' likelihood of a violent response in the 2006 scenario also showed that levels of both provocation and monitoring were independent and significant predictors, although the effect was likewise stronger for provocation (model not shown).

**Table 8.9  Predicting violent responses using provocation and absence of monitoring (logistic regression)**

| Scenario | Predictors[a] | Nagelkerke $R^2$ x 100 | b | SE | Odds ratio | Prob. |
|---|---|---|---|---|---|---|
| 2004 | — | 12.6 | | | | |
| | Absence of monitors | | .22 | .09 | 1.26 | .015 |
| | Provocation | | .71 | .10 | 2.04 | .000 |
| 2006 | — | 11.4 | | | | |
| | Absence of monitors | | .33 | .09 | 1.39 | .000 |
| | Provocation | | .57 | .09 | 1.77 | .000 |

[a] The independent variables in these models are standardized to allow comparison to later models.

increased participants' tendency to report violent behavioural intentions.

These findings are in line with the situational model proposed by SAT, which suggests that the level of provocation has a greater influence on violent action because it determines whether or not people are motivated to respond to a friction and perceive violence as an alternative means of doing so, whereas the level of monitoring can only influence the choice of whether or not to carry out a violent action after it has been perceived as an alternative. The conditional relevance of controls, a key principle of SAT, posits that the presence or absence of monitoring (an element of external control, ie deterrence) will only influence the action choices of people who perceive violence as an action alternative and then deliberate about whether or not to choose that alternative (if people act violently out of habit, controls do not play a role in their actions, as they perceive no need to control their actions and/or choose other alternatives; see section 1.3.7).

### 8.3.2  Idiosyncratic features of actors: Crime propensity

When people respond to scenarios, each 'tends towards consistency in his or her own judgements, departing in a relatively regular way from the socially defined consensus on how such judgements should be made' (Rossi and Anderson 1982: 16). In other words, there will be variation in how people respond to settings, and features of settings, but they may do so in predictable and measurable ways. For example, we have shown that crime propensity is a key personal characteristic determining differences between people in their rule-breaking behaviours, which interacts with criminogenic features of the settings in which they take part. We would therefore expect that people's crime propensity would predict differences in their likelihood of responding to criminogenic features of scenarios. Those with a higher crime propensity would be more *situationally vulnerable* to criminogenic features of settings (such as high provocation and the absence of monitoring).

Recall that crime propensity refers to a person's morality and ability to exercise self-control (see sections 1.3.4 and 3.2). SAT theorizes that a person's morality interacts with the moral context of the settings in which he or she takes part to determine, via the moral filter, whether or not he or she perceives rule-breaking as an action alternative in response to a particular motivation (eg temptation or provocation). In the case of violent rule-breaking, his or her violence-relevant morality, and the violence-relevant aspects of the moral context, will be of particular importance. If he or she perceives rule-breaking (in this case, violent rule-breaking) as an alternative, his or her ability to exercise self-control may play a role in his or her decision to act violently if he or she perceives conflict between doing so and his or her personal morality; alternatively, deterrence (eg the presence of monitors) may play a role if there is conflict between his or her doing so and the rules of the setting. Hence even in the same setting, people with different personal morality will differ in how likely they are to perceive and choose violence as an action alternative.

Findings from PADS+ scenario data support the influence of crime propensity on people's response to criminogenic factors. Across all scenario permutations participants with a higher crime propensity were more likely to report they would respond violently than participants with a lower crime propensity. Indeed, the tendency to respond violently to the 2004 scenario increased linearly, dramatically, and significantly with increasing crime propensity (Figure 8.3 and Table 8.10). This increase was less dramatic in response to the 2006 scenario, but there was still a considerable, significant, and positive, correlation between participants' crime propensity (in 2006) and their reported likelihood of responding violently to the 2006 scenario ($r_S = .38.\ p = .000$).

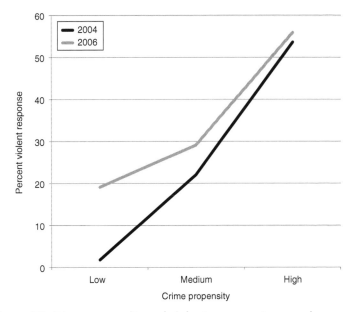

**Figure 8.3  Crime propensity and violent response to scenarios (percentage within propensity group)**

**Table 8.10  Predicting violent responses by crime propensity (logistic regression)**

| Scenario | Predictor[a] | Nagelkerke R² x 100 | b | SE | Odds ratio | Prob. |
|---|---|---|---|---|---|---|
| 2004 | Crime propensity | 23.0 | .65 | .07 | 1.92 | .000 |
| 2006[b] | Crime propensity | 13.3 | .42 | .05 | 1.53 | .000 |

[a] Crime propensity scores refer to those for the year corresponding with the scenario and are already standardized.
[b] Although the logistic regression Chi² statistic is significant, suggesting a significant difference in response by crime propensity, the Hosmer and Lemeshow statistic is just significant at the $p < .05$ level, suggesting that this particular model is not an ideal fit.

### Consistency of violent response and crime propensity

To further emphasize the association between crime propensity and violent responses to criminogenic settings, we can analyse this

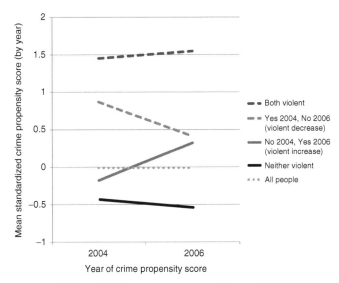

**Figure 8.4  Stability of violent response to 2004 and 2006 violence scenarios by 2004 and 2006 mean crime propensity score**

relationship over time.[15] As far as we are aware this is the first time scenario data of this kind has been analysed longitudinally, which is perhaps overdue in factorial survey studies (see Jasso 2006: 411). Since this analysis compares mean propensity scores that have been standardized within each year (see section 8.2.4), age-related changes in crime propensity are effectively controlled. This means that although crime propensity increases for the sample as a whole during this highly specific developmental phase (age 13 to 15) (see Figure 3.5), changes in mean crime propensity between 2004 and 2006 shown in Figure 8.4 represent changes in rank order relative to the rest of the sample. Figure 8.4 shows that individuals who responded more violently to the 2006 scenario than the 2004 scenario (regardless of the permutation) also showed a significant increase in their mean crime propensity relative to the rest of the sample ($t$ = -3.60, $p$ = .000), whilst those who responded less violently showed a significant decrease in their mean crime propensity

[15] Bearing in mind the differences between the 2004 and 2006 scenarios and the limitations noted earlier (see chapter 8, footnote 12).

relative to the rest of the sample ($t$ = 3.23, $p$ = .002).[16] Those who were consistent in their violent responses across years (ie who responded violently or non-violently to both scenarios) were also consistent in their crime propensity, relative to the rest of the sample (differences between mean propensity in 2004 and 2006 were not significant for these groups). This will not be further analysed here, but this finding is in line with other findings using PADS+ data that show that changes in crime propensity and criminogenic exposure predicted changes in crime involvement (Reinecke and Wikström 2012 using trajectory analysis; and Wikström 2009, using change scores).

### 8.3.3 Shared and idiosyncratic features of situations

So far scenario data has shown that young people generally agree about which features of settings are more criminogenic (greater provocation and, to a lesser extent, the absence of effective monitors); however, they also differ in how they perceive and choose action alternatives (participants with higher crime propensities were more likely to report violent behavioural intentions in response to any settings than participants with lower crime propensities). The next task is to analyse how these shared and idiosyncratic factors interact, ie to explore to what extent young people with varying crime propensities differ in their tendency to report violent behavioural intentions in response to settings with varying levels of provocation and monitoring.

In line with findings presented in earlier chapters, the scenario data shows that the extent to which young people reported they would respond violently to a provocation depended on their morality and ability to exercise self-control (their crime propensity) as well as the deterrent qualities (level of monitoring) of the setting;[17] consistent with the main arguments of SAT, crime propensity interacted with criminogenic exposure. Figure 8.5 shows the relative proportion of violent behavioural intentions reported by participants

[16] The mean crime propensity of those who responded non-violently in 2004 and violently in 2006 is lower in both years than that of those who responded violently in 2004 but non-violently in 2006. This is explicable by the finding that the 2006 scenario is more conducive to violence, particularly for participants with a low crime propensity (Table 8.7 and Figure 8.1).

[17] Similar findings using Rasch models and data from the PADS+ 2004 violence scenario are reported by Haar and Wikström (2010).

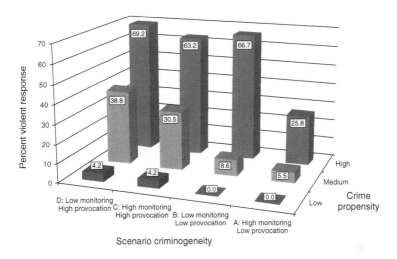

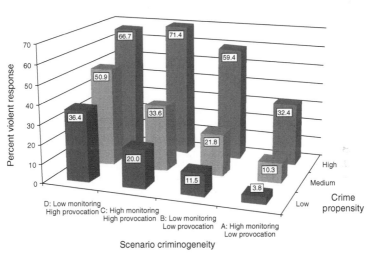

**Figure 8.5 Violent responses to 2004 (top figure) and 2006 (bottom figure) scenarios by criminogeneity and crime propensity**

with different crime propensities across the different permutations of both scenarios.

Using the permutation criminogeneity scale (see Table 8.4) to predict violent responses by each crime propensity group in both logistic regression and Chi$^2$ analyses (Table 8.11) confirms that crime propensity groups differed significantly in their likelihood to

**Table 8.11  Impact of permutation criminogeneity[a] on violent response, by crime propensity (logistic regression and Chi² analysis)**

| Crime propensity | Scenario | Logistic regression | | | Chi² | |
|---|---|---|---|---|---|---|
| | | Nagelkerke R² x 100 | Odds ratio | Prob. | Chi² | Prob. |
| Low | 2004 | — | — | *n.s.* | — | *n.s.* |
| | 2006 | 15.6 | 2.50 | .002 | 11.24[b] | .002 |
| Medium | 2004 | 17.0 | 2.54 | .000 | 57.27 | .000 |
| | 2006 | 15.0 | 2.20 | .000 | 50.56 | .000 |
| High | 2004 | 13.5 | 1.90 | .002 | 14.32 | .000 |
| | 2006 | 9.8 | 1.80 | .004 | 11.67 | .001 |

[a] Criminogeneity scale is standardized for logistic regression.
[b] Some cells have an expected count of fewer than five; however, values are included to show the general trend.

respond violently to the different permutations of the scenarios. This means that participants with different crime propensities tended to differ systematically in their likelihood of responding violently to either scenario.

Generally, as permutation criminogeneity increased, the likelihood of violent response increased regardless of crime propensity (consistent with the general agreement across the sample as to the more criminogenic setting features), although in 2004 there was no significant relationship between criminogeneity and violent responses by participants with a low crime propensity, as only two (1.8 per cent) participants with a low crime propensity (in 2004) reported a violent response to any permutation of the 2004 scenario (although both were to the more criminogenic permutations C and D). This is consistent with the argument forwarded by SAT that people with a low crime propensity are generally *situationally resistant* to criminogenic features, ie they do not see crime as an alternative even in most criminogenic settings. Wikström, Tseloni, and Karlis (2011: 1) drew a similar conclusion using entirely different data from PADS+ in a paper that showed that 'deterrence perceptions are largely irrelevant for those who lack a propensity to commit acts of crime'.

The small number of factorial surveys into criminal behavioural intentions that take moral beliefs into account support this finding. For example, in their scenario study of drink driving among a probability sample, Thurman et al. (1993: 261) found that

respondents in the general sample who are socially and morally committed to law abiding behaviour are relatively unresponsive to legal threats due to the very fact that, if they do not engage in drunk driving, then it follows that the sanctions applied to drink driving per se are a matter of little concern for them as individual drivers.

Bachman et al. (1992: 376) evaluated the impact of sanctions on, among other things, intentions to sexually offend among male college students, and reported that, although they found

a deterrent effect for the perceived risk of formal sanctions, it should be kept in mind that respondents' moral beliefs were a more important source of social control and that the effect of formal sanction threats was conditioned by moral beliefs... when the male's behaviour in the scenario was thought to be morally wrong... respondents were unaffected by instrumental concerns of cost/benefit. Their moral condemnation of the action was so strong that they could not even consider the possibility of offending.

Participants with a low crime propensity responded differently to the 2006 scenario, however. Although they still reported considerably less intention to respond violently than participants with a higher crime propensity, a much larger proportion (19.1 per cent) reported violent behavioural intentions than in 2004 (1.8 per cent) (see Figure 8.3).[18] Permutation criminogeneity did have a significant effect on the violent responses of young people with high and medium crime propensities to both scenarios (Table 8.11, Figure 8.5). However, there were differences in how young people in these crime propensity groups responded to criminogenic factors. As the graphs in Figure 8.5 suggest, and Chi[2] analysis (not shown) confirms, although criminogeneity significantly predicted a violent response to scenario permutations by participants with a high crime propensity in both 2004 and 2006, this relationship was driven entirely by the difference in response between the least criminogenic permutation (A) and the remaining permutations (the differences between responses to the latter being non-significant for both scenarios).

---

[18] Although there was considerable overlap, propensity groups did not necessarily constitute the same participants in 2004 as in 2006, as some young people's propensity changed enough to cross group thresholds.

In contrast, violent responses to the three most criminogenic permutations for young people with a medium crime propensity differed significantly, as they did to the least criminogenic permutation. This reflects the pattern observed for violent response by young people with a low crime propensity to permutations of the 2006 scenario, albeit at a lower magnitude; as permutation criminogeneity increased, the likelihood of a violent response steadily and significantly increased.

This implies that unlike their counterparts with a medium or low crime propensity, many participants with a high crime propensity required only minimal provocation to report violent behavioural intentions (around two-thirds reported violent responses to permutations with a low level of provocation; see Figure 8.5).[19] Increasing the level of provocation did little to increase their tendency to perceive and choose crime as an alternative, as for most young people with a high crime propensity, the threshold at which they did so was already crossed; when provoked, even at a minimal level, their weak violence-relevant morality meant they would perceive crime as a viable and even preferred action alternative. However, as long as provocation was minimal, the presence of monitors did significantly influence their violent action choices, suggesting they were more likely to deliberate about their actions, and were able to exercise enough self-control to counteract their motivation to act violently. When the level of provocation was increased, they were more likely to perceive no conflict between their violent intentions and the moral context, and therefore chose to act violently without deliberation, or were less able to offset their greater motivation through their weak ability to exercise self-control.

In contrast, setting criminogeneity played a more significant role in whether or not young people with a medium crime propensity (and, in the 2006 scenario, a low crime propensity) saw and chose violence as an alternative. Their stronger morality meant that greater provocation had a significant effect on whether or not they saw violence as an appropriate response option, while their greater

[19] In 2006, for example, the mean violent response likelihood reported by young people with a high crime propensity was more than 2.5 (more likely than not) in response to all permutations. Of course, a number (30–40 per cent) of young people with a high crime propensity were not classified as reporting a violent behavioural intention, especially to the least conducive permutation. However, many of these young people reported it was 'likely' they would hit or push their aggressor.

ability to exercise self-control meant the level of monitoring had a significant effect on whether or not they chose violence as a preferred response option.

This pattern of findings is robust; despite the differences in the 2004 and 2006 scenarios the findings are generally the same and support SAT's core argument concerning the interaction between crime prone people and criminogenic settings.

## 8.4 Hypothetical scenarios and the real world

Behavioural intentions are not actions but internal states and, for a range of reasons (eg interferences and changes in circumstances), do not always materialize into the intended action (see further section 1.3.5). It is logical, however, to expect that a stated intention indicates an increased likelihood of that action; a behavioural intention implies that, unless there is some form of interference, the actor will carry out the action as planned. Findings from other studies support this correspondence between behavioural intentions, as measured via response to scenarios, and real-world outcomes (eg Eagly and Chaiken 1998; Liker 1982: 139–40), although it is important to exercise caution when drawing conclusions about behavioural outcomes from scenario judgements (R. Hughes 2004). Unlike many other scenario studies, PADS+ is able to place the findings from its scenarios against a backdrop of other data and analyses, including data on participants' actual behaviour. While PADS+ scenarios provide a test of a small part of the perception–choice process—ie the situational-level interaction of individual characteristics (propensity) and setting features (provocations and deterrents) leading to action—other PADS+ data (much of which is presented throughout this book) provides evidence for the broader social and situational dynamics of crime, as posited by SAT. The fact that we can demonstrate a correspondence between participants' scenario responses and real-world behavioural outcomes, as measured using other methodologies, validates the scenario method as a means of tapping into at least the tendency for certain kinds of people to act in certain ways when faced with certain kinds of settings.

Due to the randomization of scenarios (see section 8.2.4), there were no significant differences between the groups of participants presented with the different scenario permutations in terms of any of the measures of their violent or aggressive behavioural outcomes.

This means that any observed differences in behavioural outcomes between groups who responded differently to scenarios were not due to any sampling bias.

### Self-reported assault

Participants were aged 13 and 15, respectively, when they answered the 2004 and 2006 questionnaires, in which they responded to the violence scenarios analysed in this chapter, as well as self-reported their involvement in crime during the previous year. For the analyses presented in this section, we compare responses to the scenarios with crimes reported in the same questionnaire (but see section 3.1.6 on the issue of retrospective crime reporting). We focus on self-reported assaults because these acts match the violent outcomes measured by the scenarios.[20] Each year participants were asked to report their involvement in assault using the following questions:

*Not counting events when you took money or other things from someone, have you in the last year (200X) beaten up or hit someone, for example, punched, kicked or head butted someone (do not count fights with your brothers and sisters)? (Yes/No)*

*If yes, how many times did you beat up or hit someone in the last year (200X)? (N times)*

All participants provided assault data each year they took part in the study (710 in 2004, 705 in 2006); as 693 participants took part in all five waves, only these participants have a Phase 1 total assault score. Of all the measured crime types, assault was the most prevalent in our sample, a typical finding in UK self-report studies of adolescent crime (Farrington et al. 2006; Hales et al. 2009; Sampson and Wikström 2008; Wikström and Butterworth 2006). Of the 693 participants who completed all waves of data collection, 56 per cent reported an act of assault at some point during Phase 1 (Table 3.1). A small group of very frequent violent offenders also emerged; for example 3 per cent of all young people who reported an assault during Phase 1 reported more than 60 assaults over the five-year period, equating to one assault a month, on average. However, assault frequency was highly positively skewed, with more than one-third of young people who reported an assault reporting fewer

---

[20] Although robbery is also a violent crime for which we collected self-report data, it is not comparable to the violent responses measured in the scenarios as it may be more instrumental, and is therefore not included in these comparisons.

than three assaults during the study period (fewer than one every other year, on average).

## Police-recorded violent and aggressive crime

As described in section 2.6, police records for official convictions, warnings, and reprimands were collected for 694 participants. As with all crimes and all crime types, few young people had received a formal sanction for an act of violence. As official data is less likely to record instances of minor violence (which would be captured by self-report data), and more likely to capture high frequency offenders (because the likelihood of being caught by the police increases with crime frequency—see section 3.1.2, Table 3.7, and Wikström and Butterworth 2006), only more frequent and serious violent young offenders are likely to have an official record for violent crime.

For our analyses, we measured officially recorded assault by combining several official categories of violent crime consistent with the self-report measure. Because of the small number of police-recorded violent crimes in the sample, we also included other aggressive crimes that may be analogous to violent responses to the provocations depicted in the scenarios (Table 8.12). Convictions, reprimands, and warnings during the study period were summed to give a Phase 1 total of convictions, warnings, and reprimands for assault and/or aggressive crimes during the study period (2004–08, ages 13–17). Although there may have been some variation by age, the small numbers of participants who received police sanctions for violent and aggressive crimes during the phase meant that a Phase

**Table 8.12  Police-recorded convictions, reprimands and warnings for assault and aggressive crime**

|  | Prevalence | | | Offenders only | | |
|---|---|---|---|---|---|---|
|  | N | % | N offences | Max | Mean | SD |
| Assault[a] | 23 | 3.3 | 42 | 5 | 1.83 | 1.03 |
| Aggressive crime[b] | 16 | 2.3 | 23 | 4 | 1.44 | 0.89 |
| Assault and/or aggressive crime | 34 | 4.9 | 65 | 5 | 1.92 | 1.29 |

[a] Includes battery, actual bodily harm, common assault, assault on a constable.
[b] Includes using threatening, abusive, or insulting words or behaviour with intent to cause fear or provocation of violence; using disorderly behaviour or threatening/abusive/insulting words likely to cause harassment, alarm, or distress; affray.

1 measure was more stable and preferable and captured personal tendencies towards violent and/or aggressive actions which can be analysed alongside responses to the scenarios.

### 8.4.1 Violent scenario responses and violent crime

Participants' reports of violent behavioural intentions in response to the violence scenarios were significantly associated with both their self-reported violent crime involvement and their police records for violent and aggressive crimes. Young people who reported a violent response to a scenario were significantly more likely to have self-reported an assault in the same year. For example, participants who reported a violent behavioural intention in response to the 2004 scenario (regardless of the permutation) were more than four times as likely to self-report an assault the same year as those who did not report a violent behavioural intention ($\phi = .30, p = .000$). A similar relationship was evident in 2006, although the effect was slightly weaker ($\phi = .24, p = .000$, OR = 2.9; see Table 8.13).[21]

Responses to the violence scenarios significantly predicted which young people were involved in assault, to any degree. However, we also found that violent responses to scenarios significantly

**Table 8.13  Self-reported assault prevalence (same year) by scenario response**

| Scenario year | Scenario response | Assault prevalence (%) | Chi² | Phi | Prob. | Odds ratio |
|---|---|---|---|---|---|---|
| 2004 | *All responses* | *31.7* | | | | |
| | Non-violent | 24.0 | 63.13 | .30 | .000 | 4.20 |
| | Violent | 57.1 | | | | |
| 2006 | *All responses* | *28.4* | | | | |
| | Non-violent | 21.1 | 39.31 | .24 | .000 | 2.93 |
| | Violent | 44.0 | | | | |

---

[21] Participants who reported violent responses to the 2004 scenario were also significantly more likely to report assault in 2006, and participants who reported violent responses to either scenario were significantly more likely to report assault over the whole data collection period (2004–08). This suggests some stability in violent response tendencies over time, which will not be further analysed here.

**Table 8.14  Self-reported assault frequency (same year) by scenario response**

| Scenario year | Scenario response | Mean frequency | Ratio | T[a] | Prob. | Cohen's d |
|---|---|---|---|---|---|---|
| 2004 | *All responses* | *1.01* | | | | |
| | Non-violent | 0.60 | 3.97 | 5.04 | .000 | .53 |
| | Violent | 2.38 | | | | |
| 2006 | *All responses* | *1.44* | | | | |
| | Non-violent | 0.71 | 4.20 | 4.57 | .000 | .42 |
| | Violent | 2.98 | | | | |

[a] Non-parametric tests also found significant differences between the means. These were run because the assault frequency was highly skewed.

predicted self-reported assault frequency.[22] For example, the mean assault frequency reported in both 2004 and 2006 by all participants reporting violent behavioural intentions in response to that year's scenario (regardless of the permutation) was four times higher than that of participants who did not report violent behavioural intentions (Table 8.14).

As noted previously, offenders are not caught for every crime, and more minor offences are less likely to appear in official data, which means that a police record for assault and/or aggressive crime is likely to reflect serious and/or frequent offending. Although few participants had received convictions, reprimands, or warnings by the police during Phase 1, those who reported violent behavioural intentions in response to the scenarios were significantly more likely to have done so. For example, participants who reported a violent intention in response to the 2004 violence scenario were four times more likely than those not reporting a violent response to have a police record for a violent and/or aggressive crime (Table 8.15).

[22] Violent responses to the 2004 scenario were also significantly related to assault frequencies reported in 2006, and violent responses to either scenario were significantly associated with self-reported assault frequencies over the whole data collection period (2004–08). ANOVA analysis of reported violent response likelihood for the 2006 scenario showed that only the participants who reported a violent response was 'very likely' differed significantly in their self-reported assault frequencies from other participants. This supports the decision to count only 'very likely' responses as 'violent' in our analyses.

**Table 8.15 Phase 1 police-recorded assault and/or aggressive crime prevalence by scenario response**

| Scenario year | Scenario response | Prevalence (%) | Chi² | Phi | Prob. | Odds ratio |
|---|---|---|---|---|---|---|
| 2004 | *All responses* | *4.8* | | | | |
| | Non-violent | 3.0 | 16.69 | .16 | .000 | 3.98 |
| | Violent | 7.4 | | | | |
| 2006 | *All responses* | *4.8* | | | | |
| | Non-violent | 3.4 | 6.01 | .09 | .014 | 2.35 |
| | Violent | 7.7 | | | | |

These findings confirm that a tendency to respond violently to a hypothetical scenario predicted a tendency to act violently in the real world, validating the scenario methodology.

### Low provocation scenario permutations

The scenario findings presented in this chapter show that judgements of violent behavioural intention are heavily influenced by the level of provocation in a setting. The proportion of violent responses to violence scenarios was generally significantly higher when the level of provocation was higher. The randomized scenario design meant that approximately half the participants were presented with permutations characterized by low provocation (A and B), and that this sub-sample reflected the full sample in terms of their level of violent offending.[23] Participants who responded violently to even low levels of provocation may be seen to have a lower provocation threshold for violent response, suggesting a particularly strong tendency to respond violently across a wide range of circumstances. We would therefore expect these participants to commit acts of violence, in the real world, at a particularly high rate (ie across more settings).[24]

---

[23] There were no significant differences in self-reported or police-recorded assault and/or aggressive crime prevalence or frequency between the randomly selected participants presented with high versus low provocation scenarios.

[24] Of course, some participants who responded to high provocation permutations may have reported violent behavioural intentions to low provocation permutations had these been presented to them. Therefore we cannot compare groups across the scenarios.

**Table 8.16  Self-reported assault prevalence (same year) by scenario response (low provocation scenarios only)**

| Scenario year | Scenario response | Prevalence (%) | Chi$^2$ | Phi | Prob. | Odds ratio |
|---|---|---|---|---|---|---|
| 2004 | *All responses* | *34.3* | | | | |
| | Non-violent | 28.5 | 39.85 | .34 | .000 | 9.71 |
| | Violent | 79.5 | | | | |
| 2006 | *All responses* | *27.2* | | | | |
| | Non-violent | 21.4 | 23.76 | .26 | .000 | 3.68 |
| | Violent | 50.0 | | | | |

Consistent with this, we found that 57.1 per cent of participants responding violently to any permutation of the 2004 scenario self-reported assault (Table 8.13), but the assault prevalence amongst those who responded violently to low provocation permutations was 79.5 per cent (Table 8.16).[25] Participants who responded violently to the low provocation permutations in 2004 were nearly 10 times more likely to have self-reported assault in the same year than those who did not respond violently, a much stronger effect than observed across all permutations (compare Table 8.16 and 8.13). Although the effect was not quite as strong, these relationships held true for the 2006 scenario. This means that a violent response to permutations characterized by low provocation was even more indicative of a violent response tendency in everyday life.

Not only were participants who reported violent responses to low provocation scenarios particularly more likely to self-report assaults than those who did not report a violent response, they also reported significantly more assaults (ie a higher frequency). Those who did not respond violently to the 2004 low provocation permutations reported fewer than one in that same year, while those who reported a violent response reported almost five assaults on average (Table 8.17). This is also evidenced by the larger effect size between the violent and non-violent response groups for low provocation scenarios (compare Tables 8.14 and 8.17).

---

[25] Due to the small numbers in the analysis resulting from a low prevalence rate and a reduced sub-sample size, results are only reported here for self-reported assault; however, the same trends were evident for police-recorded assault and/or aggressive crime.

**Table 8.17  Self-reported assault frequency (same year) by scenario response (low provocation scenarios only)**

| Scenario year | Scenario response | Mean frequency | Ratio | T[a] | Prob. | Cohen's d |
|---|---|---|---|---|---|---|
| 2004 | *All responses* | *1.13* | | | | |
| | Non-violent | 0.68 | 6.87 | 3.58 | .001 | .79 |
| | Violent | 4.67 | | | | |
| 2006 | *All responses* | *1.45* | | | | |
| | Non-violent | 0.75 | 5.59 | 3.22 | .002 | .53 |
| | Violent | 4.19 | | | | |

[a] Non-parametric tests also found significant differences between the means. These were run because the assault frequency was highly skewed.

A small random subsample of 169 participants responded to a low provocation scenario in *both* 2004 and 2006, while 175 responded to high provocation scenarios in both years. Within the former low provocation group, nine participants reported violent behavioural responses to both scenarios, revealing extreme violent tendency (ie a low threshold), while 137 participants in the latter high provocation group reported non-violent behavioural intentions to both, suggesting a particularly high threshold for being provoked to see violence as an alternative.[26] Although the low threshold group was very small, they exhibited marked differences in their behavioural outcomes compared to the high threshold group. All nine low threshold participants self-reported acts of assault in 2004, compared to just one-fifth of the high threshold group, and were 7.13 times more likely to have self-reported assault in 2006. These nine reported a Phase 1 mean frequency of 34 assaults, more than five times the expected rate for the sample, while the high threshold group reported a mean frequency of only three assaults. Of the nine low threshold participants, two had a police record for violent or aggressive crime during Phase 1, compared to only four of the 137 high threshold participants.

[26] There may be others in the PADS+ cohort who would be equally extreme in their judgements, but it is not possible to identify them because only a small subsample were presented with either the low provocation permutation of both the 2004 and 2006 scenarios, or the high provocation permutation of both the 2004 and 2006 scenarios (due to the randomization of scenario permutations).

## Differences between the 2004 and 2006 scenarios and behavioural outcomes

Earlier findings detailed in this chapter showed that the 2006 scenario was more conducive to violent responses than the 2004 scenario (Figure 8.1), particularly for participants with a low crime propensity (Figure 8.3). Differences between the scenarios might, in part, underlie the stronger association between violent scenario response and violent behavioural outcomes for 2004 than 2006. In particular, the violent response option for 2004 (hit) was more serious than for 2006 (push or hit), which meant participants were more likely to see violence as an option in 2006 (see section 8.3.1 for discussion). This means that a violent response to the 2004 scenario may identify participants and settings that are particularly conducive to more serious violence. Consistent with this, fewer participants willing to consider a violent response to the 2006 scenario reported an actual involvement in violence than those willing to consider a violent response to the 2004 scenario (44 per cent versus 57.1 per cent; see Table 8.13). Similarly, violent responses to the 2004 scenario were more strongly associated with official sanctions for assault and aggressive crimes than violent responses to the 2006 scenario (Table 8.15). The difference between the crime prevalence and frequency of those responding violently to ány permutation and those who responded violently to low provocation permutations was also more marked for the 2004 than the 2006 scenario. Taken together, these findings suggest the 2004 scenario may have been more sensitive to real-world violent tendencies than the 2006 scenario.

Comparison of the scenario response data with self-reported assault and police-recorded assault and/or aggressive crime data shows a significant and consistent association between behavioural intentions and behavioural outcomes. Participants' tendency to report they would commit an act of violence in response to a hypothetical scenario was reflected in their actual violent crime involvement.

In chapter 7 we showed that acts of crime occurred when certain kinds of people interacted with certain kinds of settings; our scenario data suggests that that interaction follows the model proposed by SAT by which key personal characteristics and features of settings interact to lead people to see and choose certain action alternatives. We would assume, then, that the self-reported and police-recorded acts of violence analysed here arise through the same perception–choice process in the same kinds of (crime-conducive, criminogenic) settings. That we can tap into that process using scenarios has important implications.

## 8.5  Summary and conclusion

While SAT proposes that it is the person–environment interaction that causes acts of crime to occur, the theory also proposes that this happens through a perception–choice process. In this chapter we tapped into this process for the first time, partially testing it using randomized violence scenarios to explore the role of motivators and deterrents. We found that higher levels of provocation, and lower levels of monitoring, were consistently viewed as more conducive to crime. Levels of provocation also proved more important to outcomes than levels of monitoring.

Young people with a high crime propensity were more likely to report violent behavioural intentions to any scenario permutations, and reported the most violent behavioural intentions to the most criminogenic permutations. Young people with a low crime propensity had a high threshold for perceiving violence as an alternative, which led them to report very few violent behavioural intentions, even to the most criminogenic permutations, whereas young people with a high crime propensity had a much lower threshold and perceived violence as an alternative even when levels of provocations were low.

As is rarely shown in similar scenario research, we were able to link young people's reports of violent behavioural intentions to their actual behaviours. Young people who reported violent behavioural intentions, especially to permutations with low levels of provocation, were more likely to have self-reported offences and to have a police record for violent crime. They also self-reported more acts of violent crime.

# PART 4

# The Dynamics of Rule-Breaking: Key Findings

# 9

# It's All About Interactions

It is difficult to imagine human action as anything other than an outcome of the interaction between a person and his or her environment. People do what they do because of who they are and the features of the settings in which they take part. Yet criminology still tends to be divided, theoretically and empirically, into person-oriented and environment-oriented approaches. Moreover, criminology lacks a satisfactory and generally accepted action theory that can help explain how (through what processes) the interplay between relevant personal and environmental factors affects people's acts of crime. What is needed to advance our knowledge about crime and its causes is an analytical approach that integrates key insights from person-oriented and environment-oriented theory and research within a framework of an adequate action theory, and provides clear testable implications.

In this book we have presented a new theory (Situational Action Theory (SAT)) that aims to explain the role of the person–environment interaction in crime causation, new methodologies (a space-time budget combined with a small area community survey) developed to help better study the person–environment interaction empirically, and key findings from Phase 1 (early and mid adolescence) of the Peterborough Adolescent and Young Adult Development Study (PADS+), a longitudinal study of around 700 young people in Peterborough (with a retention rate of 97 per cent over Phase 1), designed to test key propositions of SAT. Although this is a study of young people, there is no reason to believe the proposed processes explaining crime involvement would be any different for people at other ages.

## 9.1 Breaking rules

According to SAT, acts of crime are conceptualized as actions that break rules of conduct stated in law. Breaking a rule of law during early and mid adolescence was not unusual (chapter 3). Most young people reported that they had committed acts of crime, albeit, for the most part, only occasionally and of a less serious nature. A sizeable group of young people (nearly a third) also reported no crime involvement. At the other extreme, a small group of offenders started offending early in life (generally before the age of 12), were persistent and versatile in their criminality, and were responsible for the bulk of their age group's crime involvement, particularly in regard to more serious crimes. This latter group was also more likely to have a police record.

Crime involvement thus varies substantially among young people, from those who have committed no acts of crime, to those who commit occasional acts of crime, to those who commit acts of crime on a regular basis. The crucial question is *why* young people (and some much more than others) break rules of conduct stated in law.

## 9.2 It's all about interactions

The basic assumption of SAT (as outlined in chapter 1) is that acts of crime are the outcome of a perception–choice process initiated by the interaction between a person's crime propensity (determined by a person's morality and ability to exercise self-control) and exposure to criminogenic settings (determined by the setting's moral norms and their enforcement). Our findings suggest that the person–environment interaction is critical to understanding the causes of young people's crime and the patterns of young people's crime in an urban environment. We have shown that acts of crime are largely an outcome of what kinds of people take part in what kinds of settings.

*First*, we can demonstrate that *people* who have a high crime propensity and more exposure to criminogenic settings have a greater crime involvement (chapter 3). Based on the theoretical propositions of SAT, we devised measures of young people's crime propensity (a combined index of their morality and ability to exercise self-control) and criminogenic exposure (time spent in unstructured peer-oriented activities in the city or local centres or residential areas with poor collective efficacy). Our findings show that both crime propensity and criminogenic exposure were strongly correlated with young people's crime involvement, and, crucially, that there was a strong interaction effect in that levels of criminogenic exposure predicted crime involvement only for young people with higher crime propensities. Young people with a low crime propensity appeared to be highly resistant to criminogenic influences from the environment.

*Second*, we can demonstrate that *areas* (settings) that have a high presence of crime prone people *as well as* a high level of criminogenic characteristics have a greater concentration of crime (chapter 6). We identified as key criminogenic environments areas characterized by commerce and entertainment (ie the city and local centres) and, in the case of residential areas, poor collective efficacy (which was closely related to key population structural characteristics, especially social disadvantage; see chapter 4). Further analyses showed that within these social environments, key criminogenic settings included shopping locales and outdoor public spaces, and key criminogenic features of settings included the presence of delinquent peers and a lack of structured activities and adult supervision (chapter 6). More young offenders lived in disadvantaged residential areas with poor collective efficacy than in other residential areas. Crucially, we found that an area's number of resident young offenders was related to the number of resident crime prone young people (ie, young people with a weak law-relevant morality and poor ability to exercise self-control; see chapter 5). Hence an area's number of resident offenders reflects its number of crime prone residents. Although a large part of young people's crime occurred close to home, this is far from the complete picture. An exploration of young people's activity fields (see chapter 6) showed that they are highly localized and that 92 per cent of young people's activities occurred within 500 metres of certain key locations (their home, school, three best friends' homes, nearest local centre, and the city centre); moreover, 77 per cent of their crimes were committed within 500 metres of these same locations (see chapter 7).

*Third*, we can demonstrate that crimes actually tend to occur when people with a high crime propensity *converge* with criminogenic settings (chapter 7). A problem with previous analyses of the person—environment interaction is they do not demonstrate that a particular person (with a particular crime propensity) is actually in a particular setting (with particular criminogenic features) when he or she commits an act of crime. The space-time budget methodology, combined with data from a small area community survey and questionnaire data about personal characteristics (see chapter 2 for details), makes such an analysis possible. Our findings clearly show that crime prone young people predominantly offended when they were in criminogenic settings. However, our findings also show that even if crime prone young people committed most of their offences in criminogenic settings (as we have defined them), they did not offend during most of the time they spent in such settings. There are apparently also other important factors that affect settings' criminogeneity and the extent to which they trigger acts of crime. For example, we have not measured social-psychological factors, such as those that relate to social relationships and group dynamics. These factors may be critical for uncovering why crimes occur when crime prone young people converge with a particular criminogenic setting at one point in time, but not at another. Observational studies or interviews may be able to provide this kind of data. Another important factor that we have not explored is the role of substance use, which may be particularly pertinent when it comes to acts of violence and vandalism. A final set of factors we have not taken into account is differential levels of motivators (temptations and provocations) across settings. Future studies investigating any of these factors may complement our findings with a more in-depth understanding of the social psychology of criminogenic settings and the role of substance use and temptations and provocations, and thus help to refine the measurement of criminogenic settings.

*Fourth*, by using randomized scenarios we are able to show that young people with a high crime propensity were more likely to see crime as an alternative even in the least criminogenic settings, while those with a low crime propensity rarely saw crime as an alternative even in the most criminogenic settings (chapter 8). These findings are entirely consistent with SAT's proposed perception–choice process, which states that the person–environment interaction leads to acts of crime because it encourages people to see, and choose, crime as an action alternative. Moreover, we were also able to link young people's reports of violent behavioural intentions to their actual behaviours, which has rarely been established before, demonstrating the real-world significance of these scenario-based findings.

The main findings summarized above support key propositions of SAT (chapter 1). Crucially, we have shown that some young people appear to be largely situationally resistant to criminogenic influences from the environment, while others are highly situationally vulnerable to such influences. Our findings also demonstrate that it is a high rate of convergence between crime prone people and criminogenic settings that is responsible for the crime hotspots we observe in the urban landscape.

One key implication of these findings is that research that focuses purely on people or environments in explaining crime runs the risk of drawing incomplete or even incorrect conclusions. Focusing on relevant aspects of people and environments (and their kinds of interactions) means that crime policy and prevention resources can be better targeted to where they have the greatest effect. Arguably, our study makes a good case for the value of multidisciplinary approaches to the study of crime and its prevention. The most effective ways to change young people's crime involvement, according to SAT and our findings, which support it, will be through (1) measures that influence the development of their morality (moral rules and moral emotions) and ability to exercise self-control; and (2) measures that influence the moral norms, and their enforcement, of the settings in which they take part, in ways that make them less likely to see and choose crime as an action alternative. Changing relevant aspects of the person and/or the environments in which he or she takes part (changing the nature of their interaction) will change the *input* into the perception–choice process that is crucial for whether or not a person will see and choose an act of crime as an action alternative when responding to temptations or provocations. The full prevention implications of SAT and the findings from PADS+ research will be discussed elsewhere (eg, Wikström 2012).

As Ruth Kornhauser observes in her seminal study *The social sources of delinquency*, there is a need 'to search for the root causes of delinquency in social structure and situation' (1978: 235). In this book we have taken up this challenge by introducing a new integrative theory (Situational Action Theory) that links people, situations, and environments in an action theory framework, and beginning to test some of its key propositions about the social and situational dynamics of crime causation.

We have theorized (chapter 1), and explored, the *social dynamics* of young people's urban crime, that is, studied how the urban structure (patterns of residential segregation and activity differentiation), through processes of social selection, place different kinds of young people in different settings (see chapters 4 and 5, and particularly chapter 6), which, in turn, create the particular *situational dynamics* (interactions between crime prone young people and criminogenic settings) that explain why crime events happen (chapters 7 and 8) and why they are concentrated in certain locations (hot spots) in the urban landscape (chapter 6).

Our main focus in this book has remained on the situation and the contemporaneous social processes (selection) that create situations; future work needs to build upon this foundation to explore the role of processes of social and personal emergence (in its broader political-economical context) in crime causation: (1) the historical processes by which, for example, particular content and patterns of residential segregation and activity differentiation emerge that create different kinds of urban social and moral contexts (social emergence), and (ii) the developmental processes through which people acquire particular crime propensities (upon a biological foundation) as a consequence of their particular life-historical exposure to moral education and cognitive nurturing in different social and moral contexts (personal emergence).

# Appendices

# A1

# Technical Appendix

## A1.1 Calculating distance

Straight-line distances between points[1] (eg crimes, homes) were calculated using Easting and Northing coordinates on the British National Grid coordinate system. Where point data was unavailable (eg space–time budget data) central coordinates of the output area were used as proxy coordinates. The geographical rounding error introduced by this method is minor, due to the fact that output areas are generally very small (see Table 2.10) and the coordinates used represented their population adjusted centres.[2] The location (output area population-centred coordinates) of participants' main homes were used when calculating distance from home to activity (including crime) location using space–time budget data. This does not take into account young people's alternative homes (where some young people may have been living at the time of the activity in question).

## A1.2 Presentation of spatial data

In this book we use a number of mapping techniques to illustrate the spatial distribution of, and identify and compare particular areas of interest for, a range of environmental and social features (eg land use, disadvantage) and behavioural outcomes (eg crimes, activities).[3] Mapping techniques vary in their applicability, advantages,

---

[1] Euclidean metrics given by the Pythagorean formula.

[2] Taking account of the spatial distribution of residents in this way is particularly useful for output areas that are mostly rural but contain the edges or corners of settlements, especially as these output areas are largest (due to design of output areas) and therefore the most problematic for assuming the geographic centre as a proxy for location.

[3] Maps and spatial data analysis contained in this book were produced using Mapinfo Professional, v.7.8, © Mapinfo Corporation; and CrimestatIII, 3.2a (see Levine 2006).

and limitations (for an overview see Chainey and Ratcliffe 2005; Eck et al. 2005; Haining 2003; Harries 1999; Ratcliffe 2010). Thematic mapping of data aggregated to the output area (OA) level and kernel density estimation using point data were selected as the most appropriate methods for this study. All maps presented in this book use Digitised Boundary Data from the 2001 Census[4] to show the boundaries of the 518 output areas that make up the Peterborough Community Survey (PCS) study area.

As with all maps, it is essential when interpreting these maps to remember the assumptions, parameters, design decisions, and original data (quality and quantity) that have produced them (avoiding what Eck et al. (2005) termed the 'visual lure of the image'). The chloropleth and kernel density estimation maps of the spatial distribution of environmental characteristics, crimes, offender homes, and activities presented in this book are provided for visual interpretation alongside other analytical methods and statistical models, against a backdrop of knowledge about geographical and structural characteristics of the study area and particular places and locations in the city.

### A1.2.1  Chloropleth (thematic) mapping

We use chloropleth maps to present data aggregated to the output area level, such as census and PCS data. These data are displayed using thematic thresholds (class boundaries) that are carefully selected to minimize interpretation error. For example, the distributions of selected characteristics that are measured at the area level (land use, disadvantage, poor collective efficacy, disorder, and prostitution) are displayed in chapter 4, using thematic thresholds (five groups of equal range) designed to highlight key areas. In contrast, the distributions of young people's activities shown in chapter 6 are skewed to a small number of output areas so class boundaries were selected on the basis of standard deviations as opposed to equal ranges.

One drawback of chloropleth maps is that readers can be drawn erroneously to large areas (Eck et al. 2005: 24) and therefore be visually misled as to the existence, location, and extent of concentrations. The data presented in this book almost always refers to the urban part of the output area and therefore chloropleth maps

---

[4] England and Wales, Office for National Statistics, © Crown Copyright 2003.

of aggregated area level data could mislead readers due to the size of some predominantly rural output areas. To reduce this problem, the boundaries of a small number of predominantly rural output areas that contained very few or no address points were altered for presentation purposes (Figure A1.1).

Maps using aggregated data also suffer from the modifiable areal unit problem (Openshaw 1984) whereby 'the results of any

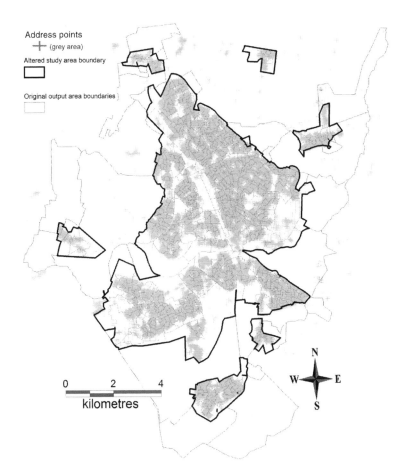

**Figure A1.1  Original and altered output area boundaries and address point locations**[a]

[a] Address point locations are reproduced by permission of Ordinance Survey on behalf of HMSO.
© Crown copyright and database right 2005. All rights reserved.

geographic aggregation process, such as the count of crimes within a set of geographic boundaries, may be as much a function of the size, shape and orientation of the geographic areas as it is of the spatial distribution of the crime data. In essence, when thematically mapped, different boundaries may generate different visual interpretations of where the hotspots may exist' (Chainey and Ratcliffe 2005: 151–2). Although unavoidable, this problem is much reduced by using such small area units as output areas. When interpreting thematic maps it is also important to avoid drawing conclusions about, for example, the residents of an area or locations within an area based on aggregate information about the area (the ecological fallacy; see W. S. Robinson 1950).

The exception to mapping aggregate (output area) data using thematic maps is Figure 7.1, when the population centre was used as proxy coordinates for space–time budget crimes (measured at the output area level) in order to layer the resultant point locations over a continuous surface map (see below) of police-recorded youth crimes (point data), and show both layers clearly on one map. As the introduced error is so small, discrepancies are only evident for locations in the largest output areas (eg those containing Hampton Centre and Thorpe Wood Police Station).

### A1.2.2 Hotspot mapping (quartic kernel density estimation)

Where point data is available, such as for police-recorded crime, kernel density estimation maps are most suitable as they may capture the greater detail of such data, avoiding problems associated with thematic mapping of aggregated data (see Chainey and Ratcliffe 2005; Chainey et al. 2008; Eck et al. 2005; Ratcliffe 2010). The single variable quartic kernel density estimation method used in this book is one of five density estimation routines available in CrimeStatIII and creates a smooth continuous surface that represents the density and spatial variation of points (eg crimes or addresses) that are distributed across the study area. In crime mapping, the resultant surfaces are often called hotspot maps in which 'a hotspot is a geographical area of higher than average crime. It is an area of crime concentration, relative to the distribution of crime across the whole region of interest' (Chainey and Ratcliffe 2005: 145–6). Such maps therefore show areas of higher and lower relative density, meaning they can be compared for differences and similarities in distribution, but not volume.[5] The thematic ranges of high and low densities displayed in this book are determined using standard deviations of the grid cells' data.[6]

Hotspots are established by determining the strength of spatial relationships, based on the premise of Tobler's (1970) first law of geography that 'everything is related to everything else, but closer things are more related' (spatial dependence). Firstly, a fine grid is created and laid over the distribution of points within the study area. The size of the cells in this grid determines the resolution and how 'grainy' the surface will appear. In order for the output to appear as smooth as possible, the study area, which is approximately 12 kilometres wide, was divided into 800 columns, providing a very fine cell width of approximately 15 metres.[7]

Secondly, intensity values for each point are then calculated within a specified search radius (bandwidth). The selection of this bandwidth has a large impact on the visual output generated from kernel density estimation, which is important as 'hotspots are often clusters of crime that can exist at different scales of interest' (Chainey and Ratcliffe 2005: 146).[8] In general, this book aims to

[5] In contrast to some other studies using the hotspots method, our primary concern was not to identify and quantify the location, relative scale, size, shape, and extent of areas of relative density (hotspots). As a result, this book will not look to Local Indicators of Spatial Association (LISA statistics) that compare local averages to global averages and highlight statistically significant differences (such as Moran's *I* and Geary's *C*, and Getis and Ord GI and GI* statistics).

[6] In Mapinfo Professional (v.7.8), the standard deviation method of creating ranges places the mean of all the cell values at the middle of the range. The ranges above or below the middle range therefore represent standard deviation(s) above or below the mean respectively. The thematic ranges of the kernel density estimation maps in this book divide the cells into 10 groups based on standard deviations, with only the groups above the mean shown shaded (grey to black) on the maps. Therefore, cells with values below the mean are white, while those above the mean are divided into five groups (the lightest group representing values from the mean to one standard deviation above the mean and the darkest group values more than four standard deviations above the mean).

[7] Chainey and Ratcliffe (2005) report an arbitrary convention to divide the shortest side of the study area into 150 cells but this is more useful for larger data-sets where the generated file sizes would be too large and smoothness of resultant maps must be compromised. In the case of this study area, this convention would result in an 80-metre cell resolution and maps would not look smooth.

[8] There is no rule as to what a suitable bandwidth is; however, it is perfectly acceptable to experiment with different bandwidth values to look at variation in the resultant surface at different scales (Bailey and Gatrell 1995), and also to refer to the geographic scale at which the hotspots need to be identified in order

show the impact of structural features and individual activity patterns on the geographical distribution of crime at the small area level. As a result, the kernel density estimation surfaces (hotspot maps) in this book were created using a bandwidth of 400 metres to reflect the small size of output areas (see Table 2.10) and make it possible to investigate (in conjunction with other data and analysis) the kinds of places around which the relative crime or activity density is highest.

Thirdly, within each 15-metre grid cell, these intensity values calculated with the 400-metre search radius are then weighted by the mathematical routine, whereby points closer to the centre contribute more to the cell's total density value. Therefore, the final grid cell values of the quartic kernel density estimation are a sum of the weighted values of all kernel estimates for each location, and represent crimes per square area (in our case, kilometres; for more information on the kernel density estimation method, see Bailey and Gatrell 1995; Chainey and Ratcliffe 2005; Eck et al. 2005; Levine 2006).

Although some sources warn that kernel density estimation maps can become misleading when based on a small number of points, there is no clear consensus as to how small a sample is too small. We assert that if the spatial distribution of even a small number of data points are significantly (and in some cases very strongly) clustered, it is still meaningful to visualize the relative density of these points using a kernel density estimation map. Some of the hotspot maps shown in this book (eg Figure 5.3) were created from only a small number of points[9] but in these cases Nearest Neighbour global tests (NNA; results not shown) confirm that clustering is significant. However, as with other methods of data presentation using a small number of observations, conclusions using these

---

to inform the bandwidth selection (Chainey and Ratcliffe 2005). As a result, the bandwidth should be selected with theory-driven aims in mind (Eck et al. 2005). A lower bandwidth allows a fine detail visualization of patterns useful for analysis of crime distributions related to routine activities (eg street corners or around specific address locations), whereas large bandwidths lead to a surface map showing a broader view of crime distribution across the study area, which might be more useful for ecological analysis (eg to compare neighbourhoods and townships in terms of their crime).

[9] Care was taken that the details of individual crimes and the locations of individual homes are not identifiable for reasons of confidentiality.

representations are cautious as the data may be less stable and contain more error.

## A1.3  Controlling for resident young people

The number of residents in an area is superfluous to the relationship between the number of resident offenders and the volume of offences (unless one expects that an area's population will differentially affect the crime rate of its resident offenders, a different question altogether). It is therefore unnecessary to control for population when carrying out this kind of analysis. Yet offender rates and crime rates are often correlated using area population as a common denominator, despite a lack of good rationale, and the fact that this shared component may actually obscure the relationship (Bollen and Ward 1980: 63–9).

On the other hand, in analyses that aim to explicate the number of resident offenders in a particular area (eg through particular causes of the causes of crime, such as an area's structural characteristics), it is important to control for the total population (and, when one is interested in resident young offenders, the number of resident young people), as population is a potentially confounding explanatory factor (it is unimpressive to conclude there are more young offenders in an area because there are more young people). In these kinds of analyses, one would ideally use an area's total population (or the total population of the target group) as an additional explanatory variable, rather than controlling for it as a common denominator (see also Bollen and Ward 1980: 60–79, for more on why and how to avoid indiscriminate use of ratios). By including population as an explanatory variable, one would subsequently not only take into account its influence on the number of resident offenders, but also analyse its unique contribution to the explanation of their concentration in particular areas.

In practice, controlling for the resident population is challenging at the output area level. We have therefore used a variety of methods to account for the number of young people, at this and more amenable levels of analysis. The only reliable data regarding the number of Peterborough residents per output area comes from the 2001 UK census, but it is clear that the resident population has changed between 2001 and the period covered by police-recorded young people's crime (2004–07), in some output areas quite significantly (see section 4.3.2). To derive the most comparable measure to our count of offender home locations, we utilized the count of resident young people in each output area who were 9 (turning 10) to 13 (turning 14) years old in 2001, and would therefore be (12 turning) 13 to (16 turning) 17 years old in 2004, the beginning of the study period.[10]

The distribution of offender home locations at the output area level proved to be modestly but significantly related to the number of resident young people ($r = .37, p = .000$)—the more young people who lived in an output area, the more young offenders (as is to be expected). This modest relationship makes it clear that the distribution of young offenders is not solely (or even substantially) driven by population density.

Counts of young people and young offenders per output area were very small, meaning that minor discrepancies had large and misleading implications. Each output area had, on average, only 21 resident young people aged 9–13 in 2001 (to a maximum of 66), and 2.5 resident police-recorded young offenders between 2004 and 2007 (to a maximum of 18). These numbers serve as a proximate gauge for *relative* rates between output areas, and therefore provide only a general impression of the number of resident young people and resident young offenders; they should not be taken to indicate actual rates (eg that, on average, one in 10 resident young people living in each output area was a young offender). Not only were the numbers very small, they were also measured at different times and calculated using different methods, such that census data reflects the distribution of five year groups in a single year (2001), while young offender data reflects eight year groups over a period varying from one to four years (commencing at any time between 2004 and 2007). For these data to be comparable in *scale*, one must assume a level of stability in where young people live, both at the personal and population level, which is unrealistic.

The problems with using this data for anything but relative rates is reflected in the fact that four output areas had more resident

---

[10] Using 9- to 13-year-olds captured the fact that, to some extent, the same young people stay in the same output areas while they age. We also explored the count of resident young people who were (12 turning) 13 to (16 turning) 17 in 2001, which captured stability in the age composition of people living in certain output areas. The two variables were highly correlated ($r = .75$), which meant comparative analyses were reasonably similar. We have chosen to use the count of 9- to 13-year-olds as it is conceptually more appropriate and also more strongly related to offender counts (hence, if anything, we overestimate its impact).

young offenders than resident young people according to these measures; one output area (in the Hamptons) had three times as many due to a clear and dramatic increase in its resident population since 2001. Thus for many analyses, census data may not be reliable enough to use as a measure of population, at least at the output area level. We have consequently developed other methods for analysing the rate of young offenders where necessary and, in many instances, focused on counts instead.

## A1.4  Quantifying time use

Quantifying space–time budget data is complex. As detailed in chapter 2, space–time budget data was collected for each young person in each year and each interview covered four days: the most recent Friday, Saturday and two additional weekdays (see Table 2.6). Although 'weekdays' refers specifically to Monday through Thursday, data from Friday is included in some analyses, where indicated, as the earlier half of Friday closely resembles other weekdays. However, Friday and Saturday are generally treated as unique days, as they present different overall patterns of time use (see section 2.5.1).

For each day, data was collected from 06:00 to 06:00 the following morning (eg Friday data included hourly data from 06:00 Friday to 06:00 Saturday). This means that any activity that occurred overnight may not be measured continuously, as it will be cut off at 06:00 the following morning. This is most problematic for measures of time spent sleeping (see section 6.1.1) but is also relevant for activities such as time spent awake with peers (for example, at a party or a club) that continued beyond 06:00 (although this amounts to fewer than 50 cases across 13,748 interview days over five years of data).

For some analyses we have subdivided days into the 10 hours between 06:00 and 16:00, and the 14 hours between 16:00 and 06:00 the following morning (for ease of presentation we refer to the former as daytime and the latter as evening time). This division captures significant differences between how time was spent before and after school on weekdays, and before and after early afternoon on weekends. This division was selected based on analysis of key changes in young people's activity patterns observable particularly after they left school on weekdays but also on weekends (see Figure 6.1 and Table 6.8). Although evening hours are traditionally conceptualized based on adult activity patterns, which demonstrate their most significant changes later in the day following normal working hours, our conceptualization captures the beginning of young people's divergent time use after school. Daytime and evening time cover different time-spans, but this is not problematic as (1) most analyses account for different rates of exposure, and (2) young people spent differing amounts of time awake in the day or evening depending on how late they slept in or stayed up (eg young people slept for many of the evening hours), therefore the two cannot and need not be equivalent.

Time use is presented in a number of ways. Exposure to particular kinds of settings is quantified using a count of hours spent by young people in those particular settings (see section 3.3.1). In many analyses we show the proportion of time spent in a particular activity in order to put certain kinds of time use into context (for example, with time use across the rest of a day, or time use in comparable activities), as well as to account for differences in group size (and hence the raw count of hours) in some comparisons. For some analyses we also report the average number of hours and/or minutes young people spent per day doing a particular kind of activity. To calculate this we have taken the mean for all (relevant) days of data collected using the space–time budget. Because each young person provided four days of data per wave (see section 2.5), there is a risk when running averages per day of under-representing the activity patterns of young people who did not take part in all five waves. While it is possible to analyse days from the individual level by first calculating the average time per day per young person, this intermediary step proved unnecessary because of the study's high retention rate (see section 2.2.3); 'average hours per day' was virtually equivalent to 'average hours per average day per participant'.

# A2

# Space–Time Budget Coding Appendix

This appendix presents the item lists and numerical codes used to record setting circumstances in PADS+ space–time budget interviews (see section 2.5 for details about the space–time budget methodology). Researchers used these lists to record a code for each domain (activity, functional place, people present, and any extra incidents occurring), for each hour of the interview period, based on participants' retrospective reports. To aid real-time coding during the interview, the items are divided into categories within each domain, with examples and notes provided where necessary. The combination of codes from each of the domains allows for very complex constructions of the circumstances of the hour while minimizing the number of codes within each domain. These codes have been specifically designed for use with the adolescents in our UK sample but most are applicable to other populations, and for reasons of replication, additions (and not deletions and alterations) should be made sparingly.[11] Consequently, while it was essential to retain comparability over time, to ensure items remained age relevant as participants aged, new items were added, but only in a way that they could be aggregated into single items that were consistent across all waves. For example, many of the employment items were added once the participants completed compulsory education, and, as participants became parents, the items detailing people present were extended to accommodate the presence of their children.

---

[11] At first inspection the item lists may appear to lack the detail necessary to capture some settings and circumstances and researchers may be tempted to add items, but it is in the combination of the domains that the context of the setting is recorded.

## A2.1 Activity

Activity refers to the main activity that occupies most of the hour. See section 2.5.1 for more details about secondary and brief activities.

---

**Domestic**

| | |
|---|---|
| Housework/chores (including cooking as a chore) | 11 |
| Gardening | 12 |
| Shopping (domestic and leisure) | 13 |
| Child care (unpaid) | 14 |
| Adult care | 15 |
| Pet care | 16 |
| Walking the dog | 17 |
| Other (including cooking for leisure) | 18 |

**Personal**

| | |
|---|---|
| Eating | 21 |
| Sleeping | 22 |
| Personal care (eg washing, dressing) | 23 |
| Medical care (appointments and treatment) | 24 |
| Ill in bed/on sofa | 25 |
| Dental care | 26 |
| Other | 20 |

**Educational**

| | |
|---|---|
| Classes and lectures | 31 |
| Homework | 32 |
| Vocational training/apprenticeship | 34 |
| Other (including detention, meetings, driving lessons) | 33 |

**Work**

| | |
|---|---|
| Voluntary work | 42 |
| Work experience | 43 |
| Construction/manual labour | 411 |
| Retail/sales | 412 |
| Catering/kitchen work | 413 |
| Hospitality/service (food/drink) | 414 |
| Engineering/electronics | 415 |
| Motor vehicle | 416 |

---

| | |
|---|---|
| Hairdressing | 417 |
| Manufacturing | 418 |
| Office work | 419 |
| Care and health | 420 |
| Other (paid) | 41 |
| **Individual sport** | |
| Boxing | 511 |
| Martial arts | 512 |
| Tennis | 513 |
| Golf | 514 |
| Motor sports | 515 |
| Badminton | 516 |
| Table-tennis | 517 |
| Athletics | 518 |
| Workout/gym class | 27 |
| Other (eg swimming, horse riding, cycling for fitness) | 519 |
| **Team sport** | |
| Rugby | 521 |
| Football | 522 |
| Cricket | 523 |
| Ice hockey | 524 |
| Land hockey | 525 |
| Basketball/netball | 526 |
| Other | 520 |
| **Clubs/societies[a]** | |
| Drama | 531 |
| Dance/orchestra/band practice | 532 |
| Art/photography/multimedia | 533 |
| Computer club | 534 |
| Guides/scouts | 535 |
| Cadets | 536 |
| Church/religious (including praying or other religious activity) | 537 |
| Political | 538 |
| Other specified club/society/organization | 539 |

*(continued)*

**Hobbies/games**

| | |
|---|---|
| Hobbies (eg collecting, painting, writing) | 541 |
| Rollerblading/ice-skating/skateboarding | 542 |
| Cycling/BMX (as a hobby) | 543 |
| Bowling | 544 |
| Darts | 545 |
| Snooker | 546 |
| Traditional games (eg board games, tag, playground) | 547 |
| Computer/console games | 548 |
| Computers (eg burning music, programming) | 549 |
| Internet (browsing) | 550 |
| Fishing | 551 |
| Fairground/theme park | 552 |
| Playing a musical instrument (including a lesson) | 553 |
| Laser quest | 554 |
| Quad bike/scooter/motocross | 555 |
| Other | 540 |

**Media consumption**

| | |
|---|---|
| Television | 561 |
| Film (TV, DVD, cinema) | 562 |
| Cartoons | 563 |
| Magazine | 564 |
| Newspaper | 565 |
| Books (excluding religious text or school work) | 566 |
| Radio/music | 567 |
| Other | 560 |

**Socializing**

| | |
|---|---|
| Face to face/hanging around/socializing | 571 |
| Phone | 572 |
| Electronic (eg email, chat rooms, IM, social networking) | 573 |
| Texting | 574 |
| Party (including house party and funeral wake) | 575 |
| Sexual activity (including alone) | 576 |
| Night clubbing | 577 |
| Other (eg writing a letter) | 570 |

**Miscellaneous**

| | |
|---|---|
| Inactive[b] | 58 |
| Transportation[c] | 59 |
| Cultural activities (eg museum) | 60 |
| Live entertainment/show/concert | 601 |
| Official meeting/appointment with a social authority (eg youth worker) | 61 |
| Watching live sport in person (ie not on TV) | 62 |

[a] For time spent at youth clubs, code the main activity, eg snooker.
[b] Inactive should be rarely used and refers only to doing nothing at all, not necessarily on one's own, but involving no form of activity/socializing, eg queuing/waiting.
[c] Excludes where socializing is the main activity and is reserved mainly for direct travel. Do not use for physical exercise or hobbies.

## A2.2  Place

Place refers to the *functional place* and is therefore often related to the ongoing activity. For example, in the same shop a participant who is shopping would be coded as in a shopping locale, while a participant who is working would be coded as in a workplace.

**Residential**

| | |
|---|---|
| Home | 10 |
| Alternative home (eg other parent's home) | 11 |
| Others' home | 20 |

**School**

| | |
|---|---|
| Classroom | 31 |
| Other place in school buildings (eg corridors, headmaster's office, dinner hall) | 32 |
| Outdoors school grounds (eg school field, including during sports lesson) | 33 |

**Shops/shopping arcades**

| | |
|---|---|
| Queensgate Shopping Centre (City centre) | 41 |
| Rivergate Shopping Centre (City centre) | 42 |
| Serpentine Green Shopping Centre (Hampton Centre) | 44 |
| Market | 45 |
| Other | 43 |

*(continued)*

**Entertainment**

| | |
|---|---|
| Games arcades | 51 |
| Theatre | 52 |
| Cinema | 53 |
| Pub/bar | 54 |
| Disco/club | 55 |
| Restaurant/cafe/takeaway | 56 |
| Theme park/fairground | 57 |
| Youth club/community centre | 58 |
| Library | 59 |
| Other | 50 |

**Sport**

| | |
|---|---|
| Peterborough United Football Club | 61 |
| Rugby ground | 62 |
| Cricket ground | 63 |
| Athletics ground | 64 |
| Ice rink | 65 |
| Snooker club | 66 |
| Golf course | 67 |
| BMX track | 68 |
| Sports/leisure centre | 69 |
| Lido/outdoor swimming pool | 70 |
| Indoor swimming pool | 71 |
| Bowling alley | 72 |
| Football ground/pitch | 73 |
| Skate park (indoors) | 74 |
| Shooting range | 75 |
| Hockey pitch | 76 |
| Tennis courts | 77 |
| Basketball courts | 78 |
| Laser quest | 79 |
| Other | 70 |

**Streets, squares and places** (use moving around codes if not stationary)

| | |
|---|---|
| Streets/street corner | 81 |
| Parks/recreation grounds/fields/forests/beach/outdoor skate park | 82 |
| Car park | 83 |
| Petrol station/garage | 84 |
| Industrial estate | 85 |
| Bus station/stop | 86 |
| Railway station | 87 |
| Airport | 88 |
| Other | 89 |

**Official building**

| | |
|---|---|
| Police station | 91 |
| Social services locale | 92 |
| Youth justice locale | 93 |
| Court | 94 |
| Other (including military base and prison) | 95 |

**Other** (do not use if workplace)

| | |
|---|---|
| Hospital | 101 |
| Doctors | 102 |
| Dentist | 103 |
| Hairdresser | 104 |
| Beauty salon | 105 |
| Church/religious centre | 106 |
| Hotel | 107 |
| Caravan site/holiday apartment | 108 |
| Other (eg museum or parent's office) | 109 |

**Moving around** (for use even if main activity is socializing)

| | |
|---|---|
| By foot | 111 |
| By bike | 112 |
| By moped/motorcycle | 113 |
| By car | 114 |

(continued)

| By bus | 115 |
|---|---|
| By train | 116 |
| By airplane | 117 |
| Other | 118 |
| **Workplace** (use only these place codes if working there oneself) | |
| Building site | 121 |
| Nursing home | 122 |
| Children's playgroup/nursery | 123 |
| Office | 124 |
| Hairdressers/beauty salon | 125 |
| Shop | 126 |
| Pub | 127 |
| Restaurant/café | 128 |
| Other person's house | 130 |
| Car garage | 131 |
| Factory | 132 |
| Other | 129 |

## A2.3  With whom

People present during an activity are divided into three main groups: family[12] (including participants' own children), peers and partners, and others (eg teachers, general public, parents' friends). Additional codes cover the myriad possible combinations of people from these groups (eg parents and friends; classmates and teacher; parent, doctor, and sibling; partner and partner's parent), many of which are duplicated to record whether a family adult or adult guardian is present (supervision). This results in some very specific codes, some of which are rarely used. To simplify the number of code combinations, we can also recommend coding the specific members present from each group separately (ie three separate code lists for family,

[12] In these code lists, a parent refers to biological, step, or adoptive parents.

peers, and others), which can capture the same detailed combinations of people and supervision and is entirely comparable.

**Alone**

| | |
|---|---|
| Alone (including in a public place) | 10 |

**Family only**

| | |
|---|---|
| Parents only (including step/adoptive parents) | 21 |
| Siblings only (if sibling is not in the role of guardian) | 22 |
| Parents + siblings only | 23 |
| Family, including adult (eg uncle, aunt, grandparent, adult sibling) | 24 |
| Family, not including adult (eg younger cousins) | 25 |
| Own child only | 26 |
| Own child + other family (including family adult) | 27 |
| Own child + other family (no family adult) | 28 |

**Family + partner**

| | |
|---|---|
| Including family adult (eg parents and partner) | 290 |
| No family adult (eg sibling and partner) | 291 |
| Own child + partner | 292 |
| Own child + partner + any other family | 293 |

**Peers only** (may also but not usually include peers who are strangers)

| | |
|---|---|
| 1 male peer | 31 |
| 1 female peer | 32 |
| 2 or more male peers | 33 |
| 2 or more female peers | 34 |
| Mixed male and female peers | 35 |

**Partner only**

| | |
|---|---|
| 1 male partner (boyfriend, husband) | 36 |
| 1 female partner (girlfriend, wife) | 37 |

**Peers + partner**

| | |
|---|---|
| Peers + partner | 38 |

**Others only**

| | |
|---|---|
| Including adult guardian (eg teacher, employer, or other responsible adult) | 41 |
| No adult guardian (eg babysitting) | 42 |

*(continued)*

**Partner + others**

| | |
|---|---|
| Including adult guardian (eg partner and doctor, or partner and partner's parent) | 43 |
| No adult guardian (eg partner and partner's sibling) | 44 |

**Family + peers**

| | |
|---|---|
| Including family adult (eg parents and peers) | 51 |
| No family adult (eg siblings and peers) | 52 |
| Including family adult and own child | 53 |
| Including own child (can also include other non-adult family) | 54 |

**Family + peers + partner**

| | |
|---|---|
| Including family adult (eg parents and partner and peers) | 55 |
| No family adult | 56 |
| Including family adult and own child | 57 |
| Including own child (can also include other non-adult family) | 58 |

**Family + others**

| | |
|---|---|
| Including family adult (eg parent and a parent's partner who is not a step-parent) | 61 |
| No family adult but including other adult guardian (eg cousin and adult family friend) | 62 |
| No family adult/adult guardian (eg sibling and someone else's child) | 63 |
| Including own child and family adult/adult guardian | 64 |
| Including own child but no family adult/adult guardian (eg own child and other's child) | 65 |

**Family + others + partner**

| | |
|---|---|
| Including family adult/adult guardian | 66 |
| No family adult/adult guardian | 67 |
| Including own child and family adult/adult guardian | 68 |
| Including own child but no family adult/adult guardian (eg own child, partner and other's child) | 69 |

**Peers + others**

| | |
|---|---|
| Including adult guardian (eg peers and a teacher, peers and their parents) | 71 |
| No adult guardian (eg a peer and their sibling) | 72 |

**Peers + others + partner**

| | |
|---|---|
| Including adult guardian | 73 |
| No adult guardian (eg partner, peers, and partner's child) | 74 |

**Family + peers + others**

| | |
|---|---|
| Including parents (eg parent, a parent's partner who is not a step-parent, and peers) | 81 |
| Including other adult guardian | 82 |
| No adult guardians (eg young family member, peer, and other small child) | 83 |

**Family + peers + partner + others**

| | |
|---|---|
| Including parents | 84 |
| Including other adult guardian | 85 |
| No adult guardian | 86 |

## A2.4  Extra incidents

Extra incidents are coded if they occur at any time, for any duration, during the hour (see section 2.5).

### A2.4.1 Alcohol and drug use

**Alcohol**

| | |
|---|---|
| Cider | 11 |
| Beer | 12 |
| Wine | 13 |
| Spirits | 14 |
| Other | 10 |
| Combination of alcohol | 15 |

**Drugs**

| | |
|---|---|
| Cannabis | 21 |
| Amphetamines, LSD, ecstasy, heroin, cocaine, crack cocaine, magic mushrooms | 23 |
| Inhalants (eg glue, aerosol spray, amyl nitrate) | 20 |
| Other | 22 |
| Combination of drugs | 30 |

## A2.4.2  Risky situations

| | |
|---|---|
| **Directly involved in an argument** | |
| Including threats | 11 |
| Not including threats | 12 |
| **Harassment/provocation** | |
| Being harassed/provoked—sexually | 20 |
| Being harassed/provoked—non-sexually | 21 |
| Harassing/provoking other—sexually | 31 |
| Harassing/provoking other—non-sexually | 32 |
| **Witnessing an argument** | |
| Including threats | 41 |
| Not including threats | 42 |
| **Witnessing harassment/provocation** | |
| Harassment/provocation—sexual | 61 |
| Harassment/provocation—non-sexual | 62 |
| **Witnessing violence** | 70 |

## A2.4.3  Victimization

| | |
|---|---|
| **Victimization—theft** | |
| Worth less than £5 | 11 |
| Worth between £5 and £25 | 12 |
| Worth between £25 and £99 | 13 |
| Worth £100 or more | 14 |
| Other/value unknown | 10 |
| **Victimization—vandalism** | |
| Worth less than £5 | 21 |
| Worth between £6 and £25 | 22 |
| Worth between £25 and £99 | 23 |
| Worth £100 or more | 24 |
| Other/value unknown | 20 |

**Victimization—violence**

| | |
|---|---|
| Minor injuries (just pain or less) | 31 |
| Minor injuries (eg bruises and marks, nose bleed; no treatment needed) | 32 |
| More serious injuries (requiring treatment from doctor) | 33 |

## A2.4.4  Offending

The situation (functional place, location, and people present) should ideally take precedence when coding the hour in which a crime takes place, even if the offence takes a short time and the participant is elsewhere or with different people for the rest of hour.

**Theft**

| | |
|---|---|
| Shoplifting | 11 |
| Directly from a person—using threats or violence | 12 |
| Directly from a person—not using threats or violence | 13 |
| Broke into a house | 14 |
| Broke into a shed/stole something from gardens/grounds | 15 |
| Broke into non-residential building | 16 |
| Broke into car | 17 |
| Stole a car | 18 |
| Stole a moped or motorcycle | 19 |
| Stole a bike | 20 |
| Driving offences | 21 |
| Other | 22 |

**Vandalism**

| | |
|---|---|
| Vehicle (car, lorry, etc.) | 31 |
| Moped/motorcycle | 32 |
| Bike | 33 |
| Private house | 34 |
| Non-residential building | 35 |
| Street lights/signs | 36 |
| Graffiti | 38 |
| Other (including arson) | 37 |

(continued)

**Violence**[a]

| | |
|---|---|
| Male/s—acquaintance | 41 |
| Female/s—acquaintance | 42 |
| Mixed sex—acquaintance | 43 |
| Male/s—known by appearance | 44 |
| Female/s—known by appearance | 45 |
| Mixed sex—known by appearance | 46 |
| Male/s—total stranger | 47 |
| Female/s—total stranger | 48 |
| Mixed sex—total strangers | 49 |

[a] If at least one of the victims is an acquaintance, code acquaintance. If at least one is known by appearance, code known by appearance.

### A2.4.5  Carrying a weapon

Carrying a weapon is only coded if the weapon is on the participant's person (ie should not refer to weapons nearby, e.g. in a young person's room while he or she is at home). Items carried that a participant intends to use as a weapon, either offensively or defensively, are also counted (eg a cricket bat carried to a fight, but not a cricket bat carried to a cricket match).

**Weapons**

| | |
|---|---|
| Gun | 10 |
| Air gun | 20 |
| Knife | 30 |
| Other sharp instrument, including improvised (eg razor, broken bottle) | 40 |
| Other blunt instrument, including improvised (eg bat, snooker ball in a sock) | 50 |

# References

Agnew, R. (2006), *Pressured into crime: An overview of General Strain Theory* (Los Angeles, CA: Roxbury Publishing Company).

Akers, R. L. (1989), 'A social behaviorist's perspective on integration of theories on crime and deviance', in S. F. Messner, M. D. Krohn, and A. E. Liska (eds), *Theoretical integration in the study of deviance and crime: Problems and prospects* (Albany, NY: State University of New York Press), 23–36.

Alexander, C. S. and Becker, H. J. (1978), 'The use of vignettes in survey research', *Public Opinion Quarterly*, 42 (1), 93–104.

Alsaker, F. D. and Flammer, A. (1999), *The adolescent experience: European and American adolescents in the 1990s* (Hillsdale, NJ: Erlbaum).

Anderson, C. A. (2004), 'An update on the effects of playing violent video games', *Journal of Adolescence*, 27 (1), 113–22.

Anderson, C. A., Carnagey, N. L., and Eubanks, J. (2003), 'Exposure to violent media: The effects of songs with violent lyrics on aggressive thoughts and feelings', *Journal of Personality and Social Psychology*, 84 (5), 960–71.

Anderson, J. (1971), 'Space–time budgets and activity studies in urban geography and planning', *Environment and Planning A*, 3 (4), 353–68.

Andorka, R. (1987), 'Time budgets and their uses', *Annual Review of Sociology*, 13 (1), 149–64.

Andresen, M. A. (2006), 'Crime measures and the spatial analysis of criminal activity', *British Journal of Criminology*, 46, 258–85.

Army Individual Test Battery (1944), 'Manual of directions and scoring' (Washington, DC: War Department, Adjutant General's Office).

Bachman, R., Paternoster, R., and Ward, S. (1992), 'The rationality of sexual offending: Testing a deterrence/rational choice conception of sexual assault', *Law & Society Review*, 26 (2), 343–72.

Baddeley, A. D., et al. (1991), 'The decline of working memory in Alzheimer's disease. A longitudinal study', *Brain*, 114, 2521–42.

Bailey, T. C. and Gatrell, A. C. (1995), *Interactive spatial data analysis* (New York, NY: Longman).

Baldwin, J. (1975), 'British areal studies of crime: An assessment', *British Journal of Criminology*, 15 (3), 211–27.

Baldwin, J. and Bottoms, A. E. (1976), *The urban criminal: A study in Sheffield* (London: Tavistock Publications).

Barker, R. G. (1968), *Ecological psychology* (Stanford, CA: Stanford University Press).

Batista-Foguet, J. M., Saris, W. E., and Tort-Martorell, X. (1990), 'Design of experimental studies for measurement and evaluation of the determinants of job satisfaction', *Social Indicators Research,* 22 (1), 49–67.

Baumer, E., et al. (2003), 'Neighborhood disadvantage and the nature of violence', *Criminology,* 41 (1), 39–72.

Bechara, A., Tranel, D., and Damasio, H. (2000a), 'Characterization of the decision-making deficit of patients with ventromedial prefrontal cortex lesions', *Brain,* 123 (11), 2189–202.

Bechara, A., Damasio, H., and Damasio, A. R. (2000b), 'Emotion, decision making and the orbitofrontal cortex', *Cerebral Cortex,* 10 (3), 295–307.

Bechara, A., et al. (1994), 'Insensitivity to future consequences following damage to human prefrontal cortex', *Cognition,* 50 (1–3), 7–15.

Bellair, P. E. (1997), 'Social interaction and community crime: Examining the importance of neighbor networks', *Criminology,* 35 (4), 677–704.

Belli, R. F., Alwin, D. F., and Stafford, F. P. (2009), 'Introduction: The application of calendar and time diary methods in the collection of life course data', in R. F. Belli, F. P. Stafford, and D. F. Alwin (eds), *Calendar and time diary: Methods in life course research* (Los Angeles, CA: Sage Publications).

Berkowitz, L. (1984), 'Some effects of thoughts on anti-and prosocial influences of media events: A cognitive-neoassociation analysis', *Psychological Bulletin,* 95 (3), 410–27.

Bichler, G., Christie-Merrall, J., and Sechrest, D. (2011), 'Examining juvenile delinquency within activity space: Building a context for offender travel patterns', *Journal of Research in Crime and Delinquency,* 48 (3), 472–506.

Block, R. L. and Block, C. R. (1995), 'Space, place and crime: Hot spot areas and hot places of liquor-related crime', in J. E. Eck and D. Weisburd (eds), *Crime and place* (Monsey, NY: Criminal Justice Press), 145–83.

Bloom, B. S. (1964), *Stability and change in human characteristics* (New York, NY: John Wiley & Sons, Inc).

Boggs, S. L. (1965), 'Urban crime patterns', *American Sociological Review,* 30 (6), 899–908.

Bollen, K. A. and Ward, S. (1980), 'Ratio variables in aggregate data analysis: Their uses, problems, and alternatives', in E. F. Borgatta and D. J. Jackson (eds), *Aggregate data: Analysis and interpretation* (Beverly Hills, CA: Sage Publications), 60–79.

Borawski, E. A., et al. (2003), 'Parental monitoring, negotiated unsupervised time, and parental trust: The role of perceived parenting practices in adolescent health risk behaviors', *Journal of Adolescent Health,* 33, 60–70.

Bottoms, A. E. and Wiles, P. (1997), 'Environmental criminology', in M. Maguire, R. Morgan, and R. Reiner (eds), *The Oxford handbook of criminology* (2nd edn; Oxford: Oxford University Press), 305–60.

Bottoms, A. E., et al. (2004), 'Towards desistance: Theoretical underpinnings for an empirical study', *The Howard Journal of Criminal Justice,* 43 (4), 368–89.

Boxford, S. (2006), *Schools and the problem of crime* (Cullompton: Willan Publishing).

Brantingham, P. J. and Brantingham, P. L. (1984), *Patterns in crime* (New York, NY: MacMillan).

—— (2008), 'Crime pattern theory', in R. Wortley and L. Mazerolle (eds), *Environmental criminology and crime analysis* (Cullompton: Willan Publishing), 78–93.

Brantingham, P. L. and Brantingham, P. J. (1981), 'Notes on the geometry of crime', in P. J. Brantingham and P. L. Brantingham (eds), *Environmental criminology* (London: Sage Publications), 27–54.

—— (1993), 'Environment, routine, and situation: Toward a Pattern theory of crime', in R. V. Clarke and M. Felson (eds), *Routine activity and rational choice: Advances in Criminological Theory, Vol 5* (New Brunswick, NJ: Transaction Publishers), 259–94.

Brooks-Gunn, J., Duncan, G. J., and Aber, J. L. (1997), *Neighborhood poverty: Vol I: Context and consequences for children* (New York, NY: Russell Sage Foundation).

Brooks-Gunn, J., et al. (1993), 'Do neighborhoods influence child and adolescent development?', *American Journal of Sociology,* 99 (2), 353–95.

Brown, A. M. (2004), 'The Edinburgh Neighbourhood Study: Implications for contemporary criminological and political discourse on community and crime' (Edinburgh: University of Edinburgh).

Brown, L. A. and Moore, E. G. (1970), 'The intra-urban migration process: A perspective', *Geografiska Annaler. Series B, Human Geography,* 52 (1), 1–13.

Browne, K. D. and Hamilton-Giachritsis, C. (2005), 'The influence of violent media on children and adolescents: A public-health approach', *The Lancet,* 365 (9460), 702–10.

Budd, T., Sharp, C., and Mayhew, P. (2005), 'Offending in England Wales: First results from the 2003 Crime and Justice Survey' (London: Home Office Research Development and Statistics Directorate).

Bunge, M. (2003), *Emergence and convergence: Quantitative novelty and the unity of knowledge* (Toronto, Canada: University of Toronto Press).

Burgess, E. W. ([1925] 1967), 'The growth of the city', in R. E. Park, E. W. Burgess, and R. D. McKenzie (eds), *The city* (Chicago, IL: University of Chicago Press), 47–62.

Bursik, R. J., Jr. (1986), 'Ecological stability and the dynamics of delinquency', in A. J. Reiss and M. Tonry (eds), *Communities and crime* (Chicago, IL: University of Chicago Press).

—— (1988), 'Social disorganization and theories of crime and delinquency: Problems and prospects', *Criminology,* 26 (4), 519–51.

Bursik, R. J., Jr. and Grasmick, H. (1993), *Neighborhoods and crime: The dimensions of effective community control* (New York, NY: Lexington).

Burt, C. (1944), *The young delinquent* (4th edn; London: University of London Press).

Burton, J., Laurie, H., and Lynn, P. (2006), 'The long-term effectiveness of refusal conversion procedures on longitudinal studies', *Journal of the Royal Statistical Society: Series A (Statistics in Society)*, 169 (3), 459–78.

CACI (2002), 'Wealth of the nation' (London: CACI).

Cancino, J. M. (2005), 'The utility of social capital and collective efficacy: Social control policy in nonmetropolitan settings', *Criminal Justice Policy Review*, 16 (3), 287–318.

Carlson, B. E. (1990), 'Adolescent observers of marital violence', *Journal of Family Violence*, 5 (4), 285–99.

Castle, I. M. and Gittus, E. (1961), 'The distribution of social defects in Liverpool', in G. A. Theodorson (ed.), *Studies in human ecology* (New York, NY: Row, Peterson and Company), 415–29.

Chainey, S. and Ratcliffe, J. (2005), *GIS and crime mapping* (London: Wiley).

Chainey, S., Tompson, L., and Uhlig, S. (2008), 'The utility of hotspot mapping for predicting spatial patterns of crime', *Security Journal*, 21 (1), 4–28.

Chilton, R. J. (1964), 'Continuity in delinquency area research: A comparison of studies for Baltimore, Detroit, and Indianapolis', *American Sociological Review*, 29 (1), 71–83.

Clarke, R. V. (1980), 'Situational crime prevention: Theory and practice', *British Journal of Criminology*, 20 (2), 136–47.

Clarke, R. V. and Felson, M. (1993), *Routine activity and rational choice: Advances in Criminological Theory, Vol 5* (Piscataway, NJ: Transaction).

Cohen, L. and Felson, M. (1979), 'Social change and crime rate trends: A routine activity approach', *American Sociological Review*, 44, 588–608.

Cohen, L., Felson, M., and Land, K. C. (1980), 'Property crime rates in the United States: A macrodynamic analysis, 1947–1977; with ex ante forecasts for the mid-1980s', *American Journal of Sociology*, 86 (1), 90–118.

Coleman, J. S. and Fararo, T. J. (1992), *Rational choice theory: Advocacy and critique*, eds J. S. Coleman and T. J. Fararo (Newbury Park, CA: Sage Publications).

Copperman, R. B. and Bhat, C. R. (2007), 'Exploratory analysis of children's daily time-use and activity patterns: Child Development Supplement to the US Panel Study of Income Dynamics', *Transportation Research Record*, 2021, 36–44.

Costanzo, C. M., Halperin, W. C., and Gale, N. (1986), 'Criminal mobility and the directional component in journeys to crime', in R. M. Figlio, S. Hakim, and G. F. Rengert (eds), *Metropolitan crime patterns* (Monsey, NY: Criminal Justice Press), 73–95.

Coulton, C. J., et al. (1995), 'Community level factors and child maltreatment rates', *Child Development,* 66 (5), 1262–76.

Countryside Agency, et al. (2004), 'Rural and urban area classification: An introductory guide' (London: Office for National Statistics).

Crosnoe, R. and Trinitapoli, J. (2008), 'Shared family activities and the transition from childhood into adolescence', *Journal of Research on Adolescence,* 18 (1), 23–48.

Crouter, A. C., et al. (1999), 'Conditions underlying parents' knowledge about children's daily lives in middle childhood: Between- and within-family comparisons', *Child Development,* 70 (1), 246–59.

Cullen, F. T., Wright, J., and Blevins, K. (2008), 'Introduction: Taking stock of criminological theory', in F. T. Cullen, J. Wright, and K. Blevins (eds), *Taking stock: The status of criminological theory. Advances in Criminological Theory, Vol 15* (New Brunswick, NJ: Transaction Publishers), 1–34.

Cullen, I. G. and Godson, V. (1975), *Urban networks: The structure of activity patterns* (Oxford: Pergamon Press).

Cullen, J. B. and Levitt, S. D. (1999), 'Crime, urban flight, and the consequences for cities', *The Review of Economics and Statistics,* 81 (2), 159–69.

Curtis, L. A. (1974), *Criminal violence: National patterns and behavior* (Lexington, MA: Lexington).

Damasio, A. R. (1994), *Descartes' error: Emotion, reason and the human brain* (London: Vintage Books).

Daneman, M. and Carpenter, P. (1980), 'Individual differences in working memory and reading', *Journal of Verbal Learning and Verbal Behavior,* 19, 450–66.

Davies, E., Habeshaw, J., and Robinson, B. (2001), *Peterborough: A story of city and country, people and places,* ed. J. Davis (Peterborough City Council: Pitkin Unichrome).

de Leeuw, E. D. and Hox, J. J. (1988), 'The effects of response-stimulating factors on response rates and data quality in mail surveys', *Journal of Official Statistics,* 4 (3), 241–9.

—— (2008), 'Self-administered questionnaires: Mail surveys and other applications', in E. D. de Leeuw, J. J. Hox, and D. A. Dillman (eds), *International handbook of survey methodology* (European Association of Methodology series; New York, NY: Psychology Press, Taylor & Francis), 239–63.

Dearing, E., et al. (2009), 'Do neighborhood and home contexts help explain why low-income children miss opportunities to participate in activities outside of school?', *Developmental Psychology,* 45 (6), 1545–62.

Denault, A. and Poulin, F. (2009), 'Intensity and breadth of participation in organized activities during the adolescent years: Multiple associations with youth outcomes', *Journal of Youth and Adolescence,* 38 (9), 1199–213.

Department for Communities and Local Government (2007), 'Generalised land use database statistics for England 2005 (enhanced basemap)' (London: Crown Copyright).

Dhami, M. K. and Mandel, D. R. (2011), 'Crime as risk taking', *Psychology, Crime & Law*, doi:10.1080/1068316X.2010.498423.

Dietvorst, A. G. J. (1994), 'Cultural tourism and time-space behaviour', in G. Ashworth and P. Larkham (eds), *Building a new heritage: Tourism, culture and identity in the New Europe* (London: Routledge), 69–89.

Dijst, M. (1999), 'Two-earner families and their action spaces: A case study of two Dutch communities', *GeoJournal*, 48 (3), 195–206.

Dillman, D. A. (1978), *Mail and telephone surveys* (New York, NY: John Wiley & Sons).

—— (1991), 'The design and administration of mail surveys', *Annual Review of Sociology*, 17 (1), 225–49.

—— (1998), *Mail and other self-administered surveys in the 21st century: The beginning of a new era* (Pullman, WA: Social and Economic Sciences Research Center, Washington State University).

—— (2000), *Mail and internet surveys: The tailored design method* (New York, NY: John Wiley & Sons).

Dillman, D. A., Smyth, J. D., and Christian, L. M. (2008), *Internet, mail, and mixed-mode surveys: The tailored design method* (New York, NY: John Wiley & Sons).

Dillman, D. A., et al. (2002), 'Survey nonresponse in design, data collection, and analysis', in R. M. Groves, et al. (eds), *Survey nonresponse* (Probability and Statistics; New York, NY: John Wiley & Sons), 3–26.

Dishion, T. J. and McMahon, R. J. (1998), 'Parental monitoring and the prevention of child and adolescent problem behavior: A conceptual and empirical formulation', *Clinical Child and Family Psychology Review*, 1 (1), 61–75.

Downes, D. (1958), *The delinquent solution* (London: Routledge and Kegan Paul).

Duncan, G. J. and Brooks-Gunn, J. (1997), *Consequences of growing up poor* (New York, NY: Russell Sage Foundation).

Duncan, G. J. and Raudenbush, S. W. (1999), 'Assessing the effects of context in studies of child and youth development', *Educational Psychologist*, 34 (1), 29–41.

Duncan, G. J., Brooks-Gunn, J., and Klebanov, P. K. (1994), 'Economic deprivation and early childhood development', *Child Development*, 65 (2), 296–318.

Duncan, T. E., et al. (2003), 'A multilevel contextual model of neighborhood collective efficacy', *American Journal of Community Psychology*, 32 (3), 245–52.

Eagly, A. H. and Chaiken, S. (1998), 'Attitude structure and function', in D. T. Gilbert, S. T. Fiske, and G. Lindzey (eds), *The handbook of social psychology* (4th edn, 1; New York, NY: McGraw Hill), 269–322.

Eccles, J. S. and Barber, B. L. (1999), 'Student council, volunteering, basket-ball, or marching band: What kind of extracurricular involvement matters?', *Journal of Adolescent Research*, 14, 10–43.

Eccles, J. S., et al. (1993), 'Development during adolescence: The impact of stage environment fit on young adolescents' experiences in schools and in families', *American Psychologist*, 48 (2), 90–101.

Eck, J. E. (1995), 'Examining Routine Activity Theory: A review of two books', *Justice Quarterly*, 12 (4), 783–97.

Eck, J. E., et al. (2005), *Mapping crime: Understanding hot spots* (Washington, DC: National Institute of Justice).

Edwards, P., et al. (2002), 'Increasing response rates to postal questionnaires: Systematic review', *British Medical Journal*, 324 (7347), 1183–92.

Ehrlich, E. ([1936] 2008), *Fundamental principles of the sociology of law* (New Brunswick, NJ: Transaction Publishers).

Eisner, M. P. and Wikström, P-O H. (1999), 'Violent crime in the urban community: A comparison of Stockholm and Basel', *European Journal on Criminal Policy and Research*, 7, 427–42.

Electoral Commission (2005), *'Understanding electoral registration: The extent and nature of non-registration in Britain'* (London: The Electoral Commission).

—— (2009), *'Interim report on case study research into the electoral registers in Great Britain'* (London: The Electoral Commission).

Elis, L. A. and Simpson, S. S. (1995), 'Informal sanction threats and corporate crime: Additive versus multiplicative models', *Journal of Research in Crime and Delinquency*, 32 (4), 399–424.

Ellis, L., Beaver, K., and Wright, J. (2009), *Handbook of crime correlates* (San Diego, CA: Academic Press).

Elster, J. (2007), *Explaining social behavior: More nuts and bolts for the social sciences* (Cambridge: Cambridge University Press).

Enders, C. K. and Tofighi, D. (2007), 'Centering predictor variables in cross-sectional multilevel models: A new look at an old issue', *Psychological Methods*, 12 (2), 121–38.

Equifax (xxxx) 'Equifax predicts problems for marketers with 2006 edited electoral roll', <www.equifax.co.uk/our_company/press_room/2006/ERproblems_Analysis.html>, accessed 13 December 2011.

Evans, J. and Frankish, K. (2009), *In two minds: Dual processes and beyond* (Oxford: Oxford University Press).

Farrington, D. P. (1988), 'Social, psychological and biological influences on juvenile delinquency and adult crime', in W. Buikhuisen and S. A. Mednick (eds), *Explaining criminal behaviour* (Leiden: E. J. Brill), 68–89.

—— (1992), 'Explaining the beginning, progress, and ending of antisocial behavior from birth to adulthood', in J. McCord (ed.), *Facts, frameworks, and forecasts: Advances in Criminological Theory, Vol 3* (New Brunswick, NJ: Transaction Publishers), 253–86.

—— (2000), 'Explaining and preventing crime: The globalization of knowledge–the American Society of Criminology 1999 Presidential Address', *Criminology*, 38 (1), 1–24.

—— (2001), 'What has been learned from self-reports about criminal careers and the causes of offending?' (London: Home Office Online Report).

—— (2002), 'Human development and criminal careers', in M. Maguire, R. Morgan, and R. Reiner (eds), *The Oxford handbook of criminology* (3rd edn; Oxford: Oxford University Press), 657–701.

Farrington, D. P. and Wikström, P-O H. (1994), 'Criminal careers in London and Stockholm: A cross-national comparative study', in E. G. M. Weitekamp and H.-J. Kerner, (eds), *Cross-national longitudinal research on human development and criminal behaviour* (Dordrecht, The Netherlands: Kluwer), 65–89.

Farrington, D. P., et al. (1990), 'Minimizing attrition in longitudinal research: Methods of tracing and securing cooperation in a 24-year follow-up study', in D. Magnusson and L. R. Bergman (eds), *Data quality in longitudinal research* (Cambridge: Cambridge University Press), 122–47.

Farrington, D. P., et al. (2006), 'Criminal careers up to age 50 and life success up to age 48: New findings from the Cambridge Study in Delinquent Development' (2nd edn; London: Home Office Research, Development and Statistics Directorate), 87.

Felson, M. (1986), 'Linking criminal choices, routine activities, informal control, and criminal outcomes', in D. B. Cornish and R. V. Clarke (eds), *The reasoning criminal: Rational choice perspectives on offending* (New York, NY: Springer-Verlag), 119–28.

—— (1987), 'Routine activities and crime prevention in the developing metropolis', *Criminology*, 25 (4), 911–32.

—— (2002), *Crime and everyday life* (3rd edn; Thousand Oaks, CA: Sage publications).

Felson, M. and Cohen, L. (1980), 'Human ecology and crime: A routine activity approach', *Human Ecology*, 8 (4), 389–406.

Fennell, D. A. (1996), 'A tourist space–time budget in the Shetland Islands', *Annals of Tourism Research*, 23 (4), 811–29.

Fishbein, M. and Ajzen, I. (1975), *Belief, attitude, intention, and behavior: An introduction to theory and research* (Reading, MA: Addison-Wesley).

Fisher, K., Gershuny, J., and Gauthier, A. (2010), 'Multinational time use study: User's guide and documentation' (Oxford: Centre for Time Use Research, University of Oxford).

Flood-Page, C., et al. (2000), 'Youth crime: Findings from the 1998/99 Youth Lifestyles Survey' (London: Home Office).

Forer, P. C. and Kivell, H. (1981), 'Space–time budgets, public transport, and spatial choice', *Environment and Planning A*, 13 (4), 497–509.

Forgas, J. P. and Laham, S. M. (2005), 'The interaction between affect and motivation in social judgments and behavior', in J. P. Forgas, K. D. Williams, and S. M. Laham (eds), *Social motivation: Conscious and unconscious processes* (Cambridge: Cambridge University Press), 168–93.

Fox, J. G. and Sobol, J. J. (2000), 'Drinking patterns, social interaction, and barroom behavior: A routine activities approach', *Deviant Behavior*, 21 (5), 429–50.

Fox, M. (1995), 'Transport planning and the human activity approach', *Journal of Transport Geography*, 3 (2), 105–16.

Friedrichs, J. and Oberwittler, D. (2007), 'Soziales kapital in wohngebieten', in A. Franzen and M. Freitag (eds), *Sozialkapital: Grundlagen und anwendungen* (Special Issue 47 of Kölner Zeitschrift für Soziologie und Sozialpsychologie edn; Wiesbaden: VS Verlag für Sozialwissenschaften), 450–86.

Fuligni, A. J. and Stevenson, H. W. (1995), 'Time use and mathematics achievement among American, Chinese, and Japanese high school students', *Child Development*, 66 (3), 830–42.

Furstenberg, F. F. (2000), 'The sociology of adolescence and youth in the 1990s: A critical commentary', *Journal of Marriage and Family*, 62 (4), 896–910.

Fuster, J. (1997), *The prefrontal cortex: Anatomy, physiology, and neuropsychology of the frontal lobe* (3rd edn; Philadelphia, PA: Lippincott Williams and Wilkins).

Gardiner, R. A. (1978), *Design for safe neighborhoods: The environmental security planning and design process* (Washington, DC: National Institute of Law Enforcement and Criminal Justice).

Gershuny, J., et al. (1986), 'Time budgets: Preliminary analyses of a national survey', *The Quarterly Journal of Social Affairs*, 2 (1), 13–39.

Gibbs, J. P. and Martin, W. T. (1962), 'Urbanization, technology, and the division of labor: International patterns', *American Sociological Review*, 27 (5), 667–77.

Gibson, C. L., et al. (2002), 'Social integration, individual perceptions of collective efficacy, and fear of crime in three cities', *Justice Quarterly*, 19 (3), 537–64.

Gibson, T. (2006), 'The 2nd Peterborough Local Transport Plan (2006–2011)' (Peterborough: Peterborough City Council).

Goldberg, E. (2001), *The executive brain: Frontal lobes and the civilized mind* (Oxford: Oxford University Press).

Goldstein, H. (2009), 'Handling attrition and non-response in longitudinal data', *Longitudinal and Life Course Studies*, 1 (1), 63–72.

Golledge, R. G. and Stimson, R. J. (1997), *Spatial behavior: A geographic perspective* (New York, NY: The Guilford Press).

Goodchild, M. F. and Janelle, D. G. (1984), 'The city around the clock: Space–time patterns of urban ecological structure', *Environment and Planning A*, 16 (6), 807–20.

Gottfredson, M. and Hirschi, T. (1990), *A General Theory of Crime* (Stanford, CA: Stanford University Press).

—— (2003), 'Self-control and opportunity', in C. Britt and M. Gottfredson (eds), *Control theories of crime and delinquency. Advances in Criminological Theory, Vol 12* (New Brunswick, NJ: Transaction Publishers), 5–19.

Goudriaan, H. and Nieuwbeerta, P. (2007), 'Contextual determinants of juveniles' willingness to report crimes: A vignette experiment', *Journal of Experimental Criminology*, 3 (2), 89–111.

Goyder, J. (1987), *The silent minority: Nonrespondents on sample surveys* (Cambridge: Polity Press).

Goyder, J., Lock, J., and McNair, T. (1992), 'Urbanization effects on survey nonresponse: A test within and across cities', *Quality and Quantity*, 26 (1), 39–48.

Goyder, J., Warriner, K., and Miller, S. (2002), 'Evaluating socio-economic status (SES) bias in survey nonresponse', *Journal of Official Statistics*, 18 (1), 1–11.

Graham, K. and Homel, R. (2008), *Raising the bar: Preventing aggression in and around bars, pubs and clubs* (Cullompton: Willan Publishing).

Graham, K., et al. (2006), 'Bad nights or bad bars? Multi-level analysis of environmental predictors of aggression in late-night large-capacity bars and clubs', *Addiction*, 101 (11), 1569–80.

Grasmick, H., et al. (1993), 'Testing the core empirical implications of Gottfredson and Hirschi's General Theory of Crime', *Journal of Research in Crime and Delinquency*, 30 (1), 5–29.

Greenwald, A. G. and Banaji, M. R. (1995), 'Implicit social cognition: Attitudes, self-esteem, and stereotypes', *Psychological Review*, 102 (1), 4–27.

Groff, E. and McCord, E. S. (2011), 'The role of neighborhood parks as crime generators', *Security Journal*, Advance online publication March 7th 2011, doi: 10.1057/sj.2011.1.

Groff, E., Weisburd, D., and Morris, N. A. (2009), 'Where the action is at places: Examining spatio-temporal patterns of juvenile crime at places using trajectory analysis and GIS', in D. Weisburd, W. Bernasco, and G. J. N. Bruinsma (eds), *Putting crime in its place: Units of analysis in geographic criminology* (New York, NY: Springer), 61–86.

Groff, E. R., Weisburd, D., and Yang, S-M. (2010), 'Is it important to examine crime trends at a local "micro" level?: A longitudinal analysis of street to street variability in crime trajectories', *Journal of Quantitative Criminology*, 26, 7–32.

Groves, R. M. and Couper, M. P. (1998), *Nonresponse in household interview surveys* (New York, NY: John Wiley & Sons).

Groves, R. M., Cialdini, R. B., and Couper, M. P. (1992), 'Understanding the decision to participate in a survey', *Public Opinion Quarterly*, 56 (4), 475–95.

Groves, R. M., et al. (2004), *Survey methodology* (New York, NY: John Wiley & Sons).

Groves, R. M., et al. (eds) (2002), *Survey nonresponse* (New York, NY: John Wiley & Sons).

Haar, D.-H. and Wikström, P-O H. (2010), 'Crime propensity, criminogenic exposure and violent scenario responses: Testing situational action theory in regression and Rasch models', *European Journal of Applied Mathematics*, 21 (4–5), 307–23.

Hägerstrand, T. (1970), 'What about people in regional science?', *Papers in Regional Science*, 24 (1), 6–21.

Haining, R. P. (2003), *Spatial data analysis: Theory and practice* (Cambridge: Cambridge University Press).

Hales, J., et al. (2009), 'Longitudinal analysis of the Offending, Crime and Justice Survey 2003–2006' (London: Home Office Research Development and Statistics Directorate).

Hall, P. (1981), *The inner city in context: The final report of the Social Science Research Council Inner Cities Working Party* (London: Heinemann).

Hanson, S. and Hanson, P. (1980), 'Gender and urban activity patterns in Uppsala, Sweden', *Geographical Review*, 70 (3), 291–9.

Harding, D. J., et al. (2011), 'Unpacking neighborhood influences on education outcomes: Setting the stage for future research', in G. Duncan and R. Murnane (eds), *Whither opportunity: Rising inequality and the uncertain life chances of low-income children* (New York, NY: Russell Sage).

Harms, T. and Gershuny, J. (2009), 'Time budgets and time use', *Working Paper Series of the German Council for Social and Economic Data* (65; Berlin: German Council for Social and Economic Data (RatSWD)).

Harries, K. D. (1974), *Geography of crime and justice* (New York, NY: McGraw Hill).

—— (1999), *Mapping crime: Principle and practice, ed. US Department of Justice* (Washington, DC: US Department of Justice).

Harris, J. R. (1995), 'Where is the child's environment? A group socialization theory of development', *Psychological Review*, 102 (3), 458–89.

—— (1998), *The nurture assumption: Why children turn out the way they do* (New York, NY: The Free Press).

Haynie, D. L. and Payne, D. C. (2006), 'Race, friendship networks, and violent delinquency', *Criminology*, 44 (4), 775–805.

Head, V. (2004), 'Ethnicity and religion in Peterborough' (Peterborough: Cambridgeshire County Council Research Group).

Heckhausen, J. and Heckhausen, H. (2008), *Motivation and action* (New York, NY: Cambridge University Press).

Herbert, D. T. (1972), *Urban geography: A social perspective* (Newton Abbot: David and Charles).

—— (1978), 'Social deviance in the city: A spatial perspective', in D. T. Herbert and R. J. Johnston (eds), *Social areas in cities: Processes, patterns and problems* (London: John Wiley & Sons), 311.

Hindelang, M. J., Gottfredson, M., and Garofalo, J. (1978), *Victims of personal crime: An empirical foundation for a theory of personal victimization* (Cambridge, MA: Ballinger Publishing Company).

Hindelang, M. J., Hirschi, T., and Weis, J. G. (1981), *Measuring delinquency* (Sage Library of Social Research, 123; Beverley Hills, CA: Sage Publications).

Hipp, J. R. (2007), 'Income inequality, race, and place: Does the distribution of race and class within neighborhoods affect crime rates?', *Criminology*, 45 (3), 665–98.

Hirschi, T. (1986), 'On the compatibility of rational choice and social control theories of crime', in D. B. Cornish and R. V. Clarke (eds), *The reasoning criminal: Rational choice perspectives on offending* (New York, NY: Springer-Verlag), 105–18.

Hirschi, T. and Gottfredson, M. (1983), 'Age and the explanation of crime', *American Journal of Sociology*, 89 (3), 552–84.

Hobbs, D., et al. (2005), 'Violence and control in the night-time economy', *European Journal of Crime, Criminal Law and Criminal Justice*, 13 (1), 89–102.

Hofferth, S. L. and Sandberg, J. F. (2001), 'How American children spend their time', *Journal of Marriage and Family*, 63, 295–308.

Hood, R. and Sparks, R. (1970), *Key issues in criminology* (London: Weidenfeld and Nicolson).

Hope, T. (1986), 'Liquor licensing and crime prevention', *Home Office Research and Planning Unit Research Bulletin* (20; London: Home Office), 5–8.

House of Commons (2002), 'The new towns: Their problems and future' (Nineteenth report of session 2001–02, 603; London: Transport, Local Government and the Regions Committee), 1–41.

Hughes, G. (2011), 'A spatial analysis of assault patterns in entertainment areas throughout the Waikato using geographic information systems' (Hamilton, New Zealand: The University of Waikato).

Hughes, K., et al. (2011), 'Environmental factors in drinking venues and alcohol-related harm: The evidence base for European intervention', *Addiction*, 106, 37–46.

Hughes, R. (2004), 'Vignette technique', in M. S. Lewis-Beck, A. Bryman, and T. Futing Liao (eds), *The SAGE encyclopedia of social science research methods* (Thousand Oaks, CA: Sage Publications), 1183–4.

Huizinga, D. and Elliott, D. S. (1986), 'Reassessing the reliability and validity of self-report delinquency measures', *Journal of Quantitative Criminology*, 2 (4), 293–327.

Ishikawa, S. and Raine, A. (2003), 'Prefrontal deficits and antisocial behavior: A causal model', in B. Lahey, T. E. Moffitt, and A. Caspi (eds), *Causes of conduct disorder and juvenile delinquency* (New York, NY: The Guilford Press), 277–304.

Janelle, D. G., Goodchild, M. F., and Klinkenberg, B. (1988), 'Space–time diaries and travel characteristics for different levels of respondent aggregation', *Environment and Planning A*, 20 (7), 891–906.

Janson, C.-G. (1980a), *Register data II-A code book* (Project Metropolitan: A longitudinal study of a Stockholm cohort, Research Report No. 15; Stockholm: Department of Sociology, Stockholm University).

—— (1980b), 'Factorial social ecology: An attempt at summary and evaluation', *Annual Review of Sociology*, 6, 433–56.

Jansson, K., et al. (2008), 'Extent and trends', in C. Kershaw, S. Nicholas, and A. Walker (eds), *Crime in England Wales 2007/8: Findings from the British Crime Survey and police recorded crime* (London: Home Office Research, Development and Statistics Directorate), 21–58.

Jasso, G. (2006), 'Factorial survey methods for studying beliefs and judgments', *Sociological Methods & Research*, 34 (3), 334–423.

Jenkins, C. R. and Dillman, D. A. (1997), 'Towards a theory of self-administered questionnaire design', in L. Lyberg, et al. (eds), *Survey measurement and process quality* (New York, NY: John Wiley & Sons), 165–96.

Jezl, D. R., Molidor, C. E., and Wright, T. L. (1996), 'Physical, sexual and psychological abuse in high school dating relationships: Prevalence rates and self-esteem issues', *Child and Adolescent Social Work Journal*, 13 (1), 69–87.

Johnson, T. P., et al. (2002), 'Culture and survey nonresponse', in R. M. Groves, et al. (eds), *Survey nonresponse* (Wiley Series in Probability and Statistics; New York, NY: John Wiley & Sons), 55–69.

Junger-Tas, J. and Marshall, I. (1999), 'The self-report methodology in crime research', *Crime & Justice*, 25, 291–367.

Juster, F. T. (1985), 'Conceptual and methodological issues involved in the measurement of time use', in F. T. Juster and F. P. Stafford (eds), *Time, goods, and well-being* (Ann Arbor, MI: Survey Research Center, The University of Michigan), 19–31.

Juster, F. T. and Stafford, F. P. (1991), 'The allocation of time: Empirical findings, behavioural models, and problems of measurement', *Journal of Economic Literature*, 29, 471–522.

—— (eds) (1985), *Time, goods, and well-being* (Ann Arbor, MI: Survey Research Center, The University of Michigan).

Kaidesoja, T. (2009), 'Bhaskar and Bunge on social emergence', *Journal for the Theory of Social Behaviour*, 39 (3), 300–22.

Katz, J. (1988), *Seductions of crime* (New York, NY: Basic Books).

Kelling, G. L. and Coles, C. M. (1996), *Fixing broken windows: Restoring order and reducing crime in our communities* (New York, NY: Touchstone).

Kennedy, L. W. and Forde, D. R. (1990), 'Routine activities and crime: An analysis of victimization in Canada', *Criminology*, 28, 137–52.

Kirk, D. S. (2008), 'The neighborhood context of racial and ethnic disparities in arrest', *Demography*, 45 (1), 55–77.

Klepper, S. and Nagin, D. (1989a), 'The deterrent effect of perceived certainty and severity of punishment revisited', *Criminology*, 27 (4), 721–46.

—— (1989b), 'Tax compliance and perceptions of the risks of detection and criminal prosecution', *Law & Society Review*, 23 (2), 209–40.

Kornhauser, R. (1978), *Social sources of delinquency: An appraisal of analytic models* (Chicago, IL: University of Chicago Press).

Kurtz, E. M., Koons, B. A., and Taylor, R. B. (1998), 'Land use, physical deterioration, resident-based control, and calls for service on urban streetblocks', *Justice Quarterly*, 15 (1), 121–49.

LaGrange, T. C. (1999), 'The impact of neighborhoods, schools, and malls on the spatial distribution of property damage', *Journal of Research in Crime and Delinquency*, 36 (4), 393–422.

Laird, R. D., et al. (2003), 'Change in parents' monitoring knowledge: Links with parenting, relationship quality, adolescent beliefs, and anti-social behavior', *Social Development*, 12 (3), 401–19.

Lander, B. (1954), *Towards an understanding of juvenile delinquency* (Columbia: Columbia University Press).

Lareau, A. and Weininger, E. B. (2008), 'Time, work, and family life: Reconceptualizing gendered time patterns through the case of children's organized activities', *Sociological Forum*, 23 (3), 419–54.

Larson, R. W. (2000), 'Toward a psychology of positive youth development', *American Psychologist*, 55 (1), 170–83.

Larson, R. W. and Verma, S. (1999), 'How children and adolescents spend time across the world: Work, play, and developmental opportunities', *Psychological Bulletin*, 125 (6), 701–36.

Larzelere, R. E. and Patterson, G. R. (1990), 'Parental management: Mediator of the effect of socioeconomic status on early delinquency', *Criminology*, 28 (2), 301–24.

Laub, J. H. and Sampson, R. J. (2003), *Shared beginnings, divergent lives: Delinquent boys to age 70* (Cambridge, MA: Harvard University Press).

Laurence, J. (2011), 'The effect of ethnic diversity and community disadvantage on social cohesion: A multi-level analysis of social capital and interethnic relations in UK communities', *European Sociological Review*, 27 (1), 70–89.

Le Blanc, M. and Fréchette, M. (1989), *Male criminal activity from childhood through youth: Multilevel and developmental perspectives*, eds A. Blumstein and D. P. Farrington (Research in criminology; New York, NY: Springer-Verlag).

Leeper Piquero, N. and Piquero, A. R. (2006), 'Control balance and exploitative corporate crime', *Criminology*, 44 (2), 397–430.

Leeper Piquero, N., Exum, M. L., and Simpson, S. S. (2005), 'Integrating the desire-for-control and rational choice in a corporate crime context', *Justice Quarterly*, 22 (2), 252–80.

LeJeune, C. and Follette, V. (1994), 'Taking responsibility: Sex differences in reporting dating violence', *Journal of Interpersonal Violence*, 9 (1), 133–40.

Lessler, J. T., Eyerman, J., and Wang, K. (2008), 'Interviewer training', in E. D. de Leeuw, J. J. Hox, and D. A. Dillman (eds), *International handbook of survey methodology* (European Association of Methodology; New York, NY: Psychology Press, Taylor & Francis), 442–60.

Letki, N. (2008), 'Does diversity erode social cohesion? Social capital and race in British neighbourhoods', *Political Studies*, 56, 99–126.

Leventhal, T. and Brooks-Gunn, J. (2000), 'The neighborhoods they live in: The effects of neighborhood residence on child and adolescent outcomes', *Psychological Bulletin*, 126 (2), 309–37.

Levine, N. (2006), 'Crime mapping and the CrimeStat program', *Geographical Analysis*, 38 (1), 41–56.

Liker, J. K. (1982), 'Family prestige judgments: Bringing in real-world complexities', in P. H. Rossi and S. L. Nock (eds), *Measuring social judgments: The factorial survey approach* (London: Sage Publications), 119–44.

Liska, A. E. and Bellair, P. E. (1995), 'Violent-crime rates and racial composition: Covergence over time', *American Journal of Sociology*, 101 (3), 578–610.

Liska, A. E., Krohn, M. D., and Messner, S. F. (1989), 'Strategies and requisites for theoretical integration in the study of crime and deviance', in S. F. Messner, M. D. Krohn, and A. E. Liska (eds), *Theoretical integration in the study of deviance and crime: Problems and prospects* (Albany, NY: University of New York Press).

Lockwood, D. (2007), 'Mapping crime in Savannah: Social disadvantage, land use, and violent crimes reported to the police', *Social Science Computer Review*, 25, 194–209.

Loeber, R. and Stouthamer-Loeber, M. (1986), 'Family factors as correlates and predictors of juvenile conduct problems and delinquency', in M. Tonry and N. Morris (eds), *Crime and Justice, Vol 7* (Chicago, IL: University of Chicago Press), 29–149.

Loeber, R. and Wikström, P-O H. (1993), 'Individual pathways to crime in different types of neighborhood', in D. P. Farrington, R. J. Sampson, and P-O H. Wikström (eds), *Integrating individual and ecological aspects of crime* (Stockholm, Sweden: Liber Forlag), 169–204.

Loeber, R. and Farrington, D. P. (1998), *Serious and violent juvenile offenders: Risk factors and successful interventions* (London: Sage Publications, Inc.).

Loeber, R., et al. (2008), *Violence and serious theft: Development and prediction from childhood to adulthood* (New York, NY: Routledge).

Logan, J. R. and Molotch, H. L. (1987), *Urban fortunes: The political economy of place* (Berkeley, CA: University of California Press).

Long, J. S. and Freese, J. (2006), *Regression models for categorical dependent variables using stata* (Texas, TX: Stata Press).

Loosveldt, G. (2008), 'Face-to-face interviews', in E. D. de Leeuw, J. J. Hox, and D. A. Dillman (eds), *International handbook of survey methodology* (European Association of Methodology series; New York, NY: Psychology Press, Taylor & Francis), 201–20.

Lüdemann, C. (2006), 'Kriminalitätsfurcht im urbanen raum: Eine mehrebenenanalyse zu individuellen und sozialräumlichen determinanten verschiedener dimensionen von kriminalitätsfurcht', *Kölner Zeitschrift für Soziologie und Sozialpsychologie, 58* (2), 285–306.

Lüdemann, C. and Peter, S. (2007), 'Kriminalität und sozialkapital im stadtteil: Eine mehrebenenanalyse zu individuellen und sozialräumlichen determinanten von viktimisierungen', *Zeitschrift für Soziologie, 36* (1), 25–42.

Magdol, L., et al. (1997), 'Gender differences in partner violence in a birth cohort of 21-year-olds: Bridging the gap between clinical and epidemiological approaches', *Journal of Consulting and Clinical Psychology, 68–78* (1), 68.

Mahoney, J. L. and Stattin, H. (2000), 'Leisure activities and adolescent antisocial behavior: The role of structure and social context', *Journal of Adolescence, 23* (2), 113–27.

Marini, M. M. and Shelton, B. A. (1993), 'Measuring household work: Recent experience in the United States', *Social Science Research, 22* (4), 361–82.

Markowitz, F. E., et al. (2001), 'Extending social disorganization theory: Modeling the relationships between cohesion, disorder, and fear', *Criminology, 39* (2), 293–320.

Marsh, H. W. and Kleitman, S. (2002), 'Extracurricular school activities: The good, the bad and the nonlinear', *Harvard Educational Review, 72*, 464–514.

Marsh, P. and Fox-Kibby, K. (1992), 'Drinking and public disorder' (London: The Portman Group).

Martin, D. (1998), '2001 Census output areas: From concept to prototype', *Population Trends,* (94), 19–24.

——(2000), 'Towards the geographies of the 2001 UK Census of Population', *Transactions of the Institute of British Geographers, 25* (3), 321–32.

Massey, D. and Denton, N. (1993), *American apartheid: Segregation and the making of the underclass* (Cambridge, MA: Harvard University Press).

Matza, D. (1964), *Delinquency and drift* (New York, NY: John Wiley and Sons Inc.).

Maund, B. (2003), *Perception* (Montreal and Kingston: McGill-Queen's University Press).

Mays, J. B. (1963), 'Delinquency areas: A re-assessment', *British Journal of Criminology*, 3, 216–30.

McCarthy, B. (2002), 'New economics of sociological criminology', *Annual Review of Sociology*, 28, 417–42.

McClintock, F. H. (1963), *Crimes of violence* (London: MacMillan).

McClintock, F. H. and Wikström, P-O H. (1992), 'The comparative study of urban violence: Criminal violence in Edinburgh and Stockholm', *British Journal of Criminology*, 32 (4), 505–20.

McIver, J. P. (1981), 'Criminal mobility: A review of empirical studies', in S. Hakim and G. F. Rengert (eds), *Crime spillover* (Beverly Hills, CA: Sage Publications), 48–53.

McNulty, T. L. and Holloway, S. R. (2000), 'Race, crime and public housing in Atlanta: Testing a conditional effect hypothesis', *Social Forces*, 79, 707–29.

McNulty, T. L. and Bellair, P. E. (2003), 'Explaining racial and ethnic differences in serious adolescent violent behavior', *Criminology*, 41 (3), 709–48.

McVie, S. (2005), 'Patterns of deviance underlying the age-crime curve: The long term evidence', *British Society of Criminology e-Journal*, 7, accessed 1 September 2011.

McVie, S. and Norris, P. (2006), 'Neighbourhood effects on youth delinquency and drug use', *Edinburgh Study of Youth Transitions and Crime* (Edinburgh: Centre for Law and Society, The University of Edinburgh).

Mears, D. P., et al. (2008), 'Social ecology and recidivism: Implications for prisoner reentry', *Criminology*, 46 (2), 301–40.

Meeks, C. B. and Mauldin, T. (1990), 'Children's time in structured and unstructured leisure activities', *Journal of Family and Economic Issues*, 11 (3), 257–81.

Mele, A. R. (2001), *Autonomous agents: From self-control to autonomy* (Oxford: Oxford University Press).

Messner, S. F. (2012), 'Morality, markets, and the ASC: 2011 presidential address to the American Society of Criminology', *Criminology*, 50 (1), 1–21.

Messner, S. F., Krohn, M. D., and Liska, A. E. (1989), *Theoretical integration in the study of deviance and crime: Problems and prospects* (Albany, NY: State University of New York Press).

Mey, M. G. and Heide, H. (1997), 'Towards spatiotemporal planning: Practicable analysis of day-to-day paths through space and time', *Environment and Planning B: Planning and Design*, 24, 709–24.

Miethe, T. D. and McDowall, D. (1993), 'Contextual effects in models of criminal victimization', *Social Forces*, 71, 741–59.

Miethe, T. D. and Meier, R. F. (1994), *Crime and its social context: Toward an integrated theory of offenders, victims, and situations* (Albany, NY: State University of New York Press).

Ministry of Justice (2008), 'Average time from arrest to sentence for persistent young offenders: January–December 2008', *Ministry of Justice Statistics Bulletin* (National Statistics).

—— (2010), 'Time intervals for criminal proceedings in magistrates' courts: December 2009', *Ministry of Justice Statistics Bulletin (National Statistics)*.

Moffitt, T. E. and Caspi, A. (1999), 'Findings about partner violence from the Dunedin Multidisciplinary Health and Development Study' (Washington, DC: US Department of Justice, National Institute of Justice).

Moffitt, T. E., et al. (2001), *Sex differences in antisocial behaviour: Conduct disorder, delinquency and violence in the Dunedin Longitudinal Study* (Cambridge: Cambridge University Press).

Morenoff, J. D. and Sampson, R. J. (1997), 'Violent crime and the spatial dynamics of neighbourhood transition: Chicago 1970–1990', *Social Forces, 76*, 31–64.

Morenoff, J. D., Sampson, R. J., and Raudenbush, S. W. (2001), 'Neighborhood inequality, collective efficacy, and the spatial dynamics of urban violence', *Criminology, 39* (3), 517–59.

Morgan, A. and Lilienfeld, S. (2000), 'A meta-analytic review of the relation between antisocial behavior and neuropsychological measures of executive function', *Clinical Psychology Review, 20* (1), 113–36.

Morris, T. (1957), *The criminal area: A study in social ecology* (London: Routledge and Kegan Paul).

Moser, C. A. and Kalton, G. (1971), *Survey methods in social investigation* (2nd edn; London: Heinemann).

Mulligan, C. B., Schneider, B., and Wolfe, R. (2005), 'Non-response and population representation in studies of adolescent time use', *Electronic International Journal of Time Use Research, 2* (1), 33–53.

Murray, D. M., Varnell, S. P., and Blitstein, J. L. (2004), 'Design and analysis of group-randomized trials: A review of recent methodological developments', *American Journal of Public Health, 94* (3), 423–32.

Muthén, L. K. and Muthén, B. O. (2009), 'Mplus User's Guide' (5.21 edn; Los Angeles, CA: Muthén & Muthén).

Nagin, D. S. and Paternoster, R. (1993), 'Enduring individual differences and rational choice theories of crime', *Law & Society Review, 27* (3), 467–96.

Nagin, D. S. and Pogarsky, G. (2003), 'An experimental investigation of deterrence: Cheating, self-serving bias, and impulsivity', *Criminology, 41* (1), 167–94.

Nelson, A. L., Bromley, R. D. F., and Thomas, C. J. (2001), 'Identifying micro-spatial and temporal patterns of violent crime and disorder in the British city centre', *Applied Geography, 21* (3), 249–74.

Niemi, I. (1993), 'Systematic error in behavioural measurement: Comparing results from interview and time budget studies', *Social Indicators Research, 30* (2), 229–44.

Nigg, J. T. and Huang-Pollock, C. L. (2003), 'An early-onset model of the role of executive functions and intelligence in conduct disorder/delinquency', in B. Lahey, T. E. Moffitt, and A. Caspi (eds), *Causes of conduct disorder and juvenile delinquency* (New York, NY: The Guilford Press), 227–53.

Noble, M., et al. (2004), 'The English Indices of Deprivation 2004: Summary' (London: Office of the Deputy Prime Minister).

Oberwittler, D. (2004), 'A multilevel analysis of neighbourhood contextual effects on serious juvenile offending: The role of subcultural values and social disorganization', *European Journal of Criminology*, 1 (2), 201–35.

Oberwittler, D. and Wikström, P-O H. (2009), 'Why small is better: Advancing the study of the role of behavioral contexts in crime causation', in D. Weisburd, W. Bernasco, and G. J. N. Bruinsma (eds), *Putting crime in its place: Units of analysis in spatial crime research* (New York, NY: Springer), 35–59.

Odgers, C. L., et al. (2009), 'The protective effects of neighborhood collective efficacy on British children growing up in deprivation: A developmental analysis', *Developmental Psychology*, 45 (4), 942–57.

Oguz, S. and Knight, J. (2011), 'Regional economic indicators: With a focus on sub-regional Gross Value Added using shift-share analysis', *Economic & Labour Market Review*, 64–105.

Ólafsson, J. O. (2004), 'Public violence in Iceland: Disentangling the agency and structural effects' (University of Cambridge, unpublished PhD dissertation).

Olds, T., et al. (2009), 'How do school-day activity patterns differ with age and gender across adolescence?', *Journal of Adolescent Health*, 44 (1), 64–72.

Openshaw, S. (1984), *The modifiable areal unit problem* (Concepts and techniques in modern geography, 38; Norwich: GeoBooks).

Osgood, D. W. and Chambers, J. M. (2000), 'Social disorganization outside the Metropolis: An analysis of rural youth violence', *Criminology*, 38 (1), 81–116.

Osgood, D. W. and Anderson, A. L. (2004), 'Unstructured socializing and rates of delinquency', *Criminology*, 42 (3), 519–49.

Osgood, D. W., Anderson, A. L., and Shaffer, J. N. (2005), 'Unstructured leisure in the after-school hours', in J. L. Mahoney, R. W. Larson, and J. S. Eccles (eds), *Organized activities as contexts of development: Extracurricular activities, after-school and community programs* (Mahwah, NJ: Lawrence Erlbaum Associates, Inc.), 45–64.

Osgood, D. W., et al. (1996), 'Routine activities and individual deviant behavior', *American Sociological Review*, 61 (4), 635–55.

Park, R. E. ([1925] 1967), 'The city: Suggestions for the investigation of human behaviour in the urban environment', in R. E. Park, E. W. Burgess, and R. D. McKenzie (eds), *The city* (Chicago, IL: University of Chicago Press), 1–46.

Park, R. E., Burgess, E. W., and McKenzie, R. D. ([1925] 1967), *The city* (Chicago, IL: University of Chicago Press).

Parker, K. F. (2001), 'A move toward specificity: Examining urban disadvantage and race-and relationship-specific homicide rates', *Journal of Quantitative Criminology,* 17, 89–110.

Parker, K. F. and Johns, T. (2002), 'Urban disadvantage and types of race-specific homicide: Assessing the diversity in family structures in the urban context', *Journal of Research in Crime and Delinquency,* 39, 277–303.

Parkinson, M., et al. (2006), 'The state of English cities: A research study' (1; London: Office of the Deputy Prime Minister).

Parsons, J. T., Siegel, A. W., and Cousins, J. H. (1997), 'Late adolescent risk-taking: Effects of perceived benefits and perceived risks on behavioral intentions and behavioral change', *Journal of Adolescence,* 20 (4), 381–92.

Pearce, D. G. (1988), 'Tourist time-budgets', *Annals of Tourism Research,* 15 (1), 106–21.

Pentland, W. E., et al. (eds) (1999), *Time use research in the social sciences* (New York, NY: Kluwer Academic/Plenum Publishers).

Peterborough City Council (2005), 'Peterborough Local Plan (first replacement) 2005' (Peterborough: Peterborough City Council).

Peterson, R. D. and Krivo, L. J. (1993), 'Racial segregation and black urban homicide', *Social Forces,* 71 (4), 1001–26.

Pettit, G. S., et al. (2001), 'Antecedents and behavior problem outcomes of parental monitoring and psychological control in early adolescence', *Child Development,* 72, 583–98.

Phillips, P. D. (1980), 'Characteristics and typology of the journey to crime', in D. E. Georges-Abeyie and K. D. Harries (eds), *Crime: A spatial perspective* (New York, NY: Columbia University Press), 167–80.

Phipps, P. A. and Vernon, M. K. (2009), 'Twenty-four hours: An overview of the recall diary method and data quality in the American Time Use Survey', in R. F. Belli, F. P. Stafford, and D. F. Alwin (eds), *Calendar and time diary: Methods in life course research* (Los Angeles, CA: Sage Publications), 109–28.

Piquero, A. R., Farrington, D. P., and Blumstein, A. (2007), *Key issues in criminal career research: New analyses of the Cambridge Study in Delinquent Development,* eds A. Blumstein and D. P. Farrington (Cambridge Studies in Criminology; Cambridge: Cambridge University Press).

Pointer, G. (2005), 'The UK's major urban areas', *Focus on people and migration* (London: Office for National Satistics).

Popper, K. (1985), *Realism and the aim of science* (London: Routledge).

Porter, S. R. (2004), 'Raising response rates: What works?', *New Directions for Institutional Research,* (121), 5–21.

Pratt, T. C. and Cullen, F. T. (2005), 'Assessing macro-level predictors and theories of crime: A meta-analysis', *Crime & Justice*, 32, 373–450.

Punch, K. (2003), *Survey research: The basics* (London: Sage Publications).

Putnam, R. D. (2007), 'E pluribus unum: Diversity and community in the twenty-first century', *Scandinavian Political Studies*, 30 (2), 137–74.

Pyle, G. F., et al. (1974), *The spatial dynamics of crime* (Research paper no. 159; Chicago: University of Chicago Press), 231.

Rallings, C., Thrasher, M., and Downe, J. (2000), 'Turnout at local government elections: Influences on levels of voter registration and electoral participation' (London: Department for Environment, Transport and the Regions).

Ratcliffe, J. (2010), 'Crime mapping: Spatial and temporal challenges', in A. R. Piquero and D. Weisburd (eds), *Handbook of quantitative criminology* (New York, NY: Springer), 5–24.

Raudenbush, S. W. (1999), 'Statistical analysis and optimal design in cluster randomized trials', *Psychological Methods*, 2 (2), 173–85.

Raudenbush, S. W. and Sampson, R. J. (1999), 'Ecometrics: Toward a science of assessing ecological settings, with application to the systematic social observation of neighborhoods', *Sociological Methodology*, 29 (1), 1–41.

Raudenbush, S. W. and Bryk, A. S. (2002), *Hierarchical linear models: Applications and data analysis methods* (2nd edn; Thousand Oaks, CA: Sage Publications).

Redline, C. D. and Dillman, D. A. (2002), 'The influence of alternative visual designs on respondents' performance with branching instructions in self-administered questionnaires', in R. M. Groves, et al. (eds), *Survey nonresponse* (Wiley Series In Probability and Statistics; New York, NY: John Wiley & Sons), 179–93.

Redline, C. D., et al. (2005), 'Factors that influence reading and comprehension of branching instructions in self–administered questionnaires', *Advances in Statistical Analysis*, 89 (1), 21–38.

Reinecke, J. and Wikström, P-O H. (2012), 'Explaining adolescent crime trajectories: Situational Action Theory tested with Growth Curve Modelling', *mimeo*.

Reiss, A. J., Jr (1971), 'Systematic observations of natural social phenomena', in H. Costner (ed.), *Sociological Methodology, Vol 3* (San Francisco, CA: Jossey-Bass), 3–33.

—— (1986), 'Why are communities important in understanding crime?', in A. J. Reiss, Jr. and M. Tonry (eds), *Crime and Justice, Vol 8: Communities and crime* (A review of research; Chicago: University of Chicago Press), 1–33.

Rhind, D. and Hudson, R. (1980), *Land use* (London: Methuen).

Rhodes, W. M. and Conly, C. (1981), 'Crime and mobility: An empirical study', in P. J. Brantingham and P. L. Brantingham (eds), *Environmental criminology* (Beverly Hills, CA: Sage Publications), 167–88.

Riley, D. (1987), 'Time and crime: The link between teenager lifestyle and delinquency', *Journal of Quantitative Criminology*, 3, 339–54.

Robinson, J. P. (1985), 'The validity and reliability of diaries versus alternative time use measures', in F. T. Juster and F. P. Stafford (eds), *Time, goods, and well-being* (Ann Arbor, MI: Institute for Social Research, The University of Michigan), 33–62.

Robinson, J. P. and Bostrom, A. (1994), 'The overestimated work week? What time diary measures suggest', *Monthly Labor Review*, 117 (8), 11–23.

Robinson, W. S. (1950), 'Ecological correlations and the behavior of individuals', *American Sociological Review*, 15, 351–7.

Roe, S. and Ash, J. (2008), 'Young people and crime: Findings from the 2006 Offending, Crime and Justice Survey' (London: Home Office Statistical Bulletin).

Roncek, D. W. (2000), 'Schools and crime', in V. Goldsmith, et al. (eds), *Analyzing crime patterns: Frontiers of practice* (Beverly Hills, CA: Sage Publications), 153–66.

Roncek, D. W. and Maier, P. A. (1991), 'Bars, blocks, and crimes revisited: Linking the theory of routine activities to the empiricism of hot-spots', *Criminology*, 29 (4), 725–53.

Ross, N. A., Nobrega, K., and Dunn, J. (2001), 'Income segregation, income inequality and mortaility in North American metropolitan areas', *GeoJournal*, 53, 117–24.

Rossi, P. H. and Nock, S. L. (1982), *Measuring social judgments: The factorial survey approach* (Beverly Hills, CA: Sage Publications).

Rossi, P. H. and Anderson, A. B. (1982), 'The factorial survey approach: An introduction', in P. H. Rossi and S. L. Nock (eds), *Measuring social judgments: The factorial survey approach* (Beverly Hills, CA: Sage Publications), 15–67.

Rossmo, D. K. (2000), *Geographical profiling* (Boca Raton, FL: CRC Press).

Sampson, R. J. (1986), 'Crime in cities: The effects of formal and informal social control', *Crime & Justice*, 8, 271–311.

—— (1987), 'Urban black violence: The effect of male joblessness and family disruption', *American Journal of Sociology*, 93 (2), 348–82.

—— (1990), 'The impact of housing policies on community social disorganization and crime', *Bulletin of the New York Academy of Medicine*, 66 (6), 526–33.

—— (1993), 'The community context of violence', in W. J. Wilson (ed.), *Sociology and the public agenda* (American Sociological Association Presidential Series; London: SAGE Publications), 259–86.

—— (1997), 'The embeddedness of child and adolescent development: A community-level perspective on urban violence', in J. McCord (ed.), *Violence and childhood in the inner city* (Cambridge: Cambridge University Press), 31–77.

—— (1999), 'What "community" supplies', in R. F. Ferguson and W. T. Dickens (eds), *Urban problems and community development* (Washington, DC: Brookings Institution Press), 241–92.

—— (2004), 'Neighborhood and community: Collective efficacy and community safety', *New Economy*, 11, 106–13.

—— (2006a), 'Collective efficacy theory: Lessons learned and directions for future inquiry', in F. T. Cullen, J. P. Wright, and K. Blevins (eds), *Taking stock: The status of criminological theory* (14; New Brunswick, NJ: Transaction Publishers), 149–67.

—— (2006b), 'How does community context matter? Social mechanisms and the explanation of crime rates', in P-O H. Wikström and R. J. Sampson (eds), *The explanation of crime: Context, mechanisms and development* (Cambridge: Cambridge University Press), 31–60.

—— (2011), 'Neighborhood effects, causal mechanisms, and the social structure of the city', in P. Demeulenaere (ed.), *Analytical sociology and social mechanisms* (Cambridge: Cambridge University Press), 227–50.

—— (2012), *Great American city: Chicago and the enduring neighborhood effect* (Chicago, IL: University of Chicago Press).

Sampson, R. J. and Wooldredge, J. D. (1987), 'Linking the micro and macro level dimensions of lifestyle-routine activity and opportunity models of predatory victimization', *Journal of Quantitative Criminology*, 3 (4), 371–93.

Sampson, R. J. and Groves, B. W. (1989), 'Community structure and crime: Testing Social-Disorganization Theory', *American Journal of Sociology*, 94 (4), 774–802.

Sampson, R. J. and Laub, J. H. (1994), 'Urban poverty and the family context of delinquency: A new look at structure and process in a classic study', *Child Development*, 65 (2), 523–40.

Sampson, R. J. and Raudenbush, S. W. (1999), 'Systematic social observation of public spaces: A new look at disorder in urban neighborhoods', *American Journal of Sociology*, 105 (3), 603–51.

Sampson, R. J. and Wikström, P-O H. (2008), 'The social order of violence in Chicago and Stockholm neighborhoods: A comparative inquiry', in S. Kalyvas, I. Shapiro, and T. Masoud (eds), *Order, conflict and violence* (Cambridge: Cambridge University Press), 97–119.

Sampson, R. J., Raudenbush, S. W., and Earls, F. (1997), 'Neighborhoods and violent crime: A multilevel study of collective efficacy', *Science*, 277 (5328), 918–24.

Sampson, R. J., Morenoff, J. D., and Earls, F. (1999), 'Beyond social capital: Spatial dynamics of collective efficacy for children', *American Sociological Review*, 64, 633–60.

Sampson, R. J., Morenoff, J. D., and Gannon-Rowley, T. (2002), 'Assessing "neighbourhood effects": Social processes and new directions in research', *Annual Review of Sociology*, 28, 443–78.

Sampson, R. J., Morenoff, J. D., and Raudenbush, S. W. (2005), 'Social anatomy of racial and ethnic disparities in violence', *American Journal of Public Health,* 95, 224–32.

Sawyer, R. K. (2005), *Social Emergence: Societies as complex systems* (Cambridge: Cambridge University Press).

Schmid, C. F. (1960a), 'Urban crime areas: Part I', *American Sociological Review,* 25, 527–42.

—— (1960b), 'Urban crime areas: Part II', *American Sociological Review,* 25, 655–78.

Schönfelder, S. and Axhausen, K. W. (2003), 'Activity spaces: Measures of social exclusion?', *Transport Policy,* 10 (4), 273–86.

Schwirian, K. P. (1974), *Comparative urban structure: Studies in the ecology of cities* (Lexington, MA: D.C. Heath & Co).

Shaw, C. and McKay, H. ([1942] 1969), *Juvenile delinquency and urban areas* (2nd edn; Chicago: University of Chicago Press).

Sherman, L. W. and Weisburd, D. (1995), 'General deterrent effects of police patrol in crime "hot spots": A randomized, controlled trial', *Justice Quarterly,* 12 (4), 625–48.

Sherman, L. W., Gartin, P., and Buerger, M. (1989), 'Hot spots of predatory crime: Routine activities and the criminology of place', *Criminology,* 27 (1), 27–55.

Siegel, A. W., et al. (1994), 'Adolescents' perceptions of the benefits and risks of their own risk taking', *Journal of Emotional and Behavioral Disorders,* 2 (2), 89–98.

Silver, E. and Miller, L. L. (2004), 'Sources of informal social control in Chicago neighborhoods', *Criminology,* 42 (3), 551–83.

Simons, R. L., et al. (2005), 'Collective efficacy, authoritative parenting and delinquency: A longitudinal test of a model integrating community and family level processes', *Criminology,* 43 (4), 989–1029.

Simpkins, S. D., et al. (2005), 'Predicting participation and outcomes in out-of-school activities: Similarities and differences across social ecologies', *New Directions for Youth Development,* 2005 (105), 51–69.

Skogan, W. G. (1986), 'Fear of crime and neighborhood change', *Communities and Crime,* 8, 203–30.

—— (1990), *Disorder and decline* (New York, NY: Free Press).

Smetana, J. G. and Daddis, C. (2002), 'Domain-specific antecedents of parental psychological control and monitoring: The role of parenting beliefs and practices', *Child Development,* 73 (2), 563–80.

Smith, D. A. and Jarjoura, G. R. (1989), 'Household characteristics, neighborhood composition and victimization risk', *Social Forces,* 68 (2), 621–40.

Smith, D. J. (2004), 'Parenting and delinquency at ages 12 to 15', *Edinburgh Study of Youth Transitions and Crime: Research Digest No. 3* (Edinburgh: Centre for Law and Society, The University of Edinburgh).

Smith, D. J. and McVie, S. (2003), 'Theory and method in the Edinburgh Study of Youth Transitions and Crime', *British Journal of Criminology,* 43 (1), 169–95.

Smith, D. J., et al. (2001), 'The Edinburgh Study of Youth Transitions and Crime: Key findings at ages 12 and 13', *Edinburgh Study of Youth Transitions and Crime Research Digest No. 1* (Edinburgh: Centre for Law and Society, The University of Edinburgh).

Smith, W. R., Glave Frazee, S., and Davison, E. L. (2000), 'Furthering the integration of routine activity and social disorganization theories: Small units of analysis and the study of street robbery as a diffusion process', *Criminology,* 38, 489–523.

Snijders, T. and Bosker, R. (1999), *Multilevel modeling: An introduction to basic and advanced multilevel analysis* (London: Sage Publications).

Stafford, F. P. (2009), 'Timeline data collection and analysis: Time diary and event history calendar methods', in R. F. Belli, F. P. Stafford, and D. F. Alwin (eds), *Calendar and time diary: Methods in life course research* (Los Angeles, CA: Sage Publications), 13–30.

Stanton, B. F., et al. (2000), 'Parental underestimates of adolescent risk behavior: A randomized, controlled trial of a parental monitoring intervention', *Journal of Adolescent Health,* 26 (1), 18–26.

Stattin, H. and Kerr, M. (2000), 'Parental monitoring: A reinterpretation', *Child Development,* 71 (4), 1072–85.

Steinberg, L. (2001), 'We know some things: Parent–adolescent relationships in retrospect and prospect', *Journal of Research on Adolescence,* 11 (1), 1–19.

—— (2011), *Adolescence* (9th edn; New York, NY: McGraw Hill).

Stewart, J. (2006), 'Assessing alternative dissimilarity indexes for comparing activity profiles', *Electronic International Journal of Time Use Research,* 3 (1), 49–59.

Stinson, L. L. (2000), '"Day of week" difference and implications for time-use research', *55th Annual Conference of the American Association for Public Opinion Research & World Association for Public Opinion Research* (Portland, Oregon), 998–1003.

Stone, A. A. and Broderick, J. E. (2009), 'Protocol compliance in real-time data collection studies: Findings and implications', in R. F. Belli, F. P. Stafford, and D. F. Alwin (eds), *Calendar and time diary: Methods in life course research* (Los Angeles, CA: Sage Publications), 243–56.

Stoop, I. A. L. (2005), *The hunt for the last respondent: Nonresponse in sample surveys* (Amsterdam: Aksant Academic Publications).

Stouthamer-Loeber, M. and van Kammen, W. B. (1995), *Data collection and management: A practical guide* (Applied Social Research Methods, 39; Thousand Oaks, CA: Sage Publications), 133.

Stucky, T. D. and Ottensmann, J. R. (2009), 'Land use and violent crime', *Criminology,* 47 (4), 1223–64.

Stuss, D. and Levine, B. (2002), 'Adult clinical neuropsychology: Lessons from studies of the frontal lobes', *Annual Review of Psychology*, (53), 401–33.

Svensson, R. (2002), 'Strategic offences in the criminal career context', *British Journal of Criminology*, 42, 395–411.

Szalai, A. (1966a), 'The multinational comparative time budget research project: A venture in international research cooperation', *American Behavioural Scientist*, 10 (4), 1–31.

—— (1966b), 'Trends in contemporary time-budget research', *International study on the main trends of research in the sciences of man* (United Nations Educational, Scientific and Cultural Organization (UNESCO)).

—— (1972), *The use of time* (The Hague: Mouton).

Taub, R. P., Taylor, D. G., and Dunham, J. D. (1984), *Paths of neighborhood change: Race and crime in urban America* (Chicago, IL: University of Chicago Press).

Taylor, R. B. (1995), 'The impact of crime on communities', *Annals of the American Academy of Political and Social Science*, 539 (3), 28–45.

—— (1996), 'Neighborhood responses to disorder and local attachments: The systemic model of attachment, social disorganization, and neighborhood use value', *Sociological Forum*, 11 (1), 41–74.

—— (2001), *Breaking away from Broken Windows: Baltimore neighbourhoods and the nationwide fights against crime, grime, fear and decline* (Boulder, CO: Westview).

—— (2002), 'Fear of crime, social ties, and collective efficacy: Maybe masquerading measurement, maybe déjà vu all over again', *Justice Quarterly*, 19 (4), 773–92.

Taylor, R. B., et al. (1995), 'Street blocks with more nonresidential land use have more physical deterioration: Evidence from Baltimore and Philadelphia', *Urban Affairs Review*, 31 (1), 120–36.

Thornberry, T. P. and Krohn, M. D. (2000), 'The self-report method for measuring delinquency and crime', *Criminal Justice*, 4, 33–83.

Thornberry, T. P., Bjerregaard, B., and Miles, W. (1993), 'The consequences of respondent attrition in panel studies: A simulation based on the Rochester Youth Development Study', *Journal of Quantitative Criminology*, 9 (2), 127–58.

Thornton, P. R., Shaw, G., and Williams, A. M. (1997), 'Tourist group holiday decision-making and behaviour: The influence of children', *Tourism Management*, 18 (5), 287–97.

Thurman, Q. C., Jackson, S., and Zhao, J. (1993), 'Drunk-driving research and innovation: A factorial survey study of decisions to drink and drive', *Social Science Research*, 22 (3), 245–64.

Timms, D. W. G. (1971), *The urban mosaic: Towards a theory of residential differentiation* (Cambridge: Cambridge University Press).

Tita, G. and Griffiths, E. (2005), 'Traveling to violence: The case for a mobility-based spatial typology of homicide', *Journal of Research in Crime and Delinquency,* 42 (3), 275–308.

Tittle, C. R. (1995), *Control balance: Toward a general theory of deviance* (Boulder, MA: Westview Press).

Tobler, W. R. (1970), 'A computer movie simulating urban growth in the Detroit region', *Economic Geography,* 46, 234–40.

Tomlinson, J., et al. (1973), 'A model of students' daily activity patterns', *Environment and Planning A,* 5, 231–66.

Tomsen, S., Homel, R., and Thommeny, J. (1991), 'The causes of public violence: Situational versus other factors in drinking related assaults', in D. Chappell, P. Grabosky, and H. Strang (eds), *Australian violence: Contemporary perspectives* (Canberra: Australian Institute of Criminology), 177–95.

Tracy, P. E., Wolfgang, M. E., and Figlio, R. M. (1990), *Delinquency careers in two birth cohorts,* eds J. A. Fox and J. G. Weis (The Plenum series in crime and justice; New York, NY: Plenum Press).

Treiber, K. (2011), 'The neuroscientific basis of Situational Action Theory', in A. Walsh and K. Beaver (eds), *The Ashgate research companion to biosocial theories of crime* (Farnham: Ashgate Press), 213–46.

Treno, A. J., et al. (2007), 'Examining multi-level relationships between bars, hostility and aggression: Social selection and social influence', *Addiction,* 103 (1), 66–77.

Tuck, M. (1989), 'Drinking and disorder: A study of non-metropolitan violence' (London: Home Office).

Updegraff, K. A., et al. (2001), 'Parents' involvement in adolescents' peer relationships: A comparison of mothers' and fathers' roles', *Journal of Marriage and Family,* 63 (3), 655–68.

Vélez, M. B. (2001), 'The role of public social control in urban neighborhoods: A multilevel analysis of victimization risk', *Criminology,* 39 (4), 837–64.

Vila, B. (1994), 'A general paradigm for understanding criminal behavior: Extending evolutionary ecological theory', *Criminology,* 32 (3), 311–60.

Waizenhofer, R. N., Buchanan, C. M., and Jackson-Newsom, J. (2004), 'Mothers' and fathers' knowledge of adolescents' daily activities: Its sources and its links with adolescent adjustment', *Journal of Family Psychology,* 18 (2), 348–60.

Wallander, L. (2008), 'Measuring professional judgements: An application of the factorial survey approach to the field of social work' (Acta Universitatis Stockholmiensis).

—— (2009), '25 years of factorial surveys in sociology: A review', *Social Science Research,* 38 (3), 505–20.

Wallis, C. P. and Maliphant, R. (1967), 'Delinquent areas in the country of London: Ecological factors', *British Journal of Criminology,* 7 (3), 250–84.

Warner, B. D. and Rountree, P. W. (1997), 'Local social ties in a community and crime model: Questioning the systemic nature of informal social control', *Social Problems*, 44, 520–36.

Warr, M. (2002), *Companions in crime: The social aspects of criminal conduct* (Cambridge: Cambridge University Press).

Weisburd, D., Morris, N., and Groff, E. (2009), 'Hot spots of juvenile crime: A longitudinal study of arrest incidents at street segments in Seattle, Washington', *Journal of Quantitative Criminology*, 25, 443–67.

Weisburd, D., et al. (2004), 'Trajectories of crime at places: A longitudinal study of street segments in the city of Seattle', *Criminology*, 42 (2), 283–322.

West, D. and Farrington, D. P. (1977), *The delinquent way of life* (London: Heineman).

Wikström, P-O H. (1985), *Everyday violence in contemporary Sweden: Situational and ecological aspects* (Stockholm, Sweden: National Council for Crime Prevention).

—— (1990), 'Age and crime in a Stockholm cohort', *Journal of Quantitative Criminology*, 6 (1), 61–84.

—— (1991), *Urban crime, criminals and victims* (New York, NY: Springer-Verlag).

—— (1995), 'Preventing city-center street crimes', *Crime & Justice*, 19, 429–68.

—— (1998), 'Communities and crime', in M. Tonry (ed.), *The handbook of crime and punishment* (New York, NY: Oxford University Press), 269–301.

—— (2005), 'The social origins of pathways in crime: Towards a developmental ecological action theory of crime involvement and its changes', in D. P. Farrington (ed.), *Integrated developmental and life course theories of offending. Advances in Criminological Theory, Vol 14* (New Brunswick, NJ: Transaction Publishers), 211–46.

—— (2006), 'Individuals, settings, and acts of crime: Situational mechanisms and the explanation of crime', in P-O H. Wikström and R. J. Sampson (eds), *The explanation of crime: Context, mechanisms and development* (Cambridge: Cambridge University Press), 61–107.

—— (2007), 'The social ecology of crime: The role of the environment in crime causation', in H. Schneider (ed.), *Internationales handbuch der kriminologie* (Berlin: de Gruyter), 333–58.

—— (2009), 'Crime propensity, criminogenic exposure and crime involvement in early to mid adolescence', *Monatsschrift fur Kriminologie und Strafrechtsreform*, 92 (2–3), 253–66.

—— (2010a), 'Explaining crime as moral action', in S. Hitlin and S. Vaysey (eds), *Handbook of the sociology of morality* (New York, NY: Springer Verlag).

—— (2010b), 'Situational Action Theory', in F. Cullen and P. Wilcox (eds), *Encyclopedia of criminological theory* (London: Sage Publications), 1000–08.

—— (2011a), 'Does everything matter? Addressing the problem of causation and explanation in the study of crime.', in J. M. McGloin, C. J. Sullivan, and L. W. Kennedy (eds), *When crime appears: The role of emergence* (New York, NY: Routledge), 53–72.

—— (2011b), 'Social sources of crime propensity: A study of the collective efficacy of families, schools and neighbourhoods', in T. Bliesener, A. Beelmann, and M. Stemmler (eds), *Antisocial behaviour and crime: Contributions of developmental and evaluation research to prevention and intervention* (Cambridge, MA: Hogrefe Publishing), 109–22.

—— (2012), 'How do you solve a problem like crime? Foundations for an effective crime prevention' Report to the Home Office (forthcoming).

Wikström, P-O H. and Loeber, R. (2000), 'Do disadvantaged neighbourhoods cause well-adjusted children to become adolescent delinquents? A study of male juvenile serious offending, individual risk and protective factors, and neighborhood context', *Criminology,* 38 (4), 1109–42.

Wikström, P-O H. and Dolmen, L. (2001), 'Urbanisation, neighbourhood social integration, informal social control, minor social disorder, victimisation and fear of crime', *International Review of Victimology*, 8, 163–82.

Wikström, P-O H. and Sampson, R. J. (2003), 'Social mechanisms of community: Influences on crime and pathways in criminality', in B. Lahey, T. E. Moffitt, and A. Caspi (eds), *Causes of conduct disorder and juvenile delinquency* (New York, NY: The Guilford Press), 118–48.

—— (2006), 'Introduction: Toward a unified approach to crime and its explanation', in P-O H. Wikström and R. J. Sampson (eds), *The explanation of crime: Context, mechanisms and development* (Cambridge: Cambridge University Press), 1–7.

Wikström, P-O H. and Butterworth, D. (2006), *Adolescent crime: Individual differences and lifestyles* (Cullompton: Willan Publishing).

Wikström, P-O H. and Treiber, K. (2007), 'The role of self-control in crime causation: Beyond Gottfredson and Hirschi's General Theory of Crime', *European Journal of Criminology,* 4 (2), 237–64.

—— (2009a), 'Violence as situational action', *International Journal of Conflict and Violence,* 3 (1), 75–96.

—— (2009b), 'What drives persistent offending? The neglected and unexplored role of the social environment', in J. Savage (ed.), *The development of persistent criminality* (Oxford: Oxford University Press), 389–420.

Wikström, P-O H., Torstensson, M., and Dolmen, L. (1997), 'Lokala problem brott och trygghet i Stockholms lan [Local crime problems and safety in Stockholm County]' (Polishögskolan report no. 4. Solna: Polishögskolan).

Wikström, P-O H., Tseloni, A., and Karlis, D. (2011), 'Do people comply with the law because they fear getting caught?', *European Journal of Criminology*, 8 (5), 401–20.

Wikström, P-O H., Weerman, F., and Bruinsma, G. (2012), 'Testing the core assumptions of Situational Action Theory: Cross-national comparison of The Hague and Peterborough', *mimeo*.

Wikström, P-O H., et al. (2010), 'Activity fields and the dynamics of crime: Advancing knowledge about the role of the environment in crime causation', *Journal of Quantitative Criminology*, 26 (1), 55–87.

Wilcox, P., Land, K. C., and Hunt, S. A. (2003), *Criminal circumstance: A dynamic multicontextual criminal opportunity theory* (New York, NY: Aldine de Gruyter).

Wilcox, P., et al. (2004), 'Busy places and broken windows? Toward defining the role of physical structure and process in community crime models', *The Sociological Quarterly Journal of Social Research*, 45, 185–207.

Wiles, P. and Costello, A. (2000), 'The "road to nowhere": The evidence for travelling criminals' (London: Home Office Research Development and Statistics Directorate).

Wilson, J. Q. and Kelling, G. L. (1982), 'Broken Windows', *Atlantic Monthly*, 249, 29–38.

Wilson, J. Q. and Herrnstein, R. J. (1985), *Crime and human nature* (New York, NY: Touchstone Books).

Wilson, W. J. (1987), *The truly disadvantaged: The inner city, the underclass, and public policy* (Chicago, IL: University of Chicago Press).

Wood, W. and Quinn, J. M. (2005), 'Habits and the structure of motivation in everyday life', in J. P. Forgas, K. D. Williams, and S. M. Laham (eds), *Social motivation: Conscious and unconscious processes* (Cambridge: Cambridge University Press).

Xie, M. and McDowall, D. (2008), 'Escaping crime: The effects of direct and indirect victimization on moving', *Criminology*, 46 (4), 809–40.

Xu, Y., Fiedler, M. L., and Flaming, K. H. (2005), 'Discovering the impact of community policing: The broken windows thesis, collective efficacy, and citizens' judgement', *Journal of Research in Crime and Delinquency*, 42, 147–86.

Zorbaugh, H. (1961), 'The natural areas of the city', in G.A. Theodorson (ed.), *Studies in human ecology* (Evanston, IL: Harper & Row), 45–9.

# Index

Printed in Germany
by Amazon Distribution
GmbH, Leipzig